Deregulation and Interdependence in the Asia-Pacific Region

NBER–East Asia Seminar on Economics
Volume 8

National Bureau of Economic Research
Tokyo Center for Economic Research
Korea Development Institute
Chung-Hua Institution for Economic Research
Hong Kong University of Science and Technology
National University of Singapore

Deregulation and Interdependence in the Asia-Pacific Region

Edited by **Takatoshi Ito and Anne O. Krueger**

The University of Chicago Press

Chicago and London

TAKATOSHI ITO is professor in the Institute of Economic Research at Hitotsubashi University, Tokyo, and a research associate of the National Bureau of Economic Research. ANNE O. KRUEGER is the Herald L. and Caroline L. Ritch Professor of Economics, senior fellow of the Hoover Institution, and director of the Center for Research on Economic Development and Policy Reform at Stanford University, and a research associate of the National Bureau of Economic Research.

The University of Chicago Press, Chicago 60637
The University of Chicago Press, Ltd., London
© 2000 by the National Bureau of Economic Research
All rights reserved. Published 2000
Printed in the United States of America
09 08 07 06 05 04 03 02 01 00   1 2 3 4 5
ISBN: 0-226-38674-0 (cloth)

Library of Congress Cataloging-in-Publication Data

Deregulation and interdependence in the Asia-Pacific region / edited by Takatoshi Ito and Anne O. Krueger.
    p. cm. — (NBER-East Asia seminar on economics ; v. 8)
    Papers presented at the eighth annual National Bureau of Economic Research East Asia Seminar on Economics (EASE8) held in Taipei in June 1997.
  Includes bibliographical references and index.
  ISBN 0-226-38674-0 (alk. paper)
  1. Industrial policy—East Asia—Congresses.
2. Deregulation—East Asia—Congresses. 3. Free trade—East Asia—Congresses. 4. Service industries—Government policy—East Asia—Case studies—Congresses. 5. Competition, International—Congresses. I. Ito, Takatoshi, 1950– II. Krueger, Anne O. III. NBER-East Asia Seminar on Economics (8th : 1997 Taipei, Taiwan) IV. NBER-East Asia seminar on economics (Series) ; v. 8.

HD3616.E183 D47 2000
338.95—dc21
                                               99-045132

Since this volume is a record of conference proceedings, it has been exempted from the rules governing critical review of manuscripts by the Board of Directors of the National Bureau (resolution adopted 8 June 1948, as revised 21 November 1949 and 20 April 1968).

Contents

Acknowledgments

This volume contains edited versions of papers presented at the NBER–East Asia Seminar on Economics' eighth annual conference, held in Taipei, Taiwan, on 19–21 June 1997.

We are indebted to members of the program committee who organized the conference, and to Chung-Hua Institution, Taipei; the Hong Kong University of Science and Technology; Korea Development Institute, Seoul; the National University of Singapore; and the Tokyo Center for Economic Research.

President Chao-Cheng Mai and Vice President Hong Hwang of the Chung-Hua Institution were the local hosts. All conference participants are grateful for the excellent organization and hospitality supporting the conference.

The National Bureau of Economic Research provided logistical support, as well as support for the North American–based conference participants and some of the Asian participants. We are greatly indebted to the NBER, as well as to the Asian institutions that support the research and this series of conferences.

Introduction

Takatoshi Ito and Anne O. Krueger

The phenomenal economic growth of the international economy over the past half-century has been in part caused by, and in part the result of, falling real and artificial barriers to international transactions among nations. Real barriers, such as transport and communications costs, have fallen sharply. It is estimated that the real cost of a three-minute phone call between London and New York, for example, is now less than 3 percent of what it was prior to World War II. Likewise, the cost of ocean shipping has dropped by about 80 percent over the same period, while air transport has become so cheap that many goods are now air-freighted between countries. As to artificial barriers, eight rounds of multilateral trade negotiations under the auspices of the General Agreement on Tariffs and Trade have resulted in a virtual elimination of quantitative restrictions on trade among industrialized countries and a reduction in average tariff rates on manufactured goods from close to 50 percent to under 5 percent.

Success in some dimensions normally brings new problems to light, and that is nowhere more true than in international trade relations. The great decline in transactions and tariff costs between countries has made producers everywhere extremely sensitive to governmental measures that impose even small cost differentials on them relative to their foreign competitors. Calls for a "level playing field" are frequently heard, with claims that foreign industries have an "unfair" advantage because of subsidies from

Takatoshi Ito is professor in the Institute of Economic Research at Hitotsubashi University, Tokyo, and a research associate of the National Bureau of Economic Research. Anne O. Krueger is the Herald L. and Caroline L. Ritch Professor of Economics, senior fellow of the Hoover Institution, and director of the Center for Research on Economic Development and Policy Reform at Stanford University, and a research associate of the National Bureau of Economic Research.

their government or cross-subsidies from domestic monopoly positions created by the home government. Appeals for protection also come from producers whose costs are increased by domestic regulatory measures for causes such as the environment. Likewise, as more goods and services have become tradable, the ability of inefficient regulatory regimes in domestic economies to handicap producers relative to their foreign competitors has increased.

Thus two fields that were formerly fairly independent—policy analysis of regulation and competition and of international economic policy—have moved closer together. One result has been calls for an international "competition" policy. Such a policy would entail an international agreement on what constitutes fair business practices and would incorporate that agreement into the World Trade Organization (WTO). Analyses of what competition policy might be and what it might do are under way throughout the world, and the topic is inherently complex.

One group of advocates of competition policy are those who believe that antidumping measures in many countries have gone far beyond their intended purpose (of preventing predatory pricing) and are used as a form of protection.[1] They believe that competition policy could replace antidumping practices with beneficial effects for the efficiency of the global trading system.

A second group of advocates believes that traditional (national) antimonopoly and antitrust laws are no longer serving their original purpose. In traditional industrial organization theory, the market share of the largest company or top three companies was an important indicator of the degree of competition in the market. However, competition can come from new entrants, imports, or substitute new products or services. The loss of monopoly power of local telephone companies with the advent of cellular telephones, and the potential threat of cable TV competition illustrates the point. Likewise, the fact that there are only three major U.S. automobile companies no longer suggests a highly concentrated industry because competition from foreign auto manufacturers severely limits any monopoly power.

Third, technological advance has made the concept of "natural monopoly," which was used as the basis for some regulation, largely obsolete. What used to be considered "natural monopolies," such as long-distance telephone service, railroads, and airlines, have been privatized with success in many countries. Fixed costs have become smaller, and advances in software technology have made it possible to increase the productivity of the existing capital stock.

---

1. See Boltuck and Litan (1991) for a good analysis of the divergence between antidumping measures used to prevent predatory pricing and the reality of antidumping measures as actually practiced in the United States.

At the same time as calls for a worldwide competition policy have increased, however, economists and others have begun questioning the efficiency of regulation for other reasons, noting that sometimes the regulated have benefited from oversight, and that sometimes regulation of "natural monopolies" has given them more market power than the enterprises would have had if left alone. The move to more efficient domestic regulation, which has resulted in deregulation in some industries, privatization in others, and changes in regulatory regimes in still others, has been one outcome. It is now widely recognized that efficient regulation takes place when social welfare is increased through government actions that, at the least cost, increase consumer welfare. In some instances, there is considerably more competition than was earlier thought, either because technology has increased the choices available or because earlier regulators simply failed to recognize potential alternatives. Indeed, in some instances, regulation itself has served as a major barrier to entry. In other instances, attempted intervention—public ownership, for example—has simply failed to achieve results even equal to those achievable with private monopoly.

Many of the sectors most affected by changes in the regulatory environment are critical to the success of exporters and significantly affect the competitive positions of producers in a number of industries. Financial services, for example, are rapidly being deregulated, in part because of the great cost advantages they provide for users of those services in countries where the costs of financial services are low. Telecommunications markets are rapidly being broken into their component parts, with competition among suppliers introduced wherever feasible. As with financial services, the availability of cheap telecommunications facilities gives yet another competitive edge to exporters.

As these changes are taking place, producers everywhere are becoming more sensitive to anything that affects their costs and margins relative to their foreign competitors. In part this is because of the great reduction in barriers to trade from the levels that earlier prevailed through transport and communications costs and through tariffs and other trade barriers.

The eighth annual National Bureau of Economic Research–East Asia Seminar on Economics was held in Taipei in June 1997 to consider these issues as they relate to the Asia-Pacific region. The papers presented at that conference provide interesting insights into the extent to which the deregulation problems of the countries of the region are similar, and into the gains that can result from improved regulatory or competitive environments for business services.

In chapter 1 Roger Noll examines the ways in which international trade considerations impinge on policy decisions regarding the regulatory environment. As he notes, trade friction over differences between regulatory regimes has increased markedly. This has led to calls for an "international competition policy" that would presumably become part of the WTO.

Such an effort might cut in two ways. On one hand, it might impose stricter regulation on industries in some countries than nationals would prefer and might indeed even be a way for some countries to protect their own industries.[2] On the other hand, there are clearly instances in which regulatory regimes impose costs "artificially" on producers in one country in ways that deprive those producers, who may be low cost, of their competitive advantage. Noll nicely illustrates this in table 1.1.

Noll starts by telling the "tale of the teleshopper," indicating how many different steps and costs, both artificial and real, may lie between the retail consumer and the producer. As he demonstrates, protection of domestic sellers can come about through such means as policies that supply low-quality access lines at high usage prices, through policies that regulate domestic package delivery, or in border delays. Thus not only have barriers to trade fallen sharply, but all sorts of economic activities that were previously of concern only for domestic economic activity now affect the ability of foreigners to compete in domestic markets. Interestingly, Noll blames these regulatory trade distortions for spurring regional and bilateral trade agreements.

Noll then discusses mechanisms for rationalizing regulatory objectives and methods. He focuses on the unnecessary costs of regulation, and ways that they can be avoided. He provides a careful analysis of the types of situations in which efficient government interventions may be called for. He examines regulatory regimes that promote competition, frameworks for preventing natural monopolists from abusing their power, and social regulation (including environmental concerns and protective standards). Noll concludes by examining ways in which competition policy, procedural reforms—especially focusing on mandatory cost-benefit analysis—and internationalization can all bring about more efficient regulatory regimes.

Whereas Roger Noll's paper focuses on the implications of internationalization for regulatory reform issues, Sadao Nagaoka examines the features of international trade that impinge on competition policy. He starts with a review of trade theory and analyzes the behavior of producers with a degree of monopoly power that might result in a reduction in social welfare, either of the producing country or of consumers in the rest of the world. He then uses that framework to analyze Japan's competition policy.

As Nagaoka points out, international trade itself generally brings about

---

2. To date, the greatest danger of protection appearing in the guise of common standards would appear to be conditions surrounding the employment of labor. Calls for labor standards are most frequently heard emanating from workers' representatives in rich countries. It is clear that raising labor costs in countries with abundant unskilled labor would deprive these countries of part of their comparative advantage. Another area where calls for common standards have been heard is environmental protection. Again, there are a number of issues, especially when there is little or no evidence of international spillovers.

greater competition for home producers than occurs when production is confined to the home market (or is protected for the home market). He examines Japanese anticartel policy, noting that it has become stricter over the years. Ironically, however, as anticartel policy has succeeded, firms have been accused of dumping in foreign markets when in fact they have been selling at lower prices due to greater competition. Instead of benefiting from price reductions, foreigners have through antidumping measures insisted on higher prices, thus reducing their own welfare when in fact it should have increased.

In addition to breaking up cartels, Japan has regulated mergers and acquisitions fairly strictly and has prevented vertical restraints of trade primarily by applying sections of the unfair trade practices law. Nagaoka concludes by noting that international regulation through national treatment is highly desirable because it will prevent rent-shifting policies that can otherwise result through regulation. He also calls for measures to contain the ability of antidumping measures to offset the gains that might otherwise result from competition policy, noting that antidumping legislation as carried out in fact works against a desirable competition policy.

In chapter 3 Frank Wolak considers how changing the regulatory regime has affected markets and price behavior in electricity. Wolak describes the changing structure of the electricity industry, once thought to be a perfect case of natural monopoly. He describes how companies behave in response to incentives after deregulation. He uses evidence on the design of electricity markets in England and Wales, Norway and Sweden, Australia, and New Zealand. Features of the market structure, the type of power generation, and the market rules are characterized for each country. Then Wolak analyzes the relationship between market rules, market structure, and the behavior of prices. He argues that although electricity is no longer considered to be a natural monopoly, it is also not perfectly competitive. Controlling market power is an important policy issue, and his analysis shows that there is no one framework that suits all situations, and that careful analysis of each situation is called for.

The next three papers consider the regulation of service industries. In chapter 4 Motoshige Itoh addresses the Japanese distribution system and the related issue of market access by foreign companies. The Japanese distribution sector was a focus of trade negotiations between the United States and Japan in the late 1980s because the United States claimed that restrictions placed on the construction of shopping malls and discount stores by the Japanese Large Scale Retail Store Law effectively created a trade barrier to imports. Statistics show that Japan had more small and medium-size stores per capita than any other advanced country. Because large retail stores carry more imported goods than small neighborhood stores, this allegedly contributed to Japan's trade surpluses.

Itoh carefully reviews structural changes in the Japanese distribution system as well as the legal situation. The Large Scale Retail Store Law was liberalized twice, in 1990 and 1994, and then abolished in 1998. Itoh attributes the change to the "motorization" of Japanese society. As more city dwellers have come to afford autos, demands for large discount stores have increased. He is skeptical of whether the liberalization of the law contributed to increased imports, attributing most of the expansion to the yen appreciation after 1985.

Itoh also analyzes changes in the distribution system since 1985 and shows that costs have been reduced not only in large discount stores but also in convenience stores (such as Seven-Eleven Japan) and specialized small stores. Itoh concludes that changes in tastes and lifestyles drove the changes in the distribution sector in Japan.

In chapter 5 Changqi Wu and Leonard Cheng consider Hong Kong's regulation of business services. Hong Kong's economy is remarkable in the extent to which it has transformed from a manufacturing-based economy to one based on services. As Hong Kong has become a major trader in services, the government has deregulated and liberalized markets for telecommunications, public transport, and electricity. Wu and Cheng characterize the shift as being primarily one "from regulation to competition."

They first trace the history of monopoly regulation in Hong Kong. Regulation seems to have started mostly in the 1950s and 1960s, along traditional lines with permitted rates of return on electricity production, local telephone service, public bus service, and transport services. But with the 1990s, deregulation came in all these industries, and the government began replacing rate-of-return regulation with measures to achieve more competition. There are now four companies competing in telecommunications (compared to one company earlier) and three bus companies, and there will shortly be two companies competing in cargo services at the airport, contrasted with the earlier monopoly positions in each of these areas.

Wu and Cheng show that rate-of-return regulation induced the electricity company to raise the capital-labor ratio more than was desirable on economic efficiency grounds. They also show that the rate of total factor productivity growth in electric power was negligible during the period when rate-of-return regulation was in effect, and that firms invested in excess capacity.

They then contrast the poor performance of the regulated electricity industry with that of the telecommunications service industry and show that regulated telecommunications was much like electricity: once deregulation and liberalization, accompanied by appropriate conditions applied to suppliers (number portability, restrictions on discrimination in access fees, etc.), had begun, the growth rate of revenues increased markedly, and Hong Kong Telecommunications announced plans for significant cutbacks in the number of employees as a cost-reducing measure, despite rapid growth in output.

Wu and Cheng regard Hong Kong as being in the midst of a transition from rate-of-return regulation to liberalization and competition within an appropriate set of guidelines. They note that some industries have advanced further than others, and that there remain a number of sheltered segments among Hong Kong's business service industries.

The other paper examining transportation services and deregulation is chapter 6, by Hirotaka Yamauchi. In his paper, Yamauchi outlines airline deregulation policy in Japan. In the old regime prior to 1986, the Ministry of Transport strictly controlled routing and airfares, viewing the industry as a natural monopoly. Japan Airlines was designated the international airline, All Nippon Airways the major domestic carrier, and Toa Domestic Airlines (now Japan Air Systems) the local route airline. Virtually no discount airfares, except for multiple-coupon discounts for the same route, were available. The U.S.-Japan Airline Service Treaty granted very favorable rights to U.S. airlines. With these handicaps, Japanese airlines did not innovate in management.

Yamauchi then describes the emergence of dynamics for deregulation and the airline industry's evolution in the 1990s. An interesting part of the story is how the movement to rectify "unequal" treatment between U.S. and Japanese airlines spilled over into domestic deregulation because allowing entry of an airline (Nippon Cargo Airlines) meant the end of the old regime. After a decade, regulations have greatly changed. By 1998, airfares in Japan were deregulated, and the U.S.-Japan Airline Service Treaty was renegotiated so that rights have been equalized.

The next four papers all examine the liberalization of the financial service sector. Two papers examine the situation in Taiwan, one paper deals with Hong Kong, and one treats Korea. Chang analyzes the deregulation of financial services in chapter 7. He starts by noting the traditional hostility of the Taiwanese authorities to services, in contrast to their preferential treatment of manufacturing industries. In consequence, there was a strong regulatory environment for financial services. This in turn resulted in a bifurcated financial system, with a formal and an informal sector. Until deregulation, the formal sector consisted almost entirely of publicly owned (or, what was the same thing, ruling party owned) banks and financial institutions. As late as 1990, 94 percent of financial institutions were publicly owned. Among the other negative effects of this structure, small and medium-size enterprises were systematically deprived of access to credit from the formal sector, even when they were in activities that were entitled to preferential credit. There is also evidence that the banking sector was inefficient in a number of ways.

In the 1990s, reforms started. A new banking law came into effect, and the process of liberalization began. Interest rates were decontrolled, private banks were permitted to enter, the foreign exchange market was significantly liberalized, and foreign banks were permitted to enter. Chang concludes that international pressures have, to a considerable extent, been responsible for deregulation, which has, in any event, not gone as rapidly as it might have. The informal sector still exists, probably because the older banks have not entirely adjusted to the new environment.

Whereas Chang concentrates on the issues that gave rise to reforms and the inefficiencies of the former system, in chapter 8 Wu and Hu analyze the effects of deregulation to date. They focus on the impact of Taiwanese financial deregulation on spreads between lending and deposit rates and differentials between official and informal interest rates. They find greater fluctuation in interest rates in both the formal and informal sectors prior to the liberalization of interest rates. Also, the spreads between lending and deposit interest rates of domestic and local foreign banks fell after 1991. They attribute this decline to the entry of private commercial banks and greater competition in the Taiwanese banking system.

The differential between informal and formal sector interest rates did not shrink, however. Wu and Hu attribute this result to the increased risk premium resulting when commercial banks could take on riskier loans, thus leading to greater riskiness of the average informal sector loan. Overall, they conclude that financial liberalization in Taiwan has increased efficiency and reduced costs in the financial system.

Kang traces the liberalization of the Korean banking system in chapter 9. In the Korean case, the chief objective seems to have been to strengthen the financial system, partly in response to foreign competition. However, the Korean authorities were aware that some banks held a number of non-performing loans in their portfolios and therefore thought that liberalization should proceed slowly so that these banks would have time to adjust.

Legislation to guide liberalization was passed in 1988, but liberalization was to take ten years and go through several phases. Kang believes that the key changes came about in the early 1990s, when interest rate ceilings were liberalized. He examines the behavior of deposit and lending rates and concludes that interest rate spreads have come down significantly for national banks but not for regional banks. Accompanying this was a drop in the profitability of banking. These results seem to be attributable to the existence of less competition at the regional level.

Kang concludes by noting that a considerable distance remains in financial liberalization, and that a recent commission on the financial sector recommended the remaining steps be undertaken in a "big bang" rather than at the gradual pace of reforms to date.

Hong Kong seems to have started with an even more rigid banking sector than Taiwan or Korea, as there had been a cartel of banks starting from the 1890s. As Kwan and Lui discuss in chapter 10, the case of Hong Kong is of special interest, not least because it is one of the large international financial centers.

Until deregulation, interest rate caps in Hong Kong had highly distortionary effects: with the Hong Kong dollar tied to the U.S. dollar, the interest rate had to be close to the U.S. rate; but since inflation was higher in Hong Kong, the resulting real interest rate was often negative. Deregulation of interest rate caps took place early in 1995, and competition among banks increased greatly. Kwan and Lui use available data to test for interest rate spreads and the profitability of banks, and they show that spreads decreased significantly. Interestingly enough, banking profitability did not decline. The authors attribute this result to the banks' response to the removal of interest rate caps: they began offering new services and simultaneously began accepting riskier loans.

Another crucial area of business services is telecommunications. Historically, telecommunications were viewed as a natural monopoly and regulated or owned by governments. Technological change has provided the means for competition and allowed movement toward more market-based services. Issues are complicated, however, because of concerns relating to network access (which may be owned by the preexisting company) and the fact that opportunities for competition differ from activity to activity within the telecommunications industry. As chapters 11 through 14, on Taiwan, Korea, China, and the United States show, no country has yet successfully completed the transition from full regulation or government ownership to private markets for telecommunications. But all four governments are trying to achieve more efficient, lower cost telecommunications services by liberalizing their regimes.

Chen views Taiwan's telecommunications liberalization as being "in process." A governmental department, the Directorate General of Telecommunications (DGT), operated and regulated all telecommunications equipment until the late 1980s. An earlier liberalization attempt in the late 1970s failed because of opposition from trade unions. During the thirty years prior to the start of liberalization in the late 1980s, there was exceptionally rapid growth in demand, and the DGT expanded telecommunications services rapidly, from 0.29 telephone mainlines per 100 inhabitants in 1950 to 32.1 in 1991 and 41.3 in 1996. Even with the rapid growth prior to 1990, demand continued to grow more rapidly still, and discontent emerged over the long waiting period for a phone and deteriorating quality of service.

In Taiwan (and in Korea, as Nam documents), telecommunications policy came into conflict with, among other things, industrial policy, as the authorities sought to induce domestic firms to produce telecommunications equipment; this often resulted in the use of outmoded equipment in operations. The DGT had taken a stake in three local suppliers, subsidiaries of foreign firms, creating a less than competitive environment for telecommunications equipment.

When liberalization did start in Taiwan in the late 1980s, international competition was a major factor behind it. Until 1996, progress with telecommunications liberalization was limited; however, the market for customer premises equipment was liberalized, as well as some related services, as competition was permitted. Moreover, a set of laws proposed in 1996 is intended to take the process much further. Among other things, the law split off the regulatory arm of the DGT from its operating arm, which then faces competition in most of its activities.

Chen reports that to date the program has been subject to numerous criticisms, both because of ambiguity as to what the law covers and because many aspects of industry operation are still regulated. The DGT continues to use rate-of-return regulation, which induces operators to invest more than is economically efficient. There is also a 20 percent limitation on permitted foreign capital. Chen notes that regulation can be inimical to the entry of new techniques and new services, especially when, as in Taiwan, different services are regulated separately. There are also questions about the extent to which Chunghwa Telecom, the operating spinoff from the DGT, is favored by the DGT in its regulations.

In considering telecommunications liberalization in Korea, Nam reports a very similar story. Telecommunications was a government monopoly, with international and domestic service provided by the government, and no separate regulatory authority until the late 1980s. The government has since moved to liberalize telecommunications but has continued with rate regulation and, in addition, has tended to set access charges more to protect the profits of new entrants than on economic efficiency grounds. Nam believes that needed (and feasible) competition has not yet been allowed to permeate the telecommunications industry.

Whereas Korea and Taiwan are in the process of liberalizing telecommunications, Lu reports that China still regulates the industry, where demand and delivery have both grown very rapidly. Foreigners are not yet permitted in the industry, and there has, to date, been little effort to begin deregulation.

As for the United States, Crandall notes that it has been deregulating and liberalizing telecommunications for thirty years without completing the process. He believes that in the United States, the political demand to provide universal access at virtually identical prices (and the cross-subsidy resulting from that) has basically impeded liberalization. As he points out, unless prices are allowed to reflect costs, one cannot expect competition to perform the regulatory role that it might otherwise. Crandall draws four key lessons from the U.S. experience: (1) rate distortions should be eliminated before introducing competition; (2) unbundling of essential facilities should be of limited duration, encouraging new entrants to build their own facilities (with greater competition resulting); (3) a date certain should be established when rates will be deregulated after entry barriers have been removed; and (4) regulations should be restricted to requiring reciprocal interconnection after rate and service deregulation occurs.

The similarities between financial deregulation, where nonperforming loans in the portfolios of existing institutions create concerns for authorities set on deregulation, and telecommunications deregulation, where pricing regulations or considerations prevent competition, are striking. As experience with deregulation and liberalization proceeds, it is likely that new means for addressing these issues will be found, and that comparative experience and international pressures will continue to push the liberalization process forward across many business service sectors.

Reference

Boltuck, Richard, and Robert Litan, eds. 1991. *Down in the dumps.* Washington, D.C.: Brookings Institution.

1

Regulatory Reform and International Trade Policy

Roger G. Noll

An unusual feature of the contemporary debate about trade policy is its focus on regulation. In the United States, regulatory policy has been politically controversial since its inception, but until the late 1970s the debate focused on either the legitimacy of government control over various aspects of private production and transactions or whether specific areas of regulation generated positive social benefits. In Europe and Japan, the parallel policy debate during most of the twentieth century was about the boundary between public and private enterprise. In most of the world, the most common political response to a perceived performance shortfall in an important industry was to nationalize it rather than to regulate it.

In the 1980s, the terms of this debate shifted to more pragmatic issues. One issue area focused on rather technocratic matters: how to develop effective policies to promote competition where possible, and how to eliminate the perverse incentives of government control where competition was not possible. The other issue area was the relationship between domestic regulation and the commitment to open economies.

As the advanced industrialized nations eased into the current regime of relatively free trade, the regulatory policy debate was internationalized in three important ways. First, opponents of regulation—especially companies opposed to environmental, health, and safety regulation—argued that regulatory policy eroded the "competitiveness" of industry and con-

Roger G. Noll is the Morris M. Doyle Professor of Public Policy, Department of Economics, Stanford University, and nonresident senior fellow at the Brookings Institution.

The author gratefully acknowledges useful comments from Scott Jacobs, Akira Kawamoto, Anne Krueger, Pietro Nivola, and Bernard Phillips, and financial support for much of the work of preparing this essay from the Markle Foundation and the Organization for Economic Cooperation and Development.

tributed to persistent trade deficits. Second, firms that were adversely affected by regulation and regulators themselves began to seek new ideas about how to reduce the financial and bureaucratic burdens of regulatory policy, a search that often led them to examine how these policies were carried out in other countries. Third, as direct trade barriers fell, and in many cases became negligible, countries began to incorporate regulatory policy into trade negotiations as a means of reducing indirect trade barriers.

In recent years, the regulatory reform debate has spilled over into many transitional and developing countries. Literally hundreds of state-owned enterprises have been privatized since the late 1980s, and in many cases privatization either was conducted in a manner that left the formally nationalized industry reasonably competitive or, at minimum, has opened the door to the possibility of competitive entry against incumbent monopolists.

This essay provides an overview of the international ramifications of the regulatory reform debate and the experiences of several countries with regulatory reform proposals. The essay also examines how international trade negotiations can play an important role in regulatory reform.

1.1   The Evolution of Regulatory Reform

In most advanced industrialized democracies, regulatory reform has been a salient political issue for two decades or more. The concept of regulatory reform is broad and somewhat vague and on occasion has been claimed by ideological proponents of either harsh or lax changes that, in reality, would be wildly inefficient. Notwithstanding these proposals, the core idea of regulatory reform—at least among scholars of business policy—is to improve the efficiency of policies that intervene in decisions about market entry, production methods, product attributes, and transactions between suppliers and customers. Reform can mean deregulation, privatization combined with the creation of a regulatory authority, or more targeted and focused regulatory reform that makes greater use of economic incentives, economic policy analysis, and policy coordination among agencies.

The debate about regulatory reform is neither empty nor sterile. Most nations have significantly changed some major regulatory policies and are considering further changes. Regulatory reform is politically salient for two main reasons. First, regulatory policies impose significant costs, and reform can reduce these costs without sacrificing regulatory objectives. Probably most of the regulatory reforms in the United States and other advanced industrialized countries that took place before 1990 were motivated primarily by the objective of improving the domestic economy by increasing the efficiency of regulated industries. Second, as direct trade barriers—tariffs and quotas on imports—have fallen, regulation has become an increasingly important source of distortions in international trade and a more frequent cause of trade conflicts. As a result, in the 1990s regulatory reform increasingly was instigated as part of a broader package of reforms that were motivated by international economic policies. For example, domestic entry prohibitions in classic infrastructural industries, such as transportation, electricity, and telecommunications, as well as domestic design requirements to protect consumer health and safety, came into conflict with trade agreements that promised openness to foreign trade and investment and "national treatment" of foreign firms. Consequently, a nation's seemingly domestic regulatory policies became the subject of international controversy.

As a result of the growing importance of the international ramifications of domestic regulation, with rising frequency regulatory policy has become an issue in international negotiations about trade and investment policies. International agreements have initiated multilateral coordination of regulatory reform. For example, the vast majority of members of the World Trade Organization (WTO) have signed the voluntary agreement to liberalize telecommunications policy, and most agreed to begin implementation before the year 2000. The European Union has adopted several reforms, some incorporated into the Treaty of Rome, to harmonize environmental, health, and safety regulations and has implemented plans to liberalize airline and telecommunications regulation. Major trade liberalization agreements typically establish dispute resolution institutions to adjudicate claims that a trading partner is attempting to gain an unfair trade advantage by using regulation as an indirect trade barrier or by applying lax regulation to businesses that produce exported products. Examples are the role of the European Court of Justice in adjudicating trade disputes arising from regulation among EU countries and of the WTO in resolving similar disputes among signatories to the GATT and successor agreements.

The elevation of regulatory policy to an issue of international economic policy is controversial. Some charge that internationalizing regulatory reform is an attempt by zealots to impose stringent regulation on nations that neither need nor want it, and to turn advocates of regulatory policies into opponents of free trade. Others contend that emphasizing the trade consequences of regulation amounts to advocacy of a regulatory "race to the bottom," whereby the nations that have done the most to pursue socially desirable regulatory policies are being forced to abandon them because regulations affect trade.

The primary objective of this essay is to examine the relationship between regulatory reform and international economic integration. This essay has two main messages. First, internationalization of regulatory reform is inevitable, and not just because the social and economic problems that give rise to regulation cross borders, as is emphasized by advocates of international environmental regulation (see, e.g., Shabecoff 1996). Even without these cross-border problems, regulation inevitably is an international issue because, when other forms of trade barriers are low, regulations can be the main source of trade distortion. Second, internationalizing regulatory reform is not likely to produce either disaster scenario: widespread overregulation or massive underregulation. Instead, internationalization of regulatory reform is a healthy development that is likely to improve the efficiency of regulation while removing trade distortions that arise from inefficient regulation.

1.2 Regulatory Policy and Market Access

The guiding principle of free trade is that national boundaries should play no role in defining the potential market for any product. Distance or differences in tastes between countries might cause a firm in one country to regard sales in another country as infeasible, but not because crossing the border creates substantial impediments to the transaction. One important feature of technological progress is that it has substantially reduced the economic costs of international transactions. An especially good example is the effect of the Internet on the ease of consumer purchases.[1] This example is especially relevant for thinking about the future of international cooperation in regulation because the extraordinarily rapid growth of electronic communications could massively restructure transactions arrangements.

The creation of the Internet has rapidly led to a circumstance in which anyone who owns a personal computer with a modem that connects to the telephone network can access millions of web sites all over the world that sell almost all consumer and office products. In many cases prices on web sites are substantially lower than ordinary retail prices, even if shipping charges are added, because web suppliers can avoid most distribution costs and can more easily engage in "just in time," "make to order," and other practices that reduce inventory costs. Especially in the United States, Internet transactions are growing very rapidly and conceivably could lead to a substantial reduction in retail stores within a few years.

For Internet retailing to work efficiently requires an array of domestic regulatory policies that do not create barriers to electronic commerce. Internet shopping requires that the user remain connected to a web site for a substantial period of time over the telecommunications network. In nations where connections are unreliable and frequently interrupted by poor service, Internet shopping is very difficult if not impossible. But even if the network has high quality, regulators can make Internet shopping unattrac-

---

1. For a more detailed discussion of trade barriers arising in Internet transactions, see Noll (1997).

tive simply by imposing excessive usage charges for telephone service or high prices on operators of web sites.[2]

Likewise, Internet shopping requires that the transportation system not be so expensive that it makes transactions financially unattractive if the buyer and seller are physically separated. If transportation is regulated in a way that imposes very high prices on small-package service or discourages fast, reliable service (such as by prohibiting such service in order to protect parcel post), most Internet shopping becomes infeasible.

In similar fashion, efficient Internet transactions typically involve the use of the banking system, as customers use credit accounts or electronic funds transfer to pay for their goods. Hence, a necessary component of Internet transactions is a supportive system of regulation of commercial transactions. And, of course, the system of taxing transactions cannot impose substantially more costs on electronic transactions than on transactions through retail stores.

Finally, environmental, health, and safety regulations determine whether a buyer legally can acquire a product. Even if the product complies with all regulations at the points of manufacture and use, a system that requires elaborate testing and documentation by the buyer if the good arrives in a shipment, as contrasted to being purchased at a retail shop, also can impose a formidable barrier to Internet transactions.

The significance of these examples is that each is far more likely to present a serious problem if a transaction is arranged across a national boundary.

Usage charges for international calling are often extremely high compared to both domestic rates and the cost of service. Indeed, many countries set very high prices for origination and termination of international calls for the purpose of generating what amounts to a large tax on foreigners to subsidize domestic telephone service or in some cases to generate general government revenues. In similar fashion, international shipping rates are often several times the price for domestic shipping over comparable distances, and many countries have prohibited entry by fast package delivery services. For example, a seven-pound parcel can be shipped by two-day delivery for $15 from New York to Los Angeles, $66 from New York to Paris, $94 from Paris to New York, or $61 over the much shorter distance from Paris to Frankfurt (all prices in U.S. dollars; OECD 1995c, 12). Likewise, in some nations financial regulations, import restrictions, tariffs and the mechanism for collecting them, and currency controls impose direct costs as well as significant bureaucratic burdens on buyers who wish to make international purchases.

2. OECD (1996b, 32). Internet access prices tend to be much lower in countries that permit competition in long-distance access and information services, such as the United States.

Finally, environmental, health, and safety regulation sometimes treats imported goods differently than domestic ones. Even when both sending and receiving countries have equivalent standards, they may not have a mutual recognition agreement, so that the same product may have to pass exactly the same test separately in every country in which it is sold (OECD 1996a). Or the product may be subject to disposal regulations that require involvement of the manufacturer or seller, so that foreign products are effectively banned, even though other disposal arrangements are easy to arrange. Environmental, health, and safety standards are a common, continuing source of trade barriers that lead to conflicts among trading partners.

The Internet shopping problem focuses on transactions in which consumers deal directly with sellers in other countries, but the revolution in electronic communications is hardly limited to this case. International specialization in production frequently causes each stage in a vertical production chain to be carried out in a different nation. Inexpensive, high-quality communications enables greater coordination and lower transactions costs at each interface in the vertical production chain. To the extent that regulatory rules interfere with these transactions, they create a potential distortion in international trade. Moreover, the importance of regulatory distortions grows as real international transactions costs decline.

Many fascinating historical disputes illustrate how, in particular, environmental, health, and safety regulation has been used to create trade barriers. *Cassis de Dijon* and *German Bottles* in the European Economic Communities (EEC) involved domestic regulations, the first about mandatory alcoholic content for liqueurs and the second about bottle recycling, that had the effect of discriminating against imports. *Canadian Red Raspberries* refers to a dispute under the old Canada-U.S. Free Trade Agreement, now incorporated into the North American Free Trade Agreement, in which Canadian raspberries could not be imported in the United States because, according to U.S. food regulation, they were not red enough. *CAFE Standards* involved a U.S. regulation that discriminated against foreign automobile manufacturers in implementing fuel efficiency regulations. *Venezuelan Gasoline,* the first case decided by the WTO, dealt with a U.S. statute on clean-burning gasoline that required greater improvements in imported gasoline than were demanded of domestic refiners.[3] The cases involving automobile fuel efficiency and reformulated gasoline are especially instructive because in both of these cases the U.S. government quite explicitly tried to rig regulatory rules to protect domestic producers from foreign competition (Vogel 1997).

An important feature of regulatory trade distortions is that bilateral and regional trade agreements can increase, rather than reduce, these trade distortions. The textbook explanation of how bilateral agreements can

---

3. In each of these cases, the regulation was found to be an unfair indirect trade barrier.

Table 1.1   **Unit Production Costs and Trade Outcomes under Alternative Regulatory and Trade Regimes**

	Country		
Cost Element	A	B	C
1. Direct production	100	100	100
2. Efficient compliance	10	15	20
3. Unit production	110	115	120
	(Produce, Export)	(Import)	(Import)
4. Efficient externality	13	5	15
5. Unit social cost	123	120	135
	(Import)	(Produce, Export)	(Import)
6. Actual compliance	25	22	14
7. Actual unit production	125	122	114
	(Import)	(Import)	(Produce, Export)
8. Actual externality	15	20	26
9. Actual unit social cost	140	142	150
	(Produce, Export)	(Import)	(Import)
10. Tariff = 25	25	25	25
11. Competitive price elsewhere	150	147	139
	(Produce)	(Produce)	(Produce)
12. B-C customs union with tariff = 10	25	25, 10[a]	25, 10[b]
13. Competitive price elsewhere	150	147, 132[c]	139, 124[d]
	(Produce)	(Import)	(Produce, Export)

Note: Entries are explained in the text.
[a]Tariffs against A and C, respectively.
[b]Tariffs against A and B, respectively.
[c]Price plus tariff of B's output in A and C, respectively.
[d]Price plus tariff of C's output in A and B, respectively.

lower economic welfare is easily extended to the case of regulatory distortions. Table 1.1 constructs an example of three countries, A, B, and C, and the actual and efficient private and social costs of a product that causes an external cost through polluting emissions in its production. The example assumes that transportation costs are zero, and that the importance of this product in the economies of the three countries is low enough that conditions in this industry have no significant effect on overall trade balances and exchange rates. At equilibrium exchange rates, the example assumes that the countries have the same direct unit production costs for a particular good, shown on line 1; however, the countries have different external costs of production and different optimal and actual regulatory regimes. Note that in the example if no country regulates production, there will be no trade because direct private production costs will be the same everywhere.

An efficient regulatory regime would pick a regulatory rule, R, that would maximize social welfare:

$$\max_{R} B(x) - C(x, R) - E(x, R),$$

where x is the rate of output and consumption, R is the set of regulatory rules, $B(\cdot)$ is the benefit of x to consumers and producers, $C(\cdot,\cdot)$ is production cost if in compliance with regulation, and $E(\cdot,\cdot)$ is the external harm created by production and consumption. Line 2 in table 1.1 is the incremental cost of production arising from compliance with the regulatory rule that solves the maximization problem. Line 3 is the total unit private cost of production under this rule, which is also the competitive equilibrium price if each country adopts an emission standard that is optimal in the sense that it equates marginal abatement cost to marginal damage from pollution. As shown on line 3, if every country regulates optimally, country A will be the low-cost producer and so will produce for all three countries.

The example assumes that the social cost of the externality is different in each country. Line 4 shows the unit external cost in each country if that country produces according to its optimal regulatory rule. This cost varies among the countries, perhaps due to differences in the countries' natural environments or perhaps because their citizens place different values on aesthetic aspects of emissions. Line 5 is the total social cost, $C + E$, in each country, including the external cost. If producers must bear the external cost, such as would be the case if polluters were charged an emission tax, line 5 would be the competitive market price for the product in each country. Because of the particular assumptions in the table, the international specialization that would occur at these market prices is that country B becomes the producer for all three nations, which is not the same as on line 3. If regulatory compliance is unusually expensive in one country, the optimal regulatory regime could produce relatively small compliance expenditure and relatively large external cost, in which case, as shown, the low-cost producer on line 3 can be a high-cost producer on line 5. Likewise, all countries may face roughly the same compliance cost, but one country may attribute a very low cost to the externality, so that it has a low social cost (although not necessarily a low production cost).

Of course, optimality in the international allocation of production requires that line 5 be the basis for international specialization. This reality causes what might be called the "Lawrence Summers problem."[4] Despite

4. While at the World Bank, Lawrence Summers took considerable political flack for making the observation that polluting industries should locate where their emissions cause the

its controversial politics, optimal international specialization would allocate production of goods that creates a local external cost to countries
that place a low value on that cost. In this case, producers in country A
have the lowest production cost; however, because country B places a low
value on the remaining external cost, it has the lowest social cost and so
is the most efficient producer. Of course, these results could be reversed
with a small change in external cost in these countries.

Lines 6 and 8 depict an actual regulatory regime, as opposed to the
theoretical ideal, showing the actual cost of compliance and external effects. Lines 7 and 9 show the international specialization that would occur
at market prices that reflect only production cost and total social cost,
respectively. Notice that, in this example, if external cost is not taken into
account, country C produces the commodity, even though it has the highest social cost of production. If social cost is taken into account, then
country A is the lowest cost producer.

The significance of these examples, of course, is that they demonstrate
the dependence of the allocation of trade on regulatory policy in a world
of putatively free trade. Lines 3, 5, 7, and 9 illustrate four possible regulatory regimes that determine the international allocation of production
among the three countries. Producers in country C can survive only in the
case depicted on lines 6 and 7: very lax domestic regulation that does not
hold the industry responsible for its external cost. Implicit in the example
is the assumption that from the perspective of producers in country C,
demand is highly elastic, so that the imposition of a significant regulatory
cost (in this case, social-welfare-maximizing regulation) would cause the
domestic industry to shut down.

Finally, lines 10 through 13 show the effects of tariffs. Lines 10 and 11
show the effect of a unit tariff of 25. If each country imposes a tariff of
25, no country engages in trade because its domestic production cost on
line 7 is lower than the import price from other countries on line 11. The
same outcome would prevail if market prices in every country reflect total
social cost, for the comparison would be between line 9 and the amount
on line 11 plus the external cost in that country. Note that producers in
countries A and B, not to mention environmental advocates, can be expected to express a great deal of quite justified indignation about a proposal to move from the high-tariff regime on line 11 to the free trade regime on line 7, for this movement would reallocate all production to
country C, which has the highest social cost due solely to its failure to
regulate effectively.

Line 13 depicts the outcome if countries B and C form a customs union

least damage, which often is in a developing country that places a higher value on economic
development and income growth than on environmental quality. The point made by Summers and the political response to it provide extremely useful insights into why regulatory
policy has become an important component of international trade negotiations.

in which they each impose a tariff of 10 on each other but maintain a tariff of 25 against country A, which A reciprocates. In this regime, country C exports to country B (inefficiently), and country A produces for itself (also inefficiently).

One can produce many other permutations of these results by assuming different regulatory regimes in different countries with respect to either the efficiency of their regulation or the extent to which external costs are internalized in market prices. As is apparent from the example, different combinations of regimes produce differences in the extent of international specialization. For example, suppose that country B regulates efficiently, with external cost fully internalized in the market price, but country C regulates inefficiently—and does not pursue a policy that causes external cost to affect price. In this case, the market price in B will be 120, while the market price in C will be 104. During negotiations over dropping the tariff from 25 to 10, country B will recognize that by doing so it is in danger of losing an efficient industry to country C and so may want to discuss regulatory reform in C as part of the trade negotiations.

The purpose of these examples is to demonstrate two crucial points. First, regulatory policy can have an effect on international trade that arises for either "good" (efficiency) or "bad" (regulatory inefficiency) reasons. Second, for either reason regulatory policy can emerge as a crucial part of trade negotiations. The differences in regulatory costs among nations arise from three sources: differences in compliance costs arising from a locally optimal policy, differences in total social costs and the extent to which external costs are reflected in market prices, and differences in the extent to which countries pursue the optimal regulatory policy. For trade negotiations to produce an improvement in the international allocation of resources, the causes of regulation-induced international specialization must be recognized and taken into account in the trade agreement.

1.3   Rationalizing Regulatory Objectives and Methods

The preceding discussion is based on the premise that some of the observed variation in the cost of regulation reflects inefficiency rather than valid policy objectives. All regulation carries the danger that it will reduce efficiency by increasing production costs without delivering offsetting social benefits; however, lax regulation can produce inefficiency by encouraging production that has low private but high social cost. In addition, all forms of regulation may further reduce economic efficiency by thwarting international competition, and especially the entry of firms into markets that are not competitive or that are served by inefficient incumbents.

A great deal of research on regulatory policy argues that in several important areas, regulation does impose unnecessary costs. If a regulation imposes costs but serves no valid social purpose, or more generally if regulatory methods serve a valid purpose but are grossly inefficient, the consequence is an inefficient domestic economy. If a poorly performing industry's inefficiency is the result of government policies, the industry is likely to receive a sympathetic political response when it seeks protection against foreign competitors that face more efficient regulation and hence lower regulatory compliance costs. Consequently, domestic regulatory reform can complement liberalized trade and foreign investment policies.

Notwithstanding the presence of some unnecessary regulatory costs, international differences in the cost of regulation may reflect valid differences in circumstances among countries. For example, a given amount of emissions will cause different amounts of damaging pollution because of physical, ecological, and climatic differences among locations. Similarly, local differences in relative factor prices (including the shadow prices of environmental resources) can cause the cost of achieving a given amount of abatement to differ across locations. Likewise, the aesthetic benefits of pollution abatement are likely to exhibit a positive income elasticity of demand and so to be valued more highly in a wealthy nation than in a poor one. All three factors are a legitimate source of comparative advantage in international trade. In short, Lawrence Summers was right!

A regulation-induced trade effect is frequently mischaracterized as a "competitiveness" issue that involves the overall trade performance of a nation, as measured by the balance of trade or domestic unemployment in export industries. Industries that produce traded goods and that experience significant regulatory compliance costs correctly perceive that regulation has reduced their ability to compete with firms that are located in countries with lower costs of compliance. Regardless of whether a nation's high regulatory compliance costs reflect efficient or inefficient regulatory decisions, an industry that faces especially stringent regulations is likely to complain about the absence of a level playing field. In some cases, political leaders who are sympathetic to the industry may call for regulatory relief to improve the industry's competitive position. In other cases, the call may be for trade barriers against nations that have less stringent regulation. The latter position can be the basis for a coalition of trade-impacted regulated industries and environmentalists in which the latter are motivated by the desire to influence pollution in other countries.

As the preceding examples of the trade effects of regulation indicate, the economics of regulation-induced trade distortion is more subtle and complex than the competitiveness argument implies. Indeed, a nation's movement to more stringent regulation can be an act to level the playing field in the sense of eliminating indirect subsidies that take the form of unpriced overuse of environmental resources in production.

Even in the absence of trade, stringent regulation causes regulated products to be more expensive and thereby shifts the composition of domestic economic activity into other, less regulated activities. If all regulations, both stringent and lax, reflect efficient responses to real problems, this shift in the composition of production is desirable: on balance, it improves the economic welfare of a nation. But if some regulations are too stringent, or others are too lax, the pattern of regulation is harmful to national economic welfare. Under a liberal trade regime, the shift in the industrial composition of domestic output is even larger because exports displace domestic production for intensely regulated products, while domestic production displaces imports for less regulated products. If regulatory rules are efficient, the change in the pattern of trade is desirable. If regulatory rules are inefficient, the result is a trade distortion.

The most efficient regulatory and international economic policies are based on distinctions between inefficient regulation and valid differences in circumstances as causes of international differences in the costs of regulatory policies. Moreover, the appropriate conceptual model for guiding policy is that the social issues that give rise to regulation may cause efficient differences among nations in the stringency and implementation cost of regulation. The latter cost differences are valid sources of comparative advantage among nations, and policy should not try to level the regulatory playing field by making private compliance costs equal in all nations. Instead, the right policy is to let trade reallocate activity to low-cost sources of supply. A nation that has especially valuable environmental resources, or that places an especially high value on avoiding illness and injuries, is better off if it adjusts the composition of its economy away from activities that lead to pollution or poor health.

Constructing an efficient trade regime, then, requires taking into account the efficiency of regulatory regimes. Consequently, regulation inevitably is part of the optimal trade regime, and regulatory reform a part of negotiating trade arrangements. If nations differ in the efficiency of their regulatory regimes, completely free trade will cause distortions of trade and a departure from the allocation of production according to comparative advantage. Hence, pursuit of free trade requires incorporating evaluations of each nation's regulatory policy and the possibility of negotiating regulatory reform in parallel with trade negotiations. If a domestic industry raises the competitiveness issue with respect to the cost of domestic regulation, the appropriate response is, first, to ascertain whether the firm really is overregulated relative to the social cost of its activities; second, to determine whether foreign competitors are underregulated by the same criteria; and, if the answers to these questions are no and yes, respectively, to address the problem by seeking to improve regulatory performance in the other nation.

1.4 Economic Analysis of Regulation

The first step in designing an efficient combination of regulation and trade policies is to distinguish between valid and excessively stringent or lax regulation and between effective and ineffective instruments for dealing with the problems that regulation is intended to solve. Economic analysis provides a means for identifying whether regulation as practiced comes reasonably close to meeting the standard of economic efficiency. By presenting a clear statement of the problem to be solved, the theoretical objective of a policy intervention, and the performance characteristics of the available policy instruments, economic efficiency analysis provides a coherent analytical method for assessing the basis for differences among nations in the costs of regulatory compliance. This section outlines the state of knowledge about the rationales for regulation and instrument choice, as well as some observations about how these issues relate to trade.[5] In cases where regulation is warranted, economic efficiency analysis identifies cost-effective methods of regulation and, therefore, is a useful tool to assist nations in harmonizing regulations so that they are not trade distorting and are compatible with liberalization of trade and foreign investment.

The economic analysis of regulation focuses on *market failure.* Market failure occurs when private transactions do not reflect the social costs and benefits of an activity. Markets are an efficient method for organizing production and distribution when the number of buyers and sellers is large, when buyers and producers are reasonably informed about the consequences of making and producing a product, and when all of the benefits and costs of producing and consuming a product are experienced only by producers and consumers. Market failure arises when a market departs significantly from any of these characteristics. The three types of market failure are imperfect information, externalities, and monopoly. A fourth market failure, ruinous competition, has been alleged but has been found to be an empty vessel. The latter two failures are the primary basis for economic regulation, or the regulation of prices, profits, and entry. The first two form the primary basis for social regulation, such as controlling pollution, improving the safety and healthfulness of products and workplaces, and requiring full disclosure of the characteristics of products.

The regulatory policy debate often focuses more on income inequality and other aspects of distributive justice than on market failure and efficiency. Contrary to the belief of many noneconomists, economic analysis is not inherently devoid of concern about distributive justice. In particular, if individuals care about distributive justice, then the effects of policy on distribution are a form of externality that, in principle, can be taken into account in policy analysis and instrument design. Economic efficiency analysis of regulatory policy can and has focused on three core distributive issues: the actual distributive effects of regulation, the role of income effects in determining evaluations of regulatory policies, and the relative effectiveness of regulation in dealing with distributive concerns. In eco-

5. This section draws heavily from Noll (1997).

nomic regulation, the primary distributive justice issue is access to core infrastructural services, such as water, electricity, and telephones, and arises in the context of "universal service" policies. In social regulation, the "Lawrence Summers problem" described above has an analogue in the idea of uncompensated reallocation of waste to communities that either have a low willingness to pay to avoid the reallocation or that lack political influence, causing their preferences to be ignored in decisions about waste disposal.[6]

1.4.1 Economic Regulation

Ruinous competition is a condition in which a competitive industry engages in price wars that bankrupt the participants or that cause wild, unpredictable price swings that prevent buyers from being able to rely on price predictability. Much of the regulation and nationalization enacted during the 1930s, such as in trucking, airlines, hydrocarbon fuels, and, in some countries, manufacturing industries, was based on the belief that the Great Depression was caused by excessive price cutting in competitive markets. Privatization and economic deregulation of these industries in several countries has generated considerable evidence that competition is efficient, regulation or nationalization is unnecessary and inefficient, and the ruinous competition argument is simply wrong.

In the United States, economic regulation was either removed or substantially relaxed in industries accounting for approximately 10 percent of gross domestic product. Recent assessments of the magnitude of the annual economic benefits of these changes (primarily in the form of lower prices to consumers) are $5 billion for airlines, $8 billion for trucking, and $3 billion for natural gas (Winston 1993). In Australia, deregulation reduced prices 20 percent in airlines (OECD 1996c). Privatization of nationalized airlines produced welfare gains equal to 1.6 percent of sales for British Airways, 22.1 percent of sales for Malaysia Airlines, and 48.5 percent for Aeromexico.[7]

Regulating industries that could be structurally competitive is certainly costly to the domestic economy, but it can distort trade as well. To the extent that these regulations apply to services used by export industries, they raise costs and distort both exports and imports. An especially good example is the regulation of international transportation, which has not been relaxed as rapidly as domestic regulation. Inefficient regulation of

---

6. Discrimination, whether in employment or product markets, can be conceptualized as a form of externality that can be dealt with by regulatory means. Whereas discrimination against foreign workers is a major issue in trade policy, its analytics are sufficiently different from other forms of market failure and regulatory intervention that it is not analyzed in this chapter.

7. Galal et al. (1994). For a thorough summary of the literature evaluating privatization activities around the world, see World Bank (1995).

international transportation has three distorting effects. First, it reduces trade in transportation services by raising its price and imposing rules that guarantee a minimum market share to domestic firms. Second, it reduces the extent of beneficial international specialization in other products as excessive transportation prices drive an unnecessary wedge between domestically produced goods and their foreign competition. Third, transportation regulation distorts input choices among transportation firms in ways that affect trade, such as by creating pressures to favor domestic equipment manufacturers and by insisting on inefficient route structures based on arbitrary distinctions between foreign and domestic terminals.

Another rationale for economic regulation of competitive industries is based on the assertion that a particular form of firm or choice of technology has a *cultural externality*. Examples are preserving democracy, a nation's cultural identity, small business (retail shops, family farms, etc.), social cohesion between rural and urban communities (through cross-subsidies for infrastructure services), or excess capacity and control in case of natural disaster or war. Some examples of this line of argument are claims that, say, foreign branches of Disneyland and McDonald's, or foreign distribution of movies and recorded music from the United States, are a form of American cultural imperialism.

These rationales are difficult to assess, for they are tautological: they define the national interest as the present market structure. In many cases, these rationales seem to be a relatively transparent excuse for protection and cartelization. The point of this form of economic regulation is not just to subsidize some users and providers but to do so by elevating prices to others, rather than by implementing a direct, targeted subsidy with a broad tax base, which is almost always a far more effective approach in the sense that it can achieve the objective of the policy at minimal social cost.

As is the case for regulations motivated by the ruinous competition rationale, economic regulation of competitive markets for the reason of cultural externalities is extremely costly. For example, in some countries retail trade is regulated by controlling entry, setting a maximum store size, and limiting shop hours, either through local zoning or national law. These regulations undermine competition by encouraging cartelization and reduce productivity by causing shops to be too small and underutilized. In the nations with the strictest regulations, Italy and Japan until reforms began in the 1990s, the number of retail outlets was roughly double the number that would be expected on the basis of other market characteristics.[8]

Another example of this form of regulation is to serve the goal of uni-

---

8. OECD (1992). Since the time of this study, Japan has begun liberalizing retail trade. See also Baily (1993), who finds that labor productivity in retail trade is twice as high in the United States as in Japan.

versal service in telecommunications and transportation by creating elaborate regulations (and in some cases a monopoly) that subsidizes rural areas by setting prices equal to average cost over a broad, heterogeneous geographic area—sometimes an entire nation—and requiring firms to serve high-cost areas as a condition of serving low-cost areas. The latter policy forces the regulator to define the boundary of a firm on the basis of the feasibility of a balanced cross-subsidy system rather than operating efficiency. Privatization, competition, and deregulation in long-distance telephony, trucking, and airlines all have been opposed on the grounds that the consequence would be denial of service to rural communities as well as on the basis of the ruinous competition argument.

The propensity to regulate retail trade and to create regulated firms of inefficient scope in communications and transportation to facilitate rural cross-subsidization could be an unfortunate precedent for the rise of electronic commerce.

The argument for protecting small shopkeepers from competition by department stores or discount retail outlets can easily be applied to electronic commerce, which is a similar innovation for increasing the convenience and reducing the cost of acquiring consumer goods. Whereas retail shop laws have had international ramifications, such as indirectly preventing successful retail chains from entering some countries, the international implications of restricting electronic commerce are surely more important. Both large department stores and discount retailers still must be physically accessible to their customers, so to the extent that there is an international ramification, it pertains to physical investment by a foreign retail chain. For electronic commerce, physical propinquity is unnecessary; a foreign retailer need not invest—or even set foot—in a country to be successful in selling goods. Hence, regulations to restrict electronic commerce, if pursued, are very likely to be a source of major trade distortions as well as international conflict.

Likewise, the universal service argument can and has been extended to insist that consumers in remote communities should be provided with Internet access, regardless of the cost of doing so. In the United States, the Telecommunications Act of 1996 states that any service enjoyed by over half of the population, or any other service so designated by a special universal service commission, is to be considered a universal service to be offered to everyone at a price equal to approximately the nationwide average cost. In the United States, the regulator—the Federal Communications Commission (FCC)—has been given the task of figuring out a way to achieve this goal while at the same time promoting competition and, eventually, deregulation in all aspects of telecommunications service, including local access. But the U.S. policy is unusual, and perhaps infeasible. More commonly, the universal service objective is regarded as requiring extensive regulation of both prices and the scope of a firm's operations.

Regardless of the validity of cultural externalities as market failures, some of these objectives usually can be attained more effectively by direct subsidy or procurement by competitive bidding than by regulations that attempt to achieve them by elevating prices and preventing competition. For example, one means to assure transportation or communications services to remote communities is to introduce competitive bidding for providing service, where the franchise specifies price and service quality and requires that all customers be served who seek service at the price, subject to penalties for noncompliance. The subsidy can be provided from general revenues (as was enacted as part of airline deregulation in the United States, although the subsidy soon disappeared because small cities did not lose service), or through a tax on sales by all firms in the industry (as is the approach of the FCC in providing a fund to subsidize universal telephone service). Many public objectives can be accomplished more cheaply, with less distortion, by resorting to the procurement model rather than regulation.

If the procurement model is adopted, the trade distortions caused by this form of regulation can be reduced. Foreign suppliers can submit the low bid to supply subsidized service, and if they are still denied the contract, the trade-distorting purpose of the regulation is exposed and can become an issue for international dispute resolution and negotiation.

Monopoly can arise from mergers, unfair trading practices, or regulatory entry barriers, in which case the cure may be simply to promote competition. Economic regulation can make sense only if the monopoly is natural, that is, if the technology underpinning the industry is such that only one firm can serve a market at minimum cost.

The rationale for most economic regulation, especially in utility industries such as communications, electricity, and water distribution, is the presence of natural monopoly somewhere in the industry. For natural monopoly to justify a regulated or nationalized monopoly, regulation or nationalization must not cause even greater inefficiency than an unfettered market. In the 1980s, two types of research findings called into question both assumptions. First, studies found little or no evidence of scale economies in many segments of supposedly natural monopolies.[9] Second, countries that allowed competitive entry and engaged in less restrictive regulation had lower prices and more productive industries. For example, relaxation of regulation in railroads and telecommunications in the United States saved consumers over $2 billion annually (Winston 1993). International comparisons find that productivity in the utility sector is substantially higher in countries with more liberal policies (Baily 1993). In partic-

---

9. See Nelson and Primeaux (1988), which finds that scale economies are small enough that they are offset by the efficiency advantages of competition in about forty U.S. cities that have competing utilities, and Bernstein (1988), which finds no significant scale economies in telephone service. See also the references in these papers.

ular, when combined with policies to facilitate transactions among retail electric utilities, free entry and almost complete deregulation in electrical generation is feasible and offers considerable cost savings. In the 1990s, over half of new generation facilities in the United States are expected to be constructed, owned, and operated by independent power producers (Utility Data Institute 1992).

Regulated monopoly produces inefficient operations for two fundamental reasons. First, historically prices in regulated monopolies have not been set in a manner that encourages monopolists to be efficient. For private monopolies, prices typically were set equal to some measure of average cost. Because as monopolies these firms had unexploited market power, increases in costs could be passed through to customers. Second, regulated monopolies, whether private or public, were regarded as a means for serving many political purposes other than providing efficient, fairly priced service. Among these purposes was subsidizing favored constituencies (including the government itself). For nationalized monopolies, another purpose was generating revenue for the government as public officials saw tariffs as taxes, rather than prices, to be allocated as part of general government revenue.[10] All of these policies served to decouple prices from costs and to distort if not destroy the incentives of the firm.

Because regulation has created inefficient operation, the case for stringently regulating even firms with natural monopoly characteristics has been seriously questioned. For example, if in an unregulated state an industry is likely to be a relatively concentrated oligopoly, it is plausible that deregulation will produce lower prices and better quality (by sharpening incentives) than regulation, even if the latter succeeds in producing a seemingly better ratio of price to average cost.

If economic regulation is retained because an incumbent's market power is likely to be substantial and durable, the agenda for regulatory reform contains two items. The first is to adopt regulations that give firms sharper incentives for reducing costs. The second is to identify the specific elements of an industry that are most plausibly a durable monopoly, and to adopt policies to assure that practices in these monopolized markets do not impede competition and reduce efficiency in other markets.

In the first category of reforms are "price cap" regulation and "earnings sharing" regulation, both of which allow regulated firms to keep some of the profits from improved efficiency.[11] The alternatives to incentive regulation are either cost-based price regulation or prices that are set by elected political officials, such as by inclusion in a statute, with no necessary connection to costs or market conditions. The difficulty with the first approach

10. For a discussion of the operations of nationalized telephone companies, see Noll (forthcoming).

11. For an excellent review of incentive regulation, see Baron (1989).

is that it rewards inefficiency by increasing allowed prices in proportion to costs. The problem with the second is that extreme politicization of prices almost always leads to massive financial losses, which are then matched by subsidies. Price-cap and earnings-sharing regulation begin with a set of prices that allows the firm roughly to break even, but to keep part of the profits it derives from cost reductions. Price-cap regulation also gives the firm flexibility to change prices as long as, according to an averaging formula, prices generally do not increase.

Telecommunications in the United States provides a useful laboratory for assessing the effects of incentive regulation. Prior to reform, the U.S. telecommunications industry was a monopoly regulated on the basis of cost-based pricing and was generally regarded as among the most efficient in the world. Nevertheless, in an attempt to improve efficiency, parts of the industry were opened to competition. The parts that were regarded as insufficiently competitive to allow deregulation were regulated by many different regulatory jurisdictions, both federal and state, and these regulatory authorities have adopted several different forms of price regulation. The results of recent research indicate that price-cap regulation has substantially increased the rate of productivity advance (Majumdar 1995) and has led to lower prices (Crandall and Waverman 1996, 213–15) and to more rapid diffusion of new technology, such as digital switches, advanced signaling, and ISDN lines (Greenstein, McMaster, and Spiller 1994).

The second category of regulatory reform attempts to minimize the extent to which regulated monopolies leverage their market power by gaining an undeserved advantage in markets that are vertically related to the monopoly, but that can be competitive. Examples are equipment sales to regulated monopolists and products for which the monopoly service is an important input. Here policy reforms include proactive intervention by competition policy agencies to scrutinize regulations for anticompetitive effects; "equal access," "equal interconnection," and "open bidding" requirements so that affiliates of the monopolist are not treated differently than their independent competitors; and "separations" requirements for unregulated activities of regulated firms.[12]

In telecommunications, several countries have successfully segmented the industry and introduced competition into several components. In most nations, equipment manufacture has been separated from services, although a "national champion" manufacturer usually still commands a large share of sales to telephone service companies, abetted by regulatory procurement practices. In many countries, radio telephony is somewhat competitive and is offered by firms other than monopoly wireline access

---

12. For a discussion of which circumstances do and do not plausibly require separations in order to introduce competition into a vertically integrated regulated monopoly, see Joskow and Noll (1999).

providers. In some countries, long-distance entry has been permitted and is successful. And a very few countries—India, New Zealand, the United Kingdom, and the United States—have not only permitted but have tried to encourage local wireline access competition, but with limited success.

In all of these cases, a major issue has been how to prevent a firm that enjoys a monopoly in one segment from leveraging that monopoly to achieve market power in other segments. For example, a competitor in long-distance or radio telephony must deal with wireline companies (usually monopolies that are either regulated or state owned) in order to complete its calls. If the wireline monopoly also provides competitive services, it can increase its market share in these services by raising the price or lowering the quality of service to its competitors. Inevitably, attempts to introduce competition into telephony have led to charges by entrants that incumbent vertically integrated firms engage in precisely these practices. One approach, vertical divestiture, has been tried in a very few countries, most notably the United States and Chile. Most countries have relied instead on regulation or competition policy to enforce nondiscriminatory behavior by the incumbent.

In several countries, competition also has been introduced in segments of the electric utility industry that had been dominated by vertically integrated monopolies.[13] One success apparently is in Norway, which created a separate state-owned power pool, Statnett Marked, to manage bulk power sales across the territorial boundaries of regional electric utilities. This reform appears to have substantially increased transactions and narrowed price differences for electricity among regions. Similar experiments in California, the eastern United States, England, Sweden, and Australia have introduced competition in generation, retail sales, or both (see Joskow 1998).

Few countries have tried any degree of vertical divestiture in electricity. The exceptions are the creation of two generation companies in England and Wales and a policy to favor nonutility companies in building new generation capacity in parts of the United States. Complete vertical separation between generation and transmission has not been mandated anywhere. Instead, governments have attempted to create "independent service organizations" that manage access to the transmission grid, including regulating the price of transmission services as well as determining the rules for independent generation sources to use the network to deliver power to their customers. This approach essentially separates the ownership of transmission networks from their management and operation.

Regulatory reform has faced difficulty in preventing regulated monopolies from dominating vertically related, potentially competitive markets.

---

13. For an excellent summary of several of these cases, including England, Norway and Sweden, and Australia, see Wolak (chap. 3 in this volume).

In the United States, policies to protect against vertical leveraging have given rise to persistent conflicts before regulatory agencies and antitrust courts for nearly a century (see Noll 1995; Joskow and Noll 1999). In the United Kingdom, which did not adopt separations remedies in telecommunications but did so to a limited degree in electricity, subsequent evaluations concluded that competition has not been extensive and intense (see Wolak, chap. 3 in this volume; Armstrong, Cowan, and Vickers 1994, esp. 355–58).

In the vast majority of the world, firms in the sectors where the natural monopoly argument is most commonly thought to apply have been state-owned enterprises. But beginning in the 1980s, several countries privatized formerly public enterprises, either as a reform measure that was an end in itself or as part of a plan to introduce competition. These experiences provide useful information about the comparative efficiency of the two organizational forms.

A recent study of generation facilities that account for over 40 percent of the world's capacity finds that private utilities produce electricity at about 5 percent lower cost than public enterprise utilities (Pollitt 1993). A study of privatization in Britain finds efficiency gains of 12 percent for British Telecom, 4 percent for National Freight, and 1.6 percent for British Airways (Vickers and Yarrow 1988). A study of British Gas concludes that privatization increased productivity by 2.3 percent; however, inconsistent results for a productivity effect were found for the regional electric utilities (Button and Weyman-Jones 1994a, 1994b). A study of privatization in Chile and Mexico found increases in economy-wide economic benefits of 50 percent for Telmex, 155 percent for Chile Telecom, and lesser but positive benefits for other cases (Galal et al. 1994). Even some urban water systems in developing countries, such as Abidjan, Buenos Aires, and Santiago, have been successfully privatized (Noll, Shirley, and Cowan forthcoming).

The lessons from reform of economic regulation in many nations are as follows. First, substantial gains in efficiency can be captured from improving the institutional environment of regulated infrastructural industries, such as by privatizing nationalized companies and adopting incentive regulation. Whereas these reforms provide direct domestic benefits in the form of lower prices for consumers, they also remove a trade distortion in that they lower the costs of export industries that make intensive use of the services of infrastructural monopolies. Second, because the case for natural monopoly is problematic, eliminating entry restrictions can introduce still greater efficiency.

These conclusions have important international ramifications. Because in many infrastructural industries only one firm has been allowed to offer service, the most plausible entrant is often the entrenched incumbent in another nation. In developing countries, privatization almost always involves at least partial ownership by a foreign company in the same industry, and other such firms have almost always been the most common source of competitive entry. In addition, in all of these industries national boundaries do not provide a basis for reasonably differentiating markets or the scope of a firm. In transportation and telecommunications, international services are arranged through mutual agreements between nations and their designated companies, and in electricity, regional power pools in Europe and North America extend across national boundaries. In these cases, formal separation of market access based on national boundaries is inefficient and precludes competitive entry by the firm that most plausibly could extend service in a monopoly service area at lowest cost. Hence, mutual relaxation of foreign investment restrictions by adjacent trading partners is a promising mechanism for speeding the evolution to competition after formal monopoly franchises have been removed.

The voluntary WTO agreement regarding access by foreign telecommunications firms is a good illustration of the connectedness of international economic policy and domestic regulation. Signatories to the agreement have committed to open at least international calling and in some cases elements of domestic service (such as long distance within the country), in most cases by the year 2000. Twenty nations have gone so far as to commit to a "single market" in telecommunications, allowing firms in these countries access to all twenty.

1.4.2   Social Regulation

Environmental protection is an example of regulation to deal with *externalities*. In this case, regulatory reform means, not deregulation, but the use of more flexible methods of regulation. In almost all countries, the standard method of regulating pollution is to set technical standards for each source.[14] These standards often are more rigorous for new production facilities than for established enterprises and so distort market entry. The stringency and cost of standards also vary among industries, further distorting the pattern of economic activity to favor less rigorously regulated sectors. For example, a study of sulfur oxide emissions in Los Angeles found that the marginal cost of abatement for the most heavily controlled sources (electric utilities) was $20,000 per ton, whereas other controlled sources faced marginal costs of abatement of around $200 (glass bottle manufacturing), and still other sources remained completely uncontrolled (dry cleaners; Hahn and Noll 1982).

Technical standards have led to two important sources of trade distor-

---

14. For an excellent review of the status of environmental regulation worldwide, see Hartman and Wheeler (1995). For an assessment of the tenacity with which the United Kingdom has clung to source-specific standards for environmental regulation, see Helm (1998).

tions. First, because such standards almost always specify the technique that must be used to reduce emissions, the standard itself can be a barrier to trade by ruling out other approaches to compliance that may be as effective but are not consistent with the standard. Second, by causing differences in compliance costs among sources within the same industry, technical standards actually can inefficiently induce imports. For example, by driving a wedge between old and new emission sources, new source performance standards create a discrete jump in the marginal private cost of production in an industry when increased production means expansion of capacity. If import prices are between the marginal costs of production at old and at new facilities, the effect can be to encourage imports to satisfy new demand, whereas efficient regulation would allow new firms to enter successfully at a price below the import price.

Because progress in environmental protection has been slow while compliance costs often have been high, some nations have begun to experiment with the use of economic incentives rather than technical standards. The two primary methods for achieving greater efficiency by introducing economic incentives into environmental regulation are emission trading and effluent fees. The advantage of both is that they are competitively neutral among industries and firms.

Emission trading in the United States began in the late 1970s with "controlled trading options" for six air pollutants, whereby two or more sources could propose regulations that reallocated pollution among them, subject to many procedural requirements and technical constraints. Despite a burdensome process, this program saved at least hundreds of millions of dollars, and more likely billions, in compliance costs without reducing environmental quality (Hahn 1989). Later, in Singapore and the United States, emission markets were used to meet international commitments under the Montreal Protocols to reduce chlorofluorocarbon emissions. In the United States, emission allowances were allocated according to historical production, but emitters were permitted to buy and sell allowances. In Singapore, emission allocations were sold at auction (O'Connor 1991). Another example is "offsets" in Germany and the United States, whereby new sources of pollution in a heavily polluted area are not permitted unless emitters reduce emissions from other facilities by more than the amount of emissions created by the new facility (Hartman and Wheeler 1995).

Effluent fees are a tax on the emission of harmful pollutants. The textbook model of effluent fees is to set the tax high enough to reflect the damage created by pollution so that polluters have a financial incentive to abate if pollution abatement is less costly than the harm it creates. Although many countries set effluent fees, these fees are almost never high enough to create a significant financial incentive to abate. Sometimes fees are selectively imposed because too few resources are allocated to enforcement or because politics enters into decisions about how much tax to levy on each source of pollution.[15]

In a few cases, effluent fees are reasonably effective. One example is water pollution control in the Netherlands (Anderson 1994; Hahn 1989). Water effluent fees are much higher in the Netherlands than elsewhere and so induce much more abatement at the source, thereby more closely approximating the least cost division of responsibility between source controls and sewage treatment. In Japan, effluent fees for sulfur dioxide emissions provide a fund for compensating victims of unhealthful air pollution (O'Connor 1993). Whether these fees are adequate is debatable, but the principle that polluters pay for the damage that they create motivates the fees.

The international consequence of incentive-based environmental regulatory reforms is to reallocate production among nations in a manner that reduces total social costs. These reforms reduce compliance costs for industries that need to control harmful pollutants. As a result, the relative production costs in these industries fall compared with firms in nations that use less efficient methods of controlling emissions, and if their products are traded, these industries gain a larger share of the world market. In some cases, the principal effect is that domestic production substitutes for exports that appeared attractive only because they were produced in a less costly regulatory environment. In other cases, the principal effect is to increase exports among industries that experience lower regulatory compliance costs. In all cases, all prices and exchange rates adjust so that some other industries experience some compensating adjustment in net imports, and total trade can either rise or fall. But in all cases, the net effect is an increase in world productivity and income as production moves in response to reductions in social costs.

Another international implication of incentive-based environmental regulation is that it beneficially affects location decisions of international firms. The relative anonymity of incentive-based environmental reforms eliminates the possibility that environmental standards will be applied in a discriminatory fashion against foreign investors. Because entry requires only that the new facility buy permits or pay emission taxes, rather than receive an emission standard and a permit to operate, incentive-based environmental regulation eliminates a source of regulatory barriers to entry.

Regulations that deal with *information imperfections* are called protective standards. This category of regulation is broad and heterogeneous. It includes product safety, drug efficacy, workplace safety, prudentiality in financial services, and protection against fraudulent advertising and prod-

---

15. E.g., Poland's effluent fee system appears not to have worked for these reasons (Wilcynski 1990).

uct labeling. At the heart of such regulations are two basic concerns. One is that one side of a market—consumers or workers—has less access to information about the quality of the product or workplace than the other side and so might be victimized. The other concern is that neither side of the market will have an adequate incentive to acquire valuable information that would be useful for evaluating products and workplaces, and that, if known, might change behavior and hence product and workplace safety.

As with environmental regulation, the issue in protective regulation is not whether such regulation is ever justified but how best to achieve regulatory objectives more efficiently. Protective standards can cause several economic problems. First, they can retard beneficial technological change by introducing inflexibility in designing products and workplaces. Second, they can prevent informed decisions that reflect individual differences in attitudes about or susceptibilities to risk. Third, they create a process that can be used by producers to create barriers to competition, especially international market access.

Reform in this area of regulation takes many forms, depending on the nature of the problem. One reform is to require full disclosure, backed by documentation of claims, so that the uninformed side of a market has more information, and then to let the market determine the appropriate degree of risk. Another reform is to adopt international standards processes so that a consumer product or workplace equipment need only prove its acceptability once, rather than separately in each country. Still another approach is to focus on performance standards rather than design standards. Performance standards allow greater variety in technical approaches to solving the same problem and so encourage cost minimization and technological progress. Finally, another approach is to subsidize product testing by independent authorities (governmental or private) and to publicize the results.

A recent OECD survey indicates that most firms in four industries (toys, lawn mowers, microwave ovens, and bicycle helmets) regard the present standards system as excessively cumbersome and costly, and about one-third indicated that some national standards processes prevented them from entering markets, even though they had satisfied equivalent standards elsewhere (OECD 1996a). The purpose of reform is to avoid these effects when they have nothing to do with the protective purposes of regulation.

1.5 Priorities for Reform

The preceding analysis focuses on specific types of regulations and institutional reforms and by implication constitutes a long list of areas in which literally every nation can find useful examples from other countries about how to make regulation more cost-effective. This section focuses on the international implications of three categories of regulatory reform: competition policy, procedural requirements such as mandatory benefit-cost analysis, and internationalization of reform. All of these policies are closely related to the efficiency concepts discussed in this essay. In the absence of any of the market failures discussed here, an unregulated competitive market is efficient.

Many hypothesized market failures that underpin regulatory policy are illusory or unimportant, in which case regulatory reform means abandoning regulation and undertaking a vigorous policy to promote competition. The presence of a significant market failure provides a rationale for continued government intervention but does not require sacrificing either competitive markets or economic efficiency. In these cases, regulatory interventions will be most effective, first, if they focus narrowly on curing the market failure while minimizing the extent to which they disrupt competition and, second, if these interventions are designed to achieve their policy objectives efficiently. Hence, even when regulation is present, there is usually a heightened role for competition policy: to assure that regulation disrupts competition to the minimum extent necessary to cure the market failure. And to help identify the most cost-effective ways to attack market failures, regulations should be developed with the aid of a comprehensive economic impact analysis.

Because regulation has become more important as a source of trade barriers, domestic regulatory policy has become a major agenda item in negotiations over trade policy. Internationalization of regulatory reform is viewed with skepticism and alarm by some advocates of liberalized trade, partly because the result of international regulatory negotiations can be the formation of an international cartel beyond the reach of domestic reform. Historical agreements about international telephone and airline services stand as continuing reminders of the pitfalls of international regulatory agreements.

Notwithstanding these problems, internationalizing regulatory policy also can facilitate the reform process and provide additional insurance against backsliding. The arena of international trade negotiations provides an opportunity for expanding the benefits of domestic reforms by pairing them with foreign reforms that grant domestic firms greater access to external markets. Once agreement is reached, international trade enforcement institutions, such as the WTO and the European Court, provide additional protection against subsequent regulatory actions that distort trade.

1.5.1 Competition Policy

Policies to promote competition are always in some tension with regulation, and effective regulatory reform usually requires rethinking how this tension should be resolved. The essence of the tension is that regulatory policy promulgates common rules of behavior for firms within a market and sometimes encourages monopoly or cartels, whereas competition policy seeks to eliminate monopoly and to force firms to operate independently. Fixing a price or a common production technology through a regulatory process is far different conceptually from insisting that each firm make price and production decisions separately and letting the competitive process determine the ultimate performance of the industry.

The anticompetitive danger of regulatory policy arises from the fact that it asks a regulatory authority to make decisions normally made by firms engaged in competition. Consequently, the power to regulate can be abused by a group of participants in a market if they can make use of the regulatory process to reduce competition among themselves, at the expense of other groups in the market. For example, a regulatory standard may reduce pollution, improve product quality, or make the workplace safer, but it may also do none of these things but instead simply require that consumers buy one type of product rather than another, benefiting the producer of that product at the expense of competitors and consumers.

Regulation often has served anticompetitive purposes by favoring domestic products over imported ones, thereby creating an indirect trade barrier. As discussed above, one example from the United States is policy regarding reformulated gasoline, whereby the details of the regulation required Venezuelan refiners to make greater improvements in their product than were required of U.S. producers of equivalent gasoline (Vogel 1997). Another example is the requirement in many countries that suppliers of infrastructural services—telephones, electric power, transportation, and so forth—be domestically owned.

Certainly the presence of these examples implies that parallel distortions in the politics of trade policy are plausible. Regulators seek to give domestic producers the advantage partly because foreign producers are less likely to be effective participants in the domestic political process, and so are less likely to be important sources of political support or opposition to a government. Indeed, not only are the employees and owners of an excluded foreign firm denied the vote, in most countries any attempt by foreigners to influence domestic politics is regarded as a criminal offense.

A second cause of regulatory favoritism toward domestic firms is that most debate about regulatory policies is narrowly focused on a particular industry, problem, or even detailed regulation. Even if a statute or an international treaty expresses the objective of avoiding anticompetitive regulations, anticompetitive outcomes are difficult to avoid if regulation inevitably arises from product-specific or industry-specific debates. Specific regulations require detailed analyses of the nature of the problem giving rise to regulation and its possible solutions. The process of undertaking such an analysis favors domestic industries: politically because they can apply direct political pressure to regulators and procedurally because they have standing before the regulators and possess information needed to assess the benefits and costs of regulation. An excluded foreign firm is unlikely to have the right to participate in these processes, and the domestic interest that would benefit from competition—buyers of regulated products—is unlikely to find it worthwhile to pay the cost to participate in the process as an advocate of foreign competitors. This problem is by no means limited to potential foreign competitors. In many cases, no firm that is not already a supplier in the industry has rights of participation in the regulatory process. Such was the case in airline regulation in the United States before deregulation (see Breyer 1982, esp. chap. 16) and is the case in telecommunications regulation in Japan (see Noll and Rosenbluth 1995).

The anticompetitive use of regulation, whether against domestic or foreign competitors, is common enough that it has been given a name: "regulatory capture." This term has an unfortunate connotation of corruption, whereby regulators consciously act on behalf of one economic interest at the expense of others and to the detriment of the economy. Whereas in some cases regulation has served as little more than a means for creating a monopoly or a cartel where otherwise competition would reign free, more subtle forms of capture probably are more important. Regulators must adopt regulations on the basis of the information available and the proposals made to them. All too often a particular regulatory issue does not capture the attention of anyone other than a few companies affected by it. If these companies propose a regulation that will reduce competition and increase their profits, the regulator may not recognize the fact or may not have enough information to ascertain whether a less anticompetitive regulation is feasible.

Competition policy can play an important role in limiting the extent to which regulatory policy has unnecessary anticompetitive effects. For example, an agency responsible for competition policy can systematically review important pending regulatory proceedings and provide its views about the effects of alternative regulations on competition. A competition policy agency also can bring actions against companies that use the regulatory process for anticompetitive purposes, as in the watershed antitrust case against the American Telephone and Telegraph Company in the United States.[16]

Regarding economic regulation, the introduction of competition into formerly monopolized infrastructural industries has raised important questions about interconnections between established firms and competitive entrants. When regulation prevents a monopolist from exercising full monopoly power in regulated markets, a strong incentive is created to le-

---

16. For details about this case and its interaction with U.S. regulatory policy, see Noll and Owen (1994).

verage the regulated monopoly into competitive areas. The means that incumbent monopolists have used to accomplish this objective are to deny competitors access to monopoly services that are essential parts of competitive services and to engage in abusive conduct, such as price discrimination, predatory pricing, or degradation of service, to undercut the success of a competitor (OECD 1994a).

In the environmental, health, and safety area, regulatory standards can create entry barriers and can facilitate the formation of cartels. For example, collaborative recycling arrangements sometimes are attractive for capturing economies of scale and coordination among manufacturers, but they can also give firms opportunities for coordinating pricing and production behavior (OECD 1994b). Likewise, product standards that differ very slightly among countries can serve solely to protect a domestic market for a single supplier, as the EEC Commission concluded in reviewing a herbicide regulation in Germany (OECD 1995a, 10–11).

When the anticompetitive policies of regulators exclude domestic suppliers, competition policy agencies have a domestic political constituency that will support their intervention; however, if regulation mainly excludes foreign competition, foreign interests face the same political liabilities in influencing both competition and regulatory policies. Their lack of effective political representation is as likely to affect one bureaucracy as another. But dispute resolution institutions created to enforce trade agreements can serve this function. These entities can be the international counterpart to domestic competition policy agencies if international agreements give them the authority to examine whether regulations anticompetitively exclude foreigners.

1.5.2   Procedural Reform: Mandatory Economic Policy Analysis

Procedural reform refers to a variety of proposals for improving the quality of regulation by improving its structure and procedures. Examples of such reforms are changes in rights of standing before regulatory authorities, the burden of proof, the standard of proof, the nature of judicial review, and the place of the regulatory authority in the hierarchy of government agencies. The structure and process of regulation are important determinants of the three major aspects of regulatory outcomes: *stringency* (how tough is the regulatory requirement?); *equity* (how are the burdens and benefits of regulation allocated across industries, geography, and demographic categories?); and *efficiency* (does the regulation achieve its purposes at lowest possible cost?).

The structure and process of regulation are important because they affect the flow of information both in the regulatory process and to citizens about the basis for a regulatory rule. In essence, structure and process determine the relative weights given to different interests and types of information in making regulatory policy (McCubbins, Noll, and Weingast

1987, 1989). An important purpose of structural reform is to improve the efficiency of regulation by making the process more open and transparent.

A prominent example of procedural reform is to require some form of economic policy analysis, which refers to a range of analytic methods for evaluating policies. The most common form is benefit-cost analysis; related methods include comparative risk analysis and cost-effectiveness analysis. The issue at stake is the extent to which economic policy analysis should play a role in the process of developing new regulations and regulatory policies.

The purpose of economic policy analysis of regulatory proposals is to provide a systematic framework for organizing relevant information for informing decisions, and to provide insight about the extent to which regulation is consistent and coherent across different areas of regulatory policy. A major criticism of regulation is that lessons from one domain of regulation are slow to spill over into others, and that different regulations, adopted at different times by different regulators, that deal with similar issues take vastly different approaches.

One study of 185 different regulatory proposals in the United States for improving health discovered no correlation between the cost-effectiveness of a proposal for saving lives and whether it was implemented (Tengs and Graham 1996). For example, this study points out that the existing standard for regulating the flammability of children's clothing has a cost of $1.5 million per life saved, but another proposal to require smoke alarms in homes with children present, which would have cost only $200,000 per life saved, was rejected. The authors found that the best estimate of total life-years saved from all of the adopted regulations was 592,000 per year at a cost of approximately $21.4 billion. Had this sum been spent in the most effective way, the total annual number of life-years saved would have been 1,230,000, or more than double the number currently being saved.

Another recent study compiled the results of ninety-one benefit-cost analyses undertaken for major regulations adopted or pending in the United States from 1990 to 1995 (Hahn 1996). The good news, according to the study, is that all fifty-four final regulations adopted, taken together, generated net benefits of nearly $300 billion in discounted present value.[17] The bad news is that thirty-one of these regulations have negative net benefits, and three had negative net benefits exceeding $10 billion.

The primary controversial issues concerning economic policy analysis are how it should be undertaken and what status it should have in the regulatory process. Proposals about the formal role of economic analysis range from establishing an agency for undertaking such analyses, to

17. The good news is not without qualification, for this finding rests on the accuracy of the assessment of the risks that gave rise to the regulation, but as Hahn (1996) points out, in many cases these risks are substantially overstated by regulatory agencies.

allowing the agency to select its targets and to have standing in regulatory proceedings, to requiring that all regulations pass a benefit-cost test before they are adopted. OECD member countries illustrate almost the full range of possibilities (OECD 1995b).

A group of U.S. economists has proposed a new role for benefit-cost analysis in environmental, health, and safety regulation (Arrow et al. 1996a, 1996b). They set out the purposes of analysis: to encourage greater consistency and transparency in regulatory policy, as well as to improve the efficiency of regulation. To this end, they propose that all major regulations be subject to mandatory benefit-cost analysis before a final regulation is adopted. In addition, they propose that all benefit-cost analyses have three features: first, the analysis should be based on a common set of assumptions about common parameters, such as the social discount rate and the value of reductions in morbidity and mortality; second, the analysis should examine the sensitivity of the magnitude of net benefits to the values of key parameters of the analysis; and third, the analysis should be subject to a system of peer review. Finally, they propose that agencies be required to justify rejecting a regulation expected to yield positive net benefits and adopting regulation that has negative net expected benefits or that achieves positive net benefits only when it uses nonstandard assumptions about key parameters. A similar proposal was made by a panel of expert advisers to the Commission of the European Communities.

Making economic policy analysis mandatory is controversial, and indeed the commission rejected the proposal of its expert panel, making reference to standard arguments against mandatory policy analysis:

> The Commission supports the thrust of this proposal. But the practicability of cost-benefit analysis has to be examined on a case by case basis. In the particular field of the environment, there is a question of what constitutes a "reasonable" balance between costs and benefits. The benefits for environment and society are mostly qualitative and often impossible to express in monetary values unlike, for example, the costs to business. The Treaty (130r(3)) also requires that the costs and benefits of *non-action* also be examined. (Commission of the European Communities 1995, 26–27)

The commission's decision to reject the proposal that all regulations must generate positive net benefits is reasonable, but the reasons given contain important misperceptions, and the decision not to require systematic economic policy analysis is not supported by these reasons.

To begin, a competent benefit-cost analysis does not ignore the costs and benefits of inaction. Benefits and costs are measured as incremental changes from the status quo, so that the net benefits of a policy change are identically equal to the net cost of inaction. Indeed, a competent benefit-cost analysis goes beyond this to estimate the incremental benefits and costs of all relevant alternatives to both the status quo and the proposed regulation.

Another important misperception is the statement by the commission that costs are easier to quantify than benefits, biasing benefit-cost analysis in favor of inaction. This statement reflects a fundamental error in the commission's reasoning: "Cost" in benefit-cost analysis does not refer to the financial cost to producers in complying with the regulation but instead to the social cost of adopting the regulation. These concepts are not the same for two basic reasons: uncertainties and unquantifiable effects affect the cost side as well as other forms of information that are essential to formulating regulations, and the presence of imprecision is a matter to be identified and explicitly taken into account, not to be ignored by sweeping analysis under the rug.

On the cost side, allocating resources to regulatory compliance, instead of other activities, also poses risks to life and the environment that are difficult to quantify. The issue of evaluating life actually demonstrates the value of careful economic analysis. Disposable family income is strongly correlated with rates of morbidity and mortality. One study estimates that if a regulatory action imposes a cost of $50 million, the regulation will cause one additional death due to the reduction in purchasing power that must occur to pay for the cost of the regulation (Viscusi 1996). And if a regulation causes a reallocation of economic activity to other products, this reallocation inevitably leads to increases in exposure to other hazards and environmental damage, in part offsetting the benefits of the regulation. Whereas the appropriate number for the value of a life saved is surely subject to considerable uncertainty, the preceding observations provide an important insight: most likely, no regulation that imposes a cost exceeding $50 million per life saved should be adopted, not because $50 million is a good estimate of the value of a life, but because a regulation that costs that much will cause at least as much indirect damage as it is intended to cure.

Mandatory economic analysis of regulatory policies is related to international trade because it facilitates identifying whether regulations promote efficiency or distort trade. An agreement among nations to use common analytical methods for evaluating regulatory proposals drives regulation in each nation toward efficient policies and thereby reduces the distortions arising from regulations of different efficiency among nations. In this sense, adopting a common efficiency metric for domestic regulatory actions has the same role in reducing trade distortions as does a common agreement to reduce tariffs in that both reduce the wedge between actual prices and social costs of production. Moreover, agreement about methods for evaluating regulations is a necessary component of a mechanism for resolving trade disputes over the ultimate purposes and effects of regulations. In particular, a competent economic analysis can distinguish regulations that have an anticompetitive purpose and distort trade from regulations that are efficient even though they have differential impacts on some imports.

1.6   International Regulatory Reform and Trade

Until recently, the regulatory reform debate has been regarded primarily as an issue of domestic economic policy. As implied by the discussion of electronic commerce and of the trade distortions created by differences in regulatory efficiency among nations, a narrow, nationalistic view of regulatory reform is not valid. As a result, recent trade negotiations and agreements inevitably have included provisions relating to regulatory issues. For example, the Uruguay Round led to an agreement that internal political constraints could not override principles of open access and created a WTO Committee on the Environment.[18]

Regulatory distortions take two conceptually distinct forms: domestic and international. This conceptual division implies a scheme for setting priorities: focus international agreements on regulatory issues that cause significant international distortions. The inefficiencies of regulation that are purely domestic are not necessarily an international priority for reform. Whereas these effects are unfortunate, the costs mostly are confined to the country that causes them. If inefficient regulation has significant international repercussions, coordination and cooperation among nations in regulatory reform have the same status as multinational arrangements for reducing direct trade barriers. Mutuality in reform creates economic benefits that are broadly shared among domestic consumers and trading partners.

As a practical matter, very little distorting regulation has purely domestic effects. International boundaries rarely define natural market barriers that cannot be crossed, and in most cases, the most efficient organization of an industry is international. For example, infrastructural industries (energy utilities, communications, transportation, and finance) all operate more efficiently if their networks are organized according to the pattern of transactions, and in a relatively open world economy, these patterns do not respect national borders. But even if markets are national or indeed local, entry by foreign firms can be an important source of price competition and productivity improvements. Many segments of retail trade are more efficient if international chains of outlets and, of course, electronic commerce are permitted. Hence, both market access for foreign-made goods and openness to foreign investment promote economic growth, and regulations that prevent either create distortions of international signifi-

---

18. For a discussion of the incorporation of environmental issues into trade agreements and enforcement organizations, see Roessler (1996a).

cance. International agreements about regulation are the natural vehicle to eliminate these distortions.

An additional advantage of internationalizing regulatory reform is that it can be used to elevate the domestic political debate about regulation from narrow issues to matters of national economic performance and international cooperation. From a political perspective, making regulatory reform an international issue is highly desirable. A common political barrier to domestic regulatory reform is that if reform is perceived as a domestic issue and is debated one issue at a time, well-organized special interests are more likely to have the political power to block it. For most specific regulatory issues, the beneficiaries of reform are numerous, but their per capita benefits are often too low or too indirect to generate significant political pressure for reform. If the reform debate is elevated to a matter of international policy that encompasses numerous reform issues, broader attention and participation from all interests is more likely, thereby reducing the ability of a single interest to block reform.

A useful analogy is to the process of setting tariffs (see Goldstein 1996). When each nation independently sets each tariff separately, the resulting tariffs are likely to be higher than those that would have been negotiated bilaterally as part of a comprehensive trade agreement. The reason is that debating tariffs one product at a time maximizes the undue influence of organized interests with a direct stake in the policy. If a tariff on a specific product is under review, the domestic industry that produces the product is likely to be intensely interested and to exercise whatever political influence it has to obtain a policy decision favorable to itself; however, because the final price of the product is less important to individual buyers than to individual producers, the former are less likely to participate in the debate. Consequently, each important trade-sensitive industry may receive and preserve a tariff or a favorable regulation when policy is debated in a purely domestic context one industry at a time, but it may receive neither protective tariffs nor protective regulations when policy is developed multinationally and covers many industries.

When each regulation is considered separately as a matter of domestic policy within a specialized agency, the government is likely to be under less pressure to adopt an efficient policy. If a regulation imposes unnecessary costs uniformly on firms in a domestic industry, sales of the industry's product may be suppressed somewhat by higher prices, but the individual firms are unlikely to suffer much because none is at a disadvantage relative to a competitor. If international trade threatens the industry, however, the industry will energetically seek relief. The politically expedient move may be to inhibit trade competition, either by using regulation as an indirect trade barrier or by banning trade while making a rhetorical attack on the lax standards of a trading partner. This approach placates the regulated industry and other interests that place high value on the regulatory policy.

The primary organized harmed interest, foreign producers, is more easily ignored because they do not participate in domestic politics.

Just as simultaneous negotiation over tariffs on all products conduces to agreements that provide freer trade, so too does simultaneous negotiation of numerous areas of regulation facilitate the elimination of regulatory indirect trade barriers. As with tariffs, the inclusion of multiple regulatory policies within the same negotiation creates more opportunities for mutually beneficial bargains to reduce distortions simultaneously on all fronts. Recent experience with multilateral negotiations bears out this belief.[19] On both the trade and regulatory fronts, with the exceptions of the Agreement on Trade in Civil Aircraft and the voluntary agreement to liberalize telecommunications access, no single-issue negotiation under the General Agreement on Tariffs and Trade (GATT) and few outside of it have produced a significant commitment to openness, and many have included new, onerous regulatory requirements. Examples of failures are the International Dairy Agreement, which establishes minimum world prices for dairy products; the Multi-Fiber Arrangement, which countenanced import quotas; and the Montreal Protocols, which set world limits on emissions of ozone-depleting chlorofluorocarbons (CFC) but prohibited reallocation among nations of either production or consumption of CFC-related products through trade or international investment.

The lesson from these examples is that incorporation of regulation into trade agreements should follow the same principles that have been generally followed with respect to tariffs and quotas. Specifically, if regulatory policy is part of an international agreement, it must reduce, not increase, distortions in the international economy and extend, not contract, the extent of liberalization. Introducing regulation into single-product negotiations tends to increase trade distortions (as regulation is used to inhibit trade). In particular, negotiations about a single product or area of regulation risk creating an alliance between protectionists and the most ardent advocates of a particular regulatory policy who seek regulations that go far beyond those that maximize net social benefits.

The same argument applies to the enforcement of agreements not to adopt anticompetitive regulations. If enforcement powers reside solely in domestic agencies, a case in which a regulation places foreign producers at a disadvantage rests on unbalanced underlying politics. Domestic producers are likely to be more effectively represented than foreigners in the agency and in the background political system within which the agency must operate. Consequently, actions to eliminate the anticompetitive international effects of regulation are likely to face more political resistance than support.

International institutions for resolving regulatory trade disputes operate

---

19. For more details on the examples presented in this paragraph, see Roessler (1996b).

in a more balanced political environment. These institutions can be a means through which nations mutually can commit to maintain procompetitive regulatory reforms. The GATT and WTO disputes about automobile fuel efficiency and reformulated gasoline illustrate how domestic regulatory agencies but not international institutions are willing to sacrifice competition as well as some of the effectiveness of regulatory policies in order to favor domestic producers.

For these reasons, internationalization of regulatory reform can succeed by enfranchising foreign producers in domestic regulatory policy across a spectrum of industries. In the context of a dispute about the trade effects of a particular regulation, intervention by an international organization often is met with cries of outrage—an intervention by foreigners into domestic policy. All international agreements entail some loss of the ability to act independently in order to achieve something else of value, which in this case is a worldwide regulatory system that is more efficient and freer of trade distortions. Such an institution generates net economic benefits to each country, even if some cases create some domestic losers. The creation of institutions for enforcing agreements to eliminate indirect trade barriers is a means to balance the political influence of these domestic losers.

The growing movement for regulatory reform throughout the world has increased the potential significance of internationalizing the reform process. If some nations operate a relatively efficient regulatory system while others do not, international cost differences arising from regulation are likely to surface as political issues in high-cost countries. Perhaps the result will be reform, but another plausible scenario is protection against "unfair" competition. Initiating multisectoral international negotiations over phased reform offers an opportunity to seize the initiative, casting the agenda in terms of improved efficiency rather than retaliation against unfair trade. Domestic reform that enfranchises competition policy agencies facilitates free trade by promoting reforms of regulatory policies that erect entry barriers. Reforms that impose mandatory benefit-cost analysis facilitate free trade by creating a stronger information base from which to challenge regulatory trade barriers in international dispute resolution institutions. Finally, designing these same dispute resolution entities to incorporate the principles of competition policy and economic policy analysis has two potential benefits: regulations are identified that have no plausible rationale other than to place foreign competition at a disadvantage, and beyond this, the degree to which differences in regulatory policy create differential regulatory efficiency is reduced. Both effects of the internationalization of regulatory reform serve the objectives of international openness and help to eliminate an important source of distortions in the international economy.

References

Anderson, Mikael Skou. 1994. Economic instruments and clean water: Why institutions and policy design matter. PUMA/REG(94)5. Paris: Organization for Economic Cooperation and Development, April.

Armstrong, Mark, Simon Cowan, and John Vickers. 1994. *Regulatory reform: Economic analysis and British experience.* Cambridge, Mass.: MIT Press.

Arrow, Kenneth J., Maureen L. Cropper, George C. Eads, Robert W. Hahn, Lester B. Lave, Roger G. Noll, Paul R. Portney, Milton Russell, Richard Schmalensee, V. Kerry Smith, and Robert N. Stavins. 1996a. *Benefit-cost analysis in environmental, health and safety regulation: A statement of principles.* Washington, D.C.: American Enterprise Institute.

———. 1996b. Is there a role for benefit-cost analysis in environmental, health, and safety regulation? *Science* 272:221–22.

Baily, Martin Neal. 1993. Competition, regulation, and efficiency in service industries. *Brookings Papers on Economic Activity: Microeconomics,* no. 2:71–130.

Baron, David. 1989. The design of regulatory mechanisms and institutions. In *The handbook of industrial organization,* ed. Richard Schmalensee and Robert Willig. New York: North-Holland.

Bernstein, Jeffrey I. 1988. Dynamic factor demands and adjustment costs: An analysis of Bell Canada's technology. *Information Economics and Policy* 3:5–24.

Breyer, Stephen. 1982. *Regulation and its reform.* Cambridge, Mass.: Harvard University Press.

Button, Kenneth, and Thomas Weyman-Jones. 1994a. Impacts of privatization policy in Europe. *Contemporary Economic Policy* 12, no. 1 (October): 23–33.

———. 1994b. X-efficiency and technical efficiency. *Public Choice* 80 (1): 83–103.

Commission of the European Communities. 1995. Comments of the Commission on the report of the Independent Experts Group on Legislative and Administrative Simplification. SEC(95) 2121 final. Brussels.

Crandall, Robert W., and Leonard Waverman. 1996. *Talk is cheap: The promise of regulatory reform in North American telecommunications.* Washington, D.C.: Brookings Institution.

Galal, Ahmed, Leroy Jones, Pankaj Tandon, and Ingo Vogelsang. 1994. *Welfare consequences of selling public enterprise: An empirical analysis.* New York: Oxford University Press.

Goldstein, Judith. 1996. International institutions and domestic politics. Stanford, Calif.: Stanford University, Center for Economic Policy Research. Working paper.

Greenstein, Shane, Susan McMaster, and Pablo T. Spiller. 1994. The effect of incentive regulation on local exchange companies' deployment of digital infrastructure. Urbana: University of Illinois, June. Working paper.

Hahn, Robert W. 1989. Economic prescriptions for environmental problems: How the patient followed the doctor's orders. *Journal of Economic Perspectives* 3, no. 2 (spring): 94–114.

———. 1996. Regulatory reform: What do the government's numbers tell us? In *Risks, costs, and lives saved: Getting better results from regulation,* ed. Robert W. Hahn. New York: Oxford University Press.

Hahn, Robert W., and Roger G. Noll. 1982. Designing a market for tradable emissions permits. In *Reform of environmental regulation,* ed. Wesley Magat. Lexington, Mass.: Lexington.

Hartman, Raymond S., and David Wheeler. 1995. Incentive regulation: Market-based pollution control for the real world. In *Regulatory policies and reform: A comparative perspective,* ed. Claudio R. Frischtak. Washington, D.C.: World Bank, Private Sector Development Department.

Helm, Dieter. 1998. The assessment of environmental policy B objectives, instruments, institutions. *Oxford Review of Economic Policy* 14, no. 4 (winter): 1–19.

Joskow, Paul L. 1998. Electricity sectors in transition. *Energy Journal* 19 (2): 25–52.

Joskow, Paul L., and Roger G. Noll. 1999. The Bell doctrine. *Stanford Law Review* 51 (5): 1249–1315.

Majumdar, Sumit K. 1995. Regulation and productive efficiency: Evidence from the U.S. telecommunications industry. Ann Arbor: University of Michigan, July. Working paper.

McCubbins, Mathew D., Roger G. Noll, and Barry R. Weingast. 1987. Administrative procedures as instruments of political control. *Journal of Law, Economics and Organization* 3 (2): 243–77.

———. 1989. Structure and process, politics and policy: Administrative arrangements and the political control of agencies. *Virginia Law Review* 75, no. 2 (March): 431–82.

Nelson, Randy A., and Walter J. Primeaux. 1988. The effects of competition on transmission and distribution costs in the municipal electric industry. *Land Economics* 64 (November): 338–46.

Noll, Roger G. 1995. The role of antitrust in telecommunications. *Antitrust Bulletin,* fall: 501–28.

———. 1997. Internationalizing regulatory reform. In *Comparative disadvantage,* ed. Pietro S. Nivola, 319–55. Washington, D.C.: Brookings Institution.

———. Forthcoming. Telecommunications in developing countries. In *Economic policy reform: The second stage,* ed. Anne O. Krueger. Chicago: University of Chicago Press.

Noll, Roger G., and Bruce M. Owen. 1994. The anticompetitive uses of regulation: *United States v. AT&T* (1982). In *The antitrust revolution,* 2d ed., ed. John E. Kwoka Jr. and Lawrence J. White, 328–75. New York: Harper Collins.

Noll, Roger G., and Frances M. Rosenbluth. 1995. Telecommunications policy: Structure, process, outcomes. In *Structure and policy in Japan and the United States,* ed. Peter F. Cowhey and Mathew D. McCubbins, 119–76. New York: Cambridge University Press.

Noll, Roger G., Mary M. Shirley, and Simon Cowan. Forthcoming. Reforming urban water systems in developing countries. In *Economic policy reform: The second stage,* ed. Anne O. Krueger. Chicago: University of Chicago Press.

O'Connor, D. 1991. Policy and entrepreneurial response to the Montreal Protocol: Some evidence from the dynamic Asian economies. Technical Paper no. 51. Paris: Organization for Economic Cooperation and Development, Development Center.

———. 1993. Managing the environment with rapid industrialization. Paris: Organization for Economic Cooperation and Development, Development Center.

OECD (Organization for Economic Cooperation and Development). 1992. Structure and change in distribution systems: An analysis of seven OECD member countries. ECO/CPE/WP1(92)7. Paris: Organization for Economic Cooperation and Development, Economics Department.

———. 1994a. Mini-roundtable on the role and enforcement of competition policy in regulated sectors. DAFFE/CLP/M(94)2/ANN4. Paris: Organization for Economic Cooperation and Development, Directorate for Financial, Fiscal and Enterprise Affairs.

———. 1994b. Role and enforcement of competition policy in regulated sectors:

Note by the Netherlands delegation. DAFFE/CLP(94)14. Paris: Organization for Economic Cooperation and Development, Directorate for Financial, Fiscal and Enterprise Affairs.

————. 1995a. Competition policy and the agro-food sector. COM/AGR/APM/TD/WP(95) 73/REV1. Paris: Organization for Economic Cooperation and Development, Directorate for Food, Agriculture and Fisheries.

————. 1995b. Control and management of government regulation. PUMA(95)9. Paris: Organization for Economic Cooperation and Development, Public Management Service.

————. 1995c. Parcel delivery in the global marketplace. Paris: Organization for Economic Cooperation and Development, Committee on Consumer Policy.

————. 1996a. Consumer product safety standards and conformity assessment: Their effect on international trade (draft). Paris: Organization for Economic Cooperation and Development, Committee on Consumer Policy.

————. 1996b. Information infrastructure convergence and pricing: The Internet. Paris: Organization for Economic Cooperation and Development, Working Party on Telecommunications and Information Services.

————. 1996c. Regulatory reform: A country study of Australia. PUMA/REG(96)1. Paris: Organization for Economic Cooperation and Development, Public Management Service.

Pollitt, Michael G. 1993. *The relative performance of publicly owned and privately owned electric utilities.* Ph.D. diss., Oxford University, Oxford.

Roessler, Frieder. 1996a. Diverging domestic policies and multilateral trade integration. In *Fair trade and harmonization: Prerequisites for free trade?* vol. 2, *Legal analysis,* ed. Jagdish Baghwati and Robert Hudec, 21–55. Cambridge, Mass.: MIT Press.

————. 1996b. Efficient and inefficient issue linkages in multilateral negotiations: A critical examination of the "trade and . . ." trend. Stanford, Calif.: Stanford University, Center for Economic Policy Research. Working paper.

Shabecoff, Philip. 1996. *A new name for peace: International environmentalism, sustainable development, and democracy.* Hanover, N.H.: University Press of New England.

Tengs, Tammy O., and John D. Graham. 1996. The opportunity costs of haphazard social investments in life-saving. In *Risks, costs, and lives saved: Getting better results from regulation,* ed. Robert W. Hahn. New York: Oxford University Press.

Utility Data Institute. 1992. *State directory of new electric power plants.* Washington, D.C.: Utility Data Institute.

Vickers, John, and George Yarrow. 1988. *Privatization: An economic analysis.* Cambridge, Mass.: MIT Press.

Viscusi, W. Kip. 1996. The dangers of unbounded commitments to regulate risk. In *Risks, costs, and lives saved: Getting better results from regulation,* ed. Robert W. Hahn. New York: Oxford University Press.

Vogel, David. 1997. Trouble for us and trouble for them: Social regulations as trade barriers. In *Comparative disadvantage,* ed. Pietro S. Nivola, 98–128. Washington, D.C.: Brookings Institution.

Wilcynski, P. 1990. Environmental management in centrally planned non-market economies of Eastern Europe. Working Paper no. 35. Washington, D.C.: World Bank, Environment Department.

Winston, Clifford. 1993. Economic deregulation: Days of reckoning for microeconomists. *Journal of Economic Literature* 31, no. 3 (September): 1263–89.

World Bank. 1995. *Bureaucrats in business.* New York: Oxford University Press.

Comment   Anne O. Krueger

This is a very rich paper, from which I learned a lot. The impression that stands out, among many others, is the great extent to which regulation and trade policy issues overlap and yet have been analyzed by two separate communities, with much less cross-fertilization than would have been desirable. Coming from the perspective of trade policy, I hope that Roger Noll's paper will make a major breach in the wall separating the two areas, and I believe that trade policy analysts will greatly benefit from this, and hopefully further, interaction.

Noll starts by noting the distinction between efficient regulation—which occurs when market failures are compensated for in a least cost way by public policy that results in an increase in social welfare—and actual regulation, which may have much higher cost because of nonoptimal regulatory behavior or because costs exceed the social benefits of regulation. Distinguishing between instances of market failures that policy can beneficially correct and instances where regulation is either inefficient or favors the regulated is a primary concern of policy analysis in the regulatory arena. In the past two decades, much regulation has been overhauled as inefficiencies have come to be recognized.

For international trade policy, the appropriate analogue would appear to be distinguishing between instances in which there are legitimate bases for protection (national defense, perhaps) and cases in which pleas for protection are based on legitimate issues (or on issues that garner political support) but come from those producers who expect to benefit privately. No producer has ever based his case for protection solely on the proposition that he alone will be better off with protection: the argument is always couched in terms of the social benefits of the industry, the unfair competition from abroad, the threat to jobs, or other aspects of the social good. A major difficulty with calls for linkages between trade and the environment has been that many of those most enthusiastically endorsing the linkage are those who would most benefit from protection.

But as Noll points out, as artificial trade barriers—primarily tariffs—have fallen, the possibility of international distortions arising out of inefficient regulation, or the interaction of inefficient regulation and protection, has made it all the more urgent to achieve efficient regulation, and in his view to achieve international agreements on regulatory regimes as well. That firms in one country are more sensitive to (artificial or economic) small cost differences because of lowered trade barriers and transport costs goes without saying.

Anne O. Krueger is the Herald L. and Caroline L. Ritch Professor of Economics, senior fellow of the Hoover Institution, and director of the Center for Research on Economic Development and Policy Reform at Stanford University, and a research associate of the National Bureau of Economic Research.

The question is the extent to which international agreements can be reached that genuinely reduce the artificial cost differences resulting from differences in national regulatory regimes (so, e.g., that there is a race to the bottom), as contrasted with the extent to which some countries will be enabled to impose their preferences on other countries in response to protectionist pressures from domestic producers. Especially for poor countries, the risk that the OECD countries may try to impose their environmental preferences (even when there are no international spillovers) on poorer countries is real. While Noll recognizes that such an outcome is possible, he is more sanguine than I am that an efficient outcome can be achieved.

It is certainly true that pressures for an international "competition" policy, or common rules of the game for producers in different countries, are growing. And the absence of common rules is used as an excuse for seeking protection. However, while market failure can justify regulation, government failure also has risks. As anyone dealing with trade policy issues is well aware, lobbyists seem to have even more disproportionate influence on trade policy than they do on matters of domestic interest.

The real challenge is to find ways to achieve international agreement on a competition (or regulatory) policy that is socially efficient and does not provide cover for protectionist measures. Anyone recognizing how difficult it has been to reach agreement even on such matters as customs procedures, scientific criteria for phytosanitary standards, and mutual recognition of standards among developed countries will naturally be less than sanguine about the prospects, at least in the next several years, for achieving an efficient international competition policy. Government failure has been more prominent than market failure in international trade.

Nonetheless, I think I agree with the conclusion: as other trade barriers and transactions costs fall, it will be increasingly important to achieve a satisfactory competition policy as protectionist pressures mount. Searching for ways to ensure that such an agreement is socially efficient is surely an endeavor where the benefit-cost ratio can be very high.

Comment   Sadao Nagaoka

This is a highly informative paper and poses a number of challenging questions for future regulatory reform. Although I support many of its conclusions, I have two reservations with regard to its international aspects.

Sadao Nagaoka is professor of management and economics at the Institute of Innovation Research of Hitotsubashi University.

International Impact of Domestic Regulation

Inefficient domestic regulation distorts resource allocation but does not necessarily harm trading partners. It does so when such regulation reduces trading or investment opportunities or when it has a negative cross-border spillover, such as acid rain. Otherwise, inefficient regulation harms only the home country. Noll, however, seems to assume that inefficient regulation pervasively reduces the welfare of trading partners. For example, he argues that a country with strict environmental regulation will lose "efficient" industry if it liberalizes trade with a country with lax environmental regulation. But from the national welfare point of view, what determines the efficient use of resources is the difference between domestic production cost and international market price. Thus free trade still benefits the country with high environmental standards.

Necessity of Internationalizing Regulatory Reform

The necessity of internationalizing regulatory reform seems to be clear when regulation limits market entry, and thus trade and investment opportunities, or when it has direct cross-border spillovers. In this case each country has a clear stake in the progress of the regulatory reform of trading partners. On the other hand, the necessity of internationalizing environmental policy and other regulations generally, as Noll seems to suggest, is not clear at all, since one country's choice of such policies does not materially harm the welfare of other countries, and efficient regulation differs between nations, depending on national conditions. If the internationalization of regulation is pursued in order to level the playing field, there is a clear danger that it will lead to inefficient regulation.

2

International Trade Aspects
of Competition Policy

Sadao Nagaoka

Competition policy has emerged as one of the high-priority policy issues in East Asian economies. Japan has strengthened its competition policy substantially in the 1990s, largely in response to U.S. demands in the Structural Impediment Initiative (SII) talks of 1989–90, but also within the overall context of regulatory reform. Both Korea and Taiwan have also substantially strengthened competition policy in recent years.[1] Competition policy has emerged as an important policy issue in regional and multilateral contexts too. The action agenda adopted at the APEC Osaka meeting of November 1995 calls for the establishment of appropriate cooperative arrangements among the competition policy authorities of the APEC economies.[2] A working group on trade and competition policy was established in the World Trade Organization (WTO) in December 1996, to study issues relating to the interaction between trade and competition policy.

These developments reflect the increasing perception of policymakers that private anticompetitive behaviors may continue to constrain "market access," even when official barriers created by border measures have come

Sadao Nagaoka is professor of management and economics at the Institute of Innovation Research of Hitotsubashi University.

The author is grateful for comments received from seminar participants.

1. The Korean Fair Trade Commission became an independent administrative agency in 1994. Taiwan enacted the Fair Trade Law in 1991 and established an enforcement agency (the Fair Trade Commission) in 1993.

2. It envisages, among other things, strengthening cooperation among the competition policy authorities of the APEC economies with regard to information exchange, notification and consultation, and development of nonbinding principles on competition policy or laws in APEC.

down.[3] In fact, the most important motivation for including competition policy on the agenda of the next round of WTO trade negotiations seems to be market access concerns. However, there has been little economic analysis of how private anticompetitive behaviors can act as trade barriers.[4] In fact, there seems to be much confusion as well as unwarranted views in this area.

This paper addresses how competition policy is and is not important for international trade. In section 2.1 I conduct a simple economic analysis of international spillovers of anticompetitive behavior. In section 2.2 I briefly review the recent development of Japanese competition policy, emphasizing its international aspects. In section 2.3 I evaluate priorities for international cooperation in competition policy based on an assessment of the importance of international spillovers of competition policy. Section 2.4 concludes.

2.1   International Spillovers of Anticompetitive Behavior

International concern has grown at the possibility that anticompetitive behavior by the private enterprises of trading partners harms trading opportunities. This section assesses how trade cartels, domestic cartels, mergers, and vertical restraints can affect foreign countries through international trade. I omit a discussion of monopolization, including predatory pricing.[5]

2.1.1   Trade Cartels and International Cartels

Trade cartels restrain international transactions.[6] They include export cartels, import cartels, and international agreements for dividing up national markets. Restriction of international trade reduces global supply and welfare and simultaneously harms the interests of trading partners.

This point is illustrated by figure 2.1 in the context of an export cartel and quantity competition. We assume here that national markets are segmented. In figure 2.1, q represents the exports of a home country and q^* the supply of the import-competing industry of a foreign country. An export cartel among the home firms shifts the reaction curve of the home

3. See, e.g., the economic report of the president of the United States for 1994 (Council of Economic Advisers 1994), as well as the report of the Group of Experts of the European Commission (1995).

4. Exceptions are Bliss (1996) and Levinsohn (1996). See also Scherer (1994).

5. Mergers and vertical restraints are, however, major means of monopolization. An extensive theoretical and empirical literature on dumping generally suggests that predatory pricing is a rarely used business strategy, in spite of many accusations (see Nagaoka 1995 for a review of the recent literature).

6. When a trade cartel is used as a means to prevent free-riding on joint investment for trade promotion, it can lead to the expansion of international trade (see Dick 1992). Here we focus only on "naked" trade cartels, the objective of which is to improve the terms of trade by limiting trade.

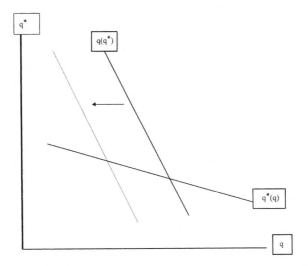

Fig. 2.1   Economic effects of a cartel

country inward, so that the output of the foreign firms expands $(dq^* > 0)$ and the market price P rises $(dP > 0)$.[7] The welfare change of the foreign country is given by

(1) $$dW^* = (P - c^*)dq^* + (q^* - q^*_H)dP,$$

where W^* is the welfare of the foreign country, c^* is the cost of production of the foreign industry, and q^*_H is the consumption of the foreign country. Because of this cartel, the foreign country, on the one hand, loses due to terms-of-trade deterioration since it is an importing country $(q^* - q^*_H < 0)$, but on the other hand, it gains due to the rent-shifting effect for the foreign industry $((P - c^*)dq^* > 0)$.

The net effect of the cartel for the foreign country, however, is always negative as long as the export cartel is voluntary since the exporters engage in the cartel only if it is profitable for them, while global welfare is reduced by the cartel unless the marginal cost of the exporters is substantially above that of the foreign industry.[8] That is,

(2) $$dW^* = d(W^* + \Pi) - d\Pi < d(W^* + \Pi) < 0,$$

where Π is the profit of the home country exporters and $W^* + \Pi$ is the sum of consumer surplus and producer surplus at market equilibrium in the foreign market. Thus a voluntary export cartel is clearly a beggar-

7. Whether the price goes up or not depends on the slope of the reaction curve of the foreign country. However, when the home firms foresee that the price will drop as a result of an export cartel, they will not engage in such a cartel.

8. $d(W^* + \Pi) = (P - c^*)dq^* + (P - c)dq = (P - c)(dq + dq^*) + (c - c^*)dq^*.$

your-neighbor policy since the home country where such a cartel originates always gains and the foreign country loses.[9] There exists a negative
international spillover of nonenforcement of competition policy against
export cartels. Identical conclusions apply to import cartels.

When export restraint is a part of an international agreement among
firms for allocating markets among themselves, all countries can lose. This
is most clear in the following symmetric case, where the home and foreign
countries are the same size, and each country has one firm with a common
production cost. In this case the firms can achieve a monopoly outcome
by each completely refraining from exporting to its competitor's market.
The welfare of both countries declines due to constrained supply, while
both firms gain.

It is important to note that the abolition of export cartels does not
necessarily improve welfare, given the presence of contingent protection,
to the extent that such cartels are used to prevent the use of contingent
protection. In particular, antidumping measures can result in stronger restriction of trade since the duties ordered are often prohibitively high. As
shown by a recent U.S. International Trade Commission report (1995),
antidumping measures often result in very large reductions in exports or
in their complete abolition, so that the trade-restraining effect of such
measures can be much larger than the monopolistic reduction of exports.[10]
Thus reform of antidumping measures is necessary to ensure that the international restriction of export cartels leads to welfare gains.

2.1.2   Domestic Cartels and Mergers

Domestic Sales Cartels and Production Cartels

When domestic and foreign markets are segmented, domestic firms can
collude to raise their sales price in the domestic market by restricting only
their sales in the domestic market. Since the price in the domestic market
is not linked with that in the foreign market, the domestic sales cartel does
not affect the equilibrium in the foreign market if the marginal cost of production is constant. With such a cartel, the foreign country does not suffer a reduction in import supply, while it can expand its exports. Thus the
foreign country's welfare definitely improves as a result of the sales cartel in
the domestic market.

When domestic and foreign markets are integrated, domestic firms have

---

9. An involuntary cartel can reduce the profits of its members due to expansion in supply
by outsiders (see Salant, Switzer, and Reynolds 1983). Such an outcome is very likely in the
case where competition is Cournot, strategic substitution holds, and outsiders have significant market share.

10. The fact that an export industry typically dislikes antidumping measures imposed on
itself also suggests that the export restrictions imposed by antidumping measures are
stronger than profit-maximizing restraint of trade.

to reduce sales in both domestic and export markets in order to raise their sales price. Thus the effect of such a cartel can be analyzed as the effect of a production cartel among domestic firms. Now we can interpret figure 2.1 as representing the global market. When the home country is an importing country and the foreign country is an exporting country ($q^* - q^*_H > 0$), it is clear that the foreign country gains from the cartel among firms in the home country. It gains both from terms-of-trade improvement and from the rent-shifting effect for its firms, as is clear from equation (1).

On the other hand, when the home country is an exporting country and the foreign country is an importing country ($q^* - q^*_H < 0$), a cartel among the home firms worsens the terms of trade of the foreign country, while the rent-shifting effect is positive for the foreign country, as in the case of an export cartel. The welfare of the foreign country is likely to decline especially when its firms are not efficient (high c^*).[11]

The above analysis shows that the international spillover from a domestic cartel tends to be positive. It can be negative only when the foreign country is a net importing country and its import price arises substantially. On the other hand, a domestic cartel harms the home country, and international trade tends to amplify this effect when markets are segmented or it is an importing country, since it invites deterioration in its terms of trade.

In spite of this clear result, policymakers often believe that a cartel abroad harms the interests of the home industry, since cartel profits are used to promote the cartel's exports. According to this "profit sanctuary" story, high profits gained by a domestic cartel are used to subsidize exports, or in other words, the cartel forces domestic consumers to cross-subsidize exports. This view is not supported by economic analysis. Domestic industry is not going to spend profits gained in the home market for export promotion unless such an act is profitable by itself. Profits in the domestic market may provide the means for artificial export promotion but not its motivation, so that a firm does not cross-subsidize consumers in one market using profits from another market.[12]

In the case of import protection, protection may promote exports, not by providing the means for cross-subsidization, but by strengthening competitiveness (Krugman 1984). Import protection shifts the global expenditure pattern in favor of the home industry, encouraging its efforts at cost reduction and learning while discouraging those of the foreign industry. However, in the case of a cartel, the exact opposite is the case. Contrary

11. High production costs for the foreign firms cause greater dependency on imports as well as low profit margins for the foreign firms.

12. Cross-subsidization may be relevant in a regulated industry, where the regulator allows the regulated firm to set its price based on its costs. In such an industry the regulated firm has an incentive to use the assets of the regulated business to expand into unregulated markets because the private cost of such activity is zero.

to the case of import protection, a cartel shifts the market away from the home industry to the foreign industry (see fig. 2.1). Consequently, cost reduction in the home industry slows while that in the foreign industry accelerates. Thus a domestic cartel is not a substitute for import protection in this regard at all, and in fact, it tends to reduce the home industry's competitiveness.

Mergers

Mergers among home firms have spillover effects on the foreign country similar to those of a combination of domestic and trade cartels, if we ignore for the time being their potential efficiency effects. This is because a consolidated firm will have more market power in both domestic and export markets and will restrict sales in each market. Thus a merger hinders exports and promotes imports if its efficiency effect is small, as pointed out by Bliss (1996). As for welfare, a merger in the import-competing industry of the home country increases the welfare of the foreign country. A merger in the export industry of the home country worsens the terms of trade of the foreign country and so can harm its welfare when foreign competing firms have high costs.

A competition policy authority typically will not allow a merger between firms if the merger creates a significant market power in the home market. Even when efficiency defenses for mergers are considered, as in the United States, a merger that will produce a firm of significantly greater market power will be approved only if it is expected to have a strong efficiency effect that can dominate the price-raising effect. Thus the regulation of mergers under competition policy tends to reduce (and can reverse) their negative as well as their positive international spillover effects.

Downstream and Upstream Effects of Cartels and Mergers

Domestic cartels in such business service sectors as international transportation and international communications, which support international trade, have a definite constraining effect on international trade because they raise the cost of such trade. Similarly, cartels among distributors in a specific industry will raise the consumer price of that industry, which in turn will reduce demand for both domestic and foreign goods in that sector. The effect of these cartels on the foreign country is just like that of tariffs on its exports (or export duties on its imported goods). Foreign downstream industry suffers from terms-of-trade deterioration and a decline in the amount of trade.[13] Thus, even if the effect of such a cartel on the foreign industry in a horizontal relationship with the domestic indus-

---

13. The home country can also lose because the monopoly transportation, communications, or distribution firm can raise its price beyond the level of the optimal tariff, ignoring the effect on domestic consumers and producers.

try is positive, its international effect may be negative if its effect on downstream foreign industry is significantly negative. Similarly, a domestic cartel can have a negative international effect if its negative effect on upstream foreign industry, such as foreign component suppliers, is large.

2.1.3 Vertical Restraints

Vertical practices may affect international trade both by constraining interbrand competition and by reducing intrabrand competition. We discuss the two cases in turn.

Interbrand Competition

Vertical restraints by incumbent domestic firms may constrain entry and growth by both foreign and domestic suppliers when they are used to increase the costs of entering and doing business in the market.[14] Such business practices as exclusive dealing, vertical integration, and refusal to deal may be used for such objectives. Foreign firms will suffer sales losses due to such anticompetitive practices by incumbent domestic firms. However, vertical restraints by incumbent firms are also used to increase the efficiency of supply.[15] It is important to note that vertical restraints by incumbent firms always reduce "market access" by a new entrant, whether such practices reduce cost of supply by incumbent firms or increase cost of supply by new entrants. When the main effect of vertical restraints is to reduce the cost of supply by incumbent firms, global welfare tends to rise, even if foreign firms suffer competitive losses.

Thus it is important to distinguish anticompetitive vertical restraints from efficient ones. Market structure plays a critical role in that regard. In particular, the following three conditions must be simultaneously present for the strategy of raising a rival's cost to be a credible profit-maximizing strategy, as pointed out by Ordover and Saloner (1989), among others. First, the foreclosing firm must have significant market power. Like predatory pricing, engaging in exclusionary practices is costly for the foreclosing firm. Thus, in order for the payoff of an exclusion strategy to be positive and to exceed that of an entry accommodation strategy, the firm must have a profitable market that can be protected from competition. Second, the foreclosing firm must be willing to pay more than the foreclosed firm in foreclosing the market. Otherwise, the foreclosure will be blocked or undone by the targeted firm. Third, the supply of the foreclosed resource

---

14. Vertical restraints may be used strategically to raise a rival's cost, in particular for exclusionary reasons (see Ordover and Saloner 1989; Ordover, Saloner, and Salop 1990; Tirole 1990).

15. Vertical restraints can be efficiency increasing in various ways (see Katz 1989). They facilitate smooth information flow across related parties and enable its efficient use. They also encourage investment by controlling ex post opportunism. They help internalize vertical or horizontal externalities such as double marginalization and free-riding on investment in reputation.

must be inelastic. Competitive output markets make the first two conditions unlikely to hold, while competitive input markets make the third condition unlikely to hold.

Intrabrand Competition

Vertical restraints such as territorial restraints may be used to price discriminate among national markets. Although the output effect of price discrimination can be positive, especially if such price discrimination is necessary to induce a firm to serve each national market, international price differentiation per se is welfare reducing. The welfare cost due to international price differences becomes larger as such differences become larger. Therefore, competition policy measures that prevent the emergence of a high degree of international price differentiation can be welfare improving.[16] Such measures include regulation of the strength of territorial restrictions imposed on distributors by a producer and prohibition of a firm from interfering with parallel imports or reverse imports.

The welfare impact of price discrimination on a foreign country depends on whether the firm sets a higher price abroad than at home, which in turn depends on consumers' willingness to pay and the degree of competition abroad relative to those at home. If a firm discriminates in favor of foreign consumers, the foreign country tends to gain from such business practices. The benefit of a lower price to its consumers tends to dominate the losses of competing firms. Thus international price discrimination can have a positive international spillover.

2.2 Recent Development of Japanese Competition Policy

2.2.1 Trade Cartels and International Division of Markets

Trade cartels that are approved by the Ministry of International Trade and Industry under the Export and Import Transaction Law[17] are exempt from the application of the Antimonopoly Law of Japan. Export cartels have accounted for more than half of the exempted cartels in terms of numbers (see fig. 2.2 and table 2.1). The number of trade cartels, however,

---

16. However, there may be good cases for price discrimination for goods embodying a large amount of R&D expenditure and among markets with significant differences of income. In the former case, price discrimination may be useful for expanding the areas for technology application, given low marginal cost, and the profits gained from price discrimination tend to encourage R&D (see Hausman and Mackie-Mason 1988). In the latter case, prohibiting price discrimination has the significant danger that the firm will choose to abandon the markets with lower incomes.

17. The law was enacted in 1952. Its objectives are to prevent unfair export transactions and to establish orderly export and import transactions. Unfair export transactions include infringing on intellectual property rights in importing countries and giving false indication of origin.

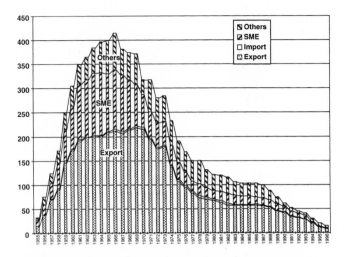

Fig. 2.2   Number of cartels exempted from the Antimonopoly Law
Note: Import is indicated by the area between small and medium-size enterprises (SME) and export.

Table 2.1   Number of Cartels Exempted from the Antimonopoly Law in Japan

Type of Exempted Cartel	1 April 1991	1 March 1997
International trade		
Export	30	4
Import	1	1
Associations of small traders	3	0
Recession or rationalization	0	0
Small and medium-size enterprises	10	0
Fishery	4	4
Transportation		
Coastal shipping	1	1
Barbershop and other services	1	1
Total	50	11

Source: JFTC (various years).
Note: Regional cartels in the same product are counted only once.

has declined substantially over time. As of March 1997, the number of trade cartels was five, of which four were export cartels.[18] The significant reduction in trade cartels reflects, first, a general reduction in the scope of exempted cartels. The Japanese government has reduced the scope of

18. The four export cartels covered textiles (quantity) to certain destinations, ceramics (design), and pearls (quality). The single import cartel covered silk products imported from China.

exemptions since the latter half of the 1980s within the context of regulatory reform. Regulatory reform has gained new momentum recently. In 1995 a cabinet decision was reached that exempted cartels be abolished in principle by the end of FY 1998. Accordingly, the exemptions for import cartels, associations of small traders, and domestic cartels for export restriction were abolished in 1998.

Second, the recent reduction in trade cartels also reflects the prohibition and phaseout of voluntary export restraints (VERs), as agreed in the Uruguay Round. Export cartels were an important means of implementing VERs and export restrictions under the Multi-Fiber Arrangement. According to a Japanese Fair Trade Commission report (JFTC 1991), preventing trade frictions was the main objective of two-thirds of export cartels (twenty out of thirty) in 1991.[19]

Trade cartels that are not approved by the government are violations of the Antimonopoly Law, even if they do not directly affect the home market. Recently, the JFTC caught such a case: the cartel coordinated by an industrial cooperative to fix the domestic wholesale prices as well as the export prices of its member's products.[20] Moreover, participation in international cartels per se is also prohibited by the Antimonopoly Law.[21]

2.2.2 Prohibition of Cartels and Regulation of Mergers

Prohibition of Cartels

The Japanese government has also strengthened its enforcement of the Antimonopoly Law against cartels by increasing the administrative surcharge on firms engaged in cartels, by more actively invoking the procedure for criminal prosecution, and by strengthening its investigative capacity (see table 2.2). The administrative surcharge was increased significantly in 1991. As a result, the surcharge on a manufacturing firm participating in a cartel was raised from 2 percent of its sales to 6 percent of its sales.[22] The average annual surcharge levied from FY 1991 to FY 1995 after the increase was 4.5 times as much as that before the increase if we exclude FY 1990, during which the cement industry was subject to a very large surcharge, and 2.2 times as much if we include that year. Criminal prosecution has been more frequently invoked. There have been four cases

19. Countervailing an import monopoly was another objective (seven out of thirty cartels).
20. In 1994 the national mosaic tile industrial cooperative was ordered by the JFTC to stop the practice of price fixing in both markets and was levied a surcharge.
21. One major case uncovered by the JFTC was an international cartel between Japanese synthetic fiber producers and European competitors in 1972, which agreed on the complete restraint of exports to each other's market as well as on quantity ceilings and minimum export prices for other markets, excluding that of the United States.
22. The surcharge of 6 percent is levied for up to three years of sales, with exceptions for retail businesses (2 percent), wholesale businesses (1 percent), and small and medium-size firms (3 percent with a further exception of 1 percent for distribution businesses).

Table 2.2   Antimonopoly Enforcement against Cartels in the 1990s

	Fiscal Year						
	1990	1991	1992	1993	1994	1995	1996	1990–96
Number of cartels acted against	13	19	30	24	21	24	15	146
Total surcharge (billion yen)	12.6	2.0	2.7	3.6	5.7	6.4	7.4	40.4
Criminal prosecution	0	1	1	0	1	1	1	5

Note: In addition to the legal measures for injunction and for levying surcharges, the JFTC issues warnings and provides guidance in cases where not enough evidence can be found to establish violation of the Antimonopoly Law. In FY 1995 alone the JFTC issued five warnings and sixteen guidances with respect to suspected cartels (twelve against price cartels and twelve against bidrigging).

from FY 1990 to FY 1995, compared with no cases in the 1980s.[23] In addition, legal exemptions from the Antimonopoly Law have been significantly streamlined. In particular, it was decided in March 1998 that the Antimonopoly Law would be amended within three years to abolish exemptions for recession cartels and rationalization cartels.

Table 2.3 shows, by industry and by customer, the number of cartels as well as the size of surcharges levied on members of cartels that were subject to legal sanctions by the JFTC from 1989 to 1995. In terms of industrial sectors, the manufacturing industry accounts for 31 percent of the cases and 60 percent of the surcharges. The construction industry accounts for 36 percent of the cases and 24 percent of the surcharges. The service and distribution sectors account for the rest. The government and other public bodies were the customers in more than half of the cartel cases. Bid rigging was the dominant form of cartel for public procurement contracts, and the construction industry contained the main offenders in bid rigging.[24] In the case of private customers, price cartels were the dominant form of cartel. Cartels in the manufacturing sector accounted for about half of the cartels selling to private customers.

Regulation of Mergers and Acquisitions

The JFTC has been relatively restrictive against mergers and acquisitions, although the new Merger Guidelines of 1999 indicate a significant liberalization of JFTC policy. A 25 percent domestic market share used to be regarded as a critical line with regard to the necessity of close scrutiny of competitive conditions. The market definition used by the JFTC has been either the national market or a regional market within Japan. Although it does consider imports in the evaluation of competition, the JFTC has never used the global market as the defined scope of the market. It has not approved the efficiency defense for mergers either.

Table 2.4 shows the domestic market shares of merged firms for the largest merger cases from 1985 to 1995. In most mergers the market share of the postmerger firm did not substantially exceed the 25 percent market share line. In three cases mergers that achieved more than 30 percent market share were approved; however, the circumstances were exceptional. In one declining market demand and low entry cost were judged to justify the

---

23. The only major case that led to criminal prosecution before the 1990s was that of a cartel in the oil-refining industry in 1974.

24. We can point out three reasons why bid rigging has been prevalent in Japanese public procurements. First, government organizations are much less concerned with cost minimization than they are with the smooth implementation of the budgeted projects. Second, defection from a cartel is much easy to detect in the case of government contracts because the government is obliged to disclose publicly the winner of the bid. As the theory of cartel stability suggests, a high detection rate of defection helps to maintain a cartel. Third, until the recent choice of open tendering, tenders had been invited only from nominated bidders.

Table 2.3   Japanese Cartels by Industry, Type, and Customer, FY 1989–95

Industry	Public Procurement (number of cases)			Private Procurement (number of cases)			Total Cases	
	Bid Rigging	Price Cartel	Others	Bid Rigging	Price Cartel	Others	Number[a]	Surcharge[a] (billion yen)
Manufacturing	14	2	0	1	25	0	42 (31)	19.7 (60)
Distribution	4	0	0	0	9	1	14 (10)	2.5 (8)
Construction	48	1	1	0	0	0	50 (36)	8.0 (24)
Service and others	11	1	0	0	14	5	31 (23)	2.5 (8)
Total	77	4	1	1	48	6	137 (100)	32.7 (100)

Source: Author's estimate based on JFTC (various years).

Note: The numbers of cases for which surcharges were levied up to the end of FY 1995 are 37 for manufacturing, 10 for distribution, 37 for construction, and 23 for service and other industry.

[a]Numbers in parentheses are industry percentages of totals.

Table 2.4   Market Shares of Major Horizontally Merged Firms, FY 1985–95

Market Share	Number of Cases
Less than or equal to 20%	11
Less than or equal to 25%	6
Less than or equal to 30%	3
More than 30%	3
Unknown	2
Total	25

Source: JFTC (various years).

Note: This table covers only major horizontal cases having the national market as market, as reported in the JFTC annual reports. When the JFTC examines several layers of markets, this table adopts the broadest market.

merger. In another a joint venture between the leading Japanese beer maker and a large foreign beer maker was approved because of regulatory restrictions on the expansion of liquor shops in Japan, and only for ten years.

Moreover, when the market share of the postmerger firm was expected to exceed the 25 percent line substantially, the JFTC often asked the merging firms to take measures that would limit their market power as a precondition for approval. For example, in 1995 the JFTC asked one chemical company undertaking consolidation to divest its shareholding in the joint production company. It asked another chemical company undertaking consolidation to liquidate its joint sales agreement with a foreign, potentially competing company.

2.2.3   Vertical Restraints

Overall Regulation

Vertical restraints have been regulated in Japan mainly under the unfair trade practices section of the Antimonopoly Law because it covers a range of business practices wider than attempted monopolization. Unfair trade practices can cover such business practices as resale price maintenance, joint refusal to deal, below-cost sales and price discrimination, exclusive dealing, and territorial restriction. Similar to the policy practices in the United States or the European Union, such conduct as exclusive dealing is not illegal per se. Legality in Japan depends on how "influential" the party requiring such a contract is as well as on how much such a practice constrains the business activities of competitors. Major exceptions in this respect are resale price maintenance, joint refusal to deal, and sales substantially below cost, which are illegal in principle, irrespective of the market position of the firm engaging in these activities. Focusing on distribution, the JFTC issued detailed guidelines on distribution and business practices in 1991, as a direct outcome of the SII talks.

Table 2.5   Unfair Business Practices Subject to JFTC Action, FY 1991–95

Type of Unfair Business Practice	Number of Cases
Resale price maintenance	20
Requirement or exclusionary contract	24
Business interference	5
Abuse of stronger bargaining position	2
Other	7
Total	58

Source: JFTC (various years).

Note: Actions include warnings, where violations were suspected but not enough evidence was obtained. The above numbers do not include unfair practices conducted by business associations that were subject to JFTC action.

Table 2.5 shows recent JFTC actions according to type of unfair business practice. Resale price maintenance accounts for one-third of the cases. Requirement or exclusionary contracts, such as exclusive dealing, account for another third. Sales restriction in international licensing can directly affect international trade. The JFTC acted in two international licensing cases in 1995, where there were agreements between Japanese firms and a Taiwanese firm that restricted sales by the Taiwanese firm in Japan even after the expiration of the licensing contract.

Exclusive Dealing

Exclusive dealing between manufacturers and distributors in Japan has sometimes been regarded as a market access barrier.[25] One of the main issues in the recent automobile trade dispute is the "closed" distribution system in Japan. In Japan all nine automakers have developed their own distribution networks, and most dealers specialize in selling the automobiles of a particular automaker. Consequently, multiple-franchise dealers have been almost nonexistent, except for those arranged by Japanese automakers themselves.[26] Similarly, the central competition policy issue in the recent film dispute was the relationship between the largest Japanese film producer and its first tier of wholesalers. These seven distributors currently sell only the films of this maker.[27]

25. In addition, Tilton (1996) points out that refusal to deal has often been used to restrain imports by Japanese firms in the basic material industry, although refusal to deal per se is not illegal.

26. The situation has been similar in Europe, where most dealers have single-franchise agreements with major automakers. In contrast, around 30 percent of dealers had multiple-franchise dealerships in the United States in 1989, although single-franchise dealers were dominant in the United States too until the 1960s.

27. On the other hand, the second tier of wholesalers, who buy films from the first tier of wholesalers for resale to small retail shops, do not specialize in handling a single brand (JFTC 1996).

Exclusive dealing contracts, when required by an influential firm,[28] are deemed an unfair business practice in Japan when they make it difficult for competitors to find alternative distribution channels. For example, the exclusive dealing contract required by a firm that possessed two-thirds of the domestic market was judged by the JFTC to be an unfair business contract. As for the automobile industry, the JFTC guided the two largest Japanese automakers to abolish the clause requiring exclusive dealing in distribution contracts in 1979. In 1991 all domestic automakers decided to abolish the prior consultation clause for distributors in selling other makers' models, in response to the JFTC's guideline on distribution. Thus producers who have relatively large market shares cannot bind distributors with contracts that bar them from dealing with competitors in Japan.[29]

From an international perspective, it is not the case that Japanese competition policy has been more favorable to exclusive dealing requirements by producers. In the United States the efficiency-improving nature of exclusive dealing is recognized, so that such practices are likely to be treated as illegal only if a firm with significant market power exercises them.[30] In Europe block exemptions have authorized exclusive dealing in automobile sales and other industries.

Parallel Imports

In the application of Japanese competition policy, not only resale price maintenance but also nonprice vertical restraints, which directly reduce price competition among distributors, have been deemed illegal without regard to the market position of the firm. Consequently, such conduct by sole import agents as asking foreign suppliers to take measures to close supply channels to parallel importers has been deemed to be a violation of the Antimonopoly Law. In recent years the JFTC took up several cases in this field involving imports of tablewares, pianos, and bags.

2.3   Implications for International Cooperation in Competition Policy

2.3.1   Welfare Measures

In considering international cooperation in competition policy, the critical issue is what welfare measure is to be used in evaluating private anti-

---

28. An influential firm as defined by the JFTC is a firm with more than 10 percent of the domestic market or a firm ranked in the top three in terms of market share.

29. The use of financial measures with an exclusionary effect, such as highly progressive rebates, is also being restricted in Japan.

30. In addition, market definition in the United States is often broader than in Japan. Two United States courts recently ruled that the largest film producer in the United States does not have market power despite its dominant market share in the U.S. market because the market was judged to be global. Consequently, the two consent decrees issued by the U.S. Fair Trade Commission, which had restricted such distribution practices as selling private-label film and requiring exclusive dealing, were lifted.

competitive practices. The appropriate measure is global welfare, and global output as its surrogate. A particular business behavior is anticompetitive domestically if it reduces the domestic supply of an industry. Similarly, a particular business behavior is anticompetitive internationally if it reduces the global supply of that industry.

Why should a global welfare criterion be used instead of a national welfare criterion? National welfare implies the adoption of different standards of competition policy with regard to anticompetitive behavior in the home market versus that in international markets or with regard to the behavior of foreign firms versus that of home firms. One example of such a policy is prohibiting cartels in the domestic market while allowing them in export markets. Another example is regarding any business practices in foreign markets as anticompetitive if the exports of home firms are constrained.

Such discriminatory application of competition policy has two major problems. First, it may undermine domestic standards. The historical evolution of the principle of competition policy from protecting competitors to protecting competition can be negatively affected. Second, when a foreign country adopts a similar policy, the national welfare of both countries can decline, just as optimal tariff policy is in fact not optimal given similar foreign behavior. The use of competition policy as a rent-shifting policy is self-destructive in these senses.

The guiding principle for securing consistency with global efficiency is to establish national treatment in the application of competition policy for domestic and foreign firms as well as for domestic and foreign consumers. Currently, national competition policy does not necessarily respect this principle, and the danger exists that political pressure to use antitrust policy in order to expand market access can further widen the gap.[31] National treatment has several important implications:

1. Extension of home competition policy to export cartels.

2. Prohibition of import cartels. Exceptions, however, may be granted in cases where the import cartel is formed as a countervailing device against an export cartel.

3. Application of the same competition policy standard to foreign and domestic firms. In the case of extraterritorial application of competition policy, the same standards will be used for foreign firms as for home firms.

Once national treatment is established and substantive standards for competition policy are agreed upon internationally, each economy will be

---

31. The U.S. government is authorized by the Congress to apply its antitrust law in an extraterritorial manner to foreign business practices that hinder the export expansion of U.S. firms (Foreign Trade Antitrust Improvement Act of 1982). It has not yet been clarified whether in applying this provision the U.S. government has to meet the same antitrust standards as those applied to domestic firms or whether it can use separate standards just for the purpose of export expansion.

willing to delegate the enforcement of competition policy to the country that can most efficiently investigate and enforce corrective actions, which would typically be the country where firms are located. It will thus encourage the development of a division of labor in enforcing competition policy, avoiding duplication and inconsistency in enforcement efforts.

2.3.2   Priorities for International Cooperation

High priority for international cooperation in competition policy could be given to the regulation of private anticompetitive conduct that has negative as well as large international effects. As discussed in section 2.2, trade cartels, including international cartels, do have negative international spillovers. The degree of spillover depends on the international market power of the cartel. The same thing applies to mergers that create international market power. In contrast, domestic cartels per se do not have substantial negative international spillovers.

As for vertical practices, what should be addressed are *efficiency-reducing* vertical practices. The degree of spillover depends on whether the market foreclosed by a firm is large in the international context. For both horizontal practices and vertical restraints, it is clear that a larger economy has more responsibility for controlling the anticompetitive behavior of its firms and for keeping its markets competitive. Firms located in a relatively small country are less likely to have international market power. Moreover, it is a time-consuming process to develop effective competition policy institutions (see Scherer 1994). Thus, international agreements on cooperation in competition policy may be framed so that differential treatment can be provided to small developing countries.

2.4   Conclusions

Competition policy, including its absence, can have important international spillovers. However, the recent focus on competition policy from a "market access" perspective can be misleading. The anticompetitive behavior that can have the most clearly negative international spillover is an export cartel. Export cartels, however, do not constrain market access. Moreover, export cartels or similar export-restraining arrangements were often used in the past to ameliorate trade frictions. Pure domestic cartels tend to improve market access and harm primarily the country that tolerates such arrangements, although when a domestic cartel is in a vertical relationship with international trade it can restrain international trade and reduce foreign welfare too. Vertical restraints can constrain market access and can have negative international spillovers. However, we have to distinguish efficiency-reducing vertical restraints from efficiency-improving restraints.

The Japanese government has substantially strengthened its competition policy in the 1990s, especially in its drastic reduction of cartels exempted from the application of the Antimonopoly Law, including trade cartels, and in its enforcement against cartels. On the other hand, Japanese competition policy used to be fairly restrictive toward mergers and acquisitions, and Japanese policy toward vertical restraints has not been significantly different from that in the United States. The recent change toward stronger enforcement of competition policy, especially against cartels, should be highly beneficial to the Japanese economy. But on the other hand, it is not clear whether this policy change can have a substantial impact on market access.

In promoting international cooperation in competition policy, it is important to have national treatment as the guiding principle, in order to avoid the danger of using competition policy as a means for rent shifting. Priority in international cooperation could be given to controlling the anticompetitive behavior of firms with international market power.

Although this paper has focused on competition policy in a narrow sense, it is very important to recognize that many WTO issues remain, the resolution of which would contribute much more to the development of competitive markets than will cooperation in competition policy itself. Unrestricted international trade and investment will make markets more competitive, so that sustaining cartels and other anticompetitive behaviors will become more difficult. A major issue in this regard is the reform of antidumping rules. Although antidumping measures have sometimes been defended by their proponents as substitutes for competition policy abroad or as transitory measures while markets remain nonintegrated, both the guiding principles as well as the actual practices of antidumping measures are widely divergent from those for competition policy interventions. The second area is the introduction of domestic and foreign competition into public utility industries, such as electricity, where vertically integrated firms used to supply monopolistically in many countries. The third area is the reform of government procurement agreements. Currently, only a limited number of WTO member countries participate in the WTO agreement on government procurement. Furthermore, the experiences of many signatory countries, including Japan, suggest that public procurement is vulnerable to bid rigging. Thus there is a substantial efficiency gain from more competition in this area too.

References

Bliss, C. 1996. Trade and competition control. In *Fair trade and harmonization: Prerequisites for free trade?* ed. J. Bhagwati and R. Hudec. Cambridge, Mass.: MIT Press.

Council of Economic Advisers. 1994. *Economic report of the president.* Washington, D.C.: Government Printing Office.

Dick, A. 1992. The competitive consequences of Japan's export cartel associations. *Journal of Japanese and International Economies* 6:275–98.

Group of Experts of the European Commission. 1995. Competition policy in the new trade order: Strengthening international cooperation and rules. Available from http://europa.eu.int/comm/dg04/index_en.htm.

Hausman, J. A., and J. K. Mackie-Mason. 1988. Price discrimination and patent policy. *Rand Journal of Economics* 19 (2): 253–65.

JFTC (Japan Fair Trade Commission). 1991. *Current status and directions for improvement in the exemption system from the application of antimonopoly law.* Tokyo: Government Printing Office.

———. Various years. *Annual report of the Fair Trade Commission.* Tokyo: Government Printing Office.

Katz, M L. 1989. Vertical contractual relations. In *Handbook of industrial organization,* ed. R. Schmalensee and R. D. Willig. Amsterdam: North-Holland.

Krugman, P. 1984. Import protection as export promotion. In *Monopolistic competition and international trade,* ed. H. Kierzkowski. Oxford: Blackwell.

Levinsohn, James. 1996. Competition policy and international trade. In *Fair trade and harmonization: Prerequisites for free trade?* ed. J. Bhagwati and R. Hudec. Cambridge, Mass.: MIT Press.

Nagaoka, S. 1995. Antidumping policy and competition. In *Regulatory policies and reform in industrializing countries,* ed. C. R. Frischtak. Washington, D.C.: World Bank.

Ordover, J. A., and G. Saloner. 1989. Predation, monopolization, and antitrust. In *Handbook of industrial organization,* ed. R. Schmalensee and R. D. Willig. Amsterdam: North-Holland.

Ordover, J. A., G. Saloner, and S. Salop. 1990. Equilibrium vertical foreclosure. *American Economic Review* 80 (1): 127–42.

Salant, S., W. Switzer, and R. J. Reynolds. 1983. Losses from horizontal merger: The effects of and exogenous change in industry structure on Cournot-Nash equilibrium. *Quarterly Journal of Economics* 97:185–99.

Scherer, F. M. 1994. *Competition policies for an integrated world economy.* Washington, D.C.: Brookings Institution.

Tilton, M. 1996. *Restrained trade: Cartels in Japan's basic materials industry.* Ithaca, N.Y.: Cornell University Press.

Tirole, J. 1990. Competition-reducing vertical restraints. In *Industrial structure in the new industrial economics,* ed. G. Bonanno and D. Brandolini. Oxford: Clarendon.

U.S. International Trade Commission. 1995. *The economic effects of antidumping and countervailing duty orders and suspension agreements.* Washington, D.C.: International Trade Commission.

Comment   Anne O. Krueger

In this paper, Sadao Nagaoka makes two important contributions: first, he analyzes competition policy and the ways in which such anticompeti-

Anne O. Krueger is the Herald L. and Caroline L. Ritch Professor of Economics, senior fellow of the Hoover Institution, and director of the Center for Research on Economic Development and Policy Reform at Stanford University, and a research associate of the National Bureau of Economic Research.

tive behavior as cartels, vertical restraints of trade, and predatory pricing can affect the welfare of home and foreign countries. Second, he then considers how Japanese competition policy has evolved in recent years.

I have little to add with regard to the first contribution, as Nagaoka's analysis covers the main issues nicely. He does point to two facts that must be borne in mind in considering competition policy: (1) predatory pricing has been relatively rare internationally except when governments themselves have undertaken policies that permitted it, and (2) even when governments break up export cartels (which should be to international, as well as national, advantage), other governments have then exercised their antidumping regulations in ways that have rendered the potential welfare gains nugatory. As an example of the first case, consider the United States, which has prohibited the formation of domestic cartels but encouraged the formation of export cartels. As an example of the second, Nagaoka notes that VERs were encouraged by importing countries and led to the formation of export cartels, especially in Japan. When the VERs were removed and the Japanese government broke up the export cartels, there were suits by importing countries on grounds of antidumping at the reduced export prices. If one considers the extent of anticompetitive behavior in international markets in the past several decades, however, there is little doubt that government-imposed anticompetitive behavior through VERs was a major source of welfare loss.

The discussion of the evolution of Japanese competition policy is also very useful. It is an irony of history that the United States, after World War II, sought competition policy in Germany and Japan in order to keep German and Japanese industries weak! Especially in light of the importance modern regulatory theory places on maintaining competition, this earlier thinking is quite remarkable.

One point that Nagaoka alludes to, on which I would have liked to have heard more, is the role of international trade in bringing about more competition. It seems self-evident that opening domestic markets to foreign competition greatly increases competitive pressures on domestic firms. Likewise, exporters selling in third markets almost surely (except in the case of international cartels) face more competition than they would selling in protected domestic markets. In terms of dealing with integrating competition policy among countries, I would therefore conjecture that there was less urgency to worrying about market shares of national markets for exporters than for producers in home markets (where the presence of foreign competition would obviously reduce the share of domestic producers). Yet most discussions of market shares seem to focus on shares of national markets held by domestic firms: does not this practice require amendment?

I would like to close by endorsing another point made by Nagaoka: that is, it is important that any international competition policy use national treatment as a guiding principle so that it cannot be used as a means for rent shifting. Nagaoka correctly urges attention to areas where firms have international market power and correctly notes that restricting the abuse of antidumping regulations would probably do more to improve the competitive environment than can possibly be achieved by coordination of competition policy. Would that this message could be received and understood by politicians!

Comment   Chong-Hyun Nam

I enjoyed reading Nagaoka's paper and think it makes a nice companion piece to chapter 1, by Roger Noll. While Noll's paper deals with broader issues of competition policy, including regulatory reforms, Nagaoka's paper focuses on narrower issues, such as cartels, mergers, and vertical restraints.

I have only a few comments to make. Beforehand, however, I think it may be useful to ask again why competition policy has recently emerged as a prominent agenda for a future round of multilateral negotiation at the WTO, and what we can expect from it. I do not know exact answers to these questions, but I can think of a couple of reasons why the subject of competition policy has gained momentum in recent years.

One is based on the fact that despite continued liberalization of trade-restricting border measures under the GATT system during the postwar period, its expected effect on trade expansion has not been fully realized in some countries. Many have argued that this is largely due to anticompetitive nonborder measures that have worked in these countries as a deterrent to market access for foreign exporters, and Japan has been frequently named as supporting evidence for their argument. They indicate that Japan's import-to-GDP ratio is the lowest among the OECD nations, about half of that for the United States, while the discrepancy between Japan's current and purchasing-power-parity-based income is the largest among the OECD nations in both absolute and relative terms. I suspect, therefore, that the main impetus behind the recent competition policy drive is U.S. and EU frustration at failing to penetrate the Japanese markets that are alleged to be the most open at the border among the OECD nations. There seems to be an expectation that once anticompetitive domestic regulations and business practices—including closed distribution systems—are lifted from Japan, that country can provide the world with vast and unexplored markets. I am not sure what kind of quantitative importance may be attached to this sort of belief, but I do think the wel-

Chong-Hyun Nam is professor of economics at Korea University.

fare gains to be reaped from a global competition policy can be sizable, especially when regulatory reforms are included in it.

Another reason for the recent prominence of competition policy is the fact that the so-called unfair trade rules currently in operation under the WTO system are utterly inadequate from the viewpoint of competition. They tend to discourage competition rather than promote it. At present, trade-related competition policies under the WTO system are reflected in antidumping and countervailing duty rules. These rules, however, are fraught with so many flaws both in theory and in practice that they have been heavily abused, most notably by the United States and the European Union. Replacement of these rules by an agreed upon global competition policy, or an agreement to use national treatment for importers, would significantly reduce trade friction and the potential for protection through antidumping measures.

Now let me turn to a few comments on some specific conclusions in Nagaoka's paper. First of all, I am puzzled by Nagaoka's conclusion that the recent competition policy drive is "misleading" in that it is focused more on market access concerns than on export cartels, arguing that export cartels deserve greater attention because they have the most clearly negative international spillovers. There is no doubt that export cartels distort trade, incurring economic costs, but it seems to me that they are not likely to be quantitatively significant compared to the economic costs associated with other anticompetitive domestic measures. Given a relatively open and competitive world trading system, as we have today, there seems to be little room left for trade cartels to exploit. Thus it seems to me that improving market access on a multilateral, reciprocal basis should and would be a major concern of the competition policy drive, and for good reason.

I am also troubled to understand Nagaoka's conclusion that domestic cartels are likely to increase market access with positive international spillovers. It may hold true in his simple model, but not in reality in general, I suppose. To be realistic, domestic cartels are unlikely to survive long unless they are protected from import competition by the government. In this circumstance, domestic cartels are likely to generate negative international spillovers instead because import protection limits market access for foreign exporters. But there can be cases in which domestic cartels come into being under natural import barriers or under some sort of domestic "regulatory capture," if I may borrow terminology from Noll's paper. Service industries such as distribution, transportation, communications, or finance may belong to such a category. A global competition policy including regulatory reforms seems to be most wanted in these circumstances because services are increasingly becoming internationally tradable goods these days.

Finally, I wonder whether we will ever be able to design and achieve a comprehensive global competition policy that can be accepted and administered by individual nations with diverse economic structures, histories, and customs. But if we could have one, the most important beneficiaries would likely be small, outward-oriented developing countries, which would enjoy improved market access as well as fewer threats from administered protection. In this regard, contrary to Nagaoka's conclusion, I think any differential treatment toward developing countries in making a global competition policy is neither necessary nor desirable. We know all too well how the special and differential treatment provided to developing countries under the GATT system eventually disserved the interests of developing countries.

3

Market Design and Price Behavior in Restructured Electricity Markets
An International Comparison

Frank A. Wolak

3.1 Introduction

Electricity supply is traditionally viewed as a natural monopoly. Economies of scale in the generation of electricity and the necessity of an extensive transmission and distribution network to deliver it to final customers seem to favor supply by a single firm for a given geographic region. However, Joskow (1987) argues that scale economies in electricity production at the generating unit level are exhausted at a unit size of about 500 MW. More recent econometric work finds that the null hypothesis of constant returns to scale in the supply of electricity (the combination of generation, transmission, and distribution) by U.S. investor-owned utilities cannot be rejected (Lee 1995).

There is also growing dissatisfaction with limited incentives for efficient operation faced by a cost-of-service-regulated or government-owned electric utility. According to this view, even if scale economies in the production of electricity exist, because of the incentives for input choice provided by the regulatory process or by state ownership the mode of production chosen by the firm does not allow them to be realized. For the case of a privately owned regulated utility, the firm earns higher returns for its share-

Frank A. Wolak is professor of economics at Stanford University and a research associate of the National Bureau of Economic Research.

The author thanks Marshall Yan for outstanding research assistance. Severin Borenstein, Jim Bushnell, and Richard Green provided very helpful comments on a previous draft. Partial financial support for this research was provided by the National Science Foundation. This paper reflects the state of electricity industry restructuring in England and Wales, Norway and Sweden, Australia and New Zealand as of 1 January 1998, unless otherwise noted. An up-to-date description of the status of electricity industry restructuring in these countries can be obtained from http://www.stanford.edu/~wolak.

holders by choosing an input mix to satisfy the demand for its output that does not minimize total production costs. For the case of a government-owned utility, the management chooses higher than cost-minimizing levels of labor or capital inputs to increase its political clout and long-term viability. Decision-making processes involving regulated utilities and regulatory bodies acting jointly or state-owned-enterprises have historically had difficulty making economically efficient new generation capacity investment choices in terms of both the size and the fuel type of the generating facility.

As consequence, regulators in the United States and worldwide have recently implemented new regulatory schemes and organizational forms in an effort to improve the incentives for efficient operation of electric utilities. Until very recently, in the United States this restructuring took the form of performance-based or incentive regulation plans, where the revenue a utility is allowed to earn is tied less to the cost of providing electricity and more to the attainment of performance goals as quantified by total factor productivity or some other measure of productive efficiency.

Other countries have undertaken more radical approaches to restructuring their electricity supply industries. Following the privatization of the majority of the generating assets of the formerly state-owned Central Electricity Generating Board, the privatization of all of the area boards (local electricity distributors), and the introduction of a market for generation in England and Wales (E&W) on 1 April 1990, many Organization for Economic Cooperation and Development (OECD) member countries have formed wholesale markets for electricity and introduced varying degrees of competition into the retail side of the electricity supply industry. Most other OECD countries are currently in the process of implementing similar reforms.

The United States has been slow to undertake this radical restructuring process. As of 1 May 1999 only three regions of the United States operate competitive wholesale markets for electricity—California, PJM (all or part of Pennsylvania, New Jersey, Maryland, Delaware, Virginia, and the District of Columbia), and New England (Massachusetts, New Hampshire, Vermont, and Maine). The California market was the first to begin operation, on 31 March 1998. As of this same date, the incumbent investor-owned utilities in California faced competition for their retail customers. As of 1 May 1999, electricity industry restructuring activity exists through most of the United States.[1] Retail competition of some form exists in all states with a competitive wholesale electricity market, as well as in many other states. Several other states in the United States have enacted

---

1. The Energy Information Agency of the U.S. Department of Energy maintains an up-to-date web site on the status of electricity industry restructuring in each state. See http://www.eia.doe.gov/cneaf/electricity/page/restructure.html.

legislation to restructure their electricity industries. The vast majority of states have ongoing activity in the regulatory body that oversees the electricity industry (usually the public utilities commission) or in the state legislature dealing with electricity industry restructuring. Only two states have no significant ongoing activity in electricity industry restructuring.

All of the industry restructurings that have taken place in the United States and abroad are consistent with the view that competition should be introduced into the electricity supply industry wherever it is technologically feasible. Only those portions of the production process most efficiently supplied by a single firm should remain regulated. The prevailing view is that the technologies for electricity generation and retailing are both such that competition is feasible. As discussed above, economies of scale in generation are exhausted at levels of production significantly below current levels of industry output. Assuming that all retailers have equal access to the transmission and distribution network and electricity from the wholesale generation market, significant increasing returns to scale in electricity retailing are unlikely to exist. On the other hand, because competition in the transmission and distribution of electricity would require duplication of the current network, these two portions of the electricity supply industry are thought to possess the features of a natural monopoly. Therefore, the transmission and distribution sectors of the electricity supply industries in all of these countries are regulated to varying degrees.

Although privatization is often part of this restructuring process, for all of the regions described in this paper both state and privately owned companies compete in the electricity generation market. Some of the countries where restructuring has taken place only have municipally owned distribution companies, whereas others have only privately owned distribution companies. The remaining countries have distribution sectors composed of a combination of privately owned and government-owned companies.

The market structure and rules governing the operation of the electricity industries in these countries are not the direct result of independent actions by market participants—generators, retailers, and customers. Consequently, it is perhaps a misnomer to call these trading arrangements markets, because most markets or exchanges arise from the voluntary actions of buyers and sellers to form a self-regulating organization to facilitate mutually beneficial trades. Each of the electricity markets that currently exist around the world is the outcome of a deliberate government policy to restructure (and often privatize) the industry. The final form of the electricity industry in United States will be the result of joint decisions by state regulatory commissions and legislatures, as well as market participants. In addition, the Federal Energy Regulatory Commission must also approve all state restructuring plans. As I discuss later, the amount of regulatory oversight in the E&W market has increased since the 1990 restructuring. The other newly established electricity markets are also subject to significant regulatory oversight. Even the New Zealand electricity supply industry, which touts its "light-handed" approach to regulation, has had a significant amount of government intervention since the market first began operation. All of the plans for establishing electricity markets in the United States mandate continual monitoring of the industry by both state and federal agencies. For all of these reasons, it is more appropriate to think of these restructured industries around the world and the proposed markets in the United States as alternative regulatory mechanisms to explicit price regulation for achieving the goals of greater economic efficiency in electricity supply.

From the perspective of economic efficiency, the optimal price for electricity should be set to mimic the market price in a competitive industry with many noncolluding firms and minimal barriers to entry. This price has several desirable properties. First, it gives firms the proper signals for the timing and magnitude of new investment expenditures. In addition, because firms have no influence over this market price, they have the maximum incentive to produce their output at minimum cost and can only earn higher profits by cost-reducing innovations not immediately imitated by competitors. The major impetus behind the liberalization of the E&W market was the belief that this new form of market organization would come closer to achieving these regulatory goals for electricity prices than the preprivatization industry structure.[2]

This new form of "regulation" of the electricity supply industry gives rise to a new set of policy-making challenges associated with achieving economically efficient prices. The problem receiving the greatest attention is market power, which I define as the ability of a firm to cause a significant increase in the market price and to profit from this price increase. Firms subject to price regulation (either based on cost of service or an incentive regulation plan) have no direct control over the prices they can charge for electricity. Therefore, the explicit exercise of market power is not possible under traditional regulatory structures because the regulator, not the firm, sets the market price. A profit-maximizing regulated utility must use other means to increase its attractiveness to prospective shareholders.

In the markets for electricity currently operating around the world, firms explicitly bid prices at which they are willing to supply electricity. The desire of privately owned generation companies to maintain and attract shareholders implies that they will attempt to exploit any potential profit-making opportunities through their bidding behavior. For this rea-

2. An important concern expressed in a 1981 study by the U.K. Monopolies and Mergers Commission was that the preprivatization market structure did not provide the proper signals for constructing the optimal amount and type of new generation capacity in a timely manner (Armstrong, Cowan, and Vickers 1994, 291).

son, from the perspective of consumer welfare, the success of a restructured electricity industry can be judged by the degree to which opportunities for significant economic profits are eliminated by the self-interested actions of producers and consumers governed by the current market rules and carried out within the existing market structure of the industry.[3]

There are many observable differences in market structure in the various restructured electricity supply industries. These differences in market structure have led to the imposition of market rules designed to mitigate the ability of firms to exercise market power in the form thought to be most prevalent given the market structure that exists in the industry. There are also many differences in market rules across these electricity industries that are due to historical reasons or engineering concerns about network integrity. The interaction of these market rules with the market structure of the industry determines whether economically efficient prices are set by these markets.

The purpose of this paper is to characterize this across-country relationship between market rules and market structure and spot prices for electricity using the restructured electricity markets in England and Wales, Sweden and Norway, the state of Victoria in Australia, and New Zealand. By studying the across-country relationship between market rules and market structure and the behavior of market-clearing prices, insights can be gained about how to set market rules to mitigate the incentives firms have to exercise market power for a given market structure.

The paper first describes the market structure and market rules governing the operation of each electricity supply industry. Because the E&W electricity market was the first established among OECD member countries, it has served as a model for much electricity industry restructuring worldwide. Consequently, I first provide a detailed discussion of the market rules and market structure of this industry. Then I describe these two aspects of the joint Norway and Sweden electricity market (Nord Pool), the Victoria Electricity market (VicPool), and the New Zealand electricity market (NZEM) in light of the discussion of the E&W market. Next I present various views of the time-series behavior of spot electricity prices in each of these markets and then relate these differences in the behavior of prices to observable differences in the market rules and market structure governing the operation of these electricity markets. This discussion focuses on linking differences in market rules and market structure to differences in the behavior of electricity prices across the countries.

Although a detailed analysis of how these across-country differences in market rules and market structure foster or mitigate the exercise of market

---

3. It is important to emphasize that firms can earn positive, zero, or negative accounting profits while earning zero economic profits. Zero economic profits implies that all factors of production are paid their opportunity cost. The opportunity cost of a piece of capital is the minimal return necessary to keep it from exiting the electricity supply industry.

power is a topic for future research, I will also point out some very preliminary evidence consistent with the exercise of market power in the time-series behavior of these spot prices. Where possible, I will attempt to link this price behavior that appears to be consistent with the exercise of market power to observable differences across the markets in the rules governing their operation and the structure of the industry.

3.2   Industry Structure in the England and Wales Electricity Market

The purpose of this section is to summarize the market structure and rules governing the operation of the E&W system. I first describe the restructuring of the electricity industry in England and Wales. I then describe the major players in the market and their relative sizes and the mix of generation capacity they own. The discussion then focuses on the rules governing the operation of the E&W electricity market. First I discuss the strategic weapons available to each of the market participants. Then I lay out the various stages of the price determination process and the potential opportunities for the exercise of market power that these rules create. I then discuss the evolution of the regulation of this market attempting to limit the market power of the two largest generators in the system.

3.2.1   Market Structure in England and Wales

Since 1 April 1990, all but a small fraction of electricity consumed in England and Wales must be sold through a mandatory day-ahead spot market for electricity with market-clearing prices set on a half-hourly basis. This market was formed as the end result of the breakup and privatization of the state-owned Central Electricity Generating Board (CEGB) and the privatization of the twelve area boards, the local electricity distribution companies, which were renamed regional electricity companies (RECs). The generating facilities of the CEGB were separated into three large companies. National Power and PowerGen took over all existing fossil fuel power stations. Nuclear power plants remained state owned, under the auspices of Nuclear Electric.[4] The national transmission grid became the National Grid Company (NGC), which was jointly owned by the twelve RECs. In addition to the three large E&W generators, Scottish nonnuclear companies (Hydro-Electric and Scottish Power), Electricity de France, and a number of independent power producers (IPPs) also sell electricity into the E&W pool. The links to the E&W market from Scotland and France are currently constrained by transmission capacity at 1.6 GW and 2.0 GW. The maximum capacity available to serve the E&W electricity

---

4. In July 1996, the U.K. government privatized the modern nuclear power stations, specifically the advanced gas-cooled reactors and the pressurized water reactor. British Energy became the holding company that owns these assets.

market is approximately 60 GW, and the peak system demand is slightly more than 49 GW.

The restructuring process has transformed the electricity supply industry into four separate subindustries: (1) generation, (2) transmission, (3) distribution, and (4) retail sales. With some minor exceptions to be noted, the electricity supply industries in all subsequent restructurings have been subdivided in the same manner.

Because the technology of generation is thought to exhibit constant or decreasing returns to scale at current levels of production, a competitive market in generation is the foundation of all the restructured electricity industries I describe. Although the rules governing the operation of the market and the numbers, plant sizes, and mix of generating technologies employed differ greatly across the various industries, the goal of all of these markets is to foster economically efficient wholesale prices for electricity.

NGC runs both the financial and physical side the E&W electricity market. It serves as both the power exchange and the independent system operator because it both determines half-hourly market-clearing spot prices for electricity and operates the national electricity transmission network, making generator dispatch decisions in real time to manage congestion on the grid and provide the ancillary services necessary to guarantee reliable power to all final customers. Originally, it was jointly owned by the RECs, but in 1995 it was separated and is currently traded on the London Stock Exchange.

Both transmission and distribution are thought to be natural monopolies, so that prices for bulk transmission provided by NGC are regulated by a price-cap mechanism. For the same reason, the distribution services provided by each of the RECs to customers in their service areas are regulated by a price-cap mechanism.

The retail side of the market is divided into franchise and nonfranchise customers. Nonfranchise customers are given the option of choosing their supplier from any of the twelve RECs as well as National Power or PowerGen directly. Initially, nonfranchise consumers were those with peak demands greater than 1 MW. On 1 April 1994, the 1 MW peak demand limit on these nonfranchise consumers was reduced to 100 kW. This size restriction on customer peak demand ceases to exist on 30 June 1999, when all residential customers will be offered this option (i.e., all customers become nonfranchise). The RECs are required to allow competitors to transfer electricity over their distribution systems at the same price they charge to themselves to provide this service to their retail customers located in their own service areas.

Since the formation of the market, National Power and PowerGen have owned the majority of generating capacity and have produced at least 54.5 percent of total electricity sold during each of the fiscal years the pool has operated through 1995/96. PowerGen and National Power, most notably, have reduced their respective capacities steadily since the pool began. National Power began the 1990/91 fiscal year with approximately 30 GW of capacity, and PowerGen had approximately 19 GW of capacity. By the beginning of the 1995/96 fiscal year, these capacities were approximately 20 and 15 GW, respectively. Contrary to this trend by the two largest generators, several IPPs have entered the market, with, in most all cases, combined-cycle gas turbine technology generation facilities. The market share of electricity sold by these two dominant producers has declined, from 45.5 percent (National Power) and 28.4 percent (PowerGen) in the 1990/91 fiscal year to 31.38 percent and 23.12 percent for the 1995/96 fiscal year.[5] There has also been a significant amount of entry by independent electricity suppliers who purchase electricity from the pool and sell it to final residential and business customers via the distribution network of the REC serving that customer's geographic area.

Another important feature of the market structure is the similarity in fuel mix between National Power and PowerGen. As of 1 April 1995, National Power's capacity had the following approximate (because of fuel-switching capabilities) fuel mix percentages, 75 percent coal, 15 percent oil, 9 percent natural gas, and 1 percent hydroelectric. PowerGen's approximate mix was 70 percent coal, 16 percent oil, 13 percent gas, and 1 percent hydroelectric.

The vast majority of an RECs customers purchase electricity at rates fixed independent of within-year variations in the pool price. Before the start of the 1998/99 fiscal year, all residential customers paid fixed prices for electricity that could vary in a mutually agreed upon manner on a daily or weekly basis, independent of fluctuations in the pool price, for the entire fiscal year. The most common form of this pricing plan for residential customers had a fixed price per megawatt-hour for all consumption during the year, plus a fixed charge. Most of the remaining residential customers pay according to a fixed price per megawatt-hour for consumption during daylight hours and another fixed price per megawatt-hour for consumption during nighttime hours, plus a fixed charge. Almost all commercial and industrial users purchase power through similar annually negotiated fixed-price contracts, which also vary on a daily or weekly basis, independent of movements in the pool price. Consequently, within-day, day-to-day, or even month-to-month movements in the pool price have no impact on the prices all but a small fraction of customers pay because the pattern of prices they face does not change for the entire fiscal year. Only a very small fraction of E&W total system load, approximately 5 percent, is pur-

---

5. Fiscal years run from 1 April to 31 March of the following calendar year. Nuclear Electric's 1995/96 fiscal year market share was 22.5 percent, power imported from Scotland and France was 8.71 percent, pumped storage was 0.7 percent, and IPPs and others was 13.6 percent (Electricity Association 1997, 26).

chased by final consumers according to variations in the half-hourly spot market price.[6]

Because RECs provide electricity to the vast majority of their customers according to rate schedules fixed well in advance of the realization of pool prices, they normally hedge against this price volatility by purchasing "contracts for differences" (CFDs). CFDs are simply financial instruments guaranteeing prices at which an agreed upon quantity of electricity can be traded at a future date.[7] CFDs have been sold by generators as well as financial institutions and traders that deal in commodity markets and derivative securities. It is important to emphasize that CFDs are not forward contracts to deliver electricity. The E&W mandatory spot market structure does not allow physical bilateral trades between generators and their customers. Unless a generating facility is dispatched by NGC as part of the day-ahead spot-market-clearing process, that plant cannot produce electricity. Consequently, if a customer and generator sign a bilateral contract for electricity supply, this does not guarantee that the generator will be dispatched in a manner that matches the customer's half-hourly demands or any prespecified rate of production. Whether or not a plant is dispatched and the rate at which it is operated in a half-hour is the decision of NGC. A plant that is dispatched by NGC (that is, not constrained on) will receive the market-clearing spot price from the E&W pool for all megawatt-hours it produces during that half-hour, regardless of the long-term contractual arrangements it has made with an REC or large customer in the CFD market.

CFDs were also used in the initial privatization process to maintain employment in the U.K. coal industry. The government required National Power and PowerGen to enter into contracts for the purchase of a higher volume of U.K. coal than they wished at higher-than-world-market prices, thus maintaining employment in the coal-mining industry. Vesting CFDs between each REC and National Power, PowerGen, and other generators were designed to compensate these generators for the higher prices they paid for U.K. coal under these coal supply contracts. The strike price of these CFDs allowed the costs of the coal contracts to be passed on to the RECs, and the structure of the REC regulatory process—a price cap with a Y-factor to pass through extraordinary cost increases—allowed these costs to be passed on to final customers in the form of higher retail prices.

6. Wolak and Patrick (1996b) describe these sorts of retail price contracts in more detail. Patrick and Wolak (1997) analyze the structure of demand under real-time prices for a sample of these customers from one of the RECs.

7. Most CFDs guarantee a fixed price for a fixed amount of electricity in the following manner. Suppose a generator and an REC write a CFD for 1 MWH of power at a strike price of £20/MWH. If the spot price of electricity is greater than £20/MWH, then the generator pays the REC the difference between the spot price and £20 for the contracted 1 MWH. If the spot price is less than £20/MWH, the REC pays the generator the difference between £20 and this spot price for the contracted 1 MWH.

In the first two years following privatization, it is estimated that CFDs covered 84.3 and 89.1 percent, respectively, of National Power's and Power-Gen's generation, declining to 72.7 and 70.6 percent over the next two years (Helm and Powell 1992). Green (1999) presents slightly larger estimates of the amount of contracts held by National Power and PowerGen over this time period using more up-to-date data.

3.2.2   Market Rules in England and Wales

For trading to take place in the E&W market, participants must know how they are compensated for the bids that they submit, particularly how market-clearing prices are determined and how dispatch decisions for generators are made. Recall that generators offer or "bid" prices at which they will provide various quantities of electricity to the E&W pool from their generating stations throughout the following day. They have two strategic weapons to influence the forty-eight half-hourly market-clearing electricity prices: (1) the daily decision for the price at which they are willing to supply electricity from a fixed portion of each generating facility and (2) the half-hourly decision whether to make that portion of each generating facility available to be called on by NGC to produce power. For example, in the E&W market firms are allowed to submit three daily prices for a given generating unit, but the amount that they are willing to supply from that unit at each of these three prices can be varied on a half-hourly basis throughout the day.

The day-ahead bid prices and availability declarations submitted by generators are input into the general ordering and loading (GOAL) program at NGC to determine the merit order of dispatching generation and reserve capacity. The lowest price generating capacity is dispatched first, unless such dispatch will compromise system integrity. Subject to this caveat, dispatching plants in this "least cost merit order" gives rise to an upward-sloping aggregate electricity supply function for each half-hour of the following day. The system marginal price (SMP) for each half-hour of the following day is the price bid on the marginal electricity generating unit ("genset") required to satisfy NGC's forecast of each half-hour's total system demand for the next day, that is, the bid where this expected demand crosses the aggregate supply curve.

The methodology and data input into NGC's forecast of demand are readily available to generators prior to their submissions of bid prices and availability declarations for the next day (Baker 1992; Electricity Pool 1997; National Grid Company 1995). This implies that generators can compute NGC's forecast of demand for all forty-eight load periods during the next day before they submit their bid prices and availability declarations. Moreover, this demand forecast that sets the SMP is perfectly price inelastic. Wolak and Patrick (1996a) argue that these two market rules have important implications for the strategies used by generators to exercise market power.

The pool purchase price (PPP), the price paid to generators per megawatt-hour in the relevant half-hour, is defined as

$$PPP = SMP + CC,$$

where the capacity charge is CC = LOLP × (VOLL − SMP), LOLP is the loss of load probability, and VOLL is the value of lost load. CC is intended to provide a signal to generators of the necessity of new generation capacity and to consumers that their consumption has a significant probability of requiring the maximum amount of generating capacity available in that load period. VOLL represents the per megawatt-hour willingness of customers to pay to avoid supply interruptions. It was set by the director general of the Office of Electricity Regulation (OFFER) at £2,000/MWH for 1990/91 and has increased annually in accordance with growth in the retail price index since that date. LOLP is determined for each half-hour as the probability of a supply interruption due to generation capacity being insufficient to meet demand. LOLP is a decreasing (at an increasing rate) function of the expected amount of excess capacity available during each half-hour period during the present day.[8] The greater the amount of capacity available relative to expected demand in any half-hour, the lower LOLP and therefore the lower CC per megawatt-hour paid to generators. Wolak and Patrick (1996b) argue that this relationship has important implications for the two largest generators' strategies for obtaining high PPPs.

The pool selling price (PSP) is the price paid mostly by RECs purchasing electricity from the pool to sell to their final commercial, industrial, and residential customers. For the purposes of determining this price, the forty-eight load periods within the day are divided into two distinct price rule regimes referred to as Table A and Table B periods. During Table A half-hours the PSP is

$$PSP = SMP + CC + UPLIFT = PPP + UPLIFT,$$

where UPLIFT is a charge used to collect costs incurred when demand and supply are actually realized each day. UPLIFT is only known after the following day's electricity demand has actually been satisfied. It is the only price uncertainty from the day-ahead perspective, and it is collected over at least twenty-eight Table A pricing periods each day. UPLIFT is zero for Table B pricing periods. Recall that the E&W market is an ex ante market in the sense that the PPP is set on a day-ahead basis using a demand forecast rather than actual demand. The costs of supplying the difference between the forecasted demand and the realized demand for the day is therefore recovered through the UPLIFT charge.

This charge also compensates generators for reserve plant available but

---

8. LOLP also depends on capacity offered in that half-hour during the seven previous days. Wolak and Patrick (1996b) describe the structure of the LOLP function in detail.

not actually used to meet demand and start-up costs. Generators are paid for being available to produce electricity according to

Availability payment/MWH = LOLP × (VOLL − max[SMP, Bid price]).

This approach to setting availability payments compensates a relatively high priced plant that is not used but is available less than a plant that bids close to the SMP. The remaining portion of UPLIFT consists of NGC's costs of ancillary services (reactive power, frequency control, hot standby, and black-start capability).

By 4 P.M. each day, the SMP, CC, and the identities of the Table A and Table B periods for all forty-eight load periods for the following day are communicated to pool participants. UPLIFT averages less than 10 percent of the PSP, and as discussed in Patrick and Wolak (1997), it can be accurately forecast on a day-ahead basis. Consequently, a large fraction of the ex post PSP is known on a day-ahead basis.

3.2.3 Regulatory Oversight in England and Wales

The Electricity Act of 1989 established OFFER, with Professor Stephen Littlechild serving as director general, to oversee the operation of the restructured U.K. electricity industry, from generation to transmission and distribution to final customers. At privatization there were no explicit controls over the PPP. Since then, Littlechild has instituted several regulatory changes in an attempt to inhibit strategic price and supply schedule offerings by generators. These include (1) an amendment of the original generation license to require generators to make public their plans on capacity availability, (2) a change in the way LOLP is calculated, (3) voluntary price caps on the time-weighted and quantity-weighted values of PPP, (4) the divestiture of generating plant, and (5) incentive mechanisms to reduce the magnitude of UPLIFT payments.

The original generation license was revised, following the Pool Price Inquiry in December 1991, to restrict the ability of generators to manipulate the PPP by reducing the capacity made available to the pool. The changes require generators to provide, for public viewing, reports containing their criteria for determining the availability of their capacity to the pool, closing generating stations, and otherwise reducing generating capacity. Each year, generators must also file detailed forecasts of the availability of each generating unit for the coming year and, at year's end, file a "reconciliation" explaining any deviations from anticipated availability. This information is also publicly available. However, "generators are under no obligation under Pool Rules to declare any of their Centrally Dispatched Generating Units (CDGUs) available to generate at any particular time, even though the CDGU may be operationally available" (Electricity Pool, n.d., 10). Wolak and Patrick (1996b) describe various other actions by the director general to encourage generators to declare capacity available.

During late 1993 and early 1994, OFFER issued reports and statements claiming that National Power and PowerGen were exercising market power to drive up pool prices. This matter was resolved with the institution of caps on time-weighted and quantity-weighted pool prices over the fiscal years 1994/95 and 1995/96 as part of a voluntary agreement, reached 11 February 1994, between National Power, PowerGen, and OFFER after Littlechild threatened to refer these generators to the Monopolies and Mergers Commission.[9] This agreement also included the divestiture of 4 and 2 GW of coal or oil generating plant by National Power and Power-Gen, respectively.

As a result of UPLIFT increases in the 1993/94 fiscal year, OFFER instituted in April 1994 the "uplift management incentive scheme" (UMIS) in an attempt to encourage NGC to minimize "avoidable costs" incurred in operating the E&W electricity market. UMIS was then replaced with the "transmission services scheme" (TSS) on 1 October 1995. TSS divided UPLIFT into the costs associated with reactive power, system constraints, transmission losses, and other ancillary services. Each category has a target level of costs, and NGC was given a share of any savings below these targets as an incentive to keep these costs down. Total ancillary services costs in all subsequent fiscal years are significantly below their 1993/94 level despite continuing growth in total annual energy production in the E&W system.

3.3   The Electricity Supply Industry in Norway and Sweden

Beginning 1 January 1996, the world's only international power exchange opened in Oslo, Norway. Statnett Marked AS, a subsidiary of the Norwegian grid company, Statnett SF, has been operating the Norwegian power market since 1993. From 1991 to 1993, Statnett SF managed both the national grid and the power market, which was introduced following the Norwegian Energy Act of 1990. With the formation of the international Nordic power market, Statnett Marked AS changed its name to Nord Pool ASA; it is currently owned 50/50 by Statnett SF and Svenska Kraftnät, the Swedish national grid operator. This power exchange integrates the Norwegian and Swedish electricity systems with ninety-six Norwegian and twenty-one Swedish participants as of March 1996. Denmark, Finland, and Russia all have participants in the market. Statnett SF is owned by the Norwegian government and Svenska Kraftnät by the Swedish government.

---

9. The Electricity Act of 1989 gives the director general the authority to refer firms to the Monopolies and Mergers Commission in order to make changes in the relevant license. Referrals can also be made under the Fair Trading Act of 1973 or the Competition Act of 1980.

3.3.1   Market Structure in Norway and Sweden

There are three major differences between the Nord Pool market structure and the E&W market structure. First is that 99 percent of installed capacity in Norway is hydropower, with the remaining capacity primarily oil and gas thermal power. In Sweden, approximately half of the total installed capacity is hydropower. Nuclear power has the next highest capacity share, approximately 30 percent. Except for a small amount of renewable generation capacity, oil and gas make up the remaining thermal power capacity. Consequently, more than 85 percent of the generation capacity in Norway and Sweden is either hydropower or nuclear power, technologies that have very low marginal costs of producing electricity. In contrast, more than 80 percent of the generating capacity in the United Kingdom is higher marginal cost coal-, oil-, or gas-fired generating technology.

The second major difference is that Nord Pool is not a mandatory pool. Generators and consumers decide whether they wish to sell or purchase electricity through this market. As a consequence, the majority of electricity in Norway and Sweden is still traded via bilateral contracts between generators and consumers, with the pool serving primarily as a wholesale market for marginal energy supplies. Nord Pool is actually composed of two markets operating simultaneously with the bilateral contract market. During any hour in the day electricity is transacted on each of these markets and through bilateral contracts. In addition, there is a futures market where weekly financial futures contracts with maturities ranging from a week ahead to three years ahead are traded. The market most like the E&W market is the daily power market (DPM), or Elspot market. Here fixed quantities of electricity are traded at prices set on a day-ahead basis for twenty-four hourly periods. Because of differences between day-ahead electricity consumption and generation plans and actual consumption and generation plans, incremental electricity must be dispatched throughout the day to meet unexpected demand and to maintain system integrity. This market for within-day electricity is called the regulation power market (RPM) in Norway and the balancing market in Sweden.

The final difference between Nord Pool and the E&W industry is that much of the generation capacity is fully or partially state owned. When the Energy Act of 1990 "deregulated" the electricity supply industry in Norway, Statkraft, the state-owned integrated electricity supplier, was broken up into separate companies providing generation, transmission, and distribution services similar to the CEGB in England and Wales, but it was not privatized. Statnett SF was created as the state-owned national grid company and system operator. Statkraft SF retained all generating plants. Statnett Marked AS was subsequently formed to run the electricity market. Statkraft SF owns approximately 40 percent of Norway's hydroelectric capacity and produces approximately 30 percent of its electricity output. The second largest producer in Norway is Hydro Energy, a subsidiary of Norsk Hydro, the largest industrial end user of electricity in Norway. It produces approximately 10 percent of Norway's electricity output. Many other smaller firms generate the remaining 60 percent of Norwegian electricity production. The vast majority of this capacity is owned by municipalities. Different from Norway, where there are more than two hundred generation companies (many of whom do not trade in the spot market), in Sweden ten large generators produce more than 90 percent of Swedish electricity. Vattenfall, the Swedish state power board, generates approximately 50 percent of the electricity produced in Sweden. In both countries, the majority of distribution assets are municipally owned. In Sweden, some of the large retail distributors also generate all or a large fraction of the electricity they distribute. For example, Sydkraft and Stockholm Energi, the two largest distribution companies, are the next largest generators after Vattenfall. In Norway, about half of the two hundred distribution companies also own generation assets.

3.3.2 Market Rules for Nord Pool

The rules governing the operation of the Nord Pool DPM differ from those for the E&W market in a number of dimensions. First, as discussed above, the DPM only trades a small fraction of the electricity produced within any hour during the day. In 1994, 14.6 TWH of electricity was sold on the spot market (1 TWH = 10^9 kWH). In 1995, this figure rose to 20.0 TWH. Total Norwegian electricity production was 113.6 TWH in 1994 and 123.5 TWH in 1995, which implies only 12.8 and 16.2 percent, respectively, of total Norwegian generation was sold through the DPM in these two years. In 1996, 40.6 TWH was sold in the new international DPM. Comparing this figure to 240.9 TWH, the total amount of generation in Norway and Sweden in 1996, implies that 16.7 percent of the production of the two countries is sold through this market. Sales in the RPM have remained stable over the three complete years Statnett Marked has operated: 5.5 TWH of sales in 1993, 6.1 TWH in 1994, 5.6 TWH in 1995, and 5.9 TWH in 1996. This is because the primary function of the RPM is to resolve imbalances between planned consumption as of the beginning of the hour and actual consumption during the hour. These consumption plans can be hedged on through bilateral contracts or on the DPM. Prices in the RPM very closely track those in the DPM, although they appear slightly more volatile. With the formation of the international DPM on 1 January 1996, the Swedish national grid company and system operator, Svenska Kraftnät, formed a similar within-day power market, which it calls the "balancing market" (*Balansetjänesten*).

The Eltermin market originally sold forward contracts for physical delivery in the future. Beginning in 1995, this market was transformed into a financial market that sells what are called Eltermin contracts, which are obligations to buy or sell a known quantity of electricity in a specific period of time at a price agreed upon at the time the contract is entered into. The contracts do not lead to physical delivery when they become due. Financial settlement is done against the DPM spot price.

Eltermin contracts are either forward or futures contracts. The forward contracts are traded for blocks of power either for thirds of the year or for the entire year. These forward contracts are CFDs on blocks of power for the contract period. When the contract becomes due it is settled against the price in the Elspot market.

Eltermin futures contracts are standardized along various dimensions. There are three different time horizons to these contracts: (1) week-long contracts, ranging from up to four to seven weeks in the future; (2) block contracts of four weeks long, for electricity delivered up to a year in the future; and (3) seasonal contracts for blocks lasting an entire season of the year, for electricity delivered over one year in advance. The final dimension of the contracts is the time period within the day that the contract is valid. There are three types of contracts along this dimension: (1) basic power, all hours in the week (168 hours); (2) day power, from 7 A.M. to 10 P.M. Monday to Friday (75 hours); and (3) night power, the remaining hours not covered by the day power contract. There is continuous trading in this market five days each week, with sellers submitting ask prices for the contracts they wish to sell, buyers submitting bid prices for the contracts they wish to purchase, and trades taking place when bid prices exceed ask prices. These contracts are purely financial contracts in the sense that financial settlement takes place daily for customers holding futures contracts, based on the day-to-day changes in the relevant Eltermin prices. During the delivery period, financial settlement of the contract takes place at the difference between the last price in the Eltermin market and that hour's price in the DPM. Volume in this market has grown significantly over time. In 1994, total trading volume over all contracts was 7.1 TWH. In 1995, this figure more than doubled to 15.5 TWH. In 1996, the figure tripled to 42.6 TWH. The greatest growth has been in the weekly and block contracts, with only moderate growth in the seasonal contracts.

The DPM is similar to the E&W market in the sense that generators submit their bids to Nord Pool on a day-ahead basis. However, because this market operates on top of the bilateral contract market, it is what Nord Pool calls a "netto-market" in the sense that each customer must be in balance during each hour the following day—its supply obligations must equal the sum of its own generation, bilateral contract purchases from other generators, and DPM purchases. The bid function submitted by a DPM market participant gives the amount of power it will actually sell or buy each hour as a function of the market-clearing price. Recall that by law all but a very small fraction of total generation in the E&W

market must be sold on the spot market during each half hour. In addition, the aggregate demand determining the market-clearing price in the E&W market is the value forecast by NGC, whereas in the DPM, the market-clearing price for each half-hour is determined at the intersection of the aggregate demand and supply bid functions. For this reason, the DPM can also be thought of as a forward market for firm delivery during the following day. Different from the E&W market, there is no uncertainty in the quantity of electricity that is traded on the spot market the next day. In the E&W market, the difference between day-ahead generation plans and actual generation is handled through the UPLIFT charge. Generators in the E&W market submit their willingness to supply a specific quantity of electricity during the following day. This means that they are at risk to sell more or less than their willingness to supply at the PPP, depending on actual market conditions. In Nord Pool, because of the presence of the RPM, the DPM is a firm financial commitment for a fixed price and quantity of electricity sold on a day-ahead basis. For this reason, one can also think of the DPM as a day-ahead market for CFDs written against the RPM price.

There is also a geographic dimension to the price-setting process in the DPM that is different from the E&W market, where there is a single price for electricity in each half-hour, except for electricity produced by constrained-on generators. Every Wednesday, Nord Pool sends to market participants either electronically or by fax two types of information about how bids should be submitted for trade in the DPM during the following week. This information defines the geographic areas of Norway and Sweden for which participants will submit bids. These bid areas are determined using historical generation and consumption data, transmission capacity, and the description of the electricity grid. If a transmission bottleneck is expected to occur between two geographic areas during the week, separate bid areas will be defined on either side of the transmission bottleneck. These bid areas can also change over the course of the week based on planned or unplanned bottlenecks in the transmission grid. The second type of information Nord Pool supplies to participants is the bid price interval, giving the highest and lowest prices that must be covered by a bid from each participant for all hours in the coming week. This is done to guarantee a unique price for each bid area. The bidder can submit a maximum of fourteen prices between these two prices, giving the amount it is willing to buy or sell as a function of these prices.

All bids by market participants must be registered in standardized bid forms, one for each bid area, and submitted electronically or by fax to Nord Pool by noon the day before actual physical delivery takes place. The bid gives the maximum hours the bid is valid (minimum one hour and maximum all of the hours a bid area is valid). These bids must be finalized by noon the day before power will be delivered on the DPM. By 2 P.M.

that same day, Nord Pool takes this information and determines the market-clearing prices for each of the twenty-four periods starting with midnight to 1 A.M. the following day and ending with the period starting at 11 P.M. and ending at midnight the day after. The system price is determined from the intersection of the aggregate electricity supply function (bids to supply electricity as a function of price) with the aggregate electricity demand function (bids to consume electricity as a function of price) without taking into account transmission constraints. If there are no transmission constraints, then all generators receive the same price for the electricity they produce.

If there are transmission constraints, generators in different bid areas receive different prices for the electricity they produce in the form of different transmission capacity fees across the different bid areas. Similarly, consumers in these bid areas purchase at different prices because of these capacity fees. In areas where generators want to sell more than can be transmitted, they will be required to pay a capacity fee to do so. Consumers in these bid areas will receive this capacity fee for all of their consumption in this area. In areas where bidders want to purchase more than generators are willing to supply, the price will be increased by a potentially different capacity fee. Generators in this area will receive this capacity fee in addition to the spot price for their generation. Prices in the surplus generation area will fall and prices in the deficit generation area will rise until the amount electricity generators in the surplus area are willing to transmit to the deficit region equals the amount consumers in the deficit region are willing to take, and both are equal to the transmission capacity between the two bid regions. These actions by Nord Pool end when all transmission bottlenecks are eliminated.[10] Bid areas that set the same prices are aggregated into common price areas. Market participants are then notified of these price areas, area prices, and the hours they are valid. Each participant is told the contractual amount of electricity it will be called on to buy or sell in each price area during each of these hours and the total amount of power transacted on the DPM during each hour. If there are no transmission bottlenecks, the entire system becomes a single price area.

The forward contract nature of the DPM is another way that it differs from the E&W spot market. In the E&W market, generators only know the market-clearing price for the next day; they do not know exactly how much electricity they will be required to supply to the spot market during each half-hour that day until the half-hour actually occurs. However, the presence of RPMs in Norway and Sweden, which operate during the next

---

10. Because of very extensive transmission networks in Norway and Sweden, transmission bottlenecks rarely occur within the two countries. The major source of bottlenecks is trading between the two countries.

day to balance any discrepancies in a generator's or consumer's contractual supply or demand obligations (including those from the DPM), fulfills this role in the Nordic power market. These unexpected deviations from plans are made up by purchases or sales into this market, so that the DPM clears the day before actual dispatch takes place. Consequently, the DPM is simply another contractual supply or consumption obligation (similar to a bilateral contract) market during the day actual supply or consumption takes place. In the E&W market, NGC serves the function of the RPM because it dispatches generation during the following day to supply the amount of electricity actually demanded (rather than the expected demand used to set the PSP) and to maintain system balance.

During each dispatch day for the DPM, an RPM operates in each country. The equation Production + Import = Consumption + Grid losses + Export must hold for each bid area. In Norway, each day before 7:30 P.M., bids are registered with the RPM. Generating stations that bid have to be able to alter their production within fifteen minutes. A bid is an option for the system operator and can take two forms. An upward regulatory bid indicates the price the market participant demands for an extra amount of power produced. A downward regulatory bid sets the price that actor is willing to pay for buying power (by producing less than planned). All bids are grouped according to price areas and sorted by price. The RPM in each bid area uses these bids to increase or decrease production in these areas. The market participant called on to increase or decrease its output is given at least fifteen minutes' notice before it must produce. It is given no indication of how long it must produce but will be given at least fifteen minutes' notice before it must shut down. When an hour of regulation has passed, the price in the RPM is fixed and one price is set for each price area. After each hour, each participant in the DPM calculates its imbalances in each price area—how much more or less than it contracted for on the DPM did it actually consume or produce in that hour? This imbalance is settled in the RPM. If a participant consumes more than planned, it must buy in the RPM, and if it consumes less than planned, it must sell in the RPM. This implies that all DPM and bilateral market participants, even if they do not submit bids to the RPM, are involved in this market.

The regulation market in Sweden operates in a different manner. By law, Svenska Kraftnät has the obligation to maintain balance between generation and load in Sweden. All consumers of electricity are required to ensure that a "balance provider" has been appointed for their point of withdrawal from the grid. Since 1 January 1995, Svenska Kraftnät has operated the "balance service," which involves agreements with approximately forty balance-responsible companies called "balance centers." These companies have the responsibility in accordance with the Balance Obligation Agreement to provide the Swedish electricity system with the same amount of electricity that the balance center's customers are consuming.

Svenska Kraftnät is responsible for the balance settlement, that is, the calculation of the imbalance, of every balance center. It then operates an hourly market for imbalances that allows trading of electricity across balance centers. Because of this congestion management scheme, Sweden is always a single bidding area in the Nord Pool bidding process.

3.3.3   Regulatory Oversight of the Nordic Power Market

Up until the formation of the international power exchange between Sweden and Norway, the Norwegian Water Resources and Energy Administration (NVE) oversaw the operations of the Nordic power market. It is still responsible for monitoring grid operations in Norway and is responsible for setting the tariffs for the local distribution companies throughout Norway. Previously, distribution tariffs were set on a cost-of-service basis, but starting in 1997, NVE implemented a version of price-cap regulation. Because Nord Pool is not required by the Swedish government to operate under any particular license, the majority of formal monitoring of Nord Pool remains with NVE.

There have been several inquiries into the reasons for high prices in Nord Pool. Following the formation of the Norwegian power market in 1991, prices were the lowest they had ever been. These prices continued until Statkraft SF publicly announced a policy of not supplying to the spot market at prices below 100 NOK/MWH. Statkraft apparently demonstrated its determination to maintain market-clearing prices above this level by punishing deviators by flooding the market and driving prices to zero. Prices subsequently stabilized at significantly higher values. Annual mean prices in the spot market have been above 100 NOK/MWH for all years following 1992. The Norwegian Competition Authority (Prisdirektoratet) investigated whether collusion between generators caused these elevated prices, but it found little evidence in favor of this claim. Other periods of extremely high prices seem to be explained by unusually dry weather conditions.

3.4   The Victoria Electricity Supply Industry

The state of Victoria has the longest running wholesale electricity market in Australia. The Victoria Power Exchange (VPX) was established under the Electricity Industry (Amendment) Act of 1994 and formally began operation on 1 July 1994. New South Wales (NSW) established a state-level wholesale market for electricity that began operation 10 May 1996. Effective 4 May 1997 interstate electricity competition between generators in NSW and Victoria to supply electricity to energy retailers in these two states began. Previously, trade between NSW and Victoria was limited to long-term contract transactions, and any short-term trades were based on system integrity considerations rather than economic considerations. The integration of these two markets to allow all feasible trades between the two states is the first stage in the establishment of the National Electricity Market for Australia, known as NEM1.

The ultimate goal of this process is to establish a single electricity market across Queensland, NSW, Victoria, and South Australia. Because the eastern seaboard of Australia is currently not a fully integrated system, modifications of the system must be completed before a competitive interstate market can be introduced. Following a process similar to the one that occurred in England and Wales, the plan is to separate transmission and distribution from generation for all of the vertically integrated and formerly government-owned utilities throughout Australia and privatize or corporatize these new entities. One outcome of this process is a harmonization of the rules governing the operation of the two markets currently in operation in Victoria and NSW. The market structures of the two electricity supply industries in Victoria and NSW are also similar in terms of the relative sizes of the generation firms and the mix of generation capacity by fuel type, although the NSW industry is a little less than twice the size (as measured by installed capacity) of the Victoria industry and the largest three generators in NSW control a larger fraction of the total generation capacity in their market than the three largest generators in Victoria control of their market. Because the NSW market has operated for a short time and shares many market rules with the Victoria market, my discussion will focus on the Victoria industry.[11]

3.4.1 Market Structure in the Victoria Electricity Supply Industry

Restructuring and privatization of the State Electricity Commission of Victoria (SECV) in 1994 took place at roughly the power station level. The generation sector was formed into five separate entities to be sold. As of 28 March 1999 when Ecogen Energy was privatized, all of the generating units formerly owned by the SECV have been sold. Buyers are from within Australia and abroad. For example, on 21 May 1996, PowerGen, the second largest E&W generating company, purchased a 49.9 percent share of Yallourn Energy, with the remaining shares purchased by investors from Japan and Australia. On 1 April 1997, Edison Mission Energy, a California-based U.S. firm, purchased the Loy Yang B station. On 4 August 1996, National Power, the largest E&W generating company at that time, purchased a 52 percent share of Hazelwood Energy.

---

11. As of 13 December 1998, the first stage of the transition to a national electricity market for Australia, NEM1, ended. The operation of VicPool ceased, and responsibility for the management of the Victoria electricity market passed to the newly formed National Electricity Market Management Company (NEMMCO), which operates an integrated market between NSW, Victoria, Queensland, Australian Capital Territory, and South Australia. The current NEMMCO market rules are very similar to the final VicPool market rules described here.

The distribution sector was formed into five privatized companies: Citi-Power, Eastern Energy, PowerCor, Solaris Power, and United Energy, which are owned by a combination of U.S. utilities and Australian companies. For example, PowerCor is owned by the U.S. firm PacificCorp, and Eastern Energy is owned by Texas Utilities. There is an accounting separation within these distribution companies between their electricity distribution business and their electricity supply business. All other retailers have open and nondiscriminatory access to the wires of the other distribution companies.

The high-voltage transmission grid initially remained in state hands but was renamed PowerNet Victoria. In early 1998, it was sold to a U.S. energy services company GPU Inc. and renamed GPU PowerNet. The VPX is separate from all of these entities. Its mission is to manage the wholesale electricity market, manage the security of Victoria's power system, and direct the development of the high-voltage transmission system. This is different from the E&W model, where NGC also owns the high-voltage transmission system in addition to providing these three services. It differs slightly from the Nord Pool model, where Stanett SF owns and operates the grid, but Nord Pool ASA, a subsidiary of Statnett SF, runs the wholesale electricity market.

The Victoria electricity supply industry is significantly smaller than either the E&W or Norway and Sweden market. Peak demand in this market is approximately 7.5 GW, and the maximum amount of generating capacity that can be supplied to the market is approximately 9.0 GW. Because of this small peak demand, and despite the divestiture of SECV generation capacity to five firms, at least three of the largest baseload generators have sufficient generating capacity to supply at least 20 percent of this peak demand.

More than 80 percent of generating plant is brown coal fired, although some capacity does have fuel-switching capabilities. Brown coal has a high moisture content and a low sulfur and ash content, but also a very low heat content relative to black coal, which is used in the NSW market and the E&W market. The brown coal power plants are located adjacent to large strip mines. Consequently, in spite of its low heat content, the very low cost of strip-mining brown coal makes these plants extremely low cost to operate. The operators of these facilities are also very reluctant to shut down these plants because more expensive fuels must be used to start them up.

The remaining generating capacity is shared equally between gas turbines and hydroelectric power. In this dimension, the market structure of the Victoria electricity supply industry is similar to the E&W market structure, where there are two large, primarily coal-fired generation companies, National Power and PowerGen, which each control more than 25 percent of total E&W system capacity.

3.4.2   Market Rules in the Victoria Power Exchange

Although there are important differences, the VPX shares several features with the E&W market. In particular, the VPX is a mandatory pool where prices are set on a half-hourly basis using bids submitted on a day-ahead basis by generators and demand-side bidders. The rules governing the operation of the VPX have changed several times since the formation of the market in 1994. The latest phase is known as VicPool III enhanced. It commenced operation on 1 September 1996. Three major changes were made to the VicPool at this time. First, daily bidding by generators replaced weekly bidding. Second, more increments were added to the allowed bid functions that generators could submit. Formerly, generators were able to bid the capacity of each generating unit into the pool in only three increments (similar to the E&W market), and up until the end of 1994 generators were only allowed to bid a single increment for each unit. In VicPool III enhanced, generators are able to bid prices for their units into the market in ten capacity increments that cannot be changed for the entire trading day—the twenty-four hour period beginning at 4 A.M. the following day. This rule is the same as the one in the E&W market because in both markets generators cannot change the price bid for each increment for the entire day but they can vary the amount they are willing to supply from that capacity increment on a half-hourly basis.

A third change in the VicPool rules is that generators now must self-commit their generation capacity. Previously, the VicPool operated on the basis of central commitment, similar to the E&W system. Under central commitment, in their bids generators are required to submit start-up costs, start-up times, and minimum on and off times. NGC in E&W (and formerly the VPX in Victoria) analyzes the costs and times presented by each generator and makes the start-up and shutdown decisions for all half-hours during the following day. Under VicPool III enhanced, generators are required to self-commit, which means that if a unit is committed by its owner, the capacity of the unit will be dispatched up to the point that the bid price for that capacity increment is less than the market-clearing price for that half-hour.

The other major difference between the VicPool and the E&W pool is that the VicPool is very close to a real-time market. Prices paid to generators are based on a real-time forecast of the total system demand in the next five-minute interval. During each five-minute period in a given half-hour this demand forecast is crossed with the aggregate supply curve for that half-hour that can satisfy this demand forecast. Ramping constraints on generating units are respected in the five-minute-ahead dispatch process. If a unit willing to supply 100 MW during a given half-hour at a certain price can only supply an additional 20 MW with five minutes' notice because of ramping constraints, the price-setting process will move further up the aggregate supply curve for that half-hour to another unit to meet any remaining unmet demand. The five-minute price can only be set by a generator that is not constrained by its ramp rate during the next five minutes. The half-hourly price of electricity is then computed as the average of the six five-minute prices set during that half-hour. All energy produced during that hour is bought and sold at this ex post spot price.[12] Longer horizon demand forecasts are used to schedule plant and make preliminary determinations of required ancillary services, such as reserve and reactive power, which are purchased under long-term contracts with generators. Because of the ex post nature of the VicPool there is no need for either a balancing market similar to that in Nord Pool or an UPLIFT charge as is the case in the E&W pool.

A participant must not update or alter the self-commitment decision, the bid prices for each capacity band, or the elbows of the capacity bands for each unit bid after 11 A.M. on the day before this bid is active. The available capacity declaration for a unit during a half-hour cannot be altered for thirty-seven hours before the start of the day that contains that half-hour period, except to reflect a change in availability of the unit due to an event or events beyond the reasonable control of that participant, in order to reflect an unexpected increase in availability of the unit, and in response to a change in market conditions that the participant could not reasonably forecast.

Because half-hourly spot prices are determined after the half-hour period, it is not known whether supply will be sufficient to meet demand when bids are submitted on a day-ahead basis. If demand exceeds or is equal to total supply during a five-minute period, then the price is set equal to the value of lost load (VOLL), which is currently set equal to AU$5,000/MWH.

There are several mechanisms for managing pool price risk in the VicPool. There is no formal futures market similar to the one that exists in Nord Pool. Generators and retailers can hedge against pool price volatility using two instruments: (1) vesting contracts and (2) contestable contracts. Each generator in the VicPool holds a vesting contract with at least one distributor. The vesting contracts cover consumption by franchise customers (those with no choice of electricity supplier) and large industrial customers on fixed-price contracts. The megawatt-hours covered under these contracts decline with the reduction in the size of the franchise market. The supply market becomes fully contestable (all customers can choose supply from any distributor) in December 2000. These vesting contracts are essentially two-sided CFDs for pool prices below $300/MWH and one-sided CFDs for pool price in excess of $300/MWH. Contestable contracts

---

12. The basic features of this price-setting process are followed by NEMMCO, established 13 December 1998.

are CFDs signed between generators and retailers to hedge the risks associated with supplying their contestable customers with electricity at prices that do not vary with the half-hourly changes in the pool price.

3.4.3   Regulatory Oversight in the Victoria Electricity Supply Industry

The Office of the Regulator General in Victoria is responsible for oversight of the Victoria electricity supply industry. It sets the prices for both transmission and distribution services, using a price-cap regulation plan. Because of the planned integration of the Australian electricity supply industry, recently there has been oversight at the national level of the VPX from the Australia Competition and Consumer Commission.

During the first two years of operation of the VPX, there were various inquiries into the exercise of market power because of sustained periods of high prices, despite a significant degree of volatility in these prices. Entry by new generators and changes in firm ownership as more new generating companies were formed from the sale of SECV units has led to much lower prices, but to an increase in relative volatility as measured by the ratio of the annual standard deviation to annual mean of VPX prices. Concern has died down about the exercise of market power in the Victoria electricity supply industry.

3.5   The New Zealand Electricity Supply Industry

Historically, the New Zealand electricity supply industry was dominated by a state-owned agency that operated the generation facilities and the bulk transmission network. Electricity supply authorities handled local distribution as local governing bodies (power boards) or under local body ownership (municipal electricity departments). This organizational structure continued largely unchanged until 1987, when the Electricity Division of the Ministry of Energy was restructured as the Electricity Corporation of New Zealand (ECNZ). At the same time, restrictions on entry into generation and wholesaling of electricity were removed. Because of excess capacity in generation, little entry took place. Despite being a state-owned enterprise, ECNZ was expected to earn a competitive rate of return on its assets. In 1988, ECNZ restructured itself into a corporate group with four subsidiaries: Production, Marketing, TransPower, and the PowerDesignBuild Group. TransPower owns and manages the national bulk transmission grid, and PowerDesignBuild offers consultancy and contracting services. At the present time ECNZ remains state owned, although eventual privatization has not been ruled out. Since 1992, TransPower has been a fully independent state-owned enterprise.

Reform of electricity distribution was spurred by the passage of the Energy Sector Reform Bill in 1992, which corporatized the electricity supply authorities and removed franchise areas, starting in 1993 for small customers, and for all customers in 1994. Ownership of the distribution network remained primarily in government hands as local government-owned trusts or local government authorities, although some privatization has taken place and more is currently under way. Open-access nondiscriminatory tariffs must be set by all distribution companies, so that other electricity retailers can supply electricity to customers. The electricity distribution ("wires") business of each distribution company is separate from its competitive supply business.

3.5.1 Market Structure in the New Zealand Electricity Industry

The New Zealand electricity system consists of two alternating current subsystems, for North and South Islands, connected by a 1,200 MW underwater high-voltage direct current cable. All capacity on South Island is hydroelectric. There is sufficient capacity on South Island to serve its annual electricity requirements, as well as to export some power to North Island, where there is both hydroelectric and thermal capacity. Approximately 75 percent of North Island demand is met from hydroelectric sources, with the remaining 25 percent split between geothermal sources and fossil fuel (coal, natural gas, and oil) sources, with the fossil fuel generation (primarily from natural gas) approximately twice that of the geothermal. Annual electricity consumption for the entire country is approximately 30 TWH per year, which is approximately one-tenth the annual consumption of England and Wales, despite the fact that the land area of New Zealand is approximately the same size as the United Kingdom. With approximately 3.5 million people in New Zealand, transmission and distribution accounts for a relatively large fraction of the cost of delivered electricity relative to the rest of the world, roughly 50 percent of the retail price of electricity.

An additional important aspect of the New Zealand system is that most of the population resides in the northern part of North Island, whereas most of the major hydroelectric resources are in the southern part of South Island. Consequently, transmission constraints between South Island and North Island can play an important role in the electricity supply process.

The generation side of the industry is dominated by the state-owned ECNZ, which prior to 1 February 1996 owned and operated more than 95 percent of total New Zealand electricity generating capacity. On 1 February 1996, in preparation for the formation of a wholesale market for electricity, Contact Energy Ltd. was formed as separate state-owned enterprise from ECNZ. It took over more than 30 percent of the generating capacity formerly owned and operated by ECNZ.[13] The government also imposed a cap on new capacity by ECNZ until its generation market share

---

13. More recently, on 1 April 1999, ECNZ was separated into three state-owned generating entities—Gensis Power Ltd., Meridan Energy Ltd., and Mighty River Power Ltd.

falls below 45 percent. It is also prohibited from owning any of the retail electricity companies. ECNZ was also required to offer a substantial fraction of its capacity in the form of "reasonably priced" CFDs. Several of the distribution companies own generating capacity, but none generates more than 250 GWH annually. Despite the retention of state ownership of ECNZ and Contact Energy, the pattern of divestiture of generation from transmission and distribution for New Zealand follows that of the other three industries.

There are currently thirty-eight electricity distribution companies providing equal access distribution services and electricity supply to customers and one electricity retailer providing electricity supply only. The state-owned corporation TransPower owns and runs the bulk transmission grid. In this capacity it is also responsible for the purchase of ancillary services.

3.5.2 Market Rules in the New Zealand Electricity Market

On 1 October 1996, a wholesale electricity market in New Zealand commenced operation under the name Electricity Market Company (EMCO). This market is a true ex post spot market. Similar to the VicPool and Nord Pool, there is separation between the power exchange, which is run by EMCO, and the system operator, which is TransPower. Similar to the Nord Pool market structure, the wholesale electricity market is not mandatory. However, because of the concentration of generating assets in the hands of ECNZ and Contact Energy, the spot market trades a large fraction of the electricity sold in New Zealand.

Because of concerns about the capacity of the high-voltage cable between North and South Islands and the level of line losses along this link, spot prices are set at reference nodes in both North and South Islands. Generators submit offer functions giving the amount of capacity they are willing to supply as a function of the price for all half-hours during the following day for each generating unit. Each generating unit can have a maximum of five price bands, and all individual generating unit offer functions must be increasing in the offer price. Purchasers submit bid functions that are decreasing in the bid price and can contain up to ten price bands. Different from the markets in England and Wales and Australia, neither the price nor the quantity bands associated with the bid and offer functions can be altered for the duration that the bid or offer curve is valid.[14] These offer and bid functions are used to perform a day-ahead prospective market, which results in a proposed dispatch schedule and forecast prices. Offer and bid functions may be freely changed up to four hours before

---

14. The price bands associated with bids and offers cannot be changed less than four hours prior to the trading period. However, if a bona fide physical reason exists, the quantity bands can be changed less than four hours prior to the trading period. However, the Market Surveillance Committee is notified of these quantity revisions and may rule on whether the revised bid was due to a bona fide physical reason.

dispatch occurs. Dispatch must meet actual loads, but to the greatest extent possible it should also match the loads obtained by using a least cost dispatch based on the latest generator offers. Prices are determined after actual demand has been satisfied by resolving the market-clearing model to meet the actual metered load at each node using the generator offer curves as of the beginning of each half-hour trading period.

The New Zealand electricity supply industry uses a full nodal-pricing model, but with a direct current power flow approximation that uses piecewise linear line loss functions. Reserve capacity procurement is integrated into the market-clearing process. Joint reserve and energy offers made by generators are input into a single market-clearing linear programming problem to produce prices for energy at each node and two classes of reserve capacity in each island. Reed, Drayton-Bright, and Ring (1998) describe the operation of the reserve capacity portion of the spot market. Energy prices are set on a half-hourly basis at more than two hundred nodes, with approximately thirty of these nodes points where generators sell into the grid.

3.5.3   Regulatory Oversight in the New Zealand Electricity Supply Industry

There is no explicit regulation of the generation, transmission, or distribution sector, aside from monitoring by the New Zealand Ministry of Commerce. As noted earlier, the New Zealand government has taken a "light-handed" approach to regulation of the industry. Parties have been left to form arrangements among themselves, with all parties being free to appeal to the courts or the Commerce Commission. There is a Market Surveillance Committee that acts as an independent monitor of the market. The EMCO rules allow the Market Surveillance Committee to recommend rule changes, cancel rule changes, investigate misconduct and breaches of market rules, and discipline market participants for undesirable behavior. The committee can also impose fines on market participants for violations of the market rules or what it determines to be undesirable practices.

3.6   An International Comparison of the Behavior of Spot Electricity Prices

This section characterizes the time-series properties of the spot electricity prices from England and Wales, Norway and Sweden, Victoria, and New Zealand electricity markets since their inception. Our goal is to characterize several dimensions of the time-series behavior of prices in these four markets. Our ultimate goal is to relate differences in these dimensions of the behavior of electricity prices across the four markets to differences in market structure and market rules across the four markets. Although this is an extremely difficult task, the analysis to be presented does appear consistent with the view that market structure and market rules cause significant differences in the behavior of spot prices for electricity across the four markets.

One of the most striking features of prices from these electricity markets is their tremendous volatility within days and across days within the week. I would like to understand the extent to which this variability in prices is forecastable and how this forecastability varies across the four markets.

Table 3.1 gives the annual average half-hourly (hourly in the case of Nord Pool) price and standard deviation of price for each year in our sample in terms of the home currency of that country. For Nord Pool, prices are quoted in Norwegian kroner per megawatt-hour. The missing entries in the table are due to the fact that the electricity market did not operate during that year. For all markets, I only have data for a portion of the year in which the market began, and data for only the first few months of 1997. The E&W market data run from 1 April 1990 to 31 March 1997. The Norwegian spot market data run from 4 May 1992 to 16 May 1997. The Victoria data begin 1 July 1994 and end 3 May 1997. The New Zealand data begin 1 October 1996 and end 31 May 1997.

Several conclusions are consistent with the results in table 3.1. First is that the mix of generation technology has an impact on both the mean and standard deviation of market prices. Prices in the two markets dominated by fossil fuel technology—E&W and Victoria—tend to be much more volatile than prices in the two markets dominated by hydroelectric capacity—Nord Pool and New Zealand. The coefficient of variation, the standard deviation divided by the mean, for almost all years in E&W and Victoria are larger than those in Nord Pool and New Zealand.

With the exception of Victoria in 1994 and 1995 versus 1996 and 1997, mean prices in the fossil-fuel-dominated markets tend to be more stable across years than prices in the hydroelectric-dominated systems.[15] Mean prices in the E&W market are much more stable across the years than those in Nord Pool. As discussed above, a major determinant of the mean of prices in hydroelectric-capacity-dominated markets is the amount of water available. If there is little water, then reservoirs tend to be low and flow volumes in rivers are reduced, so that hydroelectric generators tend to be very reluctant to sell into the spot market during the winter season and spot prices remain high until the late spring and summer, when electricity demand is much lower. The supply of energy inputs to fossil-fuel-based systems is not nearly as sensitive to local weather conditions. Because there are relatively integrated international coal, natural gas, and oil

---

15. There are several reasons to believe that there was a regime shift in the VicPool before and after 1 January 1996. Before this date, very few of the generators had been sold off, so that the SECV was effectively bidding all plants. In addition, before this date, there were high levels of vesting contracts at prices between AU$35/MWH and AU$40/MWH.

Table 3.1   Annual Means and Standard Deviations of Spot Prices of Electricity

Year	E&W		NW		VIC		NZN		NZS	
	Mean	SD	Mean	SD	Mean	SD	Mean	SD	Mean	SD
1990	17.38	5.38	n.a.	n.a.	n.a.	n.a.	n.a.	n.a.	n.a.	n.a.
1991	22.50	12.65	n.a.	n.a.	n.a.	n.a.	n.a.	n.a.	n.a.	n.a.
1992	23.42	6.28	58.10	44.38	n.a.	n.a.	n.a.	n.a.	n.a.	n.a.
1993	27.14	7.86	80.28	41.02	n.a.	n.a.	n.a.	n.a.	n.a.	n.a.
1994	24.73	18.73	182.67	49.29	36.72	18.24	n.a.	n.a.	n.a.	n.a.
1995	26.15	50.89	117.69	38.92	41.94	30.02	n.a.	n.a.	n.a.	n.a.
1996	25.18	27.85	253.52	44.62	21.11	19.30	39.36	17.00	28.53	6.53
1997	29.27	27.97	150.63	42.90	22.96	59.05	46.97	8.71	41.97	8.87

Note: E&W = England and Wales Pool, units = £/MWH; NW = Nord Pool, units = NOK/MWH; VIC = Victoria Power Exchange, units = AU$/MWH; NZN = New Zealand North Island, units = NZ$/MWH; and NZS = New Zealand South Island, units = NZ$/MWH. All prices in home currency per MWH.

markets, prices for these fuels tend to be stable across years, so that the mean price of electricity from fossil-fuel-based markets should be stable across years. The more variable annual mean prices across years and smaller variance in prices within years in hydroelectric systems versus fossil-fuel-dominated systems is consistent with this view.

There are three alternative explanations for the lower level of volatility in Nord Pool and the NZEM relative to the E&W market and the VicPool. First, both fossil-fuel-based systems, the E&W market and the VicPool, are mandatory pools, whereas the two hydroelectric-based systems, Nord Pool and the NZEM, have optional day-ahead markets. Consequently, the lower relative volatility in Nord Pool and the NZEM could be explained by holders' of bilateral contracts for electricity standing ready to sell into the spot electricity market if prices become high enough. This willingness to sell into the spot market at high prices increases the elasticity of the supply response that any generating company might face if it attempts to raise its bid prices, so that much of the adjustment to high bids in the spot market will come in the form of reduced amounts transacted rather than increased prices, as is the case in mandatory pools with little, if any, demand-side bidding such as in the E&W market, and to a lesser extent the VicPool.

A second explanation for the result in table 3.1 is that the vast majority of generating capacity in the E&W market is privately owned and an increasing (over time) fraction of the capacity in the VicPool is privately owned, whereas both Nord Pool and the NZEM are dominated by large state-owned generation companies. One would expect the large state-owned companies to pursue other objectives besides maximizing profits, whereas the major goal of the privately owned firms would be to maximize profits. Therefore, some of the volatility in the E&W market and the Vic-Pool could be explained as episodes of successful and unsuccessful attempts to exercise market power. State-owned enterprises may also be unwilling to engage in the risky bidding behavior necessary to set these occasional high prices and may instead settle for lower but more certain revenue streams than privately owned firms.

A final explanation can be traced to the differences in the bidding process across the four markets. In the E&W market and the VicPool generators can alter the quantity supplied from each bid increment on a half-hourly basis, whereas in Nord Pool and the New Zealand market both the prices and quantities associated with the hourly supply curves submitted by generators are fixed for the duration that a generating unit's supply curve is valid. The greater flexibility afforded to bidders in the E&W market and the VicPool to vary their supply curves on a half-hourly basis may allow generators to tailor their bids to set market prices that more closely follow the within-day pattern of total system load than in Nord Pool and the New Zealand market, where supply functions are generally fixed for longer periods of time during the day.

A final aspect of table 3.1 deserves comment. Consistent with the description of the differences in market structure between North and South Islands in New Zealand—cheap, abundant hydroelectric power in South Island and most of the population in North Island along with more expensive fossil-fuel-based plants—the mean price in the north is significantly higher than the mean price in the south for both years. In addition, prices in the north are also more volatile than those in the south, particularly for 1996. This reflects the use of fossil units to meet system peaks in North Island. Consequently, even for an integrated system such as the New Zealand market, the region with the greater share of total electricity production from fossil fuel units experiences greater spot price volatility.

To determine which market sells electricity at the lowest price, I convert each hourly or half-hourly price to U.S. dollars using the relevant dollar-to-home-currency exchange rate at noon that day obtained from the PACIFIC web site.[16] Table 3.2 lists the mean and standard deviation of the half-hourly or hourly prices (in the case of Nord Pool) in U.S. dollars per megawatt-hour. The E&W market consistently has the highest U.S. dollar price for electricity for the years in which I have comparable data. For both 1994 and 1995, the U.S. dollar prices in the E&W market are significantly higher than those in Nord Pool or Victoria. In both of these years, Nord Pool set lower prices on average, although in 1996 and 1997, this order reverses, with VicPool U.S. dollar prices significantly lower than U.S. dollar prices in either Nord Pool or the NZEM. These low prices in Victoria can be explained in part by the extremely inexpensive Australian brown coal and natural gas purchased to generate electricity. The coal used to produce electricity in the E&W market is considerably more expensive. U.K. coal is more costly to mine, and purchasing coal from abroad entails significant transportation costs, which increases its price in the E&W market relative to Victoria.

In order to better understand the pattern of volatility in electricity prices in home currency per megawatt-hour in the four markets, I compute the ratio of the difference between the highest and lowest prices over a given time horizon divided by the average value of prices over that same time horizon. For example, for each day in the sample, I compute the difference between the highest and the lowest price for the day and divide that by the average price for that day. Repeating this calculation for each day in the sample for each market, and computing means, standard deviations, the sample minimum, and the sample maximum, yields the values given in table 3.3. This table shows that over all time horizons the prices in the E&W market and the VicPool are considerably more variable than those

16. Policy Analysis and Computing and Information Facility in Commerce (PACIFIC) at the University of British Columbia, Faculty of Commerce and Business Administration (http://pacific.commerce.ubc.ca/xr/).

Table 3.2   Annual Means and Standard Deviations of Spot Price of Electricity Converted to U.S. Dollars

Year	E&W		NW		VIC		NZN		NZS	
	Mean	SD	Mean	SD	Mean	SD	Mean	SD	Mean	SD
1990	31.84	10.25	n.a.	n.a.	n.a.	n.a.	n.a.	n.a.	n.a.	n.a.
1991	39.80	22.71	n.a.	n.a.	n.a.	n.a.	n.a.	n.a.	n.a.	n.a.
1992	41.32	11.31	9.20	6.73	n.a.	n.a.	n.a.	n.a.	n.a.	n.a.
1993	40.80	11.91	11.28	5.62	n.a.	n.a.	n.a.	n.a.	n.a.	n.a.
1994	38.00	29.37	25.97	7.04	27.42	13.65	n.a.	n.a.	n.a.	n.a.
1995	41.10	79.15	18.50	5.89	30.95	21.94	n.a.	n.a.	n.a.	n.a.
1996	39.37	44.06	39.26	6.86	16.53	15.03	27.77	11.93	20.13	4.59
1997	47.96	46.95	22.50	7.14	17.83	46.00	32.75	6.04	29.25	6.10

Note: Prices converted to U.S. dollars per megawatt-hour using daily exchange rates. See table 3.1 note for market abbreviations.

Table 3.3   Ratio of Difference between Highest and Lowest Prices to Average
                   Price over Various Time Horizons

Horizon and Market	Mean	SD	Min	Max
Day				
NW	0.18	0.19	0.00	2.04
NZN	0.58	0.65	0.03	3.15
NZS	0.37	0.41	0.01	2.86
E&W	1.51	1.34	0.23	12.12
VIC	1.78	1.45	0.03	26.58
Week				
NW	0.44	0.38	0.04	2.21
NZN	1.49	1.04	0.23	3.31
NZS	1.06	1.00	0.18	3.90
E&W	2.83	3.29	0.54	37.84
VIC	3.97	8.51	0.80	102.22
Month				
NW	0.86	0.54	0.12	2.22
NZN	2.66	1.06	0.66	4.09
NZS	2.28	1.43	0.52	3.94
E&W	5.23	6.53	0.89	45.08
VIC	7.81	19.20	1.96	117.29
Fiscal year				
NW	2.48	0.99	1.14	4.00
NZN	n.a.	n.a.	n.a.	n.a.
NZS	n.a.	n.a.	n.a.	n.a.
E&W	18.80	15.26	4.07	46.37
VIC	43.16	72.23	4.37	151.46

Note: Mean = sample mean, SD = standard deviation, Min = sample minimum, and
Max = sample maximum. See table 3.1 note for market abbreviations.

in Nord Pool and the NZEM. By this measure of variability, VicPool
prices are more volatile than E&W prices. Nord Pool prices exhibit the
least amount of average variability over the four time horizons.

Because I do not have a complete year's worth of data for the NZEM,
I cannot compute the ratio of the difference between the highest and low-
est prices within the year divided by the average price for the year for
NZEM prices. However, the greater variability in North Island versus
South Island NZEM prices shows up in this measure of price variability
for all available time horizons. Although the average variability of these
prices is less than that magnitude in either the E&W market or the Vic-
Pool, these prices are substantially more variable than Nord Pool prices.
These results illustrate the differences in the time-series behavior of prices
in systems where fossil fuels are used to meet peak demands as in North
Island of New Zealand relative to systems where hydroelectric capacity
is used to meet system peaks as in South Island of New Zealand and
Nord Pool.

The next step in the across-country analysis of the behavior of prices focuses on the relative forecastability of the daily vector of prices in each country. This requires a model for the time-series behavior of the (48 × 1) vector of half-hourly prices or (24 × 1) hourly prices for Nord Pool, which I denote Y_t. After some preliminary analysis of each vector of prices, I settled on a time-varying mean for Y_t that depends on the day of the week and month of the sample period. I hypothesize that once M_t, the (48 × 1) ([24 × 1] for the case of Nord Pool) vector of means of Y_t, is subtracted from Y_t, the resulting stochastic process is a vector autoregressive model of order 8. The statistical model I hypothesize for Y_t is

$$(1) \qquad \Phi(L)(Y_t - M_t) = E_t,$$

Where E_t is a (48 × 1) ([24 × 1] for the case of Nord Pool) vector-valued white noise process with mean zero and covariance matrix Σ, $\Phi(L) = I - \Phi_1 L - \cdots - \Phi_p L^p$, where each Φ_i is a (48 × 48) ([24 × 24] for the case of Nord Pool) matrix of coefficients and L is the lag operator function defined by $Y_{t-k} = L^k Y_t$. The remaining discussion of the model is for case of forty-eight half-hourly prices, although the modifications necessary for twenty-four hourly prices are straightforward. Let M_{ti} denote the ith element of M_t. In terms of our above notation, $M_{ti} = X_t' \beta_i$, where X_t is a vector of day of the week and month indicator variables for load period i and β_i is the vector of coefficients associated with these indicator variables. Excluding the β_i coefficients associated with M_{ti}, for each element of M_t, there are 16,120 = 8 × (48)² elements of $\Phi_1, \Phi_2, \ldots, \Phi_8$ to estimate. Rather than present the more than 18,000 coefficient estimates (including the β_i for each of the forty-eight load periods) for this model, which are estimated by least squares applied to each of the forty-eight load period price equations, I provide several summary measures of the adequacy of this model and summarize what insights it provides about the forecastability of Y_t for each market.

To investigate the adequacy of equation (1) for each country, I compute the multivariate analogue of the Box-Pierce (1970) portmanteau statistic derived by Hosking (1980) for the (48 × 1) vector of residuals from equation (1). This statistic is computed as

$$P = T \sum_{r=1}^{M} \text{trace}(C_r' C_0^{-1} C_r C_0^{-1}), \qquad \text{where } C_r = T^{-1} \sum_{t=r+1}^{T} \hat{E}_t \hat{E}_{t-r}',$$

where $\hat{E}_t$ is the residual vector from equation (1) for period t and C_0 is the sample covariance matrix of $\hat{E}_t$. Hosking has shown that the asymptotic distribution of P is χ^2 with $N^2 \times (M - p)$ degrees of freedom, where p is the order of the autoregressive process and N is the dimension of Y_t. For all of the models estimated, I find little evidence against the null hypothesis that E_t is multivariate white noise.

Table 3.4 presents the R^2, the standard error of the regression, and the mean of the dependent variable for each of forty-eight ordinary least squares regressions of the half-hourly price on eight lags of this price and all other half-hourly prices. I find the largest R^2—all in excess of 0.84—are associated with load periods 33 to 38, which run from 4 P.M. to 7 P.M., the load periods in the day with highest prices on average as indicated by the sample mean of the PSP in each load period given in the third column. Load periods 33 to 38 are also the periods with the six largest estimated regression standard errors. The combination of these two results suggests that the explanatory power of the model is highest for those load periods $i = 33, \ldots, 38$ with the highest unconditional variance in Y_{ti}. However, despite the superior explanatory power of the model for these load periods, the level of the estimated forecast variance is higher for these load periods than for any others. Past values of Y_t therefore improve the predictive power of the load period regressions for periods 33 to 38 significantly more than they do for the other load period regressions, but despite this fact, these load periods are still the most unpredictable in terms of the estimated level of their day-ahead forecast variance. This result is consistent with the view that there are short periods within the day when the PSP is above or below its unconditional mean, and the occurrence of these extreme prices in certain load periods within a day make them more likely to occur in the same load periods in neighboring days.

Table 3.5 presents this same information for the (24×1) vector of daily Nord Pool spot prices. The most striking feature of this table is the uniformly high explanatory power of these twenty-four regressions. In all cases, the R^2 is at least 0.99, which implies that almost all of the movements in hourly prices across days in Nord Pool can be forecast. In addition, none of the hours appear to be significantly more predictable using past prices than other hours. For all hours during the day, the standard errors of the regressions are very similar in magnitude, although the hours during the day with higher average prices do have slightly larger estimated residual variances.

Table 3.6 presents the information in table 3.4 for VicPool prices. The R^2 from the forty-eight regressions used to estimate the eighth-order vector autoregressive process indicate that VicPool prices are less forecastable than Nord Pool prices. The magnitude of the R^2 are similar to those for the E&W system in table 3.4. However, different from the results in table 3.4, I find that the higher average price periods do not have higher R^2 from the regression forecasting that price. In fact, the highest average price period, load period 26, has by far the lowest $R^2 = 0.44$. Different from the case of the E&W market, the highest R^2's occur for load periods with both low and high average prices.

Because I only have a very short time series of prices for the NZEM, it is not possible to estimate an eighth-order vector autoregressive process

Table 3.4 R^2, Standard Error, and Sample Mean of Dependent Variable for Regression Forecasting Half-Hourly Pool Selling Price in England and Wales

Load Period	R^2	Standard Error of Regression	Sample Mean Price (£/MWH)
1	0.81	2.43	15.06
2	0.78	3.91	17.32
3	0.80	4.44	18.91
4	0.80	4.77	19.92
5	0.80	4.03	18.54
6	0.80	3.91	17.96
7	0.79	3.80	17.16
8	0.79	3.10	15.78
9	0.79	2.68	14.90
10	0.83	2.21	14.42
11	0.80	2.61	14.55
12	0.82	2.45	14.56
13	0.80	2.68	15.02
14	0.80	3.49	17.66
15	0.82	3.30	20.31
16	0.76	4.55	22.15
17	0.74	5.81	24.25
18	0.72	6.52	25.96
19	0.66	8.05	27.88
20	0.66	8.57	29.45
21	0.66	8.22	29.36
22	0.66	8.10	28.60
23	0.69	8.09	29.37
24	0.69	8.93	30.99
25	0.70	8.64	31.31
26	0.70	7.73	29.71
27	0.70	5.47	25.62
28	0.71	4.65	23.65
29	0.70	4.83	22.41
30	0.73	4.56	21.83
31	0.75	4.47	21.22
32	0.79	7.69	22.97
33	0.84	19.07	32.20
34	0.86	31.34	44.61
35	0.87	35.45	50.19
36	0.87	28.72	46.24
37	0.84	17.81	35.51
38	0.85	9.10	30.24
39	0.82	6.81	27.67
40	0.81	4.97	25.52
41	0.76	4.55	23.89
42	0.75	4.29	23.91
43	0.76	4.23	24.35
44	0.79	4.05	24.10
45	0.77	4.12	22.36
46	0.77	3.75	19.85
47	0.74	3.05	17.20
48	0.78	2.52	15.43

Table 3.5 R^2, Standard Error, and Sample Mean of Dependent Variable for
Regression Forecasting Hourly Spot Price in Nord Pool

Load Period	R^2	Standard Error of Regression	Sample Mean Price (NOK/MWH)
1	0.99	7.31	137.99
2	0.99	9.72	136.28
3	0.99	8.87	135.38
4	0.99	7.46	134.86
5	0.99	7.40	135.05
6	0.99	7.65	136.82
7	0.99	8.84	142.69
8	0.99	10.33	148.90
9	0.99	10.72	151.05
10	0.99	10.65	151.93
11	0.99	10.17	151.87
12	0.99	10.01	151.49
13	0.99	9.41	149.57
14	0.99	9.46	149.07
15	0.99	9.39	148.76
16	0.99	9.33	148.53
17	0.99	9.03	148.00
18	0.99	9.06	148.70
19	0.99	8.92	148.98
20	0.99	8.69	148.41
21	0.99	8.44	147.81
22	0.99	8.48	147.69
23	0.99	7.99	145.43
24	0.99	10.01	141.79

for these prices. I estimate the vector autoregression with the largest number of lags possible given the time series of prices available to me. In this case, I am able to estimate a fourth-order vector autoregressive process. Table 3.7 presents the R^2, the standard error of the regression, and the mean of the dependent variable for each of forty-eight ordinary least squares regressions of the half-hourly spot price on four lags of this price and all other half-hourly prices for North Island spot prices. Table 3.8 produces the same information for South Island spot prices. The South Island price results resemble the results for Nord Pool, consistent with the fact that South Island is dominated by hydroelectric capacity. The North Island results resemble the Nord Pool results, but they show more variability across hours in the R^2 and the standard errors of the regression than do the South Island results. This is consistent with the use of fossil fuel plants in North Island.

A final issue associated with the Y_t process is the extent to which forty-eight (twenty-four in the case of Nord Pool) distinct prices occur within

Table 3.6 R^2, **Standard Error, and Sample Mean of Dependent Variable for Regression Forecasting Half-Hourly Spot Price in VicPool**

Load Period	R^2	Standard Error of Regression	Sample Mean Price (AU$/MWH)
1	0.89	9.23	32.22
2	0.89	9.12	29.06
3	0.87	10.49	33.47
4	0.87	9.72	29.36
5	0.87	8.59	24.82
6	0.86	7.77	20.92
7	0.86	7.15	17.40
8	0.84	6.94	14.73
9	0.83	6.34	12.85
10	0.80	6.64	11.95
11	0.77	9.10	13.69
12	0.78	9.51	16.28
13	0.79	11.16	22.35
14	0.81	13.29	28.56
15	0.84	11.35	29.47
16	0.85	13.39	34.02
17	0.83	14.97	36.46
18	0.82	16.37	37.00
19	0.84	15.55	37.81
20	0.84	15.71	38.03
21	0.85	15.43	37.99
22	0.85	16.08	38.19
23	0.84	15.93	37.38
24	0.87	15.06	37.26
25	0.89	16.56	37.50
26	0.44	113.75	40.80
27	0.81	18.47	38.20
28	0.81	18.39	37.86
29	0.80	18.73	37.21
30	0.78	18.80	36.31
31	0.79	18.03	35.90
32	0.79	18.77	35.92
33	0.80	17.62	35.76
34	0.79	17.22	36.15
35	0.80	17.49	37.59
36	0.82	17.55	39.92
37	0.77	21.82	39.84
38	0.81	18.28	38.08
39	0.84	14.66	35.50
40	0.81	14.64	34.39
41	0.86	14.24	33.80
42	0.86	13.85	32.33
43	0.83	13.26	29.87
44	0.83	12.28	26.52
45	0.82	12.09	25.21
46	0.80	12.08	24.74
47	0.79	14.60	34.18
48	0.80	13.76	33.31

Table 3.7 R^2, **Standard Error, and Sample Mean of Dependent Variable for Regression Forecasting Half-Hourly Spot Prices in NZEM—North Island Reference Node**

Load Period	R^2	Standard Error of Regression	Sample Mean Price (NZ$/MWH)
1	0.98	4.06	42.55
2	0.98	4.22	41.71
3	0.97	4.19	41.09
4	0.97	4.26	40.54
5	0.97	4.14	39.61
6	0.97	3.85	38.71
7	0.96	4.48	38.42
8	0.97	3.90	38.08
9	0.97	4.20	37.87
10	0.97	4.19	38.03
11	0.96	4.19	38.28
12	0.96	4.12	38.80
13	0.96	3.91	40.11
14	0.96	4.23	42.31
15	0.96	7.20	45.34
16	0.97	10.50	50.84
17	0.96	11.02	50.33
18	0.95	11.57	49.27
19	0.97	6.43	47.35
20	0.96	7.33	47.04
21	0.98	4.84	46.46
22	0.97	5.19	46.30
23	0.97	5.30	46.22
24	0.96	6.56	46.76
25	0.96	6.30	46.14
26	0.97	5.22	46.10
27	0.96	4.45	45.30
28	0.97	4.38	45.36
29	0.97	5.06	45.14
30	0.98	5.00	45.32
31	0.97	5.32	45.24
32	0.96	7.54	46.42
33	0.93	11.18	46.17
34	0.97	7.46	47.67
35	0.94	9.36	47.08
36	0.92	10.06	47.55
37	0.95	7.49	46.60
38	0.95	6.19	45.90
39	0.96	5.35	45.33
40	0.97	4.61	45.03
41	0.98	6.38	47.00
42	0.98	6.80	47.53
43	0.98	5.19	46.35
44	0.98	5.15	46.03
45	0.96	4.33	43.63
46	0.97	3.76	42.32
47	0.97	5.07	43.44
48	0.96	5.92	41.59

Table 3.8 **R^2, Standard Error, and Sample Mean of Dependent Variable for Regression Forecasting Half-Hourly Spot Prices in NZEM—South Island Reference Node**

Load Period	R^2	Standard Error of Regression	Sample Mean Price (NZ$/MWH)
1	0.99	3.13	37.40
2	0.99	2.86	36.95
3	0.99	2.88	36.48
4	0.99	3.16	36.09
5	0.99	3.04	35.23
6	0.99	3.07	34.48
7	0.98	3.39	33.87
8	0.98	3.39	33.54
9	0.98	3.48	33.32
10	0.98	3.78	33.30
11	0.98	3.30	33.34
12	0.99	2.75	33.66
13	0.99	2.78	34.74
14	0.98	3.56	36.33
15	0.98	4.89	37.98
16	0.96	7.59	39.73
17	0.97	5.35	38.81
18	0.96	5.48	38.85
19	0.99	3.21	38.98
20	0.98	3.22	39.01
21	0.98	3.43	39.16
22	0.98	3.46	39.17
23	0.98	3.30	39.13
24	0.98	3.48	39.34
25	0.98	3.35	39.25
26	0.99	3.00	39.03
27	0.99	2.93	39.21
28	0.99	3.03	38.97
29	0.99	3.12	38.56
30	0.98	3.28	38.26
31	0.98	3.33	38.29
32	0.98	3.26	38.71
33	0.98	3.36	38.90
34	0.99	3.05	39.05
35	0.97	5.53	39.56
36	0.96	6.38	40.19
37	0.99	3.56	39.60
38	0.99	3.38	39.19
39	0.99	3.22	38.85
40	0.99	2.83	38.28
41	0.99	3.16	38.07
42	0.98	3.74	37.94
43	0.98	4.13	37.90
44	0.98	4.02	38.03
45	0.98	3.87	37.52
46	0.98	3.43	36.62
47	0.98	3.64	37.31
48	0.98	3.60	36.21

the day. Specifically, are there really forty-eight distinct sources of stochastic variation in prices over the course of the day? The way I address this question is by asking if E_t possesses a factor structure. By this I mean that E_t can be written as

$$E_t = \Delta V_t + U_t,$$

where Δ is a $48 \times G$ $(G < 48)$ matrix, V_t is a $(G \times 1)$ white noise process with mean zero and covariance matrix I_G (the identity matrix of dimension G), and U_t is a (48×48) white noise process with mean zero and covariance matrix $\sigma^2 I$, where I is a (48×48) identity matrix. The processes V_t and U_t are assumed to be uncorrelated. This structure imposes restrictions on the form of the covariance matrix of Σ. In general there are $(1/2)$ $(48)(49) = 1,176$ distinct elements of Σ. For example, if I assume that G, the number of common factors, equals one, then there are forty-eight elements of Δ and σ^2, which implies that the 1,176 elements of Σ can be written as functions of the forty-eight elements of Δ and σ^2, which implies a significant number of restrictions. The usual way to determine the extent to which there exists a factor structure for E_t is to compute the principal components of Σ and the eigenvalues associated with these principal components. Defining trace(Σ) as the total variation in Σ, by the properties of the trace operator, the sum of the eigenvalues of Σ equals trace(Σ). Consequently, I can get a measure of the extent to which a single principal component or group of orthogonal principal components explains the total variation in Σ. (Another definition often used is the determinant of Σ (det (Σ)) because det(Σ) is the product of the eigenvalues. This would involve computing the ratio of the determinant to the product of a subset of the eigenvalues.) In table 3.9, I list the eigenvalues associated with the forty-eight principal components of the white noise process driving the vector of daily E&W prices. The last column computes the cumulative sum of the eigenvalues up to the number of principal components for that row divided by the trace of Σ. This table indicates that more than 20 percent of the total variation is explained by the first principal component. However, the number of factors necessary to adequately model the structure of Σ appears to be large. For example, the cumulative number of principal components necessary to capture 90 percent of the total variation in Σ is twenty-two. The large number of factors necessary to represent a substantial fraction of the total variation in Σ is consistent with the view that there is not a single or even a small number of independent determinants of the pattern of spot prices within the day in the E&W market.

Table 3.10 repeats this calculation for the (24×1) covariance matrix of the white noise process driving Nord Pool spot prices. This table is very different from the one for E&W prices. Over 75 percent of the total variation in Σ is explained by the first principal component. It only takes three

Table 3.9   **Eigenvalues of Residual Covariance Matrix from Vector Autoregression Used to Forecast Vector of Daily Pool Selling Prices in England and Wales**

Principal Component	Eigenvalue	Percentage of Total Variance
1	12.267	0.2556
2	4.861	0.3568
3	3.926	0.4386
4	2.684	0.4945
5	2.399	0.5445
6	2.119	0.5887
7	1.684	0.6283
8	1.652	0.6582
9	1.552	0.6905
10	1.401	0.7197
11	1.108	0.7428
12	1.096	0.7656
13	1.021	0.7869
14	0.838	0.8044
15	0.772	0.8204
16	0.720	0.8355
17	0.685	0.8497
18	0.540	0.8610
19	0.502	0.8714
20	0.481	0.8814
21	0.462	0.8911
22	0.423	0.9000
23	0.420	0.9086
24	0.394	0.9168
25	0.385	0.9248
26	0.355	0.9322
27	0.326	0.9390
28	0.307	0.9454
29	0.273	0.9511
30	0.253	0.9564
31	0.242	0.9614
32	0.228	0.9661
33	0.206	0.9705
34	0.182	0.9743
35	0.161	0.9776
36	0.147	0.9807
37	0.143	0.9836
38	0.129	0.9863
39	0.115	0.9887
40	0.110	0.9910
41	0.096	0.9930
42	0.088	0.9950
43	0.086	0.9966
44	0.053	0.9978
45	0.049	0.9988
46	0.038	0.9996
47	0.014	0.9998
48	0.007	1.0000

Table 3.10   **Eigenvalues of Residual Covariance Matrix from Vector Autoregressive Model Used to Forecast Vector of Daily Spot Prices in Nord Pool**

Principal Component	Eigenvalue	Percentage of Total Variation
1	18.089	0.7537
2	2.795	0.8702
3	0.757	0.9017
4	0.481	0.9218
5	0.412	0.9389
6	0.328	0.9526
7	0.253	0.9632
8	0.197	0.9714
9	0.154	0.9778
10	0.122	0.9829
11	0.100	0.9871
12	0.064	0.9897
13	0.060	0.9923
14	0.050	0.9944
15	0.040	0.9960
16	0.023	0.9970
17	0.017	0.9977
18	0.013	0.9982
19	0.012	0.9987
20	0.011	0.9991
21	0.009	0.9995
22	0.006	0.9998
23	0.003	0.9999
24	0.002	1.0000

factors to explain more than 90 percent of the total variation in Σ. This factor structure is consistent with the view discussed earlier that there is a single dominant determinant of unexpectedly high prices within a day, uncertainly about the availability of future water supplies.

Table 3.11 presents the forty-eight eigenvalues of the estimate of Σ for VicPool prices. The story that emerges is midway between the one from Nord Pool and the one from the E&W market. Approximately half of the total variation in Σ is explained by the first principal component. Only fifteen factors, versus twenty-two in the E&W market, are required to explain more than 90 percent of the total variation in Σ.

Tables 3.12 and 3.13 present the forty-eight eigenvalues of the estimate of Σ for North Island and South Island prices, respectively. Consistent with North Island use of fossil units, the number of eigenvalues necessary to explain 90 percent of the variation in Σ is ten. Whereas for South Island this number is eight, which is consistent with it being a hydro-based system where the opportunity cost of water is the primary determinant of price movements within and across days.

Table 3.11   **Eigenvalues of Residual Covariance Matrix from Vector Autoregressive Model Used to Forecast Vector of Daily Spot Prices in VicPool**

Principal Component	Eigenvalue	Percentage of Total Variation
1	23.405	0.4876
2	4.694	0.5854
3	3.231	0.6527
4	2.208	0.6987
5	1.829	0.7368
6	1.433	0.7667
7	1.254	0.7928
8	0.927	0.8121
9	0.898	0.8308
10	0.785	0.8472
11	0.711	0.8620
12	0.567	0.8738
13	0.511	0.8844
14	0.480	0.8944
15	0.439	0.9036
16	0.381	0.9115
17	0.344	0.9187
18	0.299	0.9249
19	0.284	0.9308
20	0.262	0.9363
21	0.255	0.9416
22	0.236	0.9465
23	0.208	0.9508
24	0.190	0.9548
25	0.187	0.9587
26	0.183	0.9625
27	0.158	0.9658
28	0.145	0.9688
29	0.133	0.9716
30	0.124	0.9742
31	0.123	0.9767
32	0.120	0.9793
33	0.100	0.9813
34	0.099	0.9834
35	0.088	0.9852
36	0.085	0.9870
37	0.078	0.9886
38	0.072	0.9901
39	0.070	0.9916
40	0.066	0.9929
41	0.060	0.9942
42	0.052	0.9953
43	0.050	0.9963
44	0.044	0.9973
45	0.042	0.9981
46	0.034	0.9988
47	0.029	0.9995
48	0.026	1.0000

Table 3.12 **Eigenvalues of Residual Covariance Matrix from Vector Autoregressive Model Used to Forecast Vector of Daily Pool Selling Price in NZEM—North Island Reference Node**

Principal Component	Eigenvalue	Percentage of Total Variance
1	19.026	0.3964
2	9.216	0.5584
3	3.458	0.6604
4	3.151	0.7261
5	2.920	0.7869
6	1.729	0.8229
7	1.465	0.8535
8	1.090	0.8762
9	0.958	0.8961
10	0.764	0.9120
11	0.671	0.9260
12	0.565	0.9378
13	0.553	0.9493
14	0.478	0.9593
15	0.324	0.9660
16	0.305	0.9724
17	0.261	0.9778
18	0.198	0.9819
19	0.167	0.9854
20	0.137	0.9883
21	0.110	0.9906
22	0.096	0.9925
23	0.084	0.9943
24	0.063	0.9956
25	0.047	0.9966
26	0.046	0.9975
27	0.032	0.9982
28	0.029	0.9988
29	0.021	0.9992
30	0.016	0.9996
31	0.010	0.9998
32	0.006	0.9999
33	0.004	1.0000
34	0.000	1.0000
35	0.000	1.0000
36	0.000	1.0000
37	0.000	1.0000
38	0.000	1.0000
39	0.000	1.0000
40	0.000	1.0000
41	0.000	1.0000
42	0.000	1.0000
43	0.000	1.0000
44	0.000	1.0000
45	0.000	1.0000
46	0.000	1.0000
47	0.000	1.0000
48	0.000	1.0000

Table 3.13 **Eigenvalues of Residual Covariance Matrix from Vector Autoregressive Model Used to Forecast Vector of Daily Pool Selling Price in NZEM—South Island Reference Node**

Principal Component	Eigenvalue	Percentage of Total Variance
1	22.101	0.4604
2	9.271	0.6536
3	4.255	0.7422
4	2.379	0.7918
5	1.834	0.8300
6	1.761	0.8667
7	1.076	0.8891
8	1.055	0.9111
9	0.723	0.9262
10	0.639	0.9395
11	0.546	0.9508
12	0.369	0.9585
13	0.319	0.9651
14	0.267	0.9707
15	0.245	0.9758
16	0.207	0.9801
17	0.171	0.9837
18	0.118	0.9861
19	0.110	0.9884
20	0.094	0.9904
21	0.081	0.9921
22	0.076	0.9937
23	0.061	0.9949
24	0.051	0.9960
25	0.043	0.9969
26	0.039	0.9977
27	0.033	0.9984
28	0.027	0.9990
29	0.018	0.9993
30	0.013	0.9996
31	0.010	0.9998
32	0.005	0.9999
33	0.003	1.0000
34	0.000	1.0000
35	0.000	1.0000
36	0.000	1.0000
37	0.000	1.0000
38	0.000	1.0000
39	0.000	1.0000
40	0.000	1.0000
41	0.000	1.0000
42	0.000	1.0000
43	0.000	1.0000
44	0.000	1.0000
45	0.000	1.0000
46	0.000	1.0000
47	0.000	1.0000
48	0.000	1.0000

Several overall conclusions emerge from tables 3.4 through 3.13. The dynamics of the within-day variation in prices in the E&W market is more complex than the dynamics of the within-day variation in prices in the VicPool. Nord Pool prices show the least complex within-day price dynamics of the three markets. Nord Pool prices are also by far the most forecastable of the three price series, as measured by the R^2 of the prediction regressions. E&W market prices and VicPool prices are predictable with approximately the same average R^2 over all half-hour periods in the day. However, different from the VicPool, the highest priced load periods in the day in the E&W market are uniformly the most forecastable by this same measure. Although the short length of the New Zealand price series required estimating a more parsimonious autoregressive process for these prices, the differences in the results across North Island and South Island prices were consistent with the results obtained for E&W and VicPool prices versus Nord Pool prices.

I now characterize differences in the behavior of the spot prices within the day and week across the peak and off-peak months of the year. Figure 3.1A plots the average behavior of normalized prices throughout the day for the E&W market in winter (December, January, and February) and summer (June, July, and August). To compute the normalized price for any load period, I divide the actual price by the sample mean price of electricity in the E&W market. Figure 3.1B plots the behavior of normalized prices throughout the week in summer and winter. These plots illustrate an important feature of the behavior of prices in the E&W market. During the winter months, all weekday prices become very high during load periods 35 to 37. The average high price during weekdays (excluding Fridays) is more than 4.0 times the sample mean of the spot price in load periods 35 to 37. Wolak and Patrick (1996b) argue that this pattern of prices represents the exercise of market power by National Power and PowerGen, the two major generators in the E&W market.

Figure 3.2 presents the day and week normalized price plots for Nord Pool. There appears to be little predictable variation in spot prices within the day and across days of the week in Nord Pool. The major movements in prices appear to be across the peak and off-peak seasons, with average summer prices significantly below average winter prices within the day and within the week. This reflects the view that water scarcity is a major determinant of prices in Nord Pool.

The average pattern of prices within the day and week in the VicPool shares features with both Nord Pool and the E&W market (see fig. 3.3). For consistency with the other two figures, I have defined summer to be the months of June, July, and August and winter to be December, January, and February. For most half-hours, average prices in June, July, and August (summer) are higher than those in December, January, and February (winter). The differences in predictable price fluctuations within the day

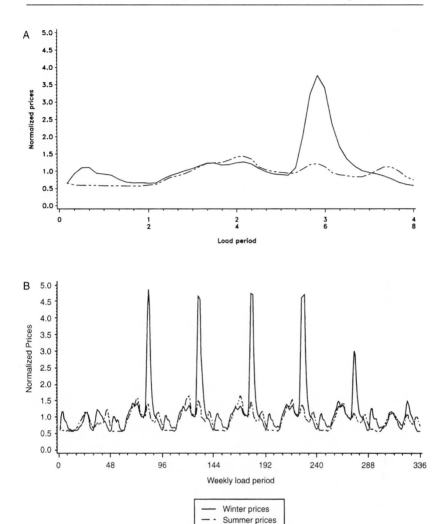

Fig. 3.1   England and Wales: average prices throughout the day (*A*) and the week (*B*)

and week across the peak and off-peak seasons is not nearly as pronounced in the VicPool as it is in the E&W market. Both seasons exhibit more predictable variation within the day and week than do E&W prices in the summer, but less than E&W prices in the winter.

Because no data exist for New Zealand for the months of June, July, and August, figure 3.4 plots the average prices in North and South Islands throughout the day and week. The pattern of average prices within the day for both islands is very similar to the pattern of prices within the day

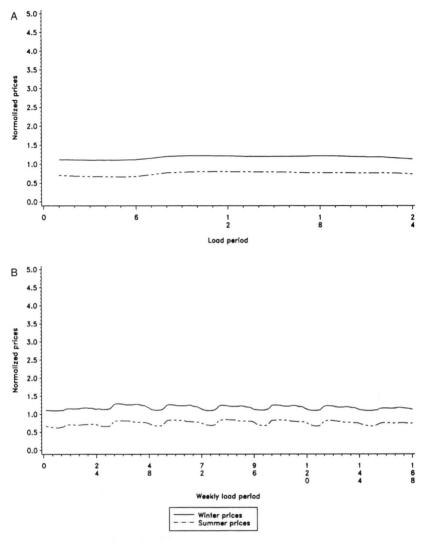

Fig. 3.2   Nord Pool: average prices throughout the day (*A*) and the week (*B*)

for Nord Pool. A similar statement can be said about the behavior of both New Zealand prices within the week.

Figures 3.5, 3.6, and 3.7 plot the period-level standard deviations of normalized prices within the day for the E&W market, Nord Pool, and the VicPool. Each point on this plot is the standard deviation of the normalized (by the overall sample mean price) price for that load period within the day for all days within that season. Figure 3.5 illustrates that although normalized prices in load periods 35 to 37 are known to be very

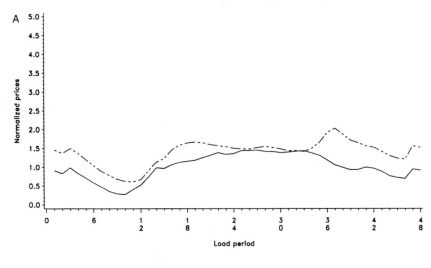

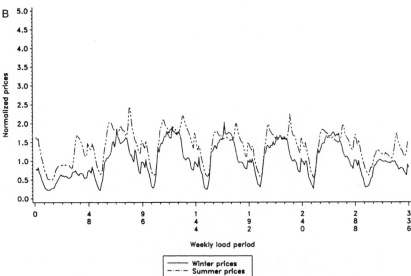

Fig. 3.3   VicPool: average prices throughout the day (*A*) and the week (*B*)

high, there is considerable uncertainty about precisely how high they will be. Figure 3.6 tells a similar story for the case of mean prices within the day for Nord Pool. The uncertainty in normalized prices is uniform within the day in both summer and winter, but the uncertainty in normalized prices is uniformly higher in the summer than the winter.

Figure 3.7 illustrates that for the most part the degree of uncertainty in normalized prices is very similar across load periods in the VicPool. The

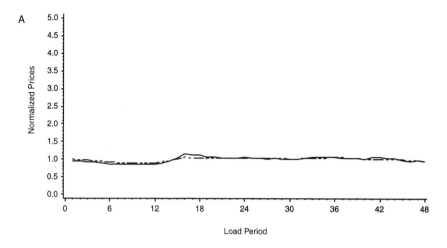

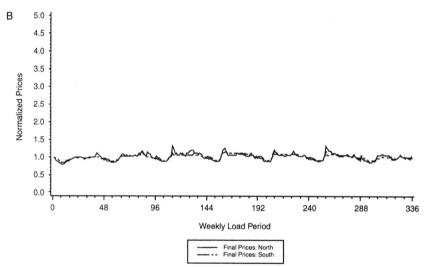

Fig. 3.4   New Zealand: average prices throughout the day (*A*) and the week (*B*)

only exception is that during the high-priced periods in December, January, and February (the months of peak demand in Victoria), the uncertainty in normalized prices is highest during the highest priced periods of the day.

Figure 3.8 computes the period-level standard deviations in normalized prices for North Island and South Island prices in New Zealand. The pattern of uncertainty in these prices is very similar to the within-day uncertainty in prices in Nord Pool. The North Island standard deviations tend to be higher than the South Island standard deviations, particularly for the peak periods of the day, reflecting the use of fossil units during these time periods in North Island.

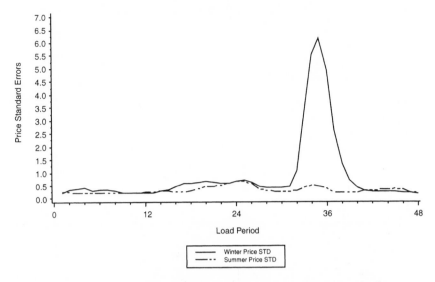

Fig. 3.5   England and Wales: standard deviation of prices throughout the day

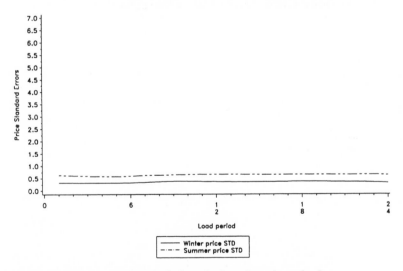

Fig. 3.6   Nord Pool: standard deviation of prices throughout the day

3.7   Market Structure and Market Rules
and the Exercise of Market Power

A significantly more detailed analysis of each of these markets is required to draw conclusions about the exercise of market power in any of these markets. However, the strong influence that both market structure and market rules appear to exert on the behavior of prices in these markets

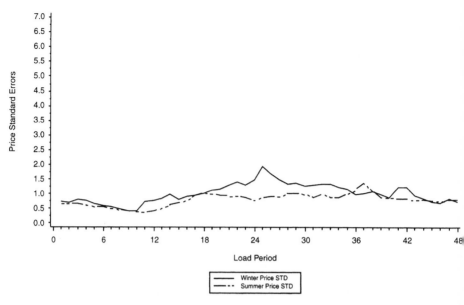

Fig. 3.7   VicPool: standard deviation of prices throughout the day

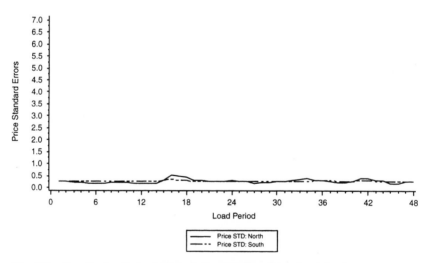

Fig. 3.8   New Zealand: standard deviation of prices throughout the day

suggests that such an across-country analysis should have significant promise to yield insights about how the interaction of market rules and market structure allows the exercise of market power.

The dramatically different pattern of average electricity prices within the day and within the week in the E&W market relative to the other three markets does lend further support to the conclusion reached in Wolak and Patrick (1996a) that the two largest generators in the E&W market—

National Power and PowerGen—possess significant market power that they are able to exercise when certain conditions in the E&W market make the residual demand they jointly face extremely large relative to the capacity of these two large generating companies.

The relatively flat pattern of average prices throughout the day in the VicPool and the very low U.S. dollar prices for electricity from this market in 1996 and 1997 seem indicative of a very competitive electricity market. The relatively high degree of volatility in prices throughout the day in the VicPool (compared to Nord Pool and the NZEM) seems to indicate that generators are sometimes successful at obtaining high prices, but just as often their efforts yield very low prices, so that on average, prices for electricity are very low. Consequently, the VicPool appears to be an example of a market where the efforts of generators to exercise market power are on average unsuccessful. The evidence on the behavior of prices appears consistent with the conclusion that it is a more competitive market than the E&W market. Further research is necessary to determine whether this apparent difference in competitiveness is due to differences in market structure of the two markets or in market rules.

Nord Pool and the NZEM present a more difficult puzzle because both markets are dominated by large state-owned enterprises. We would not expect these firms to exercise market power with the same vigor that privately owned firms do. Nevertheless, both of these electricity supply industries produce the vast majority of their power from very inexpensive hydroelectric resources, so the higher U.S. dollar prices in these two markets relative to Victoria do raise suspicions about the exercise of market power by the large state-owned firms. As discussed earlier, in the fall of 1992, Statkraft publicly announced a policy to keep spot prices above 100 NOK/MWH, although subsequently prices have fallen below this level for long periods of time. The evidence from the behavior of prices in both Nord Pool and the NZEM relative to prices in Victoria and the E&W market seems to indicate that the large state-owned generators in Nord Pool and the NZEM are price leaders with the remaining firms serving as a competitive fringe. Further analysis of both of these markets is necessary to reach a more definitive conclusion about whether these outcomes represent market power.

References

Armstrong, Mark, Simon Cowan, and John Vickers. 1994. *Regulatory reform: Economic analysis and British experience.* Cambridge, Mass.: MIT Press.

Baker, A. B. 1992. The methodology and process of forecasting nominal demand. GSMNC/ABB/DF 5.1.2.9. Coventry, England: National Grid Company, Grid System Management, National Control.

Box, G. E. P., and David A. Pierce. 1970. Distribution of residual autocorrelations in autoregressive-integrated moving average time series models. *Journal of the American Statistical Association* 65:1509–26.

Electricity Association. 1997. *Electricity industry review.* London: Electricity Association Services Limited, Business Information Center. Document available from Electricity Association, http://www.electricity.org.uk.

Electricity Pool of England and Wales. 1997. *Schedule 9: The pool rules.* Pooling and Settlement Agreement for the Electricity Industry in England and Wales, issue no. 45, version 6.20, 1 February. Binder available from Electricity Pool of England and Wales, 338 Enston Road, 10th Floor, Regent's Place, London NW1 3BP.

———. n.d. *Introduction to pool rules,* issue no. 2. Document available from Electricity Pool of England and Wales, 338 Enston Road, 10th Floor, Regent's Place, London NW1 3BP.

Green, Richard J. 1999. The electricity contract market in England and Wales. *Journal of Industrial Economics* 47 (1): 107–24.

Helm, Dieter, and Andrew Powell. 1992. Pool prices, contracts and regulation in the British electricity supply industry. *Fiscal Studies* 13 (1): 89–105.

Hosking, J. R. M. 1980. The multivariate portmanteau statistic. *Journal of the American Statistical Association* 75:602–8.

Joskow, Paul. 1987. Productivity growth and technical change in the generation of electricity. *Energy Journal* 8 (1): 17–38.

Lee, Byung-Joo. 1995. Separability test for the electricity supply industry. *Journal of Applied Econometrics* 10:49–60.

National Grid Company. 1995. *1995 Seven year statement.* Coventry, England: National Grid Company.

Patrick, Robert H., and Frank A. Wolak. 1997. Estimating customer-level demand for electricity under real time pricing. March. Document available from http://www.stanford.edu/~wolak.

Reed, E. Grant, Glenn R. Drayton-Bright, and Brendan J. Ring. 1998. An integrated energy and reserve market for New Zealand. Energy Modelling Research Group Working Paper no. EMRG-WP-98-01. Christchurch, New Zealand: University of Canterbury, Department of Management.

Wolak, Frank A., and Robert H. Patrick. 1996a. The impact of market rules and market structure on the price determination process in the England and Wales electricity market. June. Document available from http://www.stanford.edu/~wolak.

———. 1996b. Industry structure and regulation in the England and Wales electricity market. In *Pricing and regulatory innovations under increasing competition,* ed. M. A. Crew, 65–90. Amsterdam: Kluwer.

Comment   Takatoshi Ito

This is a well-structured, detailed paper on comparing structural changes in the electricity industries in selected countries and regions (Norway and Sweden, New Zealand, England and Wales, and Victoria). The following

Takatoshi Ito is professor in the Institute of Economic Research at Hitotsubashi University, Tokyo, and a research associate of the National Bureau of Economic Research.

three aspects stand out as interesting points in this paper. First, the electricity industry was considered a typical example of a natural monopoly only fifteen years ago. This is no longer true. However, perfect competition is obviously not the case. Hence the problem is how to set a "market rule" to produce efficient and fair outcomes. Second, the industry is composed of two different subindustries, power generation and power distribution (transmission). It seems to be the trend that these two subindustries can be treated differently. Power generation can be privatized more easily. Third, trade aspects of the electricity industry depend on the location of the country. Obviously, Scandinavian countries can trade electricity more easily than Japan can with its neighbors. Let me elaborate on these points, especially from the viewpoint of lessons for Asian countries.

First, it is good to see players respond to incentives, as detailed in the paper. Also, prices for electricity behave as theory predicts, according to market structure and market rules. It is shown that some larger companies reduce scale instead of expanding market share. This underscores the importance of setting the right market rule. But what is the optimal market rule? The paper indicates that the market rule depends on the type of power generation—oil, hydroelectric, or nuclear. The market rule should be designed to reflect such differences, so a country or even a region (an island) of a country has to design its own market rule.

Second, power generation and power distribution may be two different industries as far as market structure goes. Even Japan, a country often regarded as lagging in deregulation, has moved to deregulate power generation. Regular companies can sell power to the public power companies (regional monopolies). Power distribution is similar to telephone service, railroad service, or any other distribution or transportation sector. There is tension between universal service and efficient allocation of resources. Power generation can be much more competitive. Many manufacturing companies potentially have capacity in power generation that can be sold back to the power company that distributes to retail customers. It is difficult to decide how to compensate quality (penalties for blackout? Subsidies to current stability and universal service?).

Third, in thinking of trade aspects, the national boundary may not be a natural boundary of the industry. The examples in this paper, an arrangement between England and Wales and one between Norway and Sweden, show the extent and structure of a pool arrangement. A similar examination can be made, for example, of an arrangement between the regional monopolies in Japan. Another interesting aspect of the Japanese situation is that power plants were required to use domestic high-cost coal. If they were allowed to import coal, electricity prices may have been lower.

Two important aspects that are beyond the scope of this paper deserve future research. Power generation types differ in many countries. France produces more than three-quarters of its electricity from nuclear power plants, while Germany, Japan, and the United Kingdom produce about one-quarter of their power from nuclear plants. More than 60 percent of Canadian power is produced from hydroelectric power plants. These ratios reflect both the natural endowments of countries and policy decisions. An important question is whether decisions concerning types of power generation should anticipate the market structure, which is governed by the (mix of) types of power generation. Until now, decisions about electric power have not considered the competition aspects of the industry.

Alternative sources of electricity have been sought after. Locations for hydroelectric power plants have been exhausted in many advanced countries, nuclear energy carries nuclear danger, and oil-burning plants produce air pollution, although more advanced plants have cleaner technology. Whether R&D in alternative sources should be subsidized, and if so whether the funds should be cross-subsidized from existing companies (customers), is an interesting question.

Last, long after the conference in 1998, there was a prolonged blackout in New Zealand, one of the countries studied in this paper. A discussion of whether the power failure had anything to do with the market rule in that country would have been interesting.

Comment   Francis T. Lui

Frank Wolak has written a very readable paper from which I have learned a great deal. The paper consists of two parts. The first is a detailed description of the market structure, market rules, and regulatory oversight of electricity markets in four different economies. The second is an empirical investigation of various aspects of the movement of electricity prices in the four economies. I will comment on each part separately.

Knowing little about the electricity market and coming from a place where the regulatory system is relatively simple, I was surprised to learn of the elaborate institutional arrangements and regulatory schemes in the four economies. Suppose some undesirable consequences occur because of the imposition of a regulatory rule. Then there seem to be two approaches to dealing with them. One is to get rid of the regulation or barriers to entry. This allows the free market to come in again as an alternative. The other is to design and introduce a more complicated set of new regulations. These possibly incentive-compatible regulations may mitigate the undesirable effects found earlier. The sample of countries under study seems to have chosen the second way.

Francis T. Lui is director of the Center for Economic Development at the Hong Kong University of Science and Technology.

Is this a good approach? The answer is not clear to me. In Hong Kong, China Light, the power company that supplies 80 percent of the electricity, is heavily regulated. Its profits cannot exceed a certain percentage of its assets. It has therefore decided to expand capacity rapidly, with the result that the maximum capacity is far bigger than peak load demand. On the other hand, the unregulated and sole provider of gas, Town Gas, enjoys a total factor productivity growth of 2 percent per annum. Wolak has collected a lot of data about the electricity market. It would be interesting to test from the data whether a complicated regulatory system can beat the free market.

Another interesting issue is the political economy of how different places have adopted their own systems. Have they emerged because of political bargaining? Are they the intellectual products of some academics that are influential enough to implement their ideas? If political bargaining is the main reason, there is no guarantee that the resulting regulatory structure is optimal. It would be nice if the author could tell us more about the political economy background.

The empirical part of the paper uses a number of techniques to investigate various properties of electricity prices—for example, forecastability of prices, their variability, and whether their changes can be explained by just a few factors. Most of the results and interpretations seem to be reasonable. However, are the tests used powerful enough to answer the basic question, namely, how does market power depend on market structure and market rules? In a sense, we have learned that (1) the price movements are different and (2) there are many technological and institutional differences across the countries. However, can we be sure that the price behavior is due mainly to the market structure and market rules? There are only four places and four sets of observations. Is the basic question answerable?

One way to make the answer more convincing is to construct data sets from many more countries. Then more information can be used for testing hypotheses. Another way is to identify refutable hypotheses from the first part of the paper and implement a number of tests in the second part. The linkage between the two parts is not too clear in some cases. Sometimes, the differences in price movements do not seem to have much to do with market rules and market structure. For example, the prices in Nord Pool are more predictable, but there is apparently just one dominating explanatory variable, namely, whether there is enough water supply for hydroelectricity. There seems to be a need to articulate the discussion so that the linkage between the two parts of the paper is explicit and the hypotheses of the first part are tested.

All in all, I like the paper. One can learn a lot of details about the individual countries by reading it.

Competition in the Japanese Distribution Market and Market Access from Abroad

Motoshige Itoh

4.1 Introduction

The distribution system in Japan in the post-World War II period developed quite differently from those in other industrial countries.[1] One of the distinguishing features of the Japanese system is that retail and wholesale distribution is dominated by small and medium-size firms and that many goods go through long tunnels of wholesalers before they reach consumers.

The distribution channel policy pursued by manufacturers has been affected by this particular characteristic of the distribution system. When the retail sector is dominated by small retail stores, wholesalers have great influence over what goods are sold in the retail sector. Small retail stores, which do not have enough information about goods or the capability to procure goods by themselves, depend heavily on the services of wholesalers. Because there were many small retail stores, there had to be many small wholesalers. It was these small wholesalers that offered advice to retail stores and delivered goods in small lots. As a result, distribution channels had a vertically segregated structure, in which each category of goods went through a different wholesale system; for example, processed foods, fresh foods, confectioneries, paper products, dairy products, frozen foods, books, liquor, and rice were distributed by different wholesalers. Furthermore, many wholesalers were local firms, and few large wholesalers covered the entire national market. There were a large number of wholesalers in Japan.

Motoshige Itoh is professor of economics at the University of Tokyo.

1. See Ito and Maruyama (1991) and Itoh (1991) on the basic structure of the Japanese distribution system.

Under this structure manufacturers engaged in strengthening their relations with wholesalers. Close relations between manufacturers and wholesalers were called *keiretsu* relations in Japanese. A number of measures were introduced by manufacturers for developing *keiretsu* relations. These included vertical restraints such as resale price maintenance and closed territories, as well as various forms of rebate systems. Manufacturers sometimes even supplied sales staff to retail stores.[2] By these methods manufacturers constructed their *keiretsu* distribution channels. In extreme cases, such as home electric appliances and cosmetic goods, manufacturers had their own *keiretsu* retail store chains.

Several factors were responsible for the particular structure of the Japanese distribution system. The motorization process was slow in Japan, and most consumers went shopping on foot until the mid-1970s. The population was concentrated in urban areas. These factors did not allow large retail stores to spread rapidly. At the same time, small retail stores were heavily protected by various regulations. Under the Large Scale Retail Store Law, large retail stores faced high barriers to entry into local markets. This law, by retarding the spread of large retail stores, slowed structural change in the distribution system.

The Japanese distribution system had many problems from the viewpoint of competition policy. The distribution channel practices of manufacturers such as the ones mentioned above often imposed high prices on consumers. Such products as cosmetic goods, home electric appliances, and pharmaceutical products were sold under manufacturer-controlled prices in small retail stores. Discounting of these prices by large retail stores was often interrupted by manufacturers. The *keiretsu* relation established between incumbent manufacturers and wholesalers often became an entry barrier to newly introduced manufactured goods including imported goods.

Foreign manufacturers as well as foreign retailers who intended to sell their products in Japan faced this barrier. The distribution system as a barrier to market access became a trade negotiation issue. It arose in Japan-U.S. trade negotiations in individual product areas such as color film and automobiles. The Large Scale Retail Store Law was negotiated with the United States in the Structural Impediment Initiative talks of 1989–90. As a result, the Japanese government announced the deregulation of the retail sector and the reform of the Large Scale Retail Store Law.

Market access issues have also attracted attention inside Japan. It was pointed out by many people that the prices of various goods were much higher in Japan than in other countries and that the Japanese distribution system was responsible. According to this argument, if sound arbitrage

---

2. Although some of these measures are in violation of antimonopoly law in Japan, the law had not been enforced strictly until recently. Manufacturers were also skillful enough to apply these measures without violating the law.

mechanisms worked through distribution channels, the inflow of low-priced goods from abroad would have filled the price gaps. The fact that the price gaps were not filled implied that the distribution system was a barrier to imports.

The Japanese distribution system has actually been in the process of rapid structural change in the past ten years or so. The deregulation mentioned above has been a driving force behind this change, but other factors have also contributed to it. Although motorization in Japan was about fifty years behind that in the United States,[3] the number of cars in Japan has increased rapidly since the 1970s. The motorization process has contributed to an increase in the number of large retail stores and shopping centers in the suburbs and to a weakening of traditional shopping areas in towns.

Another important factor causing structural change in the distribution system has been an increase in imports, which was triggered by yen appreciation. Imports of manufactured goods have increased in particular; the share of manufactured goods in the total imports of Japan increased from 30 percent in 1985 to 60 percent in 1995. Import goods often came through newly established distribution channels and thus contributed to the growth of these new channels.

The distribution system of Japan is now in the midst of great change. Traditional channels and newly emerging channels now coexist. In spite of its rapid change, the structure of Japanese distribution is still quite different from that in the United States and in other countries.

The purpose of this paper is to explain how the traditional distribution system emerged, to analyze the mechanisms behind the structural change in the system, and to consider the implications for competition policy of the present changes in the distribution system. I will also discuss the market access issue.

The structure of this paper is as follows. Section 4.2 explains how the traditional distribution channels emerged in Japan and what implications the system has for competition. Section 4.3 then discusses the role the Large Scale Retail Store Law played in the distribution system. Section 4.4 then discusses the present structural change in the Japanese distribution system and its implications for competition policy. Brief concluding remarks are given in section 4.5.

4.2   Basic Structure of the Traditional Japanese Distribution System

Table 4.1 shows some of the basic characteristics of the Japanese distribution system as compared with those in other industrial countries in the mid-1980s. The table confirms that, as mentioned in the introduction, one

---

3. There was one car for every 5.3 people in the United States in 1930, while there was one car for every 7.5 people in Japan in 1973.

Table 4.1   **Comparison of Distribution Markets among Major Countries**

	Countries				
	Japan, 1985	West Germany, 1985:3	United States, 1982	France, 1986:1	United Kingdom, 1984
Retailers					
Shop density					
No. of shops per 1,000 km²	4,311	1,636	205	1,018	1,406
No. of shops per population of 10,000	135	67	81	102	61
No. of workers per shop	3.9	5.8	7.5	3.9[a]	6.8
Wholesalers					
Shop density					
No. of shops per 1,000 km²	1,093	505	40	290	
No. of shops per population of 10,000	34	21	16	29	
No. of workers per 1,000 retailers	85	309	196	285	
No. of workers per shop	9.7	7.0	12.6	9.9[a]	
W/R ratio	4.2	1.8[b]	1.9	1.6[a]	

Source: Ministry of International Trade and Industry (1988). Data: *Annuaire statistique de la France, Statistisches Jahrbuch, Retailing Business Monitor, Statistical Abstract of the United States, Census of Business,* and *Commercial Statistics of MITI.*
[a]1983.
[b]1984.

of the distinguishing characteristics of the traditional Japanese distribution system was the dominance of the retail and wholesale sectors by small and medium-size firms. In Japan the number of shop outlets per given population was large and the number of workers per 1,000 retailers was small. Note that the *W/R* ratio at the bottom of the table shows the ratio of total wholesale transactions to total retail transactions. The high *W/R* ratio for Japan indicates that there were a large number of wholesale transactions before goods reached retail stores.

One can think of several reasons why the distribution sector was dominated by small firms. The transport system is a crucial factor in determining the shape of the distribution system. Japan lagged behind other industrial countries in the motorization process, while public transportation, such as the railway system, subway system, and bus system, was well developed. Japan was also characterized by high population density with most of its population in urban regions. Most consumers did their routine shopping on foot and used the public transportation system for occasional shopping in larger shopping areas near a railway station or in the center of a large city. Responding to these shopping habits, a large number of

small shopping zones, which consisted of many mom-and-pop stores selling such items as drugs, fresh vegetables, fish, and meat emerged near
residential areas. Larger shopping areas near railway stations or in the
centers of large cities sold such products as clothing, jewelry, books, and
home electric appliances.

There were also a large number of small wholesalers supporting these
small retail stores. Most small retail stores were mom-and-pop stores,
where family members spent most of their working time in the store serving customers. Thus they depended on the services of wholesalers for delivery of products, pricing suggestions, and sometimes even for the display
of goods in their stores. Without the heavy support of wholesalers, they
would not have been able to run their stores.

Most of the wholesalers were also small—the better to serve small retail
stores: the type of services small retail stores were seeking could not be
provided by large wholesalers. Just like small retail stores, most small
wholesalers specialized in some category of goods. Thus there were many
segregated distribution channels, each of which specialized in some category of products.[4]

Wholesalers were classified according not only to categories of goods
but also to regions. Although Japan is a small country geographically,
most wholesalers were regional and not many were national.[5]

It is important to realize that the distribution channel policy of manufacturers depended on these characteristics of the Japanese system. Establishing close and often exclusive relations with wholesalers was essential
for manufacturers to have better control over the retail market, since
wholesalers influenced retail stores in their product choices. So-called
keiretsu distribution channels were set up by manufacturers.

For wholesalers too it was crucial to establish intimate relations with
national manufacturers. Manufacturers often offered volume rebate
schemes under which wholesalers were given rebates according to the
amount they sold.[6] Under this rebate system wholesalers had an incentive
to sell as much as possible of one manufacturer's products rather than
diversifying their sales effort to several manufacturers. Wholesalers having
good relations with manufacturers were also treated favorably in the supply of goods. In the period of rapid economic growth of the 1950s and

4. I once conducted a field study of the distribution channels for local supermarkets (Itoh
1995). One of the striking features of the wholesale distribution network for supermarkets is
that each category of product is carried by a different wholesaler. This contrasts with the
situation in the United States, where most products are carried to supermarkets by a limited
number of wholesalers who deal with all kinds of products.

5. In fact, the wholesale system often was a multilayer system, in which goods were sold
by national-level wholesalers to local wholesalers and then by local wholesalers to local retail stores.

6. In table 4.2 below, I give a typical example of a volume rebate system for the case of
cosmetic goods.

1960s best-selling products were often scarce and not all wholesalers could receive their full orders of these goods. Manufacturers discriminated among wholesalers according to how close they were to the manufacturers. This type of intimate relation sometimes went as far as the situation, as in the case of beer, where many wholesalers dealt only with a particular manufacturer's products. In Japan, even now, almost no wholesalers deal with beer from all four major manufacturers.[7]

This kind of control of distribution channels by manufacturers sometimes went as far as exclusive relations between retail stores and manufacturers. Typical cases of control of small retail stores by manufacturers involved home electric appliances and cosmetics. The largest manufacturer of home electric appliances in Japan, Matsushita, organized twenty to thirty thousand small retail stores around the nation: the majority of the sales in these stores were Matsushita products. Matsushita provided these stores with various kinds of support, such as favorable rebates (the amount of rebate increases with the store's sales of Matsushita products), favorable supply of products, and other assistance. These stores were called "Matsushita chain stores" and were located in local shopping areas. The owners of these stores had intimate relations with people in the neighborhood through various local activities. During the period when maintenance service was important for electric appliances people tended to use these neighborhood stores, which they could trust. Other manufacturers of home electric appliances followed marketing approaches similar to Matsushita's.[8]

Leading cosmetic manufacturers took an approach similar to that of home electric appliance manufacturers. They organized small retail stores all around the nation as their "chain stores": most of these stores sold only some leading manufacturer's products or at least the majority of their sales consisted of those products. Although these stores were mom-and-pop stores and therefore had no ownership relation with manufacturers, manufacturers supplied various services—for example, sales clerks. Very favorable rebate schemes were another crucial sales policy used by manufacturers. Table 4.2 illustrates the rebate schedule of one of the leading companies. The amount of rebate is quite large: up to 15 percent of the order price is returned to a retail store when the order exceeds a certain amount. Under this type of accelerating nonlinear rebate schedule retail stores have strong incentives to sell the products of one particular company.

---

7. When Suntory, the fourth-largest beer manufacturer in Japan, entered the beer market, it had difficulty finding wholesalers to deal with its products because all beer wholesalers were part of the *keiretsu* network of some incumbent beer manufacturer.

8. It should be noted that when Matsushita started its production and sales of such home electric appliances as TVs and washing machines, it could not find a well-developed distribution network for its products. Thus Matsushita constructed its own distribution channels by asking small local stores, such as radio repair shops, to become "Matsushita chain stores."

Table 4.2   **Rebate Scheme Example**

Amount of Procurement per Month (ten thousand yen)	Rebate Rate (%)
> 500	15
> 240	14
> 120	13
> 90	12
> 60	11
> 40	8
> 30	6
> 15	4

Source: Shukan Daiyamondo (Diamond Weekly; Tokyo), 3 July 1993.

The cases of home electric appliances and cosmetics, where even retail stores were organized into *keiretsu* networks by manufacturers, may be extreme. However, for many other products, one could observe manufacturers' *keiretsu* distribution channels to some extent, and manufacturers introduced various measures to support *keiretsu* networks.

Among various measures that manufacturers introduced to affect the incentives of retail stores and wholesalers, the vertical price structures the manufacturers set and the resulting retail margins were the most important tools. By vertical price structure I mean the relative position in the distribution channel of various prices, such as the manufacturer's sales price, the wholesaler's shipping price and the retail price. In the literature on vertical restraint (see, e.g., Tirole 1988, chap. 4), the importance of retail margin as an incentive mechanism is pointed out by many people. The manufacturer-wholesaler-retailer relation can be considered one type of principal-agent model, where manufacturers are principals and wholesalers and retailers are agents. Retail stores and wholesalers as agents sell products for manufacturers. Manufacturers set the retail margins of their products strategically so that retail stores and wholesalers had incentives to sell their products.

The pharmaceutical industry is perhaps where competition in retail margins went to the extreme. Table 4.3 shows retail margins for some national brand cough medicines when they were sold at the suggested price (the data are based on interviews I conducted with retail stores). It should be noted that the margins for two products are as high as 60 percent of their retail prices, whereas the margins for the other products are around 40 percent. One can imagine that retail stores had strong incentive to suggest these two high-margin products to customers. It was said that many customers coming to drugstores would ask the store pharmacist for a suggestion. Thus drugstores had strong influence on consumers' product choices in Japan.

The manufacturers selling the two products with relatively small retail

Table 4.3   **Retail Margin under Suggested Price for National Brand Cough Medicine**

Brand	Retail Margin[a] (%)
Benza-ace	40
Lulu-A	38
Sutona	60
Pavlon	64

Source: Based on author's interviews.

[a]The percentage share of the retail margin in the total sales price.

margins had established their shares of the market and formed close relations with wholesalers before the other two entered. Thus the other two, the entrants, decided to sell their products directly to retail stores and bypass the wholesale system, recognizing the difficulty of penetrating *keiretsu* wholesale networks. These two entrants chose to set high retail margins in order to give strong incentives for retail stores to sell their products.

Needless to say, a high retail margin always induces discount stores to sell at lower prices. The pharmaceutical industry in Japan was no exception. However, there were two obstacles for discounters. One was severe government regulation of the opening of new drugstores. This regulation protected traditional mom-and-pop drugstores and made the expansion of drugstore chains and sale of pharmaceuticals in large retail stores difficult (these regulations are going to be removed soon).

Another barrier to discounters was the difficulty of obtaining enough product from the manufacturers. The many mom-and-pop drugstores were an important distribution channel for manufacturers. Thus manufacturers did not like their retail margins to shrink due to discounting. So manufacturers did not supply enough product to retail stores selling at discounted prices.[9] This kind of manufacturer behavior of course violates antimonopoly law. But there are many subtle ways to discourage discounting behavior without explicitly violating the law. Moreover, the Fair Trade Commission in Japan did not regulate this behavior severely.

So far, I have been discussing the structure of the traditional Japanese distribution system by focusing on small stores. However, even large retail stores, such as department stores and general merchandising stores (GMS), which had a crucial position in the postwar distribution system in Japan, followed practices similar to those discussed above.

To understand the role of department stores in the traditional Japanese distribution system one must note the complementary relation between

9. Retail stores could obtain some products from other retail stores or from independent wholesalers. However, manufacturers sometimes put pressure on these retail stores and wholesalers not to sell their products to discounters.

department stores and small retail stores, mentioned above; that is, most consumers visited neighborhood shopping zones containing small retail stores for daily shopping and larger shopping areas in the centers of large cities for occasional shopping for such products as seasonal clothing, furniture, and some luxury goods. Department stores were in the larger shopping areas.

Due to this complementary relation between small shopping areas and department stores, department stores dealt with goods that mom-and-pop stores did not carry and stocked quite a large variety of goods. *Hyakkaten,* the Japanese expression for a department store, means "the store selling a hundred goods": in Japanese a hundred means a lot. The typical department store in Japan sold a far wider variety of goods than department stores in other industrial countries.

The size of the department store reflected the size of the city. Department stores in larger cities were much larger than those in smaller cities. Department stores in wealthy neighborhoods carried more expensive goods than other department stores. The contents of the department stores thus varied greatly depending on the characteristics of consumers in the neighborhood. It was therefore almost impossible in Japan to run department stores as chain operations. Each store was operated quite independently. The procurement of goods was not centralized and depended heavily on wholesalers and manufacturers, just as in the case of small retail stores. A large portion of department store sales were under consignment. Under consignment arrangements, department stores did not take any risk for sales because wholesalers or manufacturers took the risk of unsold goods. Prices were also set by wholesalers and manufacturers under consignment. Furthermore, more than half of the sales clerks in department stores were employees of wholesalers or manufacturers. As did small retail stores, department stores depended heavily on wholesalers and manufacturers.

GMSs grew rapidly during the 1960s and 1970s. GMSs, typically smaller in scale than department stores and with smaller customer bases were run as chain operations. The relations between GMSs and wholesalers were not like those between department stores and wholesalers. GMSs used their own sales clerks, took their own risks and set prices by themselves. The independent position of GMSs allowed them to be less influenced by manufacturers' market channel controls, and it was often the case that these GMSs played a role in changing the traditional distribution system.[10] However, as will be discussed in the next section, expansion of GMS chains has been regulated by the Large Scale Retail Store Law.

10. The conflict between Matsushita, the largest home electric appliance manufacturer, and Daiei, the largest GMS, regarding the pricing policy of Daiei was famous. Daiei's discounting of Matsushita products induced Matsushita to cease selling to Daiei.

Until the mid-1970s most Japanese consumers did not use automobiles for shopping. Most GMSs had their shop outlets near railway stations. Although they were chain operated, the Japanese GMSs had many of the features of department stores. They sold not only food and sundries but also many other goods, such as home electric appliances, apparel, and furniture. Compared with a chain store in the United States, the typical Japanese GMS sold a much greater variety (though not amount) of goods. For example, if one compares Wal-Mart, the largest chain in the United States, and Daiei, the largest chain in Japan, in the mid-1990s, the former sold about three times as much as the latter in value, while it had about ten times the number of the shop outlets. This means that sales per outlet for Daiei were about three times as large as for Wal-Mart. If one compares a typical Daiei store with a typical Wal-Mart store, one can understand why Daiei's sales per store were far larger than Wal-Mart's. Daiei carried a far greater variety of goods than Wal-Mart, which enabled Daiei to sell more in value per store.

The Japanese-style GMSs, which sold a large variety of goods and as a result sold smaller amounts of each item, could not have the level of independence that American chain stores enjoy. Japanese chain stores depended on the services of wholesalers, unlike American chain stores whose procurement is far more centralized and who often have their own centralized distribution centers. Thus, in spite of rapid growth, the Japanese GMSs did not replace the traditional wholesale system; they rather coexisted with the traditional system.

4.3   Structural Change in the Distribution System and the Large Scale Retail Store Law

The Japanese distribution system started changing rapidly in the mid-1980s. The most important driving force behind this change was the motorization of Japanese society. Although Japan lagged behind other industrial nations in the motorization process, the number of automobiles owned by people suddenly started increasing at the end of the 1970s. Many people now use automobiles for shopping. They prefer stores with parking spaces, and they now can go to stores they could not have reached on foot. In large cities the young generation, who are forced to live in suburban areas due to high land prices in the city centers, shop in stores located in the suburbs. In smaller cities and towns where the population is below fifty thousand, large shopping centers are often built in the middle of two or three of these cities to attract consumers from these cities: in Japan where residential land is constrained and the population is dense, a large shopping center can attract consumers from more than two neighboring towns. Large retail stores responded to this changing environment in the distribution industry. They opened large stores and shopping centers with large parking lots in suburban areas. By contrast, traditional mom-and-pop stores could not adjust to these changes.

However, there was a big barrier to this change. That was the Large Scale Retail Store Law, as well as other regulations on opening new store branches. Under the law, the government reconciled regional small store owners with large retail stores, concerning the opening of large store outlets in the region. Before a large store could open, there had to be approval from local store owners, and the negotiation process was controlled by the government under the law.

This law had several problems. First, it took a long time to complete the negotiation process. The length of the negotiation process depended on how strongly local shop owners resisted. It was more than usual for negotiations to take two to three years. In some cases negotiations took ten years. The long negotiation process not only retarded the opening of new shop outlets but also increased the cost of such stores.

Another problem with the law was that as a result of negotiations, the large retail store often made concessions regarding the size of the store and its opening hours. Store sizes were curtailed and stores were forced to close at seven o' clock or seven-thirty. In other words large stores were regulated in size and business hours.

Some stores bypassed these regulations by opening stores smaller than the size specified in the Large Scale Retail Store Law. Many "roadside" stores followed this strategy and opened smaller stores in the suburbs. These stores were obviously smaller than was optimal, and they faced serious problems when regulation was relaxed and larger stores entered the market.

Regulation under the Large Scale Retail Store Law was criticized by many people: academics, large retail store owners, and the mass media. However, political lobbying by small shop owners was strong enough to retard deregulation. Only when the American government requested abolishment of the law following the entry of the large U.S. toy chain store, Toys "Я" Us, was reform of the law initiated.

It should be noted that the Ministry of International Trade and Industry (MITI), which was in charge of the law, was not necessarily in a position to resist deregulation. In spite of the fact that most in MITI thought deregulation necessary, political pressure from small shop owners was strong enough to discourage reform of the law. American pressure for deregulation was actually a good chance to initiate reform.

The law has been reformed twice since then. As a result of these changes, the process of negotiation was speeded up and the business hours of large stores were extended. The reform of the law apparently hastened the structural change in the distribution system.

In spite of this deregulation it should be emphasized that not all regulation was removed. Store size is still curtailed and business hours are restricted. Further deregulation was requested both from inside and outside.

The case of the law was brought to a panel of the World Trade Organization. Before a decision was made by the panel, the Japanese government decided to abolish the law. The decision was made at the end of 1998 to abolish the Large Scale Retail Store Law and introduce a new law, the Large Scale Retail Store Location Law.

Under the new system of the Large Scale Retail Store Location Law, store size and opening hours are no longer negotiated between large stores and small local stores. However, the new law mandates that the entry of new, large retail stores be checked from the viewpoint of their environmental effects on their neighbors—including such effects as traffic congestion and noise. Although the new law is quite different in purpose from the old, there is some concern that local retail stores may use the new law as an excuse to block the entry of large stores. However, since the law has not yet been enacted as of May 1999, its effect on competitive conditions in the distribution system is yet to be seen.

4.4 Structural Change of the Distribution System and Market Access

Structural change in the Japanese distribution system triggered by motorization and deregulation made market access from abroad far easier than before. The rapid increase in the imports of manufactured goods reflected this change.

Another factor that is important when one discusses changes in market access conditions is the yen appreciation since 1985. The yen-dollar exchange rate appreciated from around 250 yen per dollar to 100 yen per dollar in the mid-1990s. The yen also appreciated in terms of its real effective exchange rate with respect to all currencies.

Yen appreciation promoted an increase in Japan's imports. Not only did the volume of imports rise, but the share of manufactured good imports also rose substantially. The share of manufactured good imports in total imports increased from about 30 percent in 1985 to about 60 percent in 1996. Before 1985 the majority of Japan's imports were primary goods that did not go through the distribution channels discussed here. But most manufactured goods imported did go through the distribution channels.

The structural change caused by motorization and deregulation obviously encouraged the expansion of imports. But at the same time, import expansion as a result of yen appreciation was a strong driving force for structural change in the distribution system. They went hand in hand.

Large stores and chain-operated stores, which are more independent of traditional distribution channels than small stores, are eager to import inexpensive foreign goods. Severe competition among these stores induces them to jump to foreign goods.

It should be noted that the new type of chain-operated stores emerged not only in suburban areas but also inside cities, the location of traditional retail stores. One of the important features of the Japanese distribution system is that many stores are still located inside cities. A large portion of the population still lives in urban areas. Although the number of mom-and-pop stores is decreasing at a rapid rate, what Japanese people call "convenience stores" are increasing in number rapidly. Most of the convenience stores were transformed from traditional mom-and-pop stores through a franchise system: the owners of the stores became members of a national franchise system of convenience stores. Under this system even small shop owners became less dependent on the traditional wholesale system.

Let me explain the case of Seven-Eleven Japan, the largest convenience store chain in Japan. This chain operation has about seven thousand stores all around the nation as of 1998. Most are run as mom-and-pop stores, but most of such services as procurement, pricing, and store management assistance are provided by the franchiser, the central office of Seven-Eleven Japan. Each store sells about three thousand items in small shops with frequent delivery of products. Some fresh foods are delivered three to four times a day. It is obvious that this system cannot use the traditional wholesale system, which is vertically segmented among different categories of goods. Thus this chain constructed a new wholesale network system by asking some wholesalers to participate. This wholesale system was constructed on the initiative of retailers, and the influence of manufacturers was weakened substantially.

Chain-operated stores—small convenience stores as well as large chain-operated stores—face strong price competition from each other. The situation is quite different from when small mom-and-pop stores were serving local consumers. Chain-operated stores cover wider regions and thus have many competitors. Furthermore, since competition is not among individual shop outlets but among chain systems as a whole, price competition is much more severe. Under this kind of rigorous price competition retail stores have little incentive to follow manufacturers' suggested prices. Retail stores now have their own pricing strategies. Due to this change in the behavior of retail stores, in some goods such as home electric appliances and processed foods, the traditional policy of manufacturers' suggested prices at each vertical stage of distribution has shifted to an "open price scheme" under which manufacturers offer no price suggestions and retail stores set their own prices freely.

Another important change in the retail sector is the emergence of many specialty retailers in such areas as music software, sporting goods, home electric appliances, books, and apparel. These retailers have many similar chain-operated stores; thus, just like large chain stores, these specialty chain stores are also relatively independent from traditional wholesale networks. They usually open their store outlets in shopping centers, and the number of shopping centers is increasing rapidly following the reform and abolishment of the Large Scale Retail Store Law.

Over all, the changes described above have increased accessibility from abroad to the Japanese retail market. Furthermore, increasing competition among retail stores as well as weaker control by manufacturers in the distribution system provides consumers with a more competitive environment. These changes certainly enhance consumer welfare.

4.5 Concluding Remarks

The traditional distribution channel in Japan was characterized by a large number of small retail stores and wholesalers. The influence manufacturers exerted through *keiretsu* distribution channels was quite strong and made access from abroad difficult. This paper has explained some of the important features of *keiretsu* distribution channels such as rebate systems, enclosure of wholesalers and retailers, and high retail margins as incentive mechanisms.

These features of the Japanese distribution system were partly due to constrained land, high population density, and a slow motorization process and partly due to various regulations enforced by the government. Although the system was efficient within the traditional economic environment, it is no longer so in the changing economic environment. Furthermore, the traditional system set high barriers to imports from abroad.

The distribution system is now, however, undergoing rapid structural change. Motorization and the resulting changes in consumer behavior triggered structural change in the distribution system. The emergence of new types of retailers accelerated the change, and the competitive environment in the distribution system made foreign access to the Japanese import market far easier. Yen appreciation since the middle of the 1980s also contributed to the change.

Deregulation of various measures, especially the abolishment of the Large Scale Retail Store Law, arose as an important policy issue for the government. It was also regarded as an important trade issue in negotiations with Japan's trade partners. Following various stages of deregulation, the Large Scale Retail Store Law was finally removed and a new law, the Large Scale Retail Store Location Law, was enacted. Since the new law has not yet gone into effect, the influence of this system change has yet to be seen. However, the increasing degree of competition among retail stores and the aggressive entry of foreign firms into the market is expected to further improve accessibility to the Japanese market.

References

Ito, Takatoshi, and Masahiro Maruyama. 1991. Is the Japanese distribution system really inefficient? In *Trade with Japan,* ed. Paul Krugman. Chicago: University of Chicago Press.

Itoh, Motoshige. 1991. The Japanese distribution system and access to the Japanese market. In *Trade with Japan,* ed. Paul Krugman. Chicago: University of Chicago Press.

———. 1995. *Nihon no Bukka ha Naze Takainoka* (Why are prices in Japan high?). Tokyo: NTT Shuppan.

Ministry of International Trade and Industry. 1988. *White paper on international trade and industry.* Tokyo: Ministry of International Trade and Industry.

Tirole, Jean. 1988. *The theory of industrial organization.* Cambridge, Mass.: MIT Press.

Comment   Thomas Gale Moore

During my time on the President's Council of Economic Advisers I became familiar with the hypothesized relationship of the distribution system in Japan to imports. The Reagan administration certainly pressured the Japanese to change their system. I am glad to learn that they are making progress on opening up their distribution system, particular with the gradual liberalization of their Large Scale Retail Store Law. Freeing up their distribution system and allowing more efficient types of retailing to flourish is in the interest of the Japanese consumer.

I do not believe that it will have much effect on U.S.-Japanese trade. It may shift somewhat the composition of trade, but the imbalance between exports and imports worldwide is a result of saving and investment balance. Japan saves much more than the United States, and a portion of the Japanese funds come to the United States as investment. We gain by this, but we *pay* for it with more imports and less exports. The actual trade deficit between the United States and Japan is a meaningless number to economists, but not to politicians.

Nevertheless, it is desirable for all that the Japanese economy continue to prosper and that its people reap the gain. A more efficient distribution system would raise the living standard of the people of that island. That might lead them to buy more goods from us, but the effect would probably not be large.

In reading Motoshige Itoh's enlightening paper, I was unsure that his statistics and arguments proved what he alleged was true. For example, Itoh cites Matsushita as having a series of chain stores that feature that manufacturer's products. These are small neighborhood stores. However,

Thomas Gale Moore is a senior fellow at the Hoover Institution, Stanford University.

Matsushita faces competition from other manufacturers. Department stores and general merchandising stores also sell electrical appliances. Thus, if the system of small shops is so inefficient, how come Matsushita employs it and why do these other outlets not bankrupt Matsushita or at least put the small stores out of business?

These small outlets probably provide considerable information to purchasers about the products. And while a shop owner has a strong incentive to push the brand names of the manufacturers that he or she handles, the proprietor must keep local customers happy. The merchant cannot sell inferior merchandise or overprice products. The local store owner and salespeople probably live close to most of their patrons and probably know them by name. Consequently, the store is likely to be very sensitive to the interests of its clientele. The existence of large rebates from manufacturers suggests that competition is keen.

Itoh argues that general merchandising stores sell a greater variety of goods than the typical American chain store. They may, but I am not convinced that his statistics demonstrate that fact. He calculates the average sales per shop for the largest chain in Japan, Daiei, and compares that to average sales at a typical Wal-Mart. What exchange rate did he use to make this conversion, a market rate, purchasing power parity, or what? But even if we agree that the sales volume is larger in a chain store in Japan, it does not follow that the variety of goods is greater. The individual items may be more expensive or the volume of sales for any one good may be higher.

As Itoh showed, the system of small retailers grew up in a market where consumers walked to local shops, especially in large cities. In the downtown part of large U.S. cities, local stores tend to be small because people find it more difficult and costly to use cars. As long as the Japanese people live in concentrated cities, shops will tend to be small. The Wal-Marts of this world are a product of suburbia with land cheap enough that large parking areas can be built. Consequently, even if the Large Scale Retail Store Law is totally repealed we would not expect that Japanese retailing would look like U.S. shopping centers.

As I mentioned earlier, the Large Scale Retail Store Law is being adjusted slowly. Nevertheless, adjustment is taking place. If the Large Scale Retail Store Law were repealed, would local government step in to protect small retailers? Probably some would: they do in the United States. However, in the United States competition for retail dollars limits the willingness of cities to exclude large retailers. In Palo Alto where I live, one of the largest retailers is Fry's, an electronic and computer store. Many residents would like to rid the city of the store, but it brings in too much money. Competition among cities does work.

I am not sure what table 4.1 shows. The data on shops per 1,000 square kilometers are meaningless; much of the United States is uninhabited. The number of shops per 10,000 people in Japan is somewhat higher than any other country listed, but as I said, Japan is a very urban country where we would expect more small shops. The number of workers per shop is the same in France and Japan. The number of employees in wholesale establishments is higher in the United States and France and lower in West Germany than in Japan. Are German wholesalers more efficient or smaller? Are U.S. wholesalers less efficient or bigger?

Finally, in the United States about 10 percent of all nonfood and non-auto retail sales are mail order. Is there much mail order in Japan? That would clearly increase competition. Basically, the evidence that Itoh presents suggests that competition is alive and well in Japan, but that the government has been trying to limit it.

Comment   Ching-hsi Chang

In this paper, Motoshige Itoh delineates the distribution system for manufactured products in Japan after World War II. The distribution market before 1970 can be characterized as a vertically separated system in which retail stores were controlled mainly by closely related wholesalers and to some extent by manufacturers. This structure was due to the characteristics of the transportation system and restriction by the government. The former included a lag in motorization, convenient public transportation systems, and densely populated urban areas. The latter took the form of the Large Scale Retail Store Law. While large retail stores faced severe barriers to entry in local markets under the law, the retail sector was dominated by small family-type retail stores serving their neighbors. Corresponding to the retail stores, a lot of local wholesalers, each in charge of a single product, had strong influence on the retailers. In extreme cases, retail stores were enclosed by manufacturers such as Matsushita and Shiseido, who had specific counters in department stores where the sales clerks were the employees of wholesalers or manufacturers. The measures that manufacturers used to control retailers were price discrimination (rebates) based on the amount of orders and order privileges during product shortages. Control by manufacturers was so effective that there was no arbitrage to exploit price margins or cheating in price collusion. Only general merchandising stores operated independently of wholesalers and manufacturers.

Since the mid-1980s, the vertically separated system has gradually been dismantled. In the late 1970s, Japan became increasingly motorized. People were able to shop in stores located in suburban areas. While the

Ching-hsi Chang is professor of economics at National Taiwan University.

Large Scale Retail Store Law still curbed the development of large shopping centers, the appreciation of the Japanese yen encouraged imports. To promote its exports, the United States initiated pressure to liberalize Japanese domestic laws.

The product distribution system is important because gains from division of labor and specialization are only realized through exchange. An effective distribution system permits greater specialization and division of labor and consequently higher economic growth. Itoh's paper on the Japanese distribution market is very informative. I am especially impressed by similarities between Japan and Taiwan. Taiwan has a similar distribution system because some Japanese companies, such as Shiseido, introduced their distribution systems to Taiwan with their products. Interestingly enough, it was also American pressure that helped deregulation in Taiwan (see my paper, chap. 7 in this volume).

I have several questions about this paper, however. First, I would like to know whether the vertically separated system before 1970 in Japan was the best distribution system or not. The question arises because small retailers were heavily protected by the government under the Large Scale Retail Store Law. What would the alternatives have been had there not been such a law? Second, the vertically separated system does not seem to be necessary for affiliations with small retail stores because close relations between wholesalers and retailers also prevailed in the department store system. In other words, a few large nationwide wholesalers could have been associated with many small retail stores. There is a fundamental question about the meaning of the separated system. Is it a product-separated or brand-separated distribution system? Since many goods go through long tunnels of wholesalers, and either wholesalers or manufacturers control the tunnels, it must be a brand-separated system. However, if people have to shop on foot, would it not be more advantageous to sell as many brands as possible in one store? On the other hand, it is not necessary for retail stores to be small under a brand-separated system because they could sell many products, each a single brand, in one retail store.

5

Hong Kong's Business Regulation in Transition

Changqi Wu and Leonard K. Cheng

5.1 Introduction

With minimum direct government intervention in private business, Hong Kong is widely regarded as the land of laissez faire. Compared with most economies in the world, the degree of direct government involvement in private business in the territory is indeed rather moderate. Nevertheless, Hong Kong does have a history of government regulation of monopolies, an aspect of economic reality that has often been overshadowed by its high degree of economic freedom.

In this paper we briefly review the history of regulation of monopolies in Hong Kong and examine the current situation. The regulated industries include electricity, telecommunications services, public transport, and airport services. These industries are not exactly alike in their economic characteristics, but they are all subject to legal or technical barriers to entry. Since the provision of these services is not under sufficiently competitive conditions, public policy toward these industries has been devised with the purpose of limiting the monopolies' exercise of market power. As in many other economies, regulation of monopoly in Hong Kong has evolved over time to cope with changes in the economic environment and structure of the industries.

In section 5.2 we provide an overview of the evolution of Hong Kong's regulation of monopolies and oligopolies. Section 5.3 analyzes the salient

Changqi Wu is assistant professor of economics at the School of Business and Management of the Hong Kong University of Science and Technology. Leonard K. Cheng is professor of economics at the Hong Kong University of Science and Technology.

The authors thank Takatoshi Ito, Thomas G. Moore, Roger Noll, and the other conference participants for their helpful comments and suggestions.

features of the scheme of control, the primary regulatory tool used in Hong Kong. The impact on firm behavior and the effectiveness of schemes of control in achieving their goals are critically appraised in section 5.4 by focusing on the electricity industry. In section 5.5 we describe the transition from regulation to market liberalization in the telecommunications service industry. Finally, the implications of the regulatory changes in Hong Kong and directions for further changes are discussed.

5.2   Evolution of the Regulation of Monopolies

The history of regulation of monopolies in Hong Kong is relatively short. It can be divided into three distinct phases: (1) before 1963, (2) 1963–95, and (3) after 1995. In the period before 1963, the regulation of monopolies was not a major issue in the government's economic policy. From 1963 to 1995, the government regulated the public utility monopolies with a series of schemes of control. Since 1995, technological changes and economic development have led the government to consider ways to bring competition to the regulated industries.

Prior to the 1960s, clearly defined and well-deliberated government policy on monopolies or near monopolies virtually did not exist. Following the economic philosophy of laissez faire, the Hong Kong government adopted a minimum interventionist approach to industries characterized as monopolies and was reluctant to play an active role in regulating them. This attitude was reflected clearly in a statement made by the government in 1921 in response to a request by the public to provide means of public transport between Victoria Harbor and Repulse Bay: "So long as the Government continues its present policy of giving reasonable facilities for private enterprise to get under way it will have done all that can be expected of it."[1] As a result, public utility services were supplied largely by private firms under government franchises.

However, that is not to say that the government never intervened in private business. As early as 1863, the then acting governor and commander-in-chief, W. T. Mercer, set rules "for the regulation of Public Vehicles and Chairs and their Drivers and Bearers, and to license the Hire of Horses, within the Colony of Hong Kong."[2] When public buses were introduced into Hong Kong in 1921, the government responded swiftly by amending the Vehicles and Traffic Regulation Ordinance. The amended ordinance gave the government new power to specify bus routes with details of the fares to be charged, the stopping places, and basic specifications of the vehicles.

1. Reported in *Hong Kong Telegraph,* 2 April 1921, and cited by Leeds (1984, 29).
2. Ordinance No. 6 of 1863, cited in Hall (1996, 2).

These and other regulations set license fees, fares, standards, and penalties for malpractice. In the process, the government benefited from royalty fees paid by franchisees. An illuminating example is the early development of public bus services in Hong Kong. When public buses first appeared in Hong Kong in 1921, a number of bus companies entered and competed for business. The government decided in 1933 to grant the exclusive right to offer public bus service in Kowloon and the New Territories to Kowloon Motor Bus (KMB). To maintain its exclusive right, KMB had to pay an amount as high as 20 percent of its gross revenue to the government as royalty during a certain period of its franchise (Leeds 1984).

The first scheme of control was introduced in 1964, about one hundred years after the first traffic regulations came into existence. It symbolized the start of the second phase of Hong Kong's regulatory history. In that year, the government decided to impose a scheme of control to regulate China Light and Power (CLP), the company that supplied electricity to Kowloon and the New Territories. Rapid expansion of industrial activities and the resulting surge in demand for electricity in Kowloon led to frequent blackouts and tariff increases. The public uproar against high tariffs and low service quality generated calls for a government takeover of CLP. Under threat of government expropriation, CLP proposed to limit its own rate of return and to set up a development fund to finance its future expansion.[3] The scheme of control was the government's response to the situation.

The scheme-of-control agreement was reached between CLP and the government in November 1964, but with retroactive effect to October 1963. The agreement, which spanned a period of fifteen years, set the maximum permitted rate of return on the average net fixed assets devoted to electricity operations at 13.5 percent. After the first scheme of control on CLP was introduced, similar schemes of control spread to other industries where suppliers of services enjoyed significant market power. The end of the 1980s was the heyday of the schemes of control, when the industries covered by the schemes included electricity supply, local telephone services, public bus services, and airport services.

As the schemes of control multiplied over the years, their drawbacks gradually became apparent. Since they did not limit price increases and returns were calculated on the basis of fixed assets, some companies took advantage of this loophole to increase tariffs and to expand their capacity, leading to high tariffs as well as excess capacity.

As Hong Kong's economy grew and technology advanced in some of the regulated industries, such as telecommunications, the government began to consider alternative regulatory mechanisms to improve the regu-

---

3. See Cameron (1982) for a detailed description of the company history of CLP.

lated industries' economic performance. Price-cap regulation, an alternative to scheme-of-control regulation, was introduced first into the local telephone network service market in 1993 in the hope that it would reward the efforts of the regulated firm to lower its costs.

Since the early 1990s, the government has taken steps to introduce competition into markets that were previously supplied by regulated monopolies. By now the competitive situation in a number of regulated industries has improved substantially. Instead of a monopoly, there are now four operators competing in the market for local fixed telecommunications services. A new bus company (Citibus) has entered the public bus market to compete against two incumbents. When the new airport at Chek Lap Kok begins operation in 1998, two firms will compete for airport cargo services compared with a monopoly at present, and three firms for ramp-handling services compared with a monopoly now. All of the schemes of control have been lifted by August 1997 except those for the electricity industry.

Given the significant role played by the schemes of control, we shall analyze this mode of regulation in greater detail in the next section. We shall examine the mechanism behind the schemes of control, identify the features that distinguish them from regulations in other economies, and evaluate their effectiveness.

5.3   Salient Features of Schemes of Control

5.3.1   Objectives of Regulation

As is well known in the economic literature, most public utilities are natural monopolies due to the economies of scale or network economies they enjoy. In other words, a sole supplier can provide the services demanded by society at the lowest possible unit cost. While efficient allocation of resources requires an output level at which consumers pay a price equal to the firm's marginal cost of production, an unregulated monopoly would maximize its profits by restricting output, thus causing the price to exceed the firm's marginal cost.

"First best" regulation implies setting price equal to marginal cost (i.e., marginal cost pricing). But given economies of scale, such a linear pricing rule will result in the firm's making a loss. If subsidies to cover losses are considered impractical due to the usual principal-agent problem, then "second best" regulation would require the firm's price to at least be equal to its average cost (i.e., average cost pricing),[4] so that the firm can break even.

If two-part tariffs are used (as they are in public utilities such as tele-

---

4. More precisely, the second-best outcome is given by the largest output level at which price is equal to average cost.

phone services and electricity), then the breakeven point will be closer to the first-best outcome than that under linear pricing.[5] In this case too, however, the calculation of marginal cost is plagued by asymmetric information that is typical of the principal-agent problem.

Schemes of control have been the Hong Kong government's main policy instruments in regulating monopolies and near monopolies in public utilities. As stated by the government, "Schemes of control exist because certain companies provide services to the public in a monopoly or semi-monopoly situation. This makes it necessary, in the public interest, for the Government to establish certain guidelines (known as schemes of control) under which these companies will operate" (see Hong Kong Government 1988, 2). This statement highlights the main motive behind schemes of control.

At the very beginning of every scheme-of-control agreement reached between a regulated firm and the government is a clause stating that the scheme of control should be devised (1) to allow the regulated company a permitted maximum return, and (2) to provide a framework under which the company's financial affairs can be monitored and tariff applications can be made. Clearly, schemes of control are a kind of rate-of-return regulation. If such regulation is effective, then a regulated firm would not be able to earn monopoly profits by charging monopoly prices, but only a return that equals to its cost of capital.

5.3.2   Basic Features

As a kind rate-of-return regulation, Hong Kong's scheme-of-control regulation has unique characteristics: (1) It specifies the permitted rate of return of the regulated firms and defines the rate base on which total returns are calculated. (2) It requires each regulated company to establish a development fund (DF) to finance future expansion and to maintain the rate of return without frequent tariff changes. (3) It sets a fixed rate of return for the entire period of the agreement, which is typically quite long.

Figure 5.1 summarizes the common features of schemes of control. A regulated firm must first submit its forecast of future demand, its investment plan, and justifications for the investment plan to the regulatory agency. After obtaining approval from the Economic Services Bureau (formerly the Economic Services Branch) of the Government Secretariat, the regulated firm can carry out its investment and production plans. Total revenue from sales, less total operating cost and taxes, will first go to investors. Debt holders receive their interest payments and equity holders re-

---

5. If the monopoly can use two-part tariffs, economic inefficiency as measured by the gap between the unit price and marginal cost would be lessened compared with that under linear pricing. However, the problem of monopoly profits will be further aggravated.

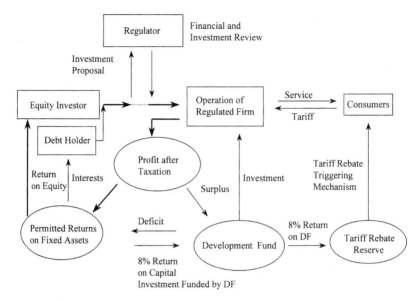

Fig. 5.1   Scheme-of-control mechanism

ceive the permitted profit as compensation for their respective supplies of capital. Any surplus (or deficit) is added to (made up by drawing down) the DF.

If the balance of the DF is insufficient to cover the shortfall in gross revenue in a particular accounting year, the government may permit the regulated firm to deduct from the DF in subsequent years any amount due to it in that year or approve an increase in tariff to cover the losses (Public Bus Services Ordinance, Cap 230, section 28). In addition, an annual charge of 8 percent on the average balance of the DF is credited to a reserve to reduce the tariff or limit tariff increases. Thus the DF serves to smooth the actual rate of return, finance capital investment, and provide rate relief.

5.3.3   Permitted Returns

By definition, permitted total returns to the regulated company depend on (1) the rate base and (2) the permitted rate of return. As stated in scheme-of-control agreements, regulated companies and their shareholders are entitled to earn returns that are reasonable in relation to the risks involved and the capital invested and retained in their businesses.

In theory, the rate of return should be based on the cost of capital, but in practice it was determined through negotiation between the government and each regulated company. This approach has led to significant variation in the permitted rates of return and in the ways in which total returns are calculated not only across industries but also across companies in the same industry.

Rate Base

In most schemes of control, fixed assets have been adopted as the rate base for the calculation of total returns. In the cases of the electricity companies CLP and Hong Kong Electric Company, the bus companies KMB and China Motor Bus (CMB), and Hong Kong Airport Terminal Service Limited, total returns are calculated on the basis of average net fixed assets. In the case of Hong Kong Airport Cargo Terminals Limited, permitted total returns are calculated on the basis of gross fixed assets. One exception is Hong Kong Telephone Company, whose total returns were calculated on the basis of shareholder equity.

Regardless of whether gross or net fixed assets are used, the assets are measured at their historical cost. In addition to acquisition costs for machinery, land, and tangible assets, fixed assets also include capitalized refurbishment and improvements, assets under construction, prepayments, and goods in transit. The costs of construction include interest paid or payable on construction loans, but only up to a maximum of 8 percent per annum on the loan's principal.

Rate of Return

For the five companies whose permitted returns were calculated on the basis of their net fixed assets, the maximum rate of return ranged from 13.5 to 18 percent per annum. The differences in the rates of returns could be attributed partly to differences in the undiversifiable risks of the industries, but they were also a result of the case-by-case approach to regulation. For example, the two regulated bus companies KMB and CMB were permitted rates of return of 16 and 15 percent, respectively. According to the government, the difference in the permitted rate of return reflected the companies' differential profitability before the imposition of the schemes of control. If that were indeed the case, then the effectiveness of regulation would be called into question. In particular, if the maximum rate of return was set at or above that corresponding to monopoly profits, the regulation clearly would have failed to achieve the primary objective of schemes of control, that is, restraining a monopolist's market power.

A crucial question is how to determine the cost of capital of regulated firms. First, these companies were unregulated monopolies before the schemes of control were introduced. If the profitability of an unregulated monopoly was used as the benchmark to set permitted return, the "opportunity cost" of an unregulated monopoly would become its cost of capital. Second, a monopoly under prospect of regulation might inflate its profits strategically in anticipation of the upcoming regulation in order to bargain for a higher permitted rate of return.

Estimating the cost of capital for a regulated industry is challenging both theoretically and operationally. In practice, two methods are often used in estimating a regulated firm's cost of equity capital, namely, the capital asset pricing model and the dividend growth model (see Armstrong, Cowan, and Vickers 1994, 183–85). In the capital asset pricing model, the cost of equity capital is measured by the risk-free rate plus the firm's risk premium. The risk premium is measured by the covariance of the returns of the individual firm's stock with that of the market portfolio.[6] The higher the covariance, the higher the risk level and the higher the required rate of return necessary to attract private capital.

The dividend growth model is based on the premise that the share price is determined by the initial dividend divided by the difference between the cost of equity capital and the rate of expected dividend growth. One can estimate the cost of equity capital by inverting that equation once the expected dividend growth rate is known or has been estimated.

Attempts to estimate the cost of capital of a regulated firm using either method are plagued by a number of difficulties, including some that are unique to Hong Kong. First, because the profitability of a regulated firm reflects the permitted rate of return, it is logically problematic to use the stock market return or dividend growth of the same firm to estimate its own cost of capital. Second, when the permitted rate of return on debt-financed capital is far above the market interest rate of long-term debt, which is the case in Hong Kong, shareholders will have an incentive to alter the debt-equity ratio to increase the net rate of return to equity. Therefore, by definition, the permitted rate of return would always be too low when compared with the "cost of equity capital" calculated in the above fashion.

The difficulty of determining the cost of capital for a regulated industry has implications for implementing rate-of-return regulation. Although economic efficiency is improved by narrowing the gap between price and marginal cost, it does not follow that the lower the permitted rate of return, the better off are consumers and society. In a simple analytical model without uncertainty, we can show that the lower the permitted rate of return (but still above the interest rate), the worse off society becomes. The underlying reason is that when the rate of return is set low, the regulated firm may increase its profits by expanding its capacity without necessarily expanding its supply. This results in greater excess capacity in the industry and a bigger waste to society.

---

6. The capital asset pricing model has been criticized recently both theoretically and empirically. See Fama and French (1992).

5.3.4 Development Funds

A development fund is an account kept by a regulated firm to enable it to maintain the permitted returns and to assist in its financing of fixed assets. So long as the fund has a positive balance, the firm is required to contribute an amount that is equivalent to 8 percent of the fund's balance to the "rate reduction reserve" to be used to reduce the tariff in the following year. Thus, when the fund grows it will lead to a reduction in prices, and when the fund shrinks it may trigger price increases in order to maintain the rate of return.

A positive balance of the fund allows the firm to draw from it to cover any shortfall in actual earnings. When the balance of the DF is too small, it may not be sufficient to serve the purpose of guaranteeing the maximum returns the regulated firm is entitled to. However, once the DF is sufficiently large, the marginal benefit of the fund as a buffer to guarantee the permitted rate of return becomes small, while the cost in terms of forced transfer to the tariff rebate reserve becomes large.

When the DF is used to expand the firm's capacity, the firm pays 8 percent interest on the amount into the rate reduction reserve, at the same rate as the DF's unused balance. Thus the additional interest cost for using the DF to finance capital investment is zero, so the real opportunity cost of using the fund for investment is the marginal benefit derived from the fund's role as a buffer to smooth actual returns. It follows that the regulated firm's dominant strategy is to expand the rate base with capital investment financed by the DF whenever the fund is sufficiently large. Furthermore, if the marginal benefits of the fund for the smoothing of returns are small because uncertainty in demand is small, then the dominant strategy would be to use the entire DF for capital expansion.

The design of the DF in schemes of control bears some resemblance to the escrow fund mechanism proposed by Vickrey (1971). When discussing the pricing of public utility services in the presence of fluctuating demand, Vickrey proposed that any actual deviation of price from marginal cost could be dealt with by establishing a dual tariff system (i.e., a "reactive" tariff and a "retention" tariff) and an escrow fund.[7] A retention tariff determines the amount of revenue that the company is entitled to retain out of the actual revenue. Any surplus would be put into an escrow fund. The company may use the escrow fund to finance investment in capacity. Thus the escrow fund provides an incentive for the company to maintain its plant capacity at an appropriate level.

---

7. Vickrey's retention tariff and reactive tariff are similar to permitted returns and actual returns except that tariffs are prices charged for services provided, whereas returns are based on fixed assets.

Despite the apparent similarities between the DF and Vickrey's escrow fund, their functions are fundamentally different. The DF is used primarily to protect the interest of regulated firms, but Vickrey's escrow fund is based on marginal cost pricing and is designed to maintain economic efficiency while avoiding the need for frequent changes in the utility's tariffs.

5.3.5   Duration of Scheme-of-Control Agreements

Schemes of control in Hong Kong take the form of long-term renewable agreements between the government and the regulated firms. The maximum permitted rates of return are fixed for the entire period of the agreements. The duration of scheme-of-control agreements, however, varies across industries. The longest period was twenty years when a scheme of control was imposed on Hong Kong Telephone Company in 1975. The effective period of the schemes of control for the two bus companies was set at ten years. The duration of the current scheme-of-control agreements for the two electricity companies is fifteen years.

Presumably, a long-term contract offers a better incentive for the regulated firm to make long-term investments than a frequently changing regulatory regime, thus providing an incentive to achieve the optimal amount of cost savings. However, such benefits associated with long-term agreements do not seem to be present in the case of Hong Kong's schemes of control. First of all, schemes of control typically contain periodic reviews and the possibility of modification of the initial agreement. The review period was set at five years for the two electricity suppliers and two years for the two public bus companies. More important, since a regulated firm can pass its costs on to the consumers, something it cannot do under price-cap regulation, the incentive to save costs is not enhanced by lengthening the agreement's duration.

Most important of all, the formulas for calculating permitted returns have given regulated firms a perverse incentive to increase capital investment beyond what is economically efficient and raised the total costs of production. As we shall see in the following section, this effect is most conspicuous in the electricity industry.

5.4   Experience with Schemes of Control: The Electricity Industry

The electricity supply industry in Hong Kong was the first industry to operate under schemes of control and will probably be the last one to leave the schemes. It provides the best illustration of the weaknesses of schemes of control. Among other questions we shall ask: (1) How did the schemes affect the firms' behavior? (2) What was the impact of the schemes on the industry's economic efficiency? (3) How effective were the schemes in achieving their objectives? Let us first provide some background information about the electricity industry before answering these questions.

5.4.1   Industry Background

Electricity in Hong Kong is supplied by two companies. The Hong Kong Electric Company Limited (HEC) supplies electricity to Hong Kong Island and the neighboring islands, while the China Light and Power Company Limited supplies electricity to Kowloon and the New Territories. The electricity generation of CLP is carried out by its associated company, the Castle Peak Power Company Limited (CAPCO), which is 60 percent owned by Exxon Energy Limited and 40 percent owned by CLP, but the associated transmission and distribution systems are wholly owned and operated by CLP.

By the end of 1996, the total installed electricity generating capacity of HEC was 2,955 MW. The total installed capacity of CAPCO was 7,515 MW. In that year, electricity sales of HEC were 8,876 million kWH. This amount represented 28 percent of total electricity sales in Hong Kong. In the same year, CLP sold 22,839 million kWH of electricity, accounting for 72 percent of the market.

The current schemes of control on CLP and HEC came into effect on 1 October 1993 and on 1 January 1994, respectively, due to differences in the two companies' financial years. Both schemes guarantee a 15 percent permitted rate of return for fifteen years. The electricity companies make forecasts of future electricity demand and submit major investment plans for approval by the Economic Services Bureau of the Government Secretariat.

The two electricity companies do not have exclusive rights to supply electricity in their respective territories, but each is the sole supplier in its own geographical area. Despite the lack of exclusive rights, there has never been any serious attempt by local or overseas investors to enter either market, and they have not made any attempt to enter each other's territories either. Their networks are interconnected by the cross-harbor cable, which is designed mainly as an emergency backup facility, not for the purpose of transmitting a large amount of electricity under normal circumstances. Given the nature of their schemes of control, however, there is really no need to enter a rival's territory so long as one's own fixed assets are allowed to grow.

5.4.2   Effect on Firm Behavior

In a competitive industry, a firm will choose the optimal combination of capital and labor to minimize its production costs. An unregulated monopoly also has the same incentive to do so because lower costs mean higher profits. A monopoly under scheme-of-control regulation, however, may not benefit directly from any cost reduction if its rate of return has already reached the permitted rate of return. Under these circumstances, the only way for the monopoly to increase its total profits is through expansion of its fixed assets.

The existence and magnitude of the distortion à la Averch-Johnson (1962) in Hong Kong's electricity industry can be empirically tested due to a peculiarity of the regulatory regime. In the period 1964–78, CLP was regulated by a scheme of control while HEC operated as an unregulated monopoly. Both firms have been regulated under similar schemes of control since 1979. The periods before and after the switch provide us with an opportunity to test Averch-Johnson's prediction.

Because capital investment can be used as a means to increase profits, we would predict that the regulated CLP employed more capital per labor than the unregulated HEC, provided that other things were equal. But other things might not be equal (e.g., the two firms operated at substantially different scales), so we would instead predict that the capital-labor ratio of CLP grew at a faster rate than that of HEC between 1964 and 1978 but that the opposite would be true after 1978.

We have found that the capital-labor ratio of the unregulated HEC remained higher than that of its regulated counterpart, CLP, throughout the period 1964–78. Nevertheless, during the fifteen-year period from 1964 to 1978, the average annual growth rate of the capital-labor ratio of CLP was 9.06 percent while that of HEC was only 7.94 percent. Furthermore, the growth rates of the two firms reversed after HEC voluntarily joined the scheme of control. In the period 1979–96, the capital-labor ratio of HEC grew at 8.82 percent per annum, faster than CLP's 8.13 percent. The changes in the firms' capital-labor ratio during these two periods are thus consistent with the prediction that regulated firms respond to schemes of control by speeding up their capital investment.

Relatedly, Peles and Whittred (1996) have demonstrated that the Hong Kong electricity companies, in response to the nature of their schemes of control, have used more fixed assets relative to current assets than U.S. electricity companies.

5.4.3   Effect on Economic Efficiency

In short, the data on capital expenditures and employment of the two electricity suppliers reveal a marked difference in their investment behavior before and after the schemes of control were imposed. While the intention of the schemes of control was to protect the consumers' interest by fixing the rate of return, the regulated electricity suppliers responded to the schemes by expanding their physical capital. The loss in economic efficiency due to such a distortion in input combination is a cost to society.

No less important than static allocative efficiency is dynamic efficiency, which measures the growth in total factor productivity (TFP) over time.

To assess the impact of the schemes of control on the regulated electricity companies, we have studied whether there are any observable changes in the TFP of the electricity firms before and after the schemes of control were introduced. Using historical data, we make two comparisons based on the estimation of the regulated firms' TPF changes: (1) the difference between the TFP changes of HEC and CLP from 1970 to 1978, when CLP was subject to a scheme of control but HEC was not,[8] and (2) the difference between the TFP growth of HEC before and after it was under the scheme of control.

The statistical results do not show any statistically significant improvement in the TFP for either company in the period 1970–78, and TFP growth remained insignificant in the period 1979–96, when both firms operated under schemes of control. That is to say, the TFP growth of electricity companies in Hong Kong was insignificant in the past three decades.

In terms of TFP, Hong Kong's electricity industry seems to have underperformed when compared with the electricity industry in the United States (see Ansar 1990; Gollop and Roberts 1981). During the 1950s and early 1960s, TFP growth of the U.S. electric power industry was on average above 4 percent annually. Even though the growth slowed down significantly in the late 1970s and the 1980s, it remained between 1 and 2 percent.[9]

To put the above findings in a broader perspective, let us compare the TFP growth of the electricity industry with that of Hong Kong's unregulated gas industry. A recent study shows that the TFP of Hong Kong China Gas grew at an average rate of about 2 percent per annum during the period 1975–95, on par with the economy-wide increase in TFP in Hong Kong (see Kwan and Png 1994). This is in sharp contrast with the situation in the electricity industry in which the TFP remained stagnant for about thirty years. While the difference in performance between the two industries may be the result of many factors, scheme-of-control regulation seems like a possible cause.

The loss in static and dynamic efficiency is better appreciated by considering the excess generation capacity of the two electricity monopolies. While schemes of control require the government regulator to review and approve the major investment projects of the electricity companies, the mechanism does not seem to have succeeded in resisting the companies' incentive to expand capacity. As a matter of fact, both companies have been investing aggressively to expand their electricity generation capacity despite excess capacity. In 1996 HEC's reserve margin—that is, the difference between installed capacity and maximum demand as a percentage of

8. The choice of a shorter period instead of the entire period 1964–78 was dictated by data availability.
9. The slowdown in the productivity growth rate in the U.S. electric power industry has often been attributed to the lack of flexibility of the regulatory regimes.

maximum demand—stood at 47 percent, which was much higher than the international norm of 30 percent. Despite the already substantial excess capacity, HEC completed the installation of a new 350 MW unit in 1997 as part of the current scheme-of-control agreement (Hong Kong Electric Company 1997).

For CLP, the situation is even more serious. The growth in demand for electricity has slowed significantly in recent years partly due to the relocation of local manufacturing industries to southern China, but the expansion of capacity continues unabated. The first of four 625 MW blocks of additional generating capacity, approved by the government in 1994, was installed in a new power station in 1996, and the second was installed in 1997. The buildup in generation capacity and the slow growth in demand have pushed the reserve margin of CLP to over 60 percent. In addition, the remaining two 625 MW blocks have been scheduled to be commissioned in 1998–2001 (Hong Kong Government 1997).

5.4.4 Effectiveness of Schemes of Control

Profitability of Electricity Companies

The first scheme-of-control agreement between CLP and the government stipulated that the regulated firm was permitted to earn a maximum rate of return of 13.5 percent on fixed assets regardless of the way in which the capital investment was financed. Later, when the scheme of control was up for renewal in 1979, the revised agreements added a new feature, namely, fixed assets financed by shareholder equity were allowed to earn a 1.5 percent premium on top of the permitted rate of return for fixed assets financed by external borrowing and "borrowing" from the DF.[10] The shareholders of the regulated companies are guaranteed not only the 15 percent rate of return but also the additional return from the difference between the permitted return on debt-financed fixed assets and the actual borrowing costs.

Using the debt and equity data reported by the two electricity companies and the assumption that the cost of borrowing was 9 percent, the net rate of return on equity would be around 20 percent, substantially higher than the 15 percent maximum permitted under the scheme.

When questioning the effectiveness of rate-of-return regulation thirty-five years ago, Stigler and Friedland (1962) suggested that one should not look only at the profit and loss accounts of the regulated firms because they would usually hide the critical information from accounting statements. Whether such a practice has actually occurred may be tested indirectly by examining the fortunes of investors in regulated firms' stocks.

---

10. External borrowing includes bank loans, supplier credits, amounts payable on leasehold land purchased on installment from the government, etc.

Using stock return data for HEC and CLP and adjusting for dividend payments, we have calculated that the stock returns on equity for both firms were on average 22.35 percent, even higher than the net rates of return during the period 1980–96. In the same period, the rates of return to shareholders of both electricity companies were higher than that of the Hang Sang Index, where most of the Hang Sang Index constituent companies were not regulated firms.

Our findings suggest that schemes of control were ineffective in protecting consumer interests because returns to shareholders of the regulated electricity companies exceeded the opportunity cost of equity capital by a very substantial margin.

Tariffs

As the other side of the coin, consumers have failed to enjoy a low-cost supply of electricity. To provide an independent piece of evidence, let us compare the levels and rates of change of CLP and HEC tariffs during the period 1963–79, when the former was regulated and the latter was not. The two firms' tariffs have moved closely during this period, suggesting that the scheme of control did not effectively alter the pricing behavior of the regulated firm CLP. An international comparison shows that the level and rate of increase of electricity prices in Hong Kong are at the high end among economies with comparable conditions (table 5.1).

Table 5.1   **Average Electricity Prices in Selected Economies**

Country	1995			1993	
	Price (HK cent/kWH)	Index	Price Change from 1993 (%)	Price (HK cent/kWH)	Index
Australia[a]	48	66	10	44	77
United States[a]	51	70	−1	51	90
Indonesia	59	81	16	51	90
Thailand	59	81	5	56	98
Malaysia	61	84	11	55	97
Korea	61	84	−5	64	114
Taiwan	62	85	−13	71	125
Singapore	64	88	16	55	96
Hong Kong	73	100	28	57	100
United Kingdom[a]	76	104	6	72	126
Philippines	89	122	14	78	137
Japan[a]	177	193	16	153	203

Data sources: Data for OECD countries are from the International Energy Agency (1997). Remaining data are from Lam (1997) and China Light and Power Company.

Note: All prices are in nominal terms and US$1 = HK$7.8. Prices of OECD countries are the average prices for industry and households.

[a]OECD countries.

In sum, the regulatory experience of the electricity industry suggests that schemes of control have failed to achieve their main objective of restraining regulated firms' monopoly power. Moreover, regulation has given rise to abnormally high excess capacity, which might have caused inefficiency in input combination and lack of productivity growth. The first reason behind the schemes' failure is the nature of rate-of-return regulation, as it gives weak incentive to regulated firms to lower cost. In addition, the formulas for calculating returns in the case of schemes of control have indeed provided a perverse incentive for regulated firms to expand their fixed assets beyond what is economically efficient and socially sensible. The second reason is asymmetric information, which makes it very difficult, if not impossible, for the regulator to monitor regulated firms effectively. As a result, it is not easy for the regulator to avoid being "captured" by regulated firms.

In the next section, we shall see a different path of development in the local telecommunications industry, where competition has gradually replaced regulation.

5.5   From Regulation to Competition: Telecommunications Services

The telecommunications service industry supplies a variety of services to different groups of customers. At the most general level, the industry can be divided into three segments: (1) local fixed telecommunications network services (FTNS), (2) mobile telecommunications services, and (3) international services. These three segments are characterized by different technologies and regulatory schemes.

The Economic Services Bureau of the Government Secretariat is responsible for setting an overall policy framework. Within this framework, the Telecommunications Authority is the regulatory body of the telecommunications industry and the administrator of the Telephone Ordinance (which governs the establishment and operation of basic telecommunications services) and the Telecommunication Ordinance (which regulates so-called nonbasic and competitive services).

Facing strong competition from neighboring regions that aspire to become the top financial and business center in the Asia-Pacific region, the government regards it as vital to have in place a good telecommunications infrastructure and to provide communications services to meet local and regional needs. The government set three policy objectives to guide the development of Hong Kong's telecommunications industry: (1) the widest range of high-quality telecommunications services should be available to the community at reasonable cost, (2) telecommunications services should be provided in the most economically efficient manner possible, and (3) Hong Kong should serve as the preeminent communications hub for the region now and into the next century (Hong Kong Government 1994).

Competition is viewed as a mechanism that engenders efficient supply of services and disciplines suppliers to ensure that prices are fair to consumers. As a result, the policy framework adopted by the government seeks to create an environment that makes entry by new suppliers possible, provides a fair rate of return to investors, and is proconsumer. Thus progressive liberalization and the licensing of competing suppliers are important aspects of the industry's development.

The three segments of the telecommunications service industry are characterized by different kinds of market structures. International telephone services are provided by Hong Kong Telecommunications International (HKTI), an unregulated monopoly. Mobile services are in a state of intensive competition. The market structure of local FTNS falls between the two extremes, experiencing a transition from a regulated monopoly to a regulated oligopoly.

5.5.1   Local Fixed Telecommunications Network Services

For quite a long time, telecommunications services have been regarded as an example of natural monopoly; that is, the most efficient service can be provided by only one service operator. Under this premise, Hong Kong Telephone Company (HKTC) was granted a fifty-year exclusive license in 1925 to provide the territory with a public telephone network. In return for this monopoly right, HKTC was required to pay a royalty to the government each year and gave concessions to the government by charging the government half of the regular tariff rates for its phone lines. In addition, HKTC was required to bear the universal telephone service obligation and seek government approval for any changes in rental charges.

The surge in demand for telephone services in the 1950s and the early 1960s outstripped HKTC's ability to provide phone services, leading to long waiting times for telephone installation. In reaction, HKTC proposed a substantial increase in rental charges to reduce waiting times and to finance the capacity expansion of the telephone network. The government initially refused the request for the rental increase but later approved a smaller increase in 1964. As part of the agreement, HKTC accepted a target return of 9 percent on average capital employed. The right of approval for any increases in the rental charges for telephone lines remained in the hands of the government.

HKTC's requests for substantial rental increases to cover rising costs in the early 1970s prompted the government to introduce a scheme of control on HKTC when its license was up for renewal in 1975. The scheme of control with HKTC, while resembling that reached between the government and CLP, had unique features. It allowed HKTC to retain its monopoly for another twenty years while limiting the maximum permitted rate of return on shareholder equity to 16 percent after taxes. After deducting total operating costs, permitted return, and taxes, 80 percent of the re-

Table 5.2   Residential Telephone Tariffs in Selected Economies (U.S. dollars)

Country	Connection			Monthly Subscription			Local Three-Minute Call		
	1995	1994	1993	1995	1994	1993	1995	1994	1993
Hong Kong	69	77.6	77.6	8.4	8	8	0	0	0
Korea	10	10	10	3.4	3.4	3.4	0.04	0.04	0.04
Singapore	56	52.4	50	5.9	5.5	5.2	0.01	0.03	0.02
Taiwan	113	228.7	255.2	2.3	4.6	4.6	0.04	0.04	0.04
United States	43	43.5	43.5	11.7	11.3	11.3	0.09	0.1	0.1

Sources: International Telecommunication Union, *ITU Statistical Yearbook* (Geneva, 1995); and International Telecommunication Union, *World Telecommunication Development Report* (Geneva, 1995, 1997).

maining surplus would go to a DF while 20 percent would go to shareholder equity in the form of bonus shares. That is to say, in contrast with the schemes of control for all other utility firms, the scheme of control on HKTC did not cap the accounting return to shareholder equity because any revenue above the permitted return would be shared by the company's shareholders and its DF. As a result, the real return to shareholders could be higher than the *maximum* permitted rate of return.

Although the DF could be used to expand HKTC's telephone network as well as to smooth its permitted returns, in practice it was used only for the latter purpose because the company had sufficient resources to finance its expansion of fixed assets. Like other DFs, the DF of HKTC represented a liability to the company and would accrue interest at the rate of 8 percent per annum on its average balance. This interest payment was deductible from the profits of HKTC and used for tariff relief.

Starting in 1993, rate-of-return regulation in the local FTNS segment was replaced by new, price-cap regulation. Under the new regulation, HKTC could revise the charges for its services on an annual basis but no more than the general inflation rate, based on the consumer price index (CPI) minus 4 percent (known as CPI-4). Rental charges for residential lines may not be increased by more than the general inflation rate less 3 percent per annum (known as CPI-3). Residential telephone tariffs from 1993 to 1995 (the year HKTC's exclusive franchise expired) are given in table 5.2. When the tariffs are compared with those of other Asian newly industrializing economies (NIEs) and the United States, we see that Hong Kong had the highest connection charges except Taiwan and the highest monthly rental fees except the United States. Despite the fact that local calls were free of charge in Hong Kong but not in the other included economies, total monthly charges were higher in Hong Kong than in the other three Asian NIEs if each household made fewer than 100 to 150 three-minute local calls per month.

From Regulation to Competition

Technological changes have made the natural monopoly argument in granting exclusive franchising increasingly irrelevant. Digital transmission and fiberoptic cable technologies have drastically reduced the cost to develop networks, thus bringing down the barriers to entry.

The expiration of the exclusive franchise of HKTC at the end of June 1995 provided an opportunity for the government to open the local telecommunications market to competition. In that year, three additional FTNS licenses were granted to Hutchison Communications Limited, New T&T Hong Kong Limited, and New World Telephone Limited for the provision of telecommunications services between fixed points in Hong Kong on a competitive basis. This move ended HKTC's seventy years of monopoly in the local fixed-line telecommunications market.

Hong Kong's approach to liberalization of the telecommunications market is different from that of other economies in two respects. First, because the exclusive franchise for international telephone services granted to HKTI will not expire until 2006, in 1995 competition was introduced only into local FTNS. Second, consistent with Hong Kong's free market philosophy, a *market-driven* open licensing approach was adopted over an alternative approach of creating a duopoly by tendering for a second network. The open licensing approach seems preferable both in promoting efficiency within the industry and ensuring that consumers enjoy the full benefits of competition.

Under the new regulatory provisions, the Telecommunications Authority has adopted a number of measures aiming to limit the market power of the dominant operator HKTC and to foster competition in the FTNS market. These measures include (1) introducing number portability to reduce customers' switching costs, (2) maintaining the universal service obligation on the dominant firm, (3) formulating tariff-setting provisions to prevent anticompetitive pricing behavior by the dominant firm, and (4) assisting new service providers in negotiation of interconnections with the dominant firm.

Number Portability. To facilitate a smooth entry by the three new FTNS operators and to create a level playing field, the Telecommunications Authority has introduced a number portability plan that allows residential and business users to keep their existing telephone numbers when they switch service providers. This measure has reduced the costs to HKTC's existing customers when they switch to a new service provider, making the services offered by the new entrants more attractive to consumers.

Universal Service Obligation. As specified in the government's position paper of 1994, *Hong Kong's Telecommunications Policy,* HKTC must carry the universal service obligation (USO) in circumstances where HKTC remains the dominant carrier, but the three new local service providers are required to pay HKTC an amount known as the "access deficit contribution" calculated on the basis of international calls to cover part of the costs of the USO (because currently local services are still cross-subsidized by international services).

In a recent report on market liberalization of local FTNS, the Consumer Council recommends that an independent universal service fund be established to subsidize the USO. This is clearly an improvement on the current system in which HKTC meets the USO while others contribute. A more important issue is to find a way to terminate the cross-subsidization of local services by international services.

Pricing Strategy. The tariffing rules set by the Telecommunications Authority state that the dominant firm HKTC is prohibited from offering to customers discriminatory tariff discounts from their published tariffs. In contrast, the three new entrants are not subject to the same constraint as long as their individual market share does not exceed 20 percent of the local telephone market.

Interconnection. Interconnection is a critical issue in the process of market liberalization because new operators can only provide their services through the incumbent firm's established network at the initial stage of entry. Current government policy is to allow the terms and conditions of the interconnection between the new entrants' networks and the fixed-link telecommunications infrastructure of HKTC to be determined through commercial negotiation on the principle that the connection charges should be based on long-run incremental costs. However, if an agreement cannot be reached, or the Telecommunications Authority considers the terms and conditions reached to be anticompetitive and against the public interest, the Telecommunications Authority has the power to determine the terms and conditions itself (Section 36A of the Telecommunication Ordinance).

HKTC and the other three FTNS suppliers reached a provisional agreement on connection charges in July 1995, and the charges were set at 9¢ per minute.[11] They have not yet reached any agreement, however, about the charges in accordance with the principles set out by the Telecommunications Authority. HKTC and NTT have sought the authority's help in determining the charges, but the determination has yet to be made.

---

11. The connection charges for mobile phones are 6.7¢ per minute, and those for value-added services are 4.2¢ per minute.

Effect of Market Liberalization

As an indirect indication of the effect of market liberalization on cost savings by the existing monopoly, let us see how HKTC responded to the opening of the local FTNS market. Hong Kong Telecom, the sole parent of both HKTC and HKTI, announced a three-year plan in March 1995 to reduce the number of its employees by 2,500, which represented 16 percent of its total workforce and the largest reduction in the company's history. Such streamlining did not seem to have adversely affected the performance of the company or services it provided. On the contrary, the growth rates of Hong Kong Telecom's revenues from local telephone services have continued to be in double digits. The 12.3 percent growth rate in revenues in the financial year ending March 1997 is even higher than in previous years (Hong Kong Telecom 1997).

As Hong Kong's experience in opening up local FTNS has demonstrated, the regulator can play an important role in the process of liberalization. Promotion of competition does not call for premature deregulation, which may set back progress toward market liberalization. Moreover, the regulator may have to be proactive and take measures to ensure that adequate competition is developing and consumers' interests are protected.

5.5.2   Mobile Telecommunications Services

Mobile telecommunications services are at present the most competitive segment of Hong Kong's telecommunications market. This segment differs from local FTNS in at least two aspects: First, there are minimum regulatory barriers to entry. The government has issued as many licenses as needed to maintain competition. Second, technologies in mobile telecommunications evolve rapidly. New entrants with better technology can penetrate the market relatively easily, thus putting competitive pressure on incumbent operators.

In 1994, the Telecommunications Authority conducted a review on the way forward with regard to the licensing and regulation of mobile telecommunications services. On the basis of the review, the authority decided to invite applications for up to four licenses for the provision of cordless access services and up to six licenses for the provision of personal communications services (PCS). This decision had a significant impact on the mobile phone business. In late 1995—almost a year before the issue of PCS licenses—the existing cellular operators responded to the threat of imminent entry by PCS (which are expected to enjoy a cost advantage) with deep cuts in tariffs and prices for handsets and with aggressive advertising campaigns to increase their customer base.

Paging services have minimal regulatory barriers to entry. There is practically no limit on the number of licenses because the Telecommunications Authority adopts a class licensing approach for mobile communications services where frequency constraints do not limit the number of potential operators. A license will be issued within days of application. Therefore, competition among paging service providers is most intense.

Mobile telecommunications services are characterized by rapid technological advances. The rapid changes in mobile communications technology illustrate the powerful force of creative destruction. A good example is the development of the CT2 Telepoint (i.e., the second-generation international standard for cordless handsets that uses digital radio technology) market in Hong Kong. Introduced into Hong Kong in 1992, CT2 generated a very positive response from consumers. Within two years of service launch, CT2 subscribership reached 170,000, representing close to 3 percent of the total population of Hong Kong. However, the CT2 system's advantages of low cost and light handsets in comparison with cellular phones quickly evaporated after cellular communications technology improved substantially. In 1996, all providers of CT2 services were out of business.

5.5.3 International Services

With an exclusive franchise that ends in 2006, HKTI enjoys a monopoly on international telecommunications circuits, telephonic services, and video-telephone services connected to the public switched telephone network.

Under both local and international pressure, in recent years the government has been pursuing opportunities to liberalize the international telecommunications segment subject to HKTI's exclusive franchise. The basic approach of the government is to define the areas to which the exclusive license applies as narrowly as possible.

In March 1995, the Telecommunications Authority announced that callback services did not constitute an infringement on HKTI's exclusive franchise. Also, as nontelephonic international services such as fax and data communications, video-conferencing, and other value-added services became increasingly popular in the business community, the authority stated in May 1996 that the simple resale of HKTI's international private lease circuits for fax and data services, private internal communications networks within companies and organizations, video-conferencing, and customer mobile terminals for mobile satellite services did not breach the terms of HKTI's monopoly on international services. As a result, these new international services have since been open to competition.

To limit the monopoly power of HKTI, the government has also allowed companies and organizations to "self-provide" their own external circuits for intracorporation traffic. In addition, companies and organizations may also provide their own international private circuits by, for example, directly leasing satellites for private use. The first self-provided external telecommunications service (SPETS) license was issued in 1995. Since then, a total of seventy-three SPETS licenses have been issued. The government has also kept future technical innovations such as international satellite cellular phone services outside of HKTI's exclusive franchise.

Given the above development, the competitive condition of the market for international services is now vastly different from what it was in 1981 when the twenty-five-year exclusive license was granted. This is an example of technological advances circumventing regulatory barriers. However, the government has been slow in responding to calls to liberalize international services and restrict the monopoly power of HKTI. The government either should find a way to end HKTI's exclusive franchise before 2006 or should seriously consider imposing price caps on the unregulated monopoly.

On 20 January 1998, however, the government announced that it had reached an agreement with Hong Kong Telecom, the parent company of HKTI, for the early surrender of HKTI's exclusive license. The liberalization measures include the following: (1) External service-based competition (such as international simple resale of voice services) will begin 1 January 1999. (2) External facility-based competition (such as IDD services over cable and satellite facilities owned by service providers other than HKTI) will begin 1 January 2000. To compensate for the early termination of HKTI's exclusive license, the government would provide cash compensation of HK$6.7 billion and terminate the royalty payment of HKTI as early as 20 January 1998. The changes in the government's position and market liberalization measures will prevent future losses in static efficiency and social waste arising from HKTI's efforts to defend its monopoly. More important, the forces of competition released by the agreement will improve dynamic efficiency by generating more and quicker innovations in international telephone services.

5.6 Conclusions

Business regulation defines the relationship between the government and business. It often alters the incentives and thus the conduct of the regulated firms. Hong Kong's business regulation is in a state of transition. Government regulation of monopolies by schemes of control in Hong Kong reached its peak in 1980s, when schemes were imposed on many public utilities, but most have now been dropped as the government has recognized their drawbacks and started to introduce competition into these industries. In sections 5.4 and 5.5, we used the electricity industry to illustrate the drawbacks of schemes of control and the telecommunications industry to illustrate the benefits of introducing competition into a regulated industry.[12]

Schemes of control in Hong Kong differ from rate-of-return regulation adopted in other economies in terms of the determination of returns, the presence of a development fund, the duration of agreements, and the price adjustment mechanism. They have failed to achieve their objectives for two reasons. First, like any rate-of-return regulation, the schemes provide a weak incentive for regulated firms to lower their costs and a perverse incentive for the firms to expand their fixed assets due to their peculiar way of determining returns (i.e., returns depending primarily on capital investment). Second, asymmetric information makes it very difficult, if not impossible, for the regulator to monitor regulated firms effectively and avoid being captured by them.

To introduce competition into the electricity industry, a necessary step would be the separation of electricity generation from its transmission and distribution. The newest technology for electricity generation and the scale of demand in Hong Kong can accommodate many small electricity firms that are able to operate at the minimum efficient scale, provided the transmission and distribution network is open to them. To achieve an open market for electricity, the government not only has to find a way to link up the transmission networks of the two geographical monopolies and have it managed by a separate company (i.e., a regulated monopoly) but also must find a way to introduce new entrants into a market that already suffers from huge excess capacity.

Failure by the government to forestall the perverse developments in this industry years ago has resulted in a messy situation from which there is no easy way out. To avoid aggravating the problem of excess capacity further, some arrangement would have to be sought to sell incumbent firms' existing capacity to new entrants. However, at present no competition and antitrust laws yet exist in Hong Kong to provide a legal basis for the government to impose such a solution.

The most competitive segment of the telecommunications industry is that for mobile communications services because the government has imposed minimal regulatory barriers to entry and because rapid technological innovations allow new entrants to put severe competitive pressure on incumbents. The local fixed telecommunications network service segment of the market comprises a dominant incumbent and three new entrants. The Hong Kong experience with this segment of the industry is that the regulator can play an important role in market liberalization by ensuring that adequate competition is developing and consumers' interests are protected.

---

12. Some studies show that direct competition between electric power companies causes firms to operate at lower average cost, sell electricity at lower prices, and avoid excess capacity. See, e.g., Primeaux (1986).

The least competitive segment is that for international telephone services. Under an agreement with the Hong Kong government in January 1998, HKTI's exclusive license on international telephone services was terminated. International services provided via HKTI will be open to competition in 1999 and international services provided via facilities of any party will be open to competition in 2000.

Looking beyond electricity and telecommunications, we can see changes in other public utility industries as well (see Cheng and Wu 1998 for details). As indicated in section 5.2 above, a new bus company has entered the public bus industry to join two incumbents, whose schemes of control were not renewed when they expired in August 1997. In addition, an open tendering system has replaced private negotiation as a mechanism for awarding bus routes. When the new Chek Lap Kok International Airport begins operation in 1998, two firms will compete for airport cargo services compared with a monopoly at present, and three firms for ramp-handling services compared with a monopoly now.

The progress in the past few years has encouraged policymakers to move ahead in the direction of regulatory reform and market liberalization. There is definitely room for both. Although the effort has already started to pay off, the pace of progress is uneven. The government has announced that it intends to open more markets to competition that until recently have been governed by exclusive franchises and will encourage further competition in markets that have already been opened.

These moves are expected to have a positive impact on productivity growth in these industries. However, the territorial monopolies in the electricity industry remain intact while they are still under schemes of control.

Even though competition in airport services will increase after the new airport is open in 1998, the nature of regulation will undergo a very fundamental, and perhaps bizarre, change. Air cargo service and ramp-handling service providers will no longer be subject to government regulation but will instead be "regulated" by the Airport Authority, a government-owned corporation that has a statutory obligation to conduct its business according to "prudential commercial principles." So far no details have been revealed about the way in which air cargo service and ramp-handling service providers will be regulated. However, if prudential commercial principles are to be the principal guidelines for the Airport Authority's business dealings with its franchisees, then the outcome would be achieved through negotiation between an upstream monopoly and a downstream duopoly or triopoly. In that case, it is not clear how well public interests will be served.

Less bizarre but equally problematic is the role of government-owned corporations in the public transport industry, namely, the Mass Transit Railway Corporation and the Kowloon Canton Railway Corporation. If these corporations continue to be primarily profit oriented, as they are now, then the government should introduce regulation to restrain their monopoly power and to protect consumers' interests.

In conclusion, to improve its regulatory regime or to bring about greater competition to industries that are traditionally regulated monopolies for the purpose of promoting economic efficiency, the government will have to formulate a comprehensive and sound public policy for each industry to guide its future initiatives.

References

Ansar, Jusmin. 1990. Multifactor productivity growth: Empirical results for a major United States utility. *Journal of Regulatory Economics* 2:251–62.

Armstrong, Mark, Simon Cowan, and John Vickers. 1994. *Regulatory reform: Economic analysis and British experience.* Cambridge, Mass.: MIT Press.

Averch, Harvey, and Leland L. Johnson. 1962. Behavior of the firm under regulatory constraint. *American Economic Review* 52 (December): 1052–69.

Cameron, Nigel. 1982. *Power: The story of China Light.* Hong Kong: Oxford University Press.

Cheng, Leonard K., and Changqi Wu. 1998. *Competition policy and regulation of business.* Hong Kong: City University of Hong Kong Press.

Fama, Eugene, and Kenneth French. 1992. The cross-section of expected stock returns. *Journal of Finance* 47 (2): 427–65.

Gollop, Frank, and Mark Roberts. 1981. The sources of economic growth in the U.S. electric power industry. In *Productivity measurement in regulated industries,* ed. Thomas G. Cowing and Rodney E. Stevenson. New York: Academic Press.

Hall, Christopher. 1996. *The uncertain hand: Hong Kong taxis and tenders.* Hong Kong: Chinese University Press.

Hong Kong Electric Company. 1997. *Hong Kong Electric Holdings Limited annual report.* Hong Kong: Hong Kong Electric Holdings Ltd.

Hong Kong Government. 1988. *The schemes of control.* Hong Kong: Government Printer.

———. Economic Services Branch. 1997. *China Light and Power's excess generating capacity.* Hong Kong: Government Printer, May.

———. Office of Telecommunications Authority. 1994. *Position paper: Hong Kong's telecommunications policy.* Hong Kong: Government Printer.

Hong Kong Telecom. 1997. *Hong Kong Telecommunications Limited annual report.* Hong Kong: Hong Kong Telecommunications Ltd.

International Energy Agency. 1997. *Electricity information.* Paris: OECD Publications.

Kwan, Y. K. Fred, and Ivan P. L. Png. 1994. Hong Kong and China Gas Company: Total factor productivity. Hong Kong: Hong Kong University of Science and Technology. Mimeograph.

Lam, Pun-Lee. 1997. *Competition in energy.* Hong Kong: City University of Hong Kong Press.

Leeds, Peter F. 1984. *The development of public transport in Hong Kong: A historical review, 1841–1974.* Hong Kong: Government Printer.

Peles, Yoram, and Gred Whittred. 1996. Incentive effects of rate of returns regulation: The case of Hong Kong electric utilities. *Journal of Regulatory Economics* 10:91–112.

Primeaux, Walter J., Jr. 1986. Competition between electric utilities. In *Electric power deregulation and the public policy,* ed. John C. Moorhouse. San Francisco: Pacific Research Institute for Public Policy.

Stigler, George, and Claire Friedland. 1962. What can regulators regulate: The case of electricity. *Journal of Law and Economics* 5:1–15.

Vickrey, William. 1971. Responsive pricing of public utility services. *Bell Journal of Economics and Management Science* 2:337–46.

Comment   Thomas Gale Moore

I learned a lot from Changqi Wu and Leonard Cheng's paper on Hong Kong's business regulation. What I found most remarkable was that Hong Kong introduced competition into the local phone market but has maintained a monopoly in the potentially more competitive international market. The authors report that HKTC was given monopoly rights for twenty years from 1975 and that 80 percent of any return over 16 percent was to go to a development fund. They also report that the development fund was exhausted in 1991. It would have been very instructive had the authors spelled out how the development fund approach actually worked. As I understand the development fund approach, the accumulated funds can be used either for investment or to lower rates to consumers. Was the HKTC development fund exhausted because it was used for investment, which incidentally would go into the rate base, justifying greater profits, or was it used to reduce rates? Since four companies have rushed in to offer competition with the phone company, the latter seems unlikely.

This brings me to a fundamental problem with regulation that is too often overlooked. The regulator gets most of its information from the regulatee. The regulated company has incentives to hire the best accountants and lawyers to make its case. The data can be presented selectively, fudged, or even made up. How much will demand grow? If it grows rapidly, more investment is needed than if it is only slowly expanding. Do the workers need ten urinals for every twenty workers or would five be enough? Does the firm need copper piping, stainless steel boilers, gold wiring, more space to park vehicles, better vehicles that break down less often, or bigger offices? Must the firm have the latest computers, connections to the Internet, its own power source in case the purchased electricity fails? I could go on, but the idea is clear.

The real question is, Can regulation be made to work? Or will it always

Thomas Gale Moore is a senior fellow at the Hoover Institution, Stanford University.

be a tool of the regulated to protect their franchises? George Stigler and Claire Friedland (1962) in a famous paper on electric utility regulation failed to find that regulation lowered rates. I did a study of electric power rates (Moore 1970) using data from the 1960s and came to the same conclusion: that is, regulation had little effect in reducing rates below what they would have been had the firm simply priced monopolistically without any controls and without fear of competition.

Primeaux has shown from examples and statistical evidence that competition in electric power can work and has worked. He has spelled this out in various studies (see Primeaux 1986). Direct competition existed between two or more electric power companies in forty-nine cities over 2,500 population in the United States in 1966. He reports that competition causes firms to operate at lower average cost. Distribution firms that have monopolies fail to exhibit lower costs than those under competition. Florida has a system of wholesale electricity competition that improves efficiency and reduces wholesale electric costs. Primeaux concludes that "direct competition is feasible between utility firms." He also reports that "competition causes firms to operate at lower costs, sell electricity at lower prices, operate without engaging in price wars, and avoid excess capacity" (Primeaux 1986, 422).

Although Hong Kong's readiness to endorse and encourage competition in local phone service is admirable, its failure to do so in the bus area is unfortunate. It has franchised four companies, each of which has a territorial monopoly. The government apparently argues that complete deregulation of public bus service is not practical because, without a monopoly franchise, "loss-incurring services cannot be provided." Before airlines were deregulated in the United States the same argument was made. The airlines "proved" that without regulation they would only serve the biggest hubs and most cities would lose service. We know that did not happen.

Trucking companies maintained that they needed regulation to continue to offer service in small communities. Actually, they failed to offer service in places where it was not profitable, and service has improved since deregulation.

Meyer and Gomez-Ibanez have shown that "the benefits of privatization and deregulation depend critically on whether effective competition can be established and maintained. . . . When competition exists, deregulation and privatization have great potential to reduce costs and improve the quality of urban bus services" (1993, 28). They go on to suggest that minibus services, shared-ride taxis, jitneys, or motorized tricycles often provide good competition. Not only does competition cut rates but it often "improves productivity and encourages more market-oriented services."

Universal service need not be mandated. It is noteworthy that Federal Express provides service to every community in the United States at a fixed rate. Clearly, the costs of serving small rural areas are much higher than those of serving big cities. Why does FedEx do this? Because it makes economic sense to market universal service.

If there are areas in Hong Kong to which bus service would not be offered because demand is too low or costs are too high, then the government could offer subsidies. It could ask for bids from bus companies to provide the service. Are jitneys permitted in Hong Kong?

I was also struck with the limited competition in the ferry market. Why not competition? The ferry market is much like the bus market or the airline market, one that could easily be competitive.

Hong Kong, which relies on trading and is one of the great ports of the world, has granted an exclusive license to one firm to provide air cargo services. This sector is much too important to be monopolized. Rate-of-return regulation will not work for the reasons that I have already outlined. This system will change to a duopoly. In addition, the government proposes that a state-owned firm do the regulating. Although I am a great supporter of privatization, I find this bizarre. This new entity will "have no obligation to reveal the methods and terms of regulation" according to the authors. Who is kidding whom? Who is paying whom? A duopoly is an improvement over a monopoly, but more competition would be better yet.

In summary, I learned a lot, especially about the problems Hong Kong is experiencing with making regulation work. The authors admit that the evidence suggests the Hong Kong program for regulation fosters more fixed assets than in the United States. They report that the electric utility companies have great excess capacity. Regulation has fostered and in fact maintained regional monopolies in buses, ferries, and electric power plants. Faith in regulation is like Samuel Johnson's remark on someone marrying for the second time, "It was the triumph of hope over experience."

References

Meyer, John, and Jose Gomez-Ibanez. 1993. Transit bus privatization and deregulation around the world: Some perspectives and lessons. In *Regulatory reform in transport: Some recent experiences,* ed. José Carbajo. World Bank symposium on Transportation Deregulation. Washington, D.C.: World Bank.

Moore, Thomas Gale. 1970. The effectiveness of regulation of electric utility prices. *Southern Economic Journal* 36 (4): 365–95.

Primeaux, Walter J., Jr. 1986. Competition between electric utilities. In *Electric power deregulation and the public interest,* ed. John C. Moorhouse, 395–423. San Francisco: Pacific Research Institute for Public Policy.

Stigler, George, and Claire Friedland. 1962. What can regulators regulate? The case of electricity. *Journal of Law and Economics* 5 (October): 1–15.

Comment   Roger G. Noll

Wu and Cheng provide some fascinating information about the history of electricity and telecommunications in Hong Kong. Their paper provides an important piece of the larger puzzle concerning the effects of neoliberal reform of infrastructural industries throughout the world. Surely the 1990s has proved to be the decade of grand experimentation in industrial policy in developed and developing countries alike. The theme of reform is broadly similar across numerous countries: to replace ubiquitous monopoly providers (usually public enterprise) with competition where possible, and to use regulatory instruments with much sharper incentives for cost minimization and technological innovation where monopoly seems durable. Nevertheless, each country has developed some unique elements of its reform policy, and variation among these countries provides interesting and useful information about how best to organize the reform.

My purpose in this comment is to place the Hong Kong case in a broader context of reform in electricity and telecommunications throughout the world. The Hong Kong case provides insights about several policy choices that reformers face in all nations. The first choice pertains to the regulatory institutions and methods for protecting consumers against monopoly abuses either permanently if monopoly is expected to endure or temporarily during the transition to a market competitive enough that regulation is no longer needed or desirable. The second decision is about the scope of permitted competition: in which markets will competitors be allowed and where will monopoly be protected? The third decision concerns the degree to which the government will be proactive in facilitating competition: will it intervene to establish regulatory rules on such matters as vertical integration and interconnection that anticipate and prevent anticompetitive actions by the incumbent monopolist, or will it rely on market opportunities, private litigation, and competition policy to sort out the ultimate industry structure and relations among horizontal competitors?

Although I cannot offer a definitive assessment of the situation in Hong Kong based solely on the essay by Wu and Cheng, my overall impression is that Hong Kong has been excessively solicitous in protecting the interests of the old monopoly enterprises. The regulatory system and background competition policy appear to be relatively timid in imposing risks on incumbent firms, with the main consequence being not only less competition than might otherwise be possible but also relatively inefficient provision of services to customers. Indeed, I interpret the performance information that the authors provide about electricity and telecommunica-

Roger G. Noll is the Morris M. Doyle Professor of Public Policy, Department of Economics, Stanford University, and nonresident senior fellow at the Brookings Institution.

tions in Hong Kong as confirming theoretical predictions from economics concerning the costly effects of regulatory rules that create perverse financial incentives and that limit the incursion of competition into the marketplace.

Regulatory System

The Hong Kong system of regulating profits and prices in these sectors is, to the best of my knowledge, unique in the world. The authors describe the system as a modified "rate-of-return" regulatory system, but this terminology surely is an injustice to the remarkable perversity of the Hong Kong approach. With all its flaws, rate-of-return regulation actually is not all that horrific a means for controlling monopoly prices. Economists rightly emphasize the superiority of price-cap regulation, but prior to the introduction of incentive regulation schemes in the 1980s, countries that practiced rate-of-return regulation enjoyed clearly superior performance in infrastructural industries, especially in telecommunications. The key weaknesses of rate-of-return regulation were that it imposed impossible information requirements on regulators and that it had the perverse effect that as regulators did a better job of solving their information problems—for example, measuring costs and demand elasticities—the distorting incentives of regulation on factor proportions (the Averch-Johnson bias in favor of capital-intensive technology) became worse. Regulators responded to this problem by imposing "used and useful" tests on capital investments, which created a burden of proof on firms to show that an investment was necessary and cost-effective before it could be added to the cost basis for setting prices. Whereas this test itself imposed impossible information requirements on regulators, at least it was likely to prevent unlimited substitution of capital for other inputs and excessive investments in quality that were predicted by the theoretical models.

The regulatory system in Hong Kong is at best a distant cousin of this system. The only connection between Hong Kong's scheme and rate-of-return regulation is that the latter is used to set a baseline revenue requirement in the short run. In reality, all forms of economic regulation must have this feature. The fundamental fact of price regulation is that unless it falls into the extreme cases of expropriation or government-protected monopoly (pure "capture" by the regulated firm), in the long run it must satisfy two criteria: nonbankruptcy of the incumbent firm and something less than monopoly pricing. Even price-cap regulation is initialized and then updated by traditional cost-based regulation. The theoretically pure price-cap system, in which prices are perpetually adjusted annually according to some arbitrary but permanent formula (such as the CPI-X), has never been implemented because no value of X has a zero probability of both bankruptcy and monopoly pricing. In fact, even a small error in

X will cumulate over even a few years to either subcompetitive or near-monopoly profits and so will require adjustment. In every case in which a price-cap formula has been adopted, within a few years it has proved to be politically unacceptable for one or another reason and has been altered. Usually, the mistake has been to make the formula too generous, arising from a persistent tendency for political authorities to underestimate the efficiency benefits of sharp incentives. Hence, over a decade or two, X generally grows as regulated firms find unpredicted ways to reduce costs when they can keep all or most of the cost reductions.

The crucial feature of the Hong Kong price regulation system is the peculiar role of the "development fund." Firms are allowed a fixed profit, determined by the product of their capital investments and an allowed rate of return. But unlike in traditional rate-of-return regulation, the profit constraint does not cap either prices or revenues. Instead, the excess of revenues over costs plus allowed profit is placed in a fund.[1] The firm can borrow from this fund at 8 percent or can save the fund. In the latter case, 8 percent of the fund is returned to ratepayers through rate reductions. Thus, if the firm invests the fund, next year it earns its allowed return on the original capital stock plus the allowed return minus 8 percent on the investment. If the firm does not invest the fund, in the next period it will earn its allowed profit on the original investment. Hence, as the authors correctly reason, investing the fund, even in useless investments ("gold plating"), always dominates saving the fund as long as the allowed rate of return is less than monopoly profits. One would predict, then, that both electricity and telecommunications firms would embark on a mad dash to invest as much as possible. In fact, this is the case. Telecommunications has invested its fund to zero, and electricity is madly adding generation facilities despite widespread excess capacity. Meanwhile, customers pay unusually high prices for both services.

The Hong Kong system is even worse than this, however. First, it lacks the feature of a standard used and useful test of rate-of-return regulation. Hence, the regulators apparently do not inquire whether an investment is worth making. As a result, overinvestment can be expected to be worse under the Hong Kong scheme than under the standard rate-of-return system. Second, once a firm invests so much that the rate-of-return constraint is no longer binding, there is an incentive for still more investment. The reason is that if any fund remains, and the firm is not reaching its rate-of-return target, it can pay itself from the fund to reach its profit target. Hence, the Hong Kong system creates an even greater incentive for excessive capital intensity, excessive quality, and gold plating than does a rate-of-return scheme that lacks a used and useful test. One wonders what in

---

1. In telecommunications, the firm keeps 20 percent of the fund as profit sharing and places 80 percent of excess profits in the fund.

the world political officials were thinking when they adopted such a ridiculously perverse system!

Competition versus Monopoly

Another important feature of the Hong Kong system is that it does not really take seriously the possibility of introducing competition. The basis for this conclusion varies somewhat in the two industries, so each needs to be discussed separately.

Electricity

In electricity, the first step in moving toward competition is to allow entry into generation. In Hong Kong, apparently entry in generation—indeed, in every aspect of the industry, including retail distribution—is technically permitted; however, the circumstances created by the perversities of the price regulation scheme make entry completely implausible. In generation, as the authors note, the two monopolies that share Hong Kong have so overinvested in capacity that no sensible company would enter, even if the government prohibited the entrants from building any more generation facilities. The reason, of course, is that the existing capacity is more than adequate to satisfy all demand for the indefinite future. Without a requirement to buy power from others, the incumbents have neither a need nor a financial incentive to buy anything from an entrant. And a requirement to buy externally would just add to the excess capacity of the system.

Thus the only viable means for introducing competition into this sector is divestiture: to split generation from transmission and distribution, and to create a market in which distribution companies buy power competitively. To accomplish this task would require two additional policies. First, because electricity distribution in Hong Kong would be a duopoly, without adding more buyers the result of a wholesale electricity market would be monopsony prices that prevent generation firms from recovering the cost of capital. Second, because generation capacity substantially exceeds demand in Hong Kong, for a long while the competitive equilibrium price also would be too low to allow the recovery of all capital costs.

To solve these problems requires some combination of the following proactive government structural policies. To reduce concentration on the demand side of the market, two possibilities could be pursued. One is further to divest the distribution companies, creating a half-dozen instead of two. Another is to use some of the development fund to connect Hong Kong generation facilities to power systems in neighboring areas of China, and to introduce competition in generation in these regions as well. The latter move might solve some of the excess capacity problem, but if it does not solve it all (or if this reform is politically infeasible), something else must be done to produce a realistic initial capitalization for generation facilities. The most efficient solution would be simply to spin off generation facilities into a number of competitive suppliers, and to subtract the depreciated book value of the generators from the rate base of the incumbents. Unfortunately, most nations have found this approach to be either illegal (an uncompensated expropriation) or politically infeasible. Assuming that this approach cannot be implemented, another possibility is a simplified version of the "efficient components pricing rule"—to auction off generation units (with limits on the number of units that could be owned by a single buyer to ensure that generation becomes structurally competitive) and then to subtract only the auction proceeds from the rate base of the incumbent companies. Generation facilities would then sell for prices based on their expected operating margins, not their book value or replacement cost (both of which are likely to be higher than their economic value). In this case, retail prices would still reflect the inefficiencies of the excessive investments of the incumbents, but at least the generation sector would face incentives for more efficient operation.

The point behind identifying the rough dimensions of a procompetitive policy in electricity is to contrast the circumstances in Hong Kong with those that one might find in a nation that was serious about improving the performance of the electricity sector through the introduction of competition. The scheme described above captures some benefits of competition immediately, and growing benefits over time as demand grows, generation equipment is retired, and new capacity begins to be added because it makes sense to do so, rather than because the peculiar incentives of the price regulation system encourage it. At the same time, it protects the investment of the incumbents, however foolish they might have been. The failure to introduce these reforms, then, has to be for reasons that go beyond the desire to assure incumbents a nice return on their existing investments. The behavior of the Hong Kong government is consistent with only two explanations: the government either is irrational or is motivated to perpetuate the inefficiency and high profitability of the status quo.

Telecommunications

Telecommunications policy in Hong Kong is not nearly as anticompetitive as electricity policy. Hong Kong has allowed competition in all elements of the industry except international calling.

The international calling system is worth a paragraph, even though Hong Kong is hardly alone in this area. Like nearly all countries, Hong Kong still succumbs to the allure of the perverse incentives of the international system for regulating prices. In brief, nearly all nations cannot resist vigorously playing the negative sum game of bloated terminating international access charges. In essence, the standard bilateral arrangement in telecommunications is that the calling party must pay half of the "official calling rate" (a bloated, monopoly price) to the local access carrier that terminates the call. Thus receiving calls is outrageously profitable, and almost everywhere these excess profits are then used to subsidize basic local access. But because both nations practice this pricing policy, each is in the position of paying roughly the same amount of subsidy for local access to the other, with one receiving some trivial net benefit if it terminates more calls than it originates. Meanwhile, both are substantially harmed by international prices that vastly exceed costs, in some cases by a factor of one hundred to one. This pricing policy not only causes a substantial deadweight loss to international callers but creates a very large incentive to spend money to evade the system on such things as "callback" and private systems.

In other aspects of telecommunications, Hong Kong has adopted most of the policies necessary to promote effective competition. First, it has adopted number portability, which reduces the switching costs of customers who change carriers. Second, it has sought to prevent anticompetitive pricing by incumbent monopolists, although the method is the crude one of demanding uniform pricing. Nevertheless, because Hong Kong is so urbanized, this policy is certainly less distorting than it would be in a nation with a large rural sector, so perhaps the simplicity of the approach is worth the relatively small distortions it will create. Third, Hong Kong has allocated spectrum in a manner that allows competition in wireless telephony. Unfortunately, the paper gives us few details here, such as how the spectrum is allocated and what technical conditions are placed on the licensees that might inhibit direct competition between wireline and wireless service. In the United States, for example, only in the 1990s were radio telephone companies permitted to use technologies that provided less mobility but had low costs, which is the necessary step if wireless and wireline services are to be close substitutes.

Unfortunately, Hong Kong has sacrificed a great deal of the potential benefits of competition by its regulations regarding universal service and interconnection pricing. The paper does not present the details of the universal service policy, so a thorough evaluation is not possible. Some key missing ingredients are as follows. First, what is the penetration of the phone system, which is relevant to assessing whether the universal service subsidy is necessary to achieve penetration among households who cannot afford it or whether it is primarily an unnecessary tax subsidy system aimed at middle-class households and businesses. Second, the paper implies, but does not actually state, that Hong Kong practices what might be called gross universal service subsidies—that is, it underprices basic access to everyone, not just to those who need it. If so, even if penetration among lower income households is nontrivial, it is achieved at a huge cost in terms of subsidies to those who do not need it, financed by excess prices on other services (like calling charges) charged to exactly the same people.

In any case, all we know from the paper is that the incumbents carry the universal service obligation and in return collect huge subsidies.

One source of this subsidy is the interconnection charge. Briefly, the interconnection charge is the price one company pays to terminate a call to a customer who is served by another company. In Hong Kong, the price that has been set by the incumbent wireline carriers is 9¢ per minute. (The authors report that the regulators have not ruled on this fee.) This price is outrageously high in comparison to costs. In most countries, the price per minute for local calls, originating and terminating in the same company, is less than this. Prices for mobile phone carriers are 6.7¢ and for value-added carriers (those who lease facilities from the incumbent carriers) are 4.2¢. These, too, are ridiculously high and are clearly designed to inhibit competition. In Hong Kong, the authors tell us that residential customers have free local calling. But a competing local access provider must pay the interconnection charge if its customer calls a customer of the incumbent.

In the pricing domain, the paper provides data from the International Telecommunication Union (ITU) about residential telephone pricing. These data are very inaccurate for the United States and so distort the comparisons. The ITU data for the United States are wrong on three counts. First, the monthly service charge is understated because it does not include the "customer access charge" for long-distance service (which is mandatory). Second, the price reported in the table is the "lifeline" price, available to households that have low incomes. The actual average monthly access price in the United States is about $18 for ordinary households and $11 for low-income households, including both local and long-distance access charges.[2] Third, the usage charge is wrong because it is actually the long-distance usage rate charged by one carrier (New York Telephone) for calls outside of a customer's local calling area (but not so far as to be picked up by a long-distance carrier). In reality, the vast majority of local customers have free local calling, and very few calls are actually charged the rate reported by the ITU. Finally, price comparisons are meaningless without including all calling prices, not just the price of a local call. The main reason for high access prices in the United States is that interconnection fees and hence prices for long-distance calls are far lower than elsewhere. Indeed, 9¢ a minute is closer to the price of a 2,500-mile long-distance call in the United States than to a local call, even for business customers who buy local measured service.

The important fact about the table of telephone prices is how low residential access charges are. One cannot imagine a circumstance in which the average cost of providing service is anywhere near this low, even if the

2. For comparisons of the entire pricing structure in Japan and the United States, see Noll and Rosenbluth (1995).

incumbent carrier is highly efficient. Hence, the Hong Kong system must feature other prices that are far above cost and that generate access subsidies. Because access demand is very price inelastic, a nation with low access prices inevitably will have a very inefficient telephone system—and an incumbent telephone company that is reluctant to make investments to provide access service to customers who do not buy the highly profitable services.

The solution to this problem is realistic pricing. One benefit of competitive entry is that it attacks massive cross-subsidy systems by attracting entrants to services that are heavily taxed. The only effective ways to stop this entry are either to prohibit it or to tax it. Apparently Hong Kong has tried the latter by imposing very high interconnection fees in order to protect an inefficient price structure.

Comparing Electricity and Telephones: A Paradox

The electricity and telephone policies seem to have quite different motives and consequences. In electricity, the policy seems consistent with a capture story: incumbent firms make supracompetitive profits, and prices seem to be very high across the board. In telecommunications, the policy is protective of incumbent wireline carriers, but not to the degree that appears to have arisen in electricity. Instead, the policy seems to be to engage in a great deal of cross-subsidization of access by international calling, radio telephony, and other things unspecified in the paper. The paradox is why these policies are so different.

The authors offer two characterizations of policy that inferentially might provide an explanation. First, the authors state early on that some aspects of these industries might be natural monopolies. The subsequent analysis of the two industries, however, is not consistent with this explanation, for generation remains monopolized even though experience elsewhere has demonstrated that it need not be. Second, the authors state that the government regards advanced telecommunications services as essential to continued economic progress in the modern world economy. But this belief, even if true, is not consistent with policy, for the effect of policy is to tax usage, which taxes advanced services, in order to subsidize ordinary telephone access.

The puzzle, then, is what in the political economy of Hong Kong has caused the divergence in policy between the two sectors? The basis for the decision to let telecommunications carriers have profit sharing, but not the electric utility, is far from obvious: why do these policies differ? Hong Kong has chosen two quite different ways to encourage inefficiency in electricity and telecommunications, with apparently different lineups of beneficiaries for these distorting policies. An interesting question is why these differences were adopted.

Reference

Noll, Roger G., and Frances M. Rosenbluth. 1995. Telecommunications policy: Structure, process, outcomes. In *Structure and policy in Japan and the United States,* ed. Peter F. Cowhey and Mathew D. McCubbins, 119–76. New York: Cambridge University Press.

6

Toward a More Liberal Sky in Japan
An Evaluation of Policy Change

Hirotaka Yamauchi

6.1 Introduction

In Japan, we are now facing a powerful policy trend reconsidering the role of the government in economic policy, and a consensus is emerging that deregulation is the only way to revitalize the economy as a whole, to recover international competitiveness, and to benefit consumers. But sometimes even those who advocate deregulation as a general economic principle will object to policy change because an individual policy is likely to hurt their interests. This tendency is a general truth all over the world, but it seems to me that we Japanese do not have as much confidence in the market mechanism as Anglo-Saxon countries, and that this is a reason why dramatic policy change cannot happen in Japan.

Naturally, transport policies in Japan are very conservative. Entry and policing have been regulated tightly in almost all transport modes and the room for effective competition among carriers is very restricted, though procompetitive policies have been adopted recently, especially since the mid-1980s.

Air transport policy is no exception. The air transport industry has been and still is regulated by the Ministry of Transport (MoT) based on the Civil Aeronautics Law, although some changes were made to introduce a competitive situation in the past decade. As is well known, the worldwide trend is to deregulate the airline industry and to promote competition in both domestic and international markets, making the markets more efficient and increasing consumer benefits. However, the changes in Japanese

Hirotaka Yamauchi is professor of transport economics in the Faculty of Commerce, Hitotsubashi University.

air transport policy are gradual and step by step and far from the total deregulation introduced in the United States in 1978.

Such cautious policy operations could be appropriate given the general dislike ordinary Japanese people have for radical policy change. The most important point, however, is whether or not the true purpose of the policy change is to reform the industrial structure significantly, and from the viewpoint of economists, this is not the case in the air transport industry. Air transport passengers hardly realize any economic benefits from the policy changes. For example, the Japanese government introduced a zone fare system in domestic markets on 1 June 1996 and fares became much more diverse than before, but some consumers criticized the diversity of fares and some complained about the fare hikes they were forced to face. The essence of this policy failure is clearly the lack of effective competition even on "double or triple trucking" routes, where two or three carriers offer services, and the difficulties faced by new carriers trying to enter markets.

The purpose of this paper is to survey and to evaluate air transport policy in Japan. In section 6.2 I investigate the history of air transport policy, and in section 6.3 I examine briefly the effect of policy changes made in the past decade. In section 6.4 international air transport aspects will be discussed, and I will try to make some assessment of the policy in section 6.5.

6.2   Regulatory Mechanisms

The Japanese air transport market developed in a strictly regulated environment. The Civil Aeronautics Law, which governs the industry, requires that firms obtain government licenses to enter the market. Airlines also need government approval for their fares, and even for their annual business plans. Naturally, international routes also require government-negotiated bilateral agreements with other countries. In this, Japan has been a traditionalist. The agreements the Japanese government has concluded with other countries are generally modeled on the old Bermuda Agreement, reached in 1944 between the United States and United Kingdom.

6.2.1   Industrial Policy in Air Transport: An Old Regime

Just after World War II, commercial aviation in Japan was banned by the Allied forces, and it was not until 1951 that a Japanese airline was allowed to commence service. In that year, the oldest airline, Japan Airlines (JAL) was founded as a private company, but in 1953 the company was reorganized as a special public corporation. The purpose of this reorganization was to strengthen JAL's international competitiveness.

Also in 1953, two domestic carriers were founded and started service. However, both companies were in poor financial condition, so the Japanese government proposed that they merge into one company and they did so in 1958. This was the birth of All Nippon Airways (ANA) and the first stage of the industrial consolidation in aviation by governmental initiative.

Besides JAL and ANA, six regional carriers were founded in the late 1950s. These carriers also suffered from deficits. Some of them were merged into ANA, but two of them, Japan Domestic Airways and Toa Airways survived until the end of the 1960s. In the second half of the 1960s, Japan Domestic developed a cooperative arrangement with ANA, as Toa did with JAL. As a result, it was thought to be appropriate that each company merge with its partner.

However, this prediction was never realized because the government changed its policy. The Cabinet Meeting Resolution Concerning Airline Operations of 1970 suggested that Japan Domestic and Toa should merge into one company and that commercial aviation in Japan should be operated by a three-company system: JAL, ANA, and Toa Domestic Airways (TDA), which was the company that Japan Domestic and Toa formed.

The government had several reasons for choosing the three-airline system over the two-airline system. First, air transport demand at that time was growing quickly, and this was part of the official reasoning for the necessity of third airline. Second, there was strong political pressure from a particular corporate group to make a third airline, and this pressure could change government policy—though this was not part of the official reasoning. In any case, the birth of TDA was the second stage of the industrial consolidation by governmental initiative.

The government not only initiated the consolidation policy but also used regulatory mechanisms to establish the three-company system. In 1972, the MoT announced the Ministry Guidance Regarding Airline Operations, which gave JAL international business and domestic trunk routes, ANA short-distance international charters and domestic operations, and TDA domestic local routes and some trunk route services.

The intention of this system was to stabilize the business condition of the three companies. According to the government's understanding at that time, the Japanese airline business was in its infancy and so unstable enough that it could not survive in a competitive environment. Since the only lucrative markets for Japanese carriers were domestic trunk routes (Sapporo-Tokyo-Osaka-Fukuoka-Naha), whether or not carriers could obtain licenses to operate on trunk routes was a crucial factor for their business.

The 1970 cabinet resolution consolidated two rather small companies into a relatively big one and made it possible to derive economies of scale. It also meant that TDA got the ability to offer proper services on large trunk routes and that it could use money from trunk routes to compensate deficits on local routes. Things were the same for the other two airlines.

JAL could make up losses incurred in international services and ANA could cross-subsidize losses on domestic local routes, both using surpluses from trunk routes.

The cabinet resolution and the 1972 ministry guidance were together called the "aviation constitution" because they determined the basic market structure of the Japanese airline industry and because airlines could not expand their business beyond the assigned fields. This "old regime" was intended to secure and nurture the capacity of all the airline companies by establishing segmented business fields for each firm. Segmentation of markets was also a common feature of Japanese industrial policy in the 1950s, 1960s, and early 1970s. In air transport, route-licensing regulation made the segmentation concrete and trunk route markets offered a base for financial stability and a source for cross-subsidization.

The old regime survived until the mid-1980s, with all three firms growing steadily within their arranged business bases. The air transport market as a whole grew rapidly with the help of the great economic expansion in Japan, and the route network was widened. Governmental intervention in the form of protection for an infant industry could be said to have functioned adequately up to this stage.

But the most serious problem of this cartel-oriented government policy was the high-cost nature of Japanese airlines brought about by protection from competition, and this problem remained even after the circumstances surrounding the airline industry changed. The government did not face up to the reality of the market and was unwilling to discard old beliefs in regulatory mechanisms. In the earlier stage, the benefits of a wider network and stability in service provision might, to some extent, have outweighed the costs of distorting allocative efficiency. This ranking of cost and benefit soon reversed, however, because as the airlines matured operational inefficiencies grew and consumers were forced to bear unnecessary cost increases.

In the 1960s and early 1970s, consolidating small companies into large ones was a common measure in Japan's general industrial policy. As a matter of form, the government-initiated mergers in the airline industry resemble the industrial policies pursued by the Ministry of International Trade and Industry in such fields as iron and automobile manufacturing. But there was a clear difference between the consolidations in the airline industry and those in other fields: while keen competition both domestically and internationally played a major role in other industries, in air transport, the leading actor was the government itself, which prevented the market from working effectively.

6.2.2   Policy Change in the Past Decade

The old air transport regime collapsed in the mid-1980s. The trigger was the conclusion of the Japan-U.S. Aviation Treaty Interim Agreement of 1985 and the signing of its memorandum of understanding. As already stated, the strategy of the Japanese government in the 1970s was to limit international scheduled carrier service to JAL, but for international air cargo transport, it was insisted that one more carrier should be allowed to provide service to meet the rapidly growing international air cargo demand. For this reason, a new airline, Nippon Cargo Airways (NCA), was formed, and it applied to the government for a route license to serve the north Pacific market. This application met with intense debate on whether or not the company should be licensed, but finally the government accepted it and started negotiating with the U.S. government over the entry of NCA into the north Pacific market. The 1985 interim agreement was the result of this negotiation.

The interim agreement admitted the new entry of NCA; moreover, it allowed other new carriers, from both Japan and the United States, to start scheduled passenger service. Naturally, to make this possible, it was necessary for the government to end JAL's scheduled international service monopoly among Japanese carriers. Around this time, calls for the liberalization of the Japanese domestic air industry also strengthened, and the Council for Transport Policy (an official advisory committee to the minister) announced its opinion that the old regime formed in the first half of the 1970s should be abolished, and that a more procompetitive air transport policy should be pursued. The content of its detailed advice was as follows:

1. International routes should be served by multiple carriers.
2. Competition on domestic routes should be promoted by new entry into particular city-pair markets.
3. JAL should be completely privatized.

After receiving the report, the Japanese government immediately issued a cabinet resolution abolishing the old regime. But with respect to domestic competition, the council argued that "an American style of deregulation does not suit the circumstances of Japan" because of the capacity limitations of Tokyo International (Haneda) Airport and Osaka International (Itami) Airport and the different competitive strengths of airlines. It is very common in every country that airport congestion problems impede fair market competition, but it seemed to be some kind of legacy from the paternalistic government policy of the old days that airlines' competitive strengths were taken into account in adopting a liberal policy.

Implementing a competition policy in the domestic market, the government set up a system whereby several carriers could enter each city-pair market. Under the criteria adopted, three companies could offer service on routes that carried one million passengers or more annually, and two companies on routes that carried 700,000 passengers or more annually. These criteria have been gradually relaxed since the introduction of the system.

The government has insisted that domestic aviation has become more competitive because of the new aviation policy adopted in 1986. However, the system has met strong criticisms that the government's regulation of fare approval and entry licensing has remained basically unchanged, so even though several carriers compete on the same routes, these routes are subject to an entirely uniform fare structure except for inclusive tour fares.

The government persisted in fare regulation in the early 1990s, while trying to evade criticism by relaxing entry conditions into double- or triple-trucking routes. The main reason why the government persisted in price regulation is that it knew intense competition between carriers would make it difficult to maintain thin local routes through cross-subsidies and it feared such a situation. Long-time regulation had created vested interests in subsidized areas, and these interests kept putting political pressure on the government. It was in 1995 that the MoT finally adopted a policy that made it easier to offer discounted fares. However, this policy could not calm the critics, and there emerged strong calls for further liberalization of airfares. Responding to these demands, the government adopted a zone fare system in 1996.

The zone fare system adopted in Japan is similar to that adopted by the European Community (now the European Union) before the third package of the Common Air Transport Policy was implemented in 1993. The system involves establishing a fixed price range and allowing carriers to set their airfares within that range at their own discretion. For example, carriers can set relatively high prices in peak travel periods and offer promotional fares during off-peak periods. Needless to say, this system allows carriers to respond to particular demand periods with a flexible fare structure. Carriers can introduce and set all types of discount fares, including advance purchase fares, to meet demand in different periods.

The upper limit of the permitted fare zone is initially calculated on the basis of the airlines' cost level. The lower end of the range is set at 25 percent less than the upper limit. This range is for normal fares. The carrier can set discount fares at most 50 percent below the lower limit. Logically, the deepest discount fare could be set at 62.5 percent off the upper limit fare, though it is not likely that such fares emerge. The possibility that fares diversify and are lower on average depends on the effectiveness of competition in each market. Again, the crucial point is barrier to new entries.[1]

As stated above, the MoT is maintaining the authority to issue route licenses, and this means the air transport market in Japan is still under regulation. But of course regulation is not the only barrier to new entry. Actually, the biggest problem is, as mentioned earlier, the limited capacity of Haneda Airport (airport capacity limitation in the Osaka area disappeared with the completion of Kansai International Airport). Haneda is

1. For details, see section 6.3 and Yamauchi (1996).

the biggest profit engine for domestic carriers, and any restriction on the number of landing slots poses a serious obstacle to new market entry.

In Japan, the MoT allocates landing slots for domestic flights, and there has been a widespread outcry over the opaqueness of the decision-making process. Mainly economists insist that the process should be based on an open and visible bidding system, or determined by a price mechanism such as peak load pricing. However, the MoT has expressed its concern that a bidding system or other market-oriented allocation mechanism would benefit those carriers with the largest current market shares and capital reserves and would only increase market differentials among the competing carriers.

The concern of the government could be reasonable, if we agreed that the purpose of air transport policy in Japan is to nurture the industry. However, Japanese air carriers have grown up, and this paternalistic policy stance has left the overwhelming problem of high costs among the carriers. It is market forces that drive airlines to be more efficient and more competitive, and effective competition among efficient carriers could produce benefits for consumers.[2]

6.3   An Evaluation of Market Competition

In this section I investigate briefly the changes caused by the new policy in the market structure of air transport in Japan.[3]

6.3.1   Demand Structure

The air transport market in Japan has been developing steadily. The five-year growth rates in the number of air passengers are 9.7 (1975–80), 1.6 (1980–85), 8.3 (1985–90), and 3.7 percent (1990–95). The trend is that air demand increase rates exceeded GDP growth rates except for the first half of 1980s, when the capacity of Haneda Airport was a bottleneck hindering supply increase. Thereafter, the expansion plan for Haneda was implemented, and capacity has been increased gradually.[4] As a result, the air transport market in Japan is not small for the geographical size of the country. Total revenue passenger kilometers in the domestic market are about 65 billion, which is one-tenth of that in United States, and the 78 million passengers on domestic routes are equivalent to one-sixth of the U.S. market (these data are for 1995).

---

2. On 5 December 1996, the MoT announced a new policy guideline, which is directed toward a more procompetitive situation. I will discuss this policy in section 6.5 briefly.

3. A more comprehensive analysis is done in Yamauchi and Murakami (1995).

4. The first phase of this expansion plan, including the opening of a new runway (called the New A), was completed in July 1988, and this spring another new runway (called the New C) was opened. New C expanded capacity substantially (13.8 percent), and this triggered new competition not only among incumbent carriers but also from new entrants.

Using time-series data for 1974–95, I estimated the aggregate demand function as follows:

$$\ln RPK = 10.157 - 0.741 \ln RFARE$$
$$(5.430) \quad (-3.665)$$

$$+ \; 1.292 \; \ln RGDP, \qquad \text{adjusted } R^2 = 0.982,$$
$$(12.782)$$

where RPK is revenue passenger kilometers, RFARE is real airfare (domestic yields per revenue passenger kilometer, deflated by the consumer price index), and RGDP is real GDP.[5]

Simple aggregate demand function analysis indicates that the long-term price elasticity of domestic air travel is about -0.74 and the long-term income elasticity is about $+1.29$. Compared with estimates by Ohta (1981), who suggests that the price and income elasticities are -0.83 and $+1.66$, respectively, our estimates show that income elasticity decreased because a newer data set was used. In any case, air travel in Japan's domestic market is a so-called normal good.

The most important feature of air transport demand in Japan is the concentration on Tokyo-related routes. Needless to say, Haneda Airport located in Tokyo is the busiest airport: it deals with about 55.1 percent of total air passengers in Japan (see fig. 6.1), although routes that originate or terminate at Haneda account for only 17.9 percent of all routes. Many dense markets are among the Haneda-related routes (see fig. 6.2), which include the Tokyo-Sapporo route, whose annual traffic is 7.6 million passengers, and the Tokyo-Fukuoka route, with 6.2 million passengers. As is well known, Tokyo-Sapporo is the biggest market in the world, and Tokyo-Fukuoka also ranks high by route density.[6] On the other hand, Osaka (Kansai)-Sapporo is the only route ranked among the ten biggest domestic markets in Japan other than Tokyo-related routes.

These features of Japan's air transport demand suggest that operating directly to and from Haneda is a crucial factor in an airline's ability to make profits. It may be possible for Japanese air carriers to operate healthy non-Tokyo routes, but it is clear that their high-cost nature prevents them from doing so, given the lack of workable competition.

6.3.2 Operators

Including the big three carriers, eight scheduled airline companies operate in Japan. Two, Japan Asia Airlines (JAA) and NCA, offer only international service, and two others, Japan Trans-Ocean Airlines (JTA) and Ja-

---

5. I estimated several other functional forms including a dummy variable that stands for significant fatal accidents, but the simplest one, cited above, was the best fit.

6. The top three markets in the United States are New York–Los Angeles, New York–Chicago, and New York–Washington, D.C. Annual traffic on each of these routes is between 2.5 and 2.7 million passengers.

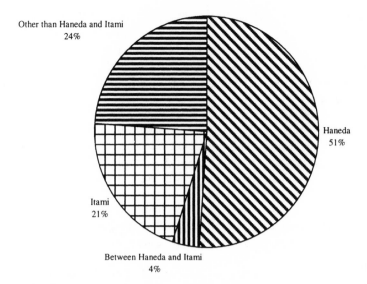

Fig. 6.1   Passenger shares of Haneda, Itami, and other airports

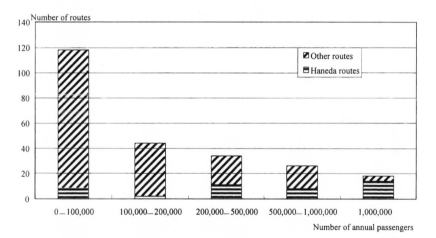

Fig. 6.2   Route structure of air transport in Japan

pan Air Commuter (JAC), are solely domestic carriers. The remaining company, Air Nippon (ANK), is mainly domestic but recently started one international route: Fukuoka-Taipei.

The biggest airline in Japan is JAL. In 1995, JAL carried about 72.4 billion RPK in domestic and international markets, which is half to a third of the traffic of an American megacarrier. The second carrier ANA's output was about 43.8 billion RPK, and that of Japan Air Systems (JAS; formerly TDA) was 13.7 billion RPK.

When the Japanese economy enjoyed an overheated business boom from the end of the 1980s to the beginning of the 1990s, the airlines also made big profits. After that period, as the economy decelerated, the business condition of the airlines declined too, and they began to accrue big deficits. Only now are business conditions in the air transport market becoming stable, but as we shall see later, airlines are still undergoing business restructuring.

As pointed out in section 6.2, one purpose of tight regulation in Japanese air transport market is to maintain cross-subsidization between trunk routes and local routes. This means that air carriers whose main business is in local markets may well have a lot of unprofitable routes, but since in Japan profit and loss accounts by route are not transparent, we cannot analyze the cross-subsidization mechanism in detail. Sometimes it is said that two-thirds of JAS's routes are loss making, and this assertion then grounds objections to a system of free entry and exit. According to the general claim, under such a system, routes for which demand is thin and that are therefore unprofitable will likely be abandoned, and the welfare of passengers on such routes without substitutable transport modes will suffer.

But from the viewpoint of economists, the best solution to this problem is to maintain services by general subsidy from the government. Such measures have been implemented in the United States as the Essential Air Service Program and are also provided in the third package of the Common Air Transport Policy in the European Union. The Japanese government is now groping for a new direct subsidy system to be implemented at the next stage of air transport liberalization.[7]

6.3.3   Market Structure

In the old regime, ANA had a major share of the domestic market, but since 1986 its share has gradually declined. As figure 6.3 shows, ANA's share dropped from 57.4 percent in 1985 to 47.2 percent in 1994. In a sense, this was a result of the liberalization of domestic air transport markets, but it should be noted that the shares of ANA's competitors did not increase dramatically. JAL and JAS raised their shares from 23.3 to 26.7 percent and 17.2 to 19.9 percent, respectively, but at the same time, ANK, which is a subsidiary of ANA, increased its share by 2.5 percentage points. ANA transferred its unprofitable routes to its subsidiary to make its own financial position healthier. In conclusion, the policy adopted in the mid-1980s has not led to a radical change in market structure.

There are some reasons why ANA has not lost share dramatically. ANA has a strong sales network and brand loyalty in the domestic market,

---

7. In April 1998, the Council for Transport Policy submitted a report on the further liberalization of air transport markets, in which it was proposed that a new subsidy program be established.

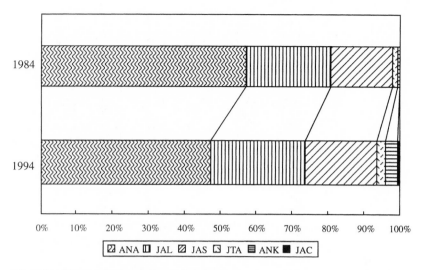

Fig. 6.3   Changes in domestic market shares
Note: Share percentages are as follows: For 1984: ANA, 57.4; JAL, 23.3; JAS, 17.2; JTA,
1.4; ANK, 0.7; JAC 0. 0. For 1994: ANA, 47.2; JAL, 26.7; JAS, 19.9; JTA, 2.5; ANK, 3.2;
JAC, 0.5.

which were nurtured under the old regime and are probably the main reasons for ANA's competitive strength. Moreover, until very recently, fare
competition has been banned, and new competitors had no effective way
to challenge incumbent carriers. In a sense, this was a legacy of the old
regulatory environment.

Another reason why shares did not change greatly is airport capacity
limitations. As stated earlier, Haneda Airport, the biggest profit center for
carriers, does not have enough capacity; and the number of landing slots
at the airport has not increased much, although an expansion project is
now under way. In such a situation, an incumbent carrier that has a lot of
slots at Haneda can use its advantageous position in competing with other
carriers, because the regulator treats the vested interest of the incumbent
carrier as something unchangeable.

On the other hand, it is also true that the percentage of passengers in
city-pair markets with multiple carriers increased. Figure 6.4 shows
changes in the percentage of passengers by market type: single-trucking,
double-trucking, and triple-trucking routes. After the policy change, the
share of passengers on multiple-trucking routes increased steadily, reaching about 72 percent in 1994. In a sense, this means that most passengers
had a choice of carrier. But as stated above, carriers were not allowed
flexibility in fare setting, even passengers with access to two or more airlines did not enjoy any benefits from competition.

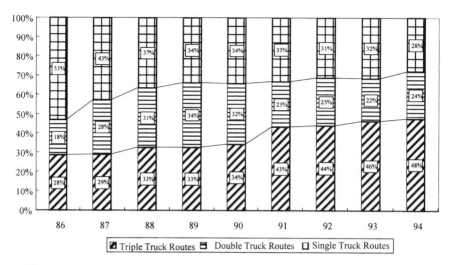

Fig. 6.4   Passenger shares by market type

6.3.4   Airfare Trends

The trend in average domestic airfare since the mid-1970s is shown in figure 6.5. In the figure, the average fare is calculated by dividing total revenue by total revenue passenger kilometers for all carriers. Until recently, domestic airfares were tightly regulated, and the level of the average fare remained relatively stable at least in nominal terms during the 1980s, after a hike in 1980 (a result of the second oil crisis in the previous year). The fact that prices remained stable in nominal terms means that they declined in real terms in general. We can identify a downward trend in airfares since 1990 in nominal as well as in real terms. In this period, fares were still under regulation, but carriers could offer travel agents discount fares for inclusive tour programs. Travel agents might well have used this kind of fare not only for tour programs but also for seat-only sales, even if it was illegal. So we cannot deny the possibility that the downward fare trend in 1990 was triggered by a relaxation of entry requirements introduced in the mid-1980s, with a time lag. But it should be noted that in this period the Japanese economy was in depression, and the fare decrease could be a result of the weak economy. At any rate, air passengers in Japan did not realize any benefits from competition, and their dissatisfaction led to demands for a relaxation of fare regulation.

As noted above, a zone fare system was introduced after 1 June 1996. Judging from its early results, we cannot say that consumers' expectations were realized. Fares under the new system were almost the same among carriers, and on some routes, fares actually rose. For example, the ¥43,100 ($399) normal round-trip fare for the Tokyo-Sapporo route rose by ¥5,400 to ¥6,600 ($50 to $60; the increase depends on the carrier and the period

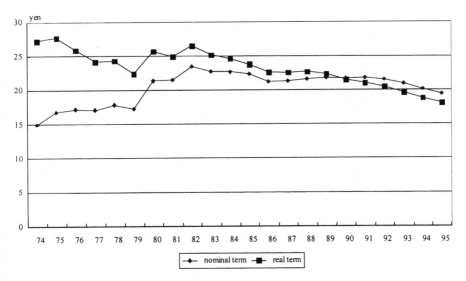

Fig. 6.5   Trend in average airfare

Note: Average airfare was calculated as total passenger revenue divided by total revenue passenger kilometers.

of use). In addition, since the carriers abolished round-trip discounts with no restrictions, the degree of the price rise was significant. Although fares for some routes fell, these were few in number and only a small percentage of passengers enjoyed the benefits.

Criticism of the new fare structure was particularly vocal among local business travelers, who are among the airlines' best customers—for example, discount fares had been offered only for the off-season. The airlines attempted to dodge criticism by saying that they would in the future be offering an even greater array of discount fares. Over the several weeks following the system's commencement, JAS dropped its fares on some routes, expanded the scope of its discount fares, and eased restrictions. The other airlines followed suit immediately.

In spring 1997, the MoT reported a comparison of the average domestic fare under the new zone fare system with that of the previous year (see fig. 6.6). According to MoT data, the average fare, which is revenue divided by revenue passenger kilometers, declined by 2.3 percent in nominal terms. Since general consumer prices remained fairly stable during this period, we can regard this decline as a real price decrease. A price drop of 2.3 percent does not seem trivial because the annual rate of decline in U.S. domestic airfares since deregulation has been 2.8 percent in real terms.[8] However, it is not clear that this price decline was brought about mainly

8. According to Air Transport Association data, the average U.S. airfare in 1977 was 13.4¢ per passenger mile, and this declined to 8.07¢ in 1995 (calculated in constant 1982 dollars).

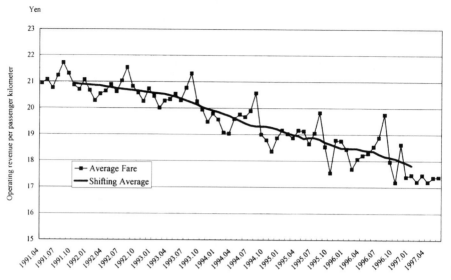

Fig. 6.6   Domestic average airfare (in nominal terms)

through the new fare zone system. As stated above, the average domestic fare started to decline in 1990, and the price fall between 1994 and 1995 was 3.5 percent in both nominal and real terms.

Judging from aggregate data, it is true that domestic airfares in Japan have tended to decline at a nontrivial rate, but consumers cannot see benefits from these fare changes. We may point out several reasons for this discrepancy between what is suggested by the data and what consumers feel. The most important point seems to be that the absolute airfare level in Japan is higher than in any other country, especially the United States.[9]

6.3.5   Cost Behavior

One of the purposes of the 1986 policy change was to strengthen the airlines' competitiveness or to make them efficient by promoting competi-

9. Note that international comparisons of domestic airfares are always difficult. E.g., the MoT of Japan reported that normal fares in Japan are generally lower than in the United States and that advance purchase discount fares are almost at the same level as in the United States, comparing similar routes. According to a news release from the Air Transport Association, however, 92.0 percent of all air passengers in the United States made use of some kind of discounted fare, and the average discount was 67.0 percent off the full fare (ATA Press Release no. 115, December 1995). Thus the simple comparison of published fares is almost meaningless. Moreover, the average domestic yield of U.S. carriers in 1995 was about 8.04 yen per passenger kilometer (12.86¢ per passenger mile). On the other hand, the yield of Japanese carriers was 19.4 yen. If we compare these yields without any manipulation, the average fare in Japan is more than twice as high as in the United States. But the average route length in U.S. domestic markets is longer than in Japan, and the average fare is thought to decline as route length grows. So in this case too, a simple comparison has no meaning.

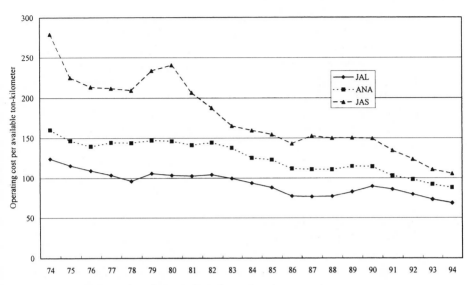

Fig. 6.7   Changes in unit costs (in real terms)

tion among air carriers. This would benefit consumers through market competition. Did the policy change affect the airlines' cost level?

Figure 6.7 shows changes in the big three carriers' unit costs in real terms. Unit costs are determined not only by the operational efficiency of the carrier but also by route structure and air fleet structure. As the average route length grows, unit cost might well decline, and also bigger aircraft could lower average cost. Because airlines in Japan have not had complete freedom to adjust their route structures, it is not proper to compare these three unit costs with each other in a straightforward way. So the trend of costs is more important to observe.

Figure 6.7 shows a downward slope for all unit cost curves. But since the declining trend started far before the regulatory policy change, we cannot conclude that the policy change had a positive effect on airline efficiency. By a brief statistical cost test done by the author, it was shown that the unit costs of JAL and ANA might have been affected by the new policy but that JAS's unit cost might not have been (see Yamauchi 1997, appendix).

JAL entered into many domestic city-pair markets after the new policy was introduced. JAL's new markets were relatively large ones because, as stated earlier, the MoT adopted a standard for new entry based on annual number of passengers carried. This made it possible for JAL to use wide-body aircraft on new routes as in international markets, and so JAL could also enjoy the economies associated with large aircraft. The increased number of domestic routes reduced average route length, which could be a factor that increased cost. But JAL was always under pressure in international markets to compete with foreign low-cost carriers and, moreover, was completely privatized under the new policy. These elements are likely to have offset the bad effects of entering new domestic markets.

The reason why the new policy decreased ANA's unit cost seems very clear: ANA started international service to Washington, D.C., and other American cities in 1986. Generally speaking, international routes are longer than Japanese domestic routes, and larger aircraft are used in order to make operations more efficient. Entry into international markets might reduce average cost, and this was probably the case for ANA's cost behavior.

As stated above, we cannot say that the average cost of JAS was influenced by the new policy. With respect to route structure, JAS had flown both trunk routes and local routes under the old regime. The new policy made it possible for JAS to enter new markets, but its route structure was not changed. JAS was also allowed to commence international operation, and it started some routes. Its new international routes were, however, short range and could have become a factor in decreasing costs.

Judging from this brief cost analysis and the changes observed in the situation, we can say that the cost behavior of JAS could reflect the net effect of newly introduced competitive policy in Japan because its route network characteristics were unchanged. By contrast, the new policy changed ANA's route structure greatly, and caused JAL's complete privatization. These elements were likely to bring down their cost levels, and probably it is appropriate to distinguish these effects from the pure competitive pressures released by the policy, because these elements can affect the cost level technically—although complete privatization would have some competitive aspects. In summary, the new air transport policy introduced in 1986 generated favorable effects on Japanese air carriers' average costs overall, but it is not clear whether or not these effects were brought about through the substantial competitive process expected from the economists' view point.[10]

6.3.6 Competitive Strategy and Entry Barriers

In evaluating deregulation policy in the United States, it is always pointed out that carriers have adopted several new competitive strategies to establish advantageous market positions and that these strategies have decreased the validity of the deregulation policy. Above all, it is said that the most influential strategies are computer reservation systems (CRSs), frequent flyer programs (FFPs), and hub and spoke network systems (HSNSs). CRSs made it possible for airlines to adopt detailed marketing plans and, consequently, segmented pricing strategies, while we can also

---

10. This analysis is tentative. I plan to analyze the airlines' cost structure more thoroughly.

regard CRSs as a tool allowing consumers to get the information necessary to make rational choices. FFPs brought consumers many benefits, in the form of price discounts; on the other hand, it increased the cost to an air passenger of switching airline companies. In other words, FFPs are a very powerful way for airlines to capture their customers.

With respect to CRSs and FFPs, Japanese air carriers are in the infant stage. Each carrier group has its own CRS but has failed to use that system, at least for domestic operations. A large portion of air tickets are sold by travel agents, in the form of inclusive tours. In these cases, it is travel agents who determine prices, not airlines. This means that Japanese airlines do not have the power or the ability to segment their market and to set prices for each market. This aspect of Japanese airline operation seems to be quite different from that of foreign carriers. Japanese airlines have not been especially active in introducing FFPs. Until recently, their FFPs were quite limited and far from being used strategically in a competitive environment. For example, all domestic FFPs were separate from international FFPs, and domestic awards were poor. In spring 1997, the airlines introduced new comprehensive FFPs, patterned on American programs, but it is too early to determine the effects of these new programs.

It is obvious that the strongest barrier to new competition is the landing slot shortage at Haneda Airport. In the United States, the HSNSs adopted by larger carriers led to concentration at hub airports, and some studies pointed out that this concentration works as an effective entry barrier (e.g., see U.S. GAO 1996). In Japan, as stated above, the major routes are connected to Haneda, and the key factor in each airline's ability to be profitable is its landing slot allocation at Haneda. Although the landing capacity of Haneda has expanded gradually, at any given time all slots are fully utilized by incumbent carriers. In this situation, it is hardly possible for a new competitor to enter the domestic market successfully and be an active competitor. Therefore, slot allocation at Haneda is an essential factor in promoting competition in the domestic air transport market.

In allocating landing slots at Haneda, the MoT's approach is as follows. First, landing slots at Haneda are property belonging to the state, and the government has the power to allocate them at its own discretion. Second, landing slots should be allocated in connection with route licenses or business plan approval. Thus, if a carrier wants to get a new landing slot, it first should offer a new service to the MoT. Then it can get a slot only when the MoT approves the proposed service as meeting the "public necessity and convenience" condition or contributing to the "public interest" and as not disturbing the supply-demand balance in the market.[11] The last requirement, called the "supply-demand balance regulation," is specified

---

11. Of course, in addition to these requirements, technological conditions including safety standards should be also satisfied.

in the Civil Aeronautics Law and is interpreted as the main source of the central government's discretionary power.[12]

Clearly, this allocation procedure will never promote effective competition because it is the MoT and not the airlines that decides what kinds of products and how much output should be supplied. As stated in section 6.2, since 1986 the MoT has tried to facilitate double or triple trucking of existing carriers. This policy, however, cannot generate a competitive environment as long as landing slots at Haneda are allocated at administrative discretion.

Faced with the sharp economic decline after the collapse of the "bubble economy," economists began to claim that the rigid Japanese administrative process and wide-ranging regulatory framework were obstacles to the self-supporting recovery of the Japanese economy. This argument spurred a social movement eager for administrative reform, and through this movement, the landing slot allocation at Haneda Airport came into the limelight. A new runway at Haneda was approaching completion, and it would clearly bring a substantial increase in the number of landing slots— enough to influence competitive conditions in the domestic air transport industry.

Responding to public opinion, the MoT established a consultative committee to consider slot allocation at Haneda. At the same time several proposals were made to establish wholly new, independent airlines and to allow entry into major domestic routes (e.g., Tokyo-Sapporo and Tokyo-Osaka) with cheaper fares. The committee recommended that new slots be allocated independent of route licenses or approval of business plans and that the allocating procedure be transparent and procompetitive. In particular, it was proposed that newcomers be given priority in getting Haneda's slots. The MoT accepted these proposals, and some slots were reserved for new entrants.[13] But crucial issues remained—among them, how to allocate the remaining slots to the three incumbent groups.

The MoT's decision was as follows: slots at Haneda would be allocated to the three carrier groups in inverse proportions to each carrier's landing slot share. Moreover, some slots given to ANA were conditioned on the destinations being fixed in order to ensure service provision to thin routes and new airports. This procedure was the same as under conventional slot allocation.

The MoT insisted that the landing slot inequality at Haneda was a legacy of tight regulation and that it was the MoT's role to rectify it. As shown in figure 6.8, ANA and its subsidiaries use about 49 percent of all

12. This is the interpretation maintained by Masahiro Yamaguchi, an ex-bureaucrat of the MoT; he drafted this law in 1952.
13. Until new airlines are ready to operate, reserved slots are provisionally used by incumbent carriers.

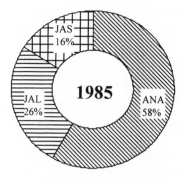 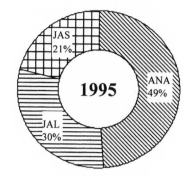

Fig. 6.8   Slot shares at Haneda Airport

Haneda's landing slots. Although ANA's slot share decreased over the past decade, it might be reasonable for other airlines to claim that ANA has a competitive advantage in an essential input factor for airline operation. In some economic analyses of the air transport market, it is pointed out that hub dominance by an airline is likely to be an impediment to effective competition.

The slot allocation rule adopted at this time by the MoT met with criticism. The contention was that the MoT intended to rectify artificially or administratively differentials in business opportunity that had been built up through tight regulation with a long history. Some pointed out that concentration at Haneda was not as serious as the experience in the United States and that if trading of landing slots among carriers were allowed, allocative efficiency would be improved through this buy-sell process, although some considerations would be necessary for newly established airlines.[14] Now the proposal is being made that some portion of the existing slots be taken away from carriers and reallocated in order to mobilize this scarce resource. From the economist's point of view, some kind of price mechanism should be adopted to increase efficiency and to keep the reallocation process open and transparent.

6.3.7   Welfare Change

In economic analysis, a policy change should be evaluated by the magnitude of welfare effects the change would bring. In transport market analysis, a method to estimate passengers' compensating variations using

14. E.g., U.S. GAO (1996) reports that at O'Hare Airport in Chicago, which is a typical congested airport, American and United occupied 87 percent of all landing slots. As for noncongested airports, there are examples at which one carrier occupies more than 80 percent of all slots. The GAO report also claims that the buy-sell rule adopted by the federal government for congested airports was likely to reduce competition.

modal choice functions has been developed and adopted in many studies.[15] The modal choice function is a discrete choice model shown in the form of a probability, which is a function of an indirect utility function. We can estimate the probability of modal choice by specifying the indirect utility function. If a new policy changes the values of, for instance, fare levels, service quality, or other variables composing the indirect utility function, the probability that passengers choose a particular transport mode will change. We can calculate compensating variations by integrating this probabilistic change, multiplying the reciprocal of the marginal utility of income, and summing up this value for every transport mode.

Unfortunately, I could not properly estimate a welfare change caused by the regulatory change mainly because of lack of data. There are two ways to estimate a multinominal logit model: one using aggregate data, the other using disaggregate choice data. Theoretically, it is said that the latter choice is a better one. In Japan, we cannot get the data needed for aggregate estimation of modal choice through published sources, and estimating a logit model with disaggregate data would require a questionnaire survey to obtain stated preference data. The Japan Transport Economic Research Center (1991), an extradepartmental body of the MoT, has published estimated results of nested logit mode choice models. A special study group composed of transportation engineers did this research in cooperation with the MoT, and the MoT used the results in making a new transport plan during the 1990s. Since the mode choice models adopted in this research are part of a four-stage transport demand projection and did not take account of economic analysis, we cannot use them to evaluate welfare change. If we try to estimate welfare gains (gross consumer surplus) caused by the introduction of the zone fare system quite roughly, the results are as follows.[16]

According to the simple demand function given in section 6.3.1, the long-term price elasticity of air travel in Japan is -0.741, and the average airfare decreased 2.3 percent after the introduction of the zone fare system. A quite simple calculation gives the result that the decrease in prices gives birth to a demand increase of about 1.7 percent, income being held constant, and thus all passengers enjoy somewhat cheaper fares. The resulting change in aggregate consumer surplus would be about ¥29.3 billion ($266 million) per year. This estimated gain seems very small compared with the gains reported in several studies of airline deregulation in the United States.[17] As stated earlier, we cannot conclude that this price reduc-

---

15. The method is developed in Small and Rosen (1981). On its application, see Morrison and Winston (1986).

16. It should be noted that the following analysis is tentative and not conclusive.

17. Morrison and Winston (1986) estimate "total annual benefit to travelers of $5.7 billion or 35 percent of actual 1977 airline revenue of $16.3 billion." Morrison and Winston's estimation is comprehensive, and we cannot make a simple comparison.

tion was brought about solely by the new regulatory system; therefore, the estimation here is hypothetical.

6.4 Revolution of International Air Transport

International air transport is carried out based on bilateral agreements that reflect the reciprocal rights and interests of each country. As often pointed out, in the bilateral system each country asserts its rights and interests, and so the equilibrium of negotiation is likely to result in a traffic level lower than is efficient. This is because the country with less competitive, less efficient carriers might well try to protect its airlines and try to delimit markets within which its carriers can make profits.

An international cartel, initiated by the International Air Transport Association (IATA), stabilized international airfares and avoided substantial competition. It is true that IATA itself still exists and that traffic conferences of IATA are held regularly to set fares route by route, but IATA's ability to tame competition has been much reduced and its main role has sifted to cooperative functions such as acting as the clearinghouse for debt and credit between airlines. As a result, the degree of competition in international markets depends on the bilateral agreements, especially the capacity control clauses of these agreements.

The Japanese government has held to a rather traditional policy stance in international aviation negotiations. However, as stated above, air transport policy reached a turning point in 1986, when the Council for Transport Policy, which consisted of neutral members, submitted a report that showed a new direction for aviation policy of Japan. With respect to international aviation, the report advised that multiple designations should be extended to markets on a reciprocal basis. The background of this council's report was the provisional agreement with the United States made in the previous year, in which new carriers from both Japan and the United States were allowed to enter markets. By this agreement, ANA and JAS became international carriers, and United Airlines, American Airlines, and Delta Airlines started to fly in Japan-U.S. markets.

Indeed, this provisional agreement was not a liberal agreement that gave carriers much freedom of capacity and price setting, but it should be noted that it triggered a change in Japanese air transport policy. And this was the starting point for a relaxation of conditions for new entry and a capacity expansion in international air transport markets with other countries. This is very clear, if we think of the Japan-U.S. negotiation process.

The Japan-U.S. provisional agreement did not become a liberal agreement because the Japanese government believed that there existed an inequality of rights and interests in the Japan-U.S. bilateral agreement, and that this inequality hampered fair competition in the air transport market between the two countries. The Japanese government insisted as follows. First, in the original agreement, the United States had unlimited fifth freedom rights ("beyond rights") beyond Japan, while Japan had only one point of that right beyond the United States. Second, the number of full-right carriers for the United States was greater than for Japan. Full-right carriers can increase or decrease capacity without advance notice. Third, there was an imbalance in capacity shares in north Pacific markets. Fourth, as a result, U.S. carriers had higher market shares than Japanese carriers over the Pacific.

If this characterization were accurate, it would have been quite natural for the Japanese government to insist that liberalizing the agreement with the United States would benefit U.S. carriers. However, not all of these assertions are thought to be appropriate. As many researchers point out, at least as far as imbalances in capacity share and market share, one cause of such imbalances is that Japanese carriers failed to expand their capacity. It is true that beyond rights are unequal between the two countries, but these rights are not as attractive to Japanese carriers as to U.S. carriers because there seems to be no lucrative market for Japanese carriers in beyond-U.S. routes.

Generally speaking, complaints from foreign countries about Japanese international aviation policy focus on the difficulty of entering the Japanese markets or increasing their capacity. These complaints are thought to stem partly from Japan's policy itself and largely from airport congestion problems.[18]

The negotiating process between Japan and the United States shows that it is not easy to liberalize international air transport through bilateral agreements. In order to conclude liberal agreements, a coincidence of interests between the countries or substantial concessions by one country are needed. In the case of the liberal agreement concluded between the Netherlands and the United States in the summer of 1992, the United States was after the symbolic effects of this agreement on other European countries and the Netherlands made use of the negotiation to strengthen the global alliance of KLM and Northwest Airlines.

Any equilibrium based on a point of compromise will be unstable; thus a new apparatus is needed in order to liberalize regulatory frameworks in the international setting. Some proponents suggest that a multilateral agreement or treaty would be better scheme for achieving institutional change directed to a more liberal environment in international aviation. In a multilateral setting, unified standards for regulatory operations would be concluded, and regulatory operations would become more transparent. Apparently, this trend contributes to liberalization. The U.S. government points out its validity, proposing it in some international organizations.

18. For a detailed discussion of the U.S.-Japan bilateral agreement, see Yamauchi and Ito (1996).

At this time, several multilateral agreements in international aviation have been concluded. The Chicago Convention in 1944, the starting point of the international aviation system after World War II, itself is a multilateral treaty, although it has no economic regulatory framework. In 1980, the United States and the European Civil Aviation Conference (ECAC) signed a memorandum of understanding on passenger-fare-setting rules. Since the ECAC is the representative organization of the aviation departments of European countries, this memorandum of understanding was the first multilateral agreement relating to economic regulations on airlines. In 1992, the Council of Transport Ministers in the European Community (now the European Union) adopted the third package of the Common Air Transport Policy, which deregulated the whole European air transport market substantially. This was a typical multilateral agreement to liberalize international aviation.

Ideally, a multilateral scheme is the most favorable apparatus for liberalizing and developing international air transport. However, it should be noted that it is extremely difficult to get to a multilateral framework. In the EU case, where the Common Air Transport Policy was introduced, the new system was strongly initiated by the European Commission, the administrative body of the European Union. This is because the Common Air Transport Policy brings the commissioners huge benefits in the form of centralized authority over policy operations. Actors as aggressive as these commissioners are rare in general economic settings. A particular country cannot be a promoter of multilateral agreements because there emerge keen conflicts of interest. The multilateral approach was discussed at the International Civil Aviation Organization meeting in 1994, but only limited approval was obtained. In conclusion, to liberalize international aviation, a multilateral approach is the right way, but to accomplish it, gradual reform will be needed.

Another apparatus for liberalizing international air transport is competition in a domestic market itself. As pointed out by Kasper (1996), in the United States, air carriers started to optimize their route networks and operations when faced with the competitive environment created by deregulation in 1978, and now the route networks to be optimized include international routes. The globalization of national economies as a whole make it crucial for airlines to construct global networks in order to be competitive. This in turn requires a more liberal framework for international aviation. We can see evidence of such an industry-oriented procompetitive policy in the United States. In any case, the important thing is not who advocates the policy, but how good is the market performance, or allocative efficiency, brought about by the policy.

Regrettably, in the case of the Japanese air transport industry, competition in the domestic market is not severe enough to force the airlines to pursue new international markets in order to optimize their networks or make them more attractive to passengers. In fact, although ANA always expresses its desire to extend its international routes, these extension plans seem to be within an existing bilateral framework. The high-cost nature of Japanese carriers makes it more attractive to remain within the existing framework, and also limited competition in the market keeps carriers in inefficient operation.

6.5 Outlook for Japan's Air Transport Policy: A Conclusion

On 5 December 1996, the MoT announced a new direction for transport policy, including air transport. The contents of the announcement were as follows. The supply-demand balance clause included in the Civil Aeronautics Law would be abolished in a year or so. The new landing slots created by completion of the new runway at Haneda Airport would be allocated through a transparent process and in a procompetitive way, and some portion of the existing slots would be transferred among airlines to make competition more workable. In a sense, this statement can be regarded as a drastic policy change, because the supply-demand balance clause gives administrative power to the MoT and the capacity limit at Haneda is the bottleneck hindering effective competition.

The supply-demand balance clause provides that a new entry or an incremental flight by an incumbent carrier will be approved if and only if the authority judges that the balance of supply and demand in the market will not be disturbed by the new entry or additional flight. This is a quantitative control on supply, and the clause has effectively blocked new entry. The clause has also given the MoT wide-ranging administrative discretion because, according to the clause, it is not airline managers but government officials who decide whether there is excess demand or not. Thus the abolition of the clause could mean much more room for effective competition than in the present situation, and this prospect could be strengthened by the new policy statement on slot allocation at Haneda.

However, it should be noted that the MoT's "new new policy" is not an American-type total deregulation policy. It is possible that the present licensing scheme will remain substantially, although its statutory expression might differ from the present one. Therefore, the wide range of administrative discretion may remain unchanged. The trigger for the "new new policy" was a policy recommendation made by the Deregulation Subcommittee of the Administrative Reform Committee, which is a consultative committee for the prime minister. The subcommittee advocated more comprehensive deregulation, but the MoT did not agree with the original proposal. Since the "new new policy" is the result of compromise between the subcommittee and the MoT, it is ambiguous what direction the MoT will take.

In this paper, it was shown that Japan's air transport policy has evolved gradually to a more liberal and procompetitive approach. However, the speed of the evolution has been very slow. In the domestic market, the legacy of the old regime remains, and the market structure has hardly changed. The effects of regulatory change in the past decade were evaluated, but the results are not clear, and the estimated welfare gain is very small.

Japan is still a traditionalist in international aviation policy. It is true that faced with policy change, airlines were forced to restructure their businesses and make them lean, but it seems to me that the airlines' response to the new situation has been "too little, too slow."[19]

In March 1998, Japan and the United States agreed to a new memorandum of understanding. In the negotiation process, while the United States government strongly insisted that Japan accept a liberal agreement, since the Japanese government refused it persistently the memorandum of understanding was not said to be a liberal agreement. The official reason why Japan opposed a liberal agreement was that there remained inequalities of rights and interests in the bilateral agreement mentioned in section 6.4.

However, the essence of the memorandum of understanding was to introduce greater competition into the north Pacific market. The new agreement allows full-right carriers to choose any city-pair market between the two countries if there is no landing slot problem, to exercise beyond rights more freely than at present, and to make use of code sharing even between same-country carriers. Moreover, the agreement equalizes the number of full-right carriers between the two countries, which meets Japan's complaint about inequality in the original bilateral agreement, while for non-full-right carriers, flight increases are allowed. The new agreement was reached with substantial compromises by both countries, but it is certain that competition among carriers will increase, and increased competition will benefit consumers as well as the air carriers themselves.

It is often pointed out that the Japanese government has always behaved in a paternalistic manner, especially in the industrial policy field, and probably this is true for the air transport industry. Given that the American economy was revitalized through competitive market processes and that newly industrializing countries are strengthening their international competitiveness quickly, Japan's stance in industrial and regulatory policy should not be the same as in previous days. And clearly, air transport policy is no exception.

19. On the airlines' strategy for the new situation, see Yamauchi (1993).

References

Japan Transport Economic Research Center. 1991. *21seiki no Wagakuni no Kotsu Juyo* (Transport demand in 21st century). Tokyo: Japan Transport Economic Research Center.

Kasper, Daniel M. 1996. U.S.-Japan aviation relations: Where do we go from here? *TEIKUOFU,* no. 76 (spring): 16–21.

Masui, Kenichi, and Hirotaka Yamauchi. 1990. *Kohku Yuso* (Air transport). Kyoto: Koyo Shobo.

Morrison, Steven, and Clifford Winston. 1986. *The economic effects of airline deregulation.* Washington, D.C.: Brookings Institution.

Ohta, Masaki. 1981. *Kokuyuso no Keizaigaku* (Economics of air transport). Tokyo: Waseda University Press.

Small, Kenneth A., and Harvey S. Rosen. 1981. Applied welfare economics with discrete choice models. *Econometrica* 49 (spring): 105–30.

U.S. GAO (General Accounting Office). 1996. *Airline deregulation: Barriers to entry continue to limit competition in several key domestic markets.* Washington, D.C.: General Accounting Office.

Yamauchi, Hirotaka. 1993. Flying low. *Look Japan* 39, no. 453 (December): 18–19.

———. 1996. Experiencing some turbulence: The piecemeal deregulation of Japan's air transport market leaves major problems rumbling in the sky. *Look Japan* 42, no. 487 (October): 16–17.

———. 1997. Air transport policy in Japan: Limited competition under regulation. In *Asia Pacific air transport: Challenges and policy reforms,* ed. Christopher Findley, Chia Lin Sien, and Karmjit Singh. Singapore: Institute of Southeast Asian Studies.

Yamauchi, Hirotaka, and Takatoshi Ito. 1996. Air transport policy in Japan. In *Flying high: Liberalizing civil aviation in the Asia Pacific,* ed. Gary C. Hufbauer and Christopher Findley. Washington, D.C.: Institute for International Economics.

Yamauchi, Hirotaka, and Hideki Murakami. 1995. Air transport in Japan: Policy change and its evaluation. *Keizai Bunseki,* no. 143 (December): 85–126.

Comment   Takatoshi Ito

Hirotaka Yamauchi gives a good description of the deregulation process in the airline industry in Japan. He covers the prolonged process of deregulation up to the current state (1997–98). Airlines in Japan, before 1986, were severely limited in their pricing and routing (like their American counterparts before the U.S. deregulation of 1978). It is interesting to note (as described in detail by Yamauchi) that the domestic deregulation of 1986 was triggered by international negotiations in which Japan pushed to introduce a new cargo airline. Hence, even the deregulation of the late

Takatoshi Ito is professor in the Institute of Economic Research at Hitotsubashi University, Tokyo, and a research associate of the National Bureau of Economic Research.

1980s was the result of international pressure rather than of an internal debate.

The paper is modest in its critical evaluation of the deregulation process. I would argue that deregulation was too slow. If the MoT had been bold enough to deregulate prices and routes completely in the mid-1980s, when they abandoned the old regime (JAL for international routes, ANA for domestic routes, and TDA for regional routes), the airline companies would have been forced to compete fiercely at a time when business as a whole was still booming. Instead, their costs—increased wages for pilots and flight attendants (rent sharing with workers) and burdens from inefficient subsidiaries—increased during the "bubble economy" period in the late 1980s. This made Japanese airlines less competitive by international standards. As the U.S. airline industry consolidated in the early 1990s, it became apparent that it was more cost-effective in competition over the Pacific. The share of U.S. carriers significantly increased in the 1990s.

Major innovations in U.S. airline services, such as HSNSs, deep discounts with early purchases and conditions, and effective use of CRSs, have not developed in Japan. Routing and pricing had been deregulated in steps in the mid-1990s. As of spring 1998, discounts of up to 50 percent off the regular fare became possible. Routing innovation has not taken place. Airfares have been declining markedly.

What is needed in evaluating Japanese airline policy is a quantitative evaluation of consumer benefits from various deregulation measures. Yamauchi's paper scratches the surface of this issue when he shows the trend of average domestic airfare measured as operating revenue divided by passenger kilometers (fig. 6.5). Ideally, airfares should be compared for each market or for the same distances, since marginal cost declines as distance grows. Difficulties in estimating consumer benefits remain. The value of increased frequency of service, through check-in, and other innovations in airline service is difficult to capture.

Advocates of deregulation faced resistance in Japan. Those who are against deregulation cite the danger of cutting service to remote islands (due to the end of cross-subsidization), thus threatening universal service, and the potentially increased probability of airline accidents due to cuts in maintenance costs. The role of economists is to provide objective evaluations of these claims and accurate accounts of the U.S. experience with airline deregulation.[1] This paper is a first step toward this kind of critical evaluation of deregulation.

---

1. On the U.S. experience with airline deregulation, see, e.g., Bailey, Graham, and Kaplan (1985) and Morrison and Winston (1986).

References

Bailey, E. E., D. R. Graham, and D. P. Kaplan. 1985. *Deregulating the airlines.* Cambridge, Mass.: MIT Press.
Morrison, S., and C. Winston. 1986. *The economic effects of airline deregulation.* Washington, D.C.: Brookings Institution.

Comment   Changqi Wu

The relationship between the development of the airline industry and the evolution of national air transport policy is full of controversy. There seem no compelling efficiency reasons, such as the economies of scale that give rise to natural monopolies in the electricity supply industry, to justify tight government regulation. Nevertheless, governments all over the world have taken measures, in one period or another, to regulate and to protect the air transport industry from its birth. European countries under the flag carrier system legitimized the state ownership of airlines with hidden government subsidies. In the United States, it was through airmail delivery that government subsidies were sneaked in. In all those years, the airline industry was under tight regulation regarding routes, landing slots, and fares. The lack of competition led to high airfares and less frequent service. Air travel became a luxury enjoyed by only a few.

Starting in 1978 in the United States, a fundamental change took place in the airline industry. Since then, "deregulation" and "open sky" have become the buzzwords of air transport policymakers. The deregulation of the airline industry has raised new questions and challenges and enriched the literature of regulatory economics and antitrust economics. Studies of problems in the airline industries, old and new, improve our understanding.[1] Unfortunately, the bulk of this literature is based on the experiences of the United States and European countries. Little has been written on what has happened in Japan.

Hirotaka Yamauchi provides a concise review of the evolutionary process that has taken place in the Japanese domestic airline industry over the past forty-five years. He also highlights the three phases of this evolution and comments critically on two policy initiatives of the Japanese government. These initiatives have helped to shape the current market structure of the airline industry in Japan.

Unlike the big bang approach to deregulation taken in the U.S. airline industry, the market liberalization process in Japan has been slow and

Changqi Wu is assistant professor of economics at the School of Business and Management of the Hong Kong University of Science and Technology.

1. For a good summary of the early debates, see Bailey, Graham, and Kaplan (1985).

piecemeal. The author discusses the three phases in air transport policy: (1) In the 1972–86 period, the relatively free entry of the 1950s was replaced by a so-called aviation constitution that put in place a market structure of three airlines. These airlines divided all routes and created essentially a monopoly in each of three segmented markets. (2) In the 1986–96 period, the territorial monopolies were challenged and replaced by controlled competition among domestic airlines over routes, fares, and services. (3) From 1996 onward, a new initiative was introduced. As we learn from the paper, the 1996 policy initiative clearly represents a more profound policy shift than the previous ones. It is expected to bring fundamental changes to the industry in the years to come. However, it seems to be too early at this stage, as the author points out, for these changes to have any significant effects that are empirically testable. Partly for this reason, he devotes much of the paper to discussing the rather limited policy changes in 1986. In the following, I shall comment on Yamauchi's study.

Market Structure and Competition

Because competition between airlines is largely based on routes, it is weak unless more than one airline serves the same route. One of the most important policy issues is whether the government should allow multiple carriers to serve the same route. This issue has arisen again and again in Japan over the past forty-five years. For instance, after a number of new airlines entered the market in the 1950s, it was the Japanese government that facilitated the creation of a superstable market structure that divided the whole domestic market into three different market segments. The MoT then allocated these routes among three airlines.

The MoT was clearly aware in the 1970s that following rapid growth in demand for air travel, the market was large enough to accommodate more competing airlines. At the same time, it was concerned about the degree of concentration in the industry. That explains why the MoT insisted on the creation of a third airline instead allowing the mergers of the two weak airlines into the two stronger ones in 1970. Nevertheless, the MoT through its administrative instructions made sure that there was no effective route competition among the airlines. Instead, the three airlines operated as separate monopolies, each in its segmented market. The experience of Japan's airline industry provides one more piece of evidence that government-engineered market structure changes do not lead to effective competition. Neither consumers nor society as a whole benefited from the potential improvement in economic efficiency.

Airfare Scheme as a Barrier to Entry

In a competitive market, the balance of demand and supply conditions establishes the price level. A price level maintained by a cartel arrangement is higher than that determined by competitive market conditions. Thus it cannot be sustained without an enforcement mechanism. Government regulation of the airfare system not only endorsed this airfare system but might actually have created it. The tight regulation of airfares constituted a major barrier to entry in the sense that potential entrants could not use price as a means to attract customers and expand their market shares.

After the new policy initiative in 1986, there existed a limited degree of competition over airfare. The author describes briefly the trend in average airfare level calculated based on total revenue and total passenger kilometers traveled. If the author had provided detailed information on changes in airfares and how the airlines set their fares, readers would have a better clue to whether airfares were used as competitive weapons. Readers could also assess the impact of competition if given detailed information on changes in prices on different types of routes. It would be particularly interesting to link airfares with operating costs of airlines, given the differences in cost structure among Japanese airlines. In the 1996 policy initiative, MoT introduced into the domestic market a zone fare system that allows diversities of airfares on different routes. This may improve economic efficiency as long as these fares are set by a well-designed auction mechanism.

Analysis of Cost of Japanese Airlines

In an attempt to assess the effect of government policy changes in 1986, the author has estimated the parameters of a model for Japanese carriers' unit costs. What is not clear in this exercise is the time period covered. The discussion of the economic reasons for the cost reduction seems murky. The author attempts to explain the decline in unit cost by economies of scale due to differences in aircraft size. Because a large aircraft can carry more passengers than a small one, large airlines therefore enjoy more benefits from economies of scale. When looking at the measurement of unit cost, we can see that it is both numbers of passengers and travel distances that matter. One should distinguish the impacts from the two sources. As pointed out by the author, international competition plays a crucial role in determining the unit cost level of Japanese airlines. Airlines exposed to international competition are forced to be competitive in the international market. They can learn from their experiences in international operations to improve their competitive positions on domestic routes. These airlines can definitely benefit from such experiences in terms of more efficient flight scheduling and other aspects of management. It is not very clear why this reason is used to explain the unit cost decline of JAL but not that of ANA. As stated in the discussion, ANA entered the international market as a result of the 1986 government policy initiative. After obtaining long-haul flight routes, ANA also faced the pressure of international competition. Such pressure should have contributed positively to cost-cutting efforts at ANA. One possible way to capture this effect is to introduce a dummy variable to capture the difference in characteristics of the airlines.

Vertical Relations between Airlines, Travel Agencies, and Airports

As we learn from other papers in this volume, there existed various degrees of inefficiency in the Japanese distribution system. Those deficiencies may constitute a kind of barrier to entry, protecting upstream manufacturers from potential entrants and alleviating competition among incumbents. The relation between the airlines and the travel agencies can also be regarded as such a vertical relation. The author's discussion of the relation between airlines and the ticketing agencies is interesting. Given the fact that there are only three airlines and must be a large number of travel agencies, it is surprising to learn that travel agencies determine the level of airfares. Unless these travel agencies are well organized or there are professional associations to coordinate prices, it is hard to imagine that airfares are determined by travel agencies instead of airlines.

Another interesting issue is how to allocate airport landing slots. In addition to the typical efficient allocation issue, airlines may also use landing rights and landing slots as a kind of barrier to entry. The experiences with deregulation in the United States and theoretical studies show that it is possible to design an efficient auction mechanism (Grether, Isaac, and Plott 1989). Unfortunately, the author does not provide information detailed enough for readers to understand how landing slots were allocated at Japanese airports.

Overall this is a useful paper. Yamauchi not only analyzes the evolution of the airline industry in Japan but also makes predictions about future developments. I am sure readers can benefit from his insights into the evolution of the policy environment in Japan.

References

Bailey, E. E., D. R. Graham, and D. P. Kaplan. 1985. *Deregulating the airlines.* Cambridge, Mass.: MIT Press.

Grether, D. M., R. M. Isaac, and C. R. Plott. 1989. *The allocation of scarce resources: Experimental economics and the problem of allocating airport slots.* Underground Classics in Economics. Boulder, Colo.: Westview.

7

The Reform of the Business Service Sector
The Case of Taiwan's Financial System

Ching-hsi Chang

Reform of financial services has been one of the major development devices used in Asian newly industrializing countries (NICs) in the 1990s. Although the service sector has been recognized as a key to growth by many great economists, the sector is viewed with hostility by intellectuals and society in general. In Taiwan, the sector has long been discriminated against by industrial policy. The reform of the Taiwanese business service sector is treated as a key stimulus to the country's further economic development, but there are some structural dilemmas in the reform program. Using the financial system as an example, this paper illuminates the reform policies and the recent problems of the business service sector in Taiwan. Section 7.1 will briefly depict the significance of and the hostility to the business service sector. Section 7.2 reviews the financial system in Taiwan, followed by a brief account of the liberalization of the financial sector by the government in section 7.3. Section 7.4 compares financial development in Japan, Korea, and Taiwan. It is shown that a couple of Taiwan's structural problems have gone unnoticed. Section 7.5 addresses these problems. A final section provides some concluding remarks.

7.1 The Significance of and Hostility to the Business Service Sector

According to Adam Smith, economic development is driven by the division of labor and specialization, and the division of labor is limited by the extent of the market. To extend the market, money is used as a medium

Ching-hsi Chang is professor of economics at National Taiwan University.

The author is grateful to Kenneth Lin and Kelly Olds for their valuable suggestions, Hwang-Ruey Song and Ching-Chih Lu for their able assistance, and the National Science Council in Taiwan for its financial support.

of exchange to replace barter transactions (Smith [1776] 1976, chaps. 3 and 4).

Adam Smith is arguing that the market will be extended by decreasing transactions costs. In the reduction of transactions costs, using money as a medium of exchange is a revolution. The development and specialization of the business service sector is likewise vital. The business service sector concerned here primarily performs intermediation or *transaction services* and is closely related to what Wallis and North (1986) defined as the "transaction sector." The business service sector is important because gains from the division of labor and specialization are only realized through exchange. "The development of specialized banking, finance, trade, and other transaction functions are the necessary requirements of enhancing productivity" (Wallis and North 1986, 121). Economic growth is therefore closely tied to the reduction of exchange costs and the increase of the business service sector that permit the realization of gains from greater specialization and the division of labor.

Although the business service sector plays an important intermediating role in realizing gains of exchange, the hostility to the sector has long been widespread.

Chinese tradition discriminates against merchants, calling them the last of the four classes of people (intellectuals, farmers, artisans, and merchants). People are used to looking down on merchants, regarding commerce as a lowly occupation and using the terms "vile" and "mean" to describe it. This is not only prevalent in the East but also common in the West. Adam Smith stated that in the rude state of society, "to trade was disgraceful to a gentleman" (1976, 2:442). Throughout history, as F. A. Hayek cited William H. McNeill's statement, "merchants were objects of very general disdain and moral opprobrium . . . , a man who bought cheap and sold dear was fundamentally dishonest. . . . Merchant behaviour violated patterns of mutuality that prevailed within primary groupings." And Eric Hoffer once remarked, "The hostility, in particular of the scribe, towards the merchant is as old as recorded history" (Hayek 1988, 90).

In the advanced Western societies, such statements as "activities such as barter and exchange and more elaborate forms of trade, the organization or direction of activities, and shifting about of available goods for sale in accordance with profitability, are still not always even regarded as *real work*" (Hayek 1988, 92) may only be found in history. In Taiwan, the emphasis on industry at the expense of commerce is being revealed in industrial policy. The 1960 Act for Encouraging Investment and the subsequent 1992 Act for Upgrading Industry provide tax holidays, accelerated depreciation, and lower interest rates. Basically these acts apply only to the manufacturing sector, which is designated as "productive." Both acts preclude service industries from enjoying all benefits. It was not until 1995 that the construction industry was recognized as a "productive" industry and authorized to enjoy the privileges provided by the Act for Upgrading Industry. Electrical rates are set to discriminate against merchants. The manufacturing sector enjoys a one-third discount on the electricity bill paid by household, but service industries must pay one-third more. Until 1996, some cabinet members in Taiwan still publicly appealed to young people to not work for service companies such as McDonald's; they should instead work in "productive" factories.

7.2   The Financial System in Taiwan

The financial system in Taiwan has three significant features. The first is its "financial dualism." The dual financial system consists of a formal system and an informal system, or the curb markets (see table 7.1). The former includes all institutions and markets established according to financial laws or rules and subject to regulation by the financial authorities. The informal system is composed of all the markets not set up according to formal financial laws or rules. It engages in lending and borrowing activities without being under the direct regulation or supervision of the financial authorities, though it is tolerated by them.

The financial authorities regarding the formal system, with the exception of the credit associations and credit departments of farmer and fishery associations, are the Ministry of Finance (MOF) and the Central Bank of China. Prior to 1995, the Cooperative Bank of Taiwan was authorized by MOF and the central bank to be the auditing agency for credit cooperatives. The direct authorities over the credit departments of farmer and fishery associations are the Ministry of the Interior and the Council of Agriculture. Each of the three kinds of credit co-ops operates on a small scale in a fairly small geographic area. They were privileged substitutes for commercial banks when private banks were completely prohibited before 1990. The financial conditions of most co-ops are shaky. Many of them have had runs; a few have even suffered bankruptcy, especially after the liberalization of private banks. Some of them have been taken over by Cooperative Bank of Taiwan or merged into other institutions. There are still many frail credit co-ops that may fail in the near future.

Taiwan has had significant curb financial markets for a long time. After World War II, the Nationalist government expropriated all Japanese businesses, included organized financial institutions, to make up the state-owned enterprises that constituted more than 90 percent of medium-sized and large nonagricultural industries in the island at that time. Curb markets evolved from the traditional financial sector and were prohibited from becoming modern financial institutions. They grew along with the early development of the private nonagricultural sector, which overtook the public sector by the mid-1960s. In 1964–66, private businesses relied on curb markets for about half of the funds they needed, according to statis-

Table 7.1   Financial System in Taiwan

Formal Financial System	Informal Financial System
Financial institutions	Market-specific organizations
Monetary institutions	Installment credit companies
Central Bank of China (Taiwan)[p]	Leasing companies
(Full service) domestic banks	Investment companies
Commercial banks	Rotating credit co-ops
Specialized banks[p]	Credit unions
Foreign banks (local branches)	Other unorganized markets
Medium business banks	Types of transactions
Cooperatives	Secured borrowing and lending
Cooperative Bank of Taiwan[p]	Unsecured borrowing and lending
Credit cooperative associations	Loans against postdated checks
Credit departments of farmer	Deposits with firms
associations[p]	Mutual loans and savings
Credit departments of fishery	Financial installment credits
associations[p]	Financial leasing
Other financial institutions	Others
Postal Remittances and Savings[p]	Participants
Investment and trust	Moneylenders
Investment and trust companies	Pawnbrokers
Units of commercial banks	Others
China Development Corp.[k]	
Insurance companies	
Life insurance companies	
Property and casualty insurance	
companies	
Central Reinsurance Corp.[k]	
Financial markets	
Money market	
Bill financial companies	
Capital market	
Taiwan Stock Exchange Corp.[k]	
Fuh-Hwa Securities Finance[k]	
Securities dealers	
Brokers	
Traders	
Offshore banking centers	
Units of domestic banks	
Units of foreign banks	
Foreign exchange market	
Foreign currency call-loan market	

[p] Publicly controlled.
[k] KMT controlled.

tics gathered by the central bank (see fig. 7.1). Since then, the curb market ratio fluctuated around 35 percent through 1990 and dropped to below 25 percent after the new banks commenced operations in the early 1990s. The average interest rate of loans in the curb markets is about two and half times that in commercial banks, as shown in figure 7.2.

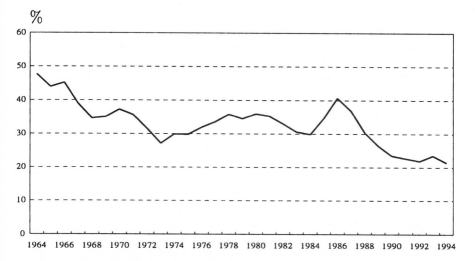

Fig. 7.1 Share of curb market in private sector
Source: Central Bank of China, Economic Research Department, *Flow of Funds in Taiwan District, Republic of China* (Taipei, 1995).

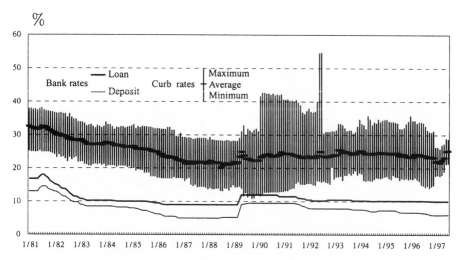

Fig. 7.2 Interest rates
Source: Central Bank of China, *Financial Statistics Monthly* (various issues).
Note: The bank loan rate is the maximum interest rate on short-term unsecured loans; the bank deposit rate is the interest rate on one-year time savings deposits. The curb rate is the interest rate on unorganized, unsecured loans in Taipei.

The curb markets themselves improved the efficiency of the financial system's operation and credit allocation. Shea and Kuo (1984) use 1965–82 data to estimate the contribution and costs of the informal system. They find that efficiency improvements by curb markets increased GDP by 1.23 percent on average during the period. At the same time, compared to the "most" efficient resource allocation under financial dualism, only 0.11 percent of GDP was lost. Shea (1994, 272) himself admits that the assumptions used for the estimation overstated the actual efficiency contribution. Besides, these estimates were done under prohibition of private banks and financial repression. Compared to a competitive market, there are two major costs of financial repression and dualism: inefficiencies and inequities.

The first effect is allocative inefficiency of funds. According to Shea's studies (see Patrick 1994), Taiwan's financial deepening was a cause of its rapid real economic growth (326), which was propelled by small business (358). However, despite rhetoric about helping small business, the relationship between the government and small business was especially negative (363). The focus of government credit programs was big enterprises and big projects (355). Small business was excluded from the organized market and had to bear the burden of substantially higher interest costs in the curb markets. Moreover, these static costs are surely smaller than the dynamic consequences of inefficient investment allocation.

The second effect is increasing inequality of income and wealth. Repression created economic rents. The huge rents created static distribution effects and dynamic development effects. The power to allocate credit on preferential terms creates potential for abuse, corruption, and other political economy problems. As Patrick observes "In Korea and Taiwan, . . . occasional scandals and anecdotal evidence . . . suggest . . . a considerable portion appears to have gone to support the state apparatus—the political parties and leadership in what were after all, rather authoritarian regimes"(1994, 337–38). Dynamically, rent-seeking activities exhibit very natural increasing returns, and rent seeking, particularly public rent seeking by government officials, is likely to hurt innovative activities more than everyday production (Murphy, Shleifer, and Vishny 1993). Further, because consumer loans, except housing loans which could be sought from formal institutions using the real estate as collateral, had to rely on the curb markets, there were further inefficiencies and inequities in the form of less improvements in welfare—less consumption—than in measured GNP performance (Patrick 1994, 367–68). These kinds of consumer loans were completely ignored in the central bank's statistics on curb markets, which are shown in figure 7.1.

The other two features characterizing the Taiwanese financial system are intertwined. The first of these features is the absolute majority of publicly owned institutions in the formal system. In fact, the financial dualism was due to the exclusive publicly owned banks in the formal financial system coupled with the fact that the government has turned a blind eye to the informal markets. Before 1990, there were only three private banks in the formal system, all of which were licensed to overseas Chinese. The second of these features is the many KMT-owned (or at least controlled) financial institutions. KMT is the abbreviation for the Kuomintang, the ruling party of Taiwan since the end of World War II.

Table 7.2 shows the number of Taiwanese formal financial institutions and branches between 1961 and 1995. Before the liberalization brought about the new Bank Law of 1989, which took effect after 1992, there were virtually no structural changes in the formal system, except the establishment of investment and bill companies, and the intrusion of KMT institutions. Table 7.3 shows the total assets of formal financial institutions in 1990 and 1995, reflecting their relative importance. In these two tables, the financial institutions are classified into three groups, namely, publicly controlled, KMT controlled, and privately controlled institutions. KMT-controlled institutions are isolated from the other groups because, on the one hand, the KMT is the ruling party, having possessed exclusive political power for fifty years in Taiwan, so that there is almost no difference between the KMT party and the Nationalist government, while on the other hand, the institutions controlled by the KMT are different from publicly controlled institutions in terms of their legal status.

The structure and development of the Taiwanese financial system, both formal and informal systems, has been well depicted by Shea (1994) and Yang (1994), except the misleading picture presented of KMT- and state-controlled enterprises and privatization, to be discussed below. Over time the share of publicly controlled financial institutions has been decreasing and those of the other two groups increasing. In 1995, the government controlled 67 percent of all kinds of formal financial institutions in number as well as in assets, the ruling party (KMT) held 3 percent in number and nearly 5 percent in assets and the private sector possessed 30 percent in number and 28 percent in assets.[1] In the financial service sector, the KMT operates almost all types of formal financial institutions, many of which are monopolies or oligopolies authorized by itself (the ruling party). Several informal financial institutions are also owned by the KMT, as shown in table 7.4 (see also Bruton 1993; Baum 1994). All these KMT financial businesses, and numerous other businesses, are under the control of its seven holding companies or investment companies like the China Development Corporation. The Central Investment Holding Company, one of the biggest holding companies in Taiwan, was listed in a political encyclopedia as the only example of a political party's receiving its funds through an enterprise (Delury 1987, 1077).

Government interventions in the financial sector can be classified into

---

1. Stock securities, including Taiwan Stock Exchange Corporation, which is controlled by the KMT, are not included in table 7.3.

Table 7.2   Number of Formal Financial Institutions in Taiwan

Type and Control[a]	1961 Co.	1961 Bra.	1961 Units	1961 Ratio	1970 Co.	1970 Bra.	1970 Units	1970 Ratio	1980 Co.	1980 Bra.	1980 Units	1980 Ratio	1990 Co.	1990 Bra.	1990 Units	1990 Ratio	1995 Co.	1995 Bra.	1995 Units	1995 Ratio
Domestic banks																				
Public	9	247	256	1.00	11	365	376	0.98	12	505	517	0.98	13	678	691	0.94	13	929	942	0.68
KMT									1	1	2	0.00	1	16	17	0.02	3	91	94	0.07
Private	1	0	1	0.00	2	6	8	0.02	2	9	11	0.02	2	27	29	0.04	18	341	359	0.26
Sum	10	247	257	1.00	13	371	384	1.00	15	515	530	1.00	16	721	737	1.00	34	1,361	1,395	1.00
Local branches of foreign banks																				
Public																				
KMT																				
Private			1	1.00			7	1.00			21	1.00			43	1.00			58	1.00
Sum			1	1.00			7	1.00			21	1.00			43	1.00			58	1.00
Medium business banks																				
Public	1	41	42	0.50	1	46	47	0.41	1	71	72	0.42	1	91	92	0.33	1	110	111	0.24
KMT																	1	52	53	0.12
Private	7	35	42	0.50	7	61	68	0.59	7	91	98	0.58	7	184	191	0.67	6	284	290	0.64
Sum	8	76	84	1.00	8	107	115	1.00	8	162	170	1.00	8	275	283	1.00	8	446	454	1.00
Credit cooperative associations																				
Public																				
KMT																				
Private	80	73	153	1.00	83	139	222	1.00	75	199	274	1.00	74	399	473	1.00	73	556	629	1.00
Sum	80	73	153	1.00	83	139	222	1.00	75	199	274	1.00	74	399	473	1.00	73	556	629	1.00

Credit departments of farmer and fishery associations

Category	(1)	(2)	Total	Prop.	(1)	(2)	Total	Prop.	(1)	(2)	Total	Prop.	(1)	(2)	Total	Prop.	(1)	(2)	Total	Prop.
Public	291	94	385	1.00	295	98	393	1.00	283	441	724	1.00	309	744	1,053	1.00	312	930	1,242	1.00
KMT																				
Private																				
Sum	291	94	385	1.00	295	98	393	1.00	283	441	724	1.00	309	744	1,053	1.00	312	930	1,242	1.00

Investment and trust companies

Category	(1)	(2)	Total	Prop.	(1)	(2)	Total	Prop.	(1)	(2)	Total	Prop.	(1)	(2)	Total	Prop.	(1)	(2)	Total	Prop.
Public			1				0				1	0.04	6	1	7	0.13			10	0.19
KMT							1				3	0.12	6	2	8	0.15			3	0.06
Private			0				17				22	0.85	34	5	39	0.72			41	0.76
Sum			1	1.00			18	1.00			26	1.00	46	8	54	1.00			54	1.00

Postal savings system

Category	(1)	(2)	Total	Prop.	(1)	(2)	Total	Prop.	(1)	(2)	Total	Prop.	(1)	(2)	Total	Prop.	(1)	(2)	Total	Prop.
Public	1	450	451	1.00	1	609	610	1.00	1	951	952	1.00	1	1,201	1,202	1.00	1	1,268	1,269	1.00
KMT																				
Private																				
Sum	1	450	451	1.00	1	609	610	1.00	1	951	952	1.00	1	1,201	1,202	1.00	1	1,268	1,269	1.00

Life insurance companies

Category	(1)	(2)	Total	Prop.	(1)	(2)	Total	Prop.	(1)	(2)	Total	Prop.	(1)	(2)	Total	Prop.	(1)	(2)	Total	Prop.
Public	3	5	8	1.00	3	6	9	0.26	3	6	9	0.15	3	6	9	0.12	3	6	9	0.08
KMT																	1	0	1	0.01
Private					6	20	26	0.74	6	46	52	0.85	12	55	67	0.88	27	77	104	0.91
Sum	3	5	8	1.00	9	26	35	1.00	9	52	61	1.00	15	61	76	1.00	31	83	114	1.00

Property insurance companies

Category	(1)	(2)	Total	Prop.	(1)	(2)	Total	Prop.	(1)	(2)	Total	Prop.	(1)	(2)	Total	Prop.	(1)	(2)	Total	Prop.
Public	2	7	9	0.50	2	10	12	0.29	2	12	14	0.20	3	14	17	0.17	3	16	19	0.16
KMT					1	0	1	0.02	1	1	2	0.03	1	4	5	0.05	1	5	6	0.05
Private	6	3	9	0.50	11	17	28	0.68	11	43	54	0.77	16	60	76	0.78	19	78	97	0.80
Sum	8	10	18	1.00	14	27	41	1.00	14	56	70	1.00	20	78	98	1.00	23	99	122	1.00

(*continued*)

Table 7.2   (continued)

Type and Control[a]	1961				1970				1980				1990				1995			
	Co.	Bra.	Units	Ratio	Co.	Bra.	Units	Ratio	Co.	Bra.	Units	Ratio	Co.	Bra.	Units	Ratio	Co.	Bra.	Units	Ratio
Bill and securities finance companies																				
Public									2	2	4	0.50	2	11	13	0.62	2	15	17	0.37
KMT									2	2	4	0.50	2	6	8	0.38	2	8	10	0.22
Private																	10	9	19	0.41
Sum									4	4	8	1.00	4	17	21	1.00	14	32	46	1.00
Total																				
Public	308	844	1,152	0.85	314	1,134	1,448	0.80	305	1,988	2,293	0.81	333	2,751	3,084	0.76	336	3,283	3,619	0.67
KMT						1	1	0.00	6	5	11	0.00	6	32	38	0.01	9	158	167	0.03
Private	94	112	206	0.15	109	250	359	0.20	106	426	532	0.19	116	802	918	0.23	156	1,441	1,597	0.30
Sum	402	956	1,358	1.00	424	1,384	1,808	1.00	417	2,419	2,836	1.00	455	3,585	4,040	1.00	501	4,882	5,383	1.00

Sources: Central Bank of China, *List of Financial Institutions* (Taipei, 1996), and Central Bank of China, *Financial Statistics Monthly* (various issues).

Note: Co. = number of companies; Bra. = number of branches.

[a] "Public" means publicly controlled financial institutions, which include, in addition to undisputed ones, International Commercial Bank of China, Taiwan Business Bank, Directorate General of Post Remittances and Savings Bank, credit departments of farmer and fishery associations, Taiwan Development and Trust Co., China Bills Finance Co., International Bills Finance Co., Taiwan Fire and Marine Insurance Co., Chung Kuo Insurance Co., and Taiwan Life Insurance Co. "KMT" means KMT-controlled institutions, which include Sinopad Commercial Bank, United World Chinese Commercial Bank, Chinatrust Commercial Bank, Kaohsiung Business Bank (after 1995), China Development Corp., China United Trust and Investment Co. (before 1994), Chung Hsing Bills Finance Co., Fuh-Hwa Securities Finance Co., Central Insurance Co., and Shin Fu Life Insurance Co.

Table 7.3   Total Assets of Financial Institutions in Taiwan (million NT dollars)

Type	1990				1995			
	Public	KMT	Private	Total	Public	KMT	Private	Total
Central bank	2,646,854 (1.000) [0.272]			2,646,854 (1.000) [0.210]	3,100,536 (1.000) [0.197]			3,100,536 (1.000) [0.132]
Domestic banks	6,323,824 (0.901) [0.649]	220,991 (0.032) [0.643]	472,398 (0.067) [0.190]	7,017,213 (1.000) [0.558]	10,921,453 (0.750) [0.693]	934,287 (0.039) [0.848]	2,709,153 (0.211) [0.411]	14,564,893 (1.000) [0.621]
Local branches of foreign banks			313,645 (1.000) [0.126]	313,645 (1.000) [0.025]			603,101 (1.000) [0.092]	603,101 (1.000) [0.026]
Credit cooperatives			879,120 (1.000) [0.353]	879,120 (1.000) [0.070]			1,764,234 (1.000) [0.268]	1,764,234 (1.000) [0.075]
Credit departments of farmer associations	632,079 (1.000) [0.065]			632,079 (1.000) [0.050]	1,359,532 (1.000) [0.086]			1,359,532 (1.000) [0.058]
Credit departments of fishery associations	11,075 (1.000) [0.001]			11,075 (1.000) [0.001]	28,056 (1.000) [0.002]			28,056 (1.000) [0.001]
Investment and trust companies	24,514 (0.052) [0.003]	62,172 (0.132) [0.181]	383,651 (0.816) [0.154]	470,337 (1.000) [0.037]	57,361 (0.146) [0.004]	52,702 (0.134) [0.048]	282,353 (0.720) [0.043]	392,416 (1.000) [0.017]
Bill finance companies	19,024 (0.543) [0.002]	16,010 (0.457) [0.047]		35,034 (1.000) [0.003]	37,812 (0.421) [0.002]	23,167 (0.258) [0.021]	28,827 (0.321) [0.004]	89,806 (1.000) [0.004]

(continued)

Table 7.3 (continued)

Type	1990				1995			
	Public	KMT	Private	Total	Public	KMT	Private	Total
Securities finance companies		42,349 (1.000) [0.123]		42,349 (1.000) [0.003]		83,686 (0.767) [0.076]	25,369 (0.233) [0.004]	109,055 (1.000) [0.005]
Property and casualty insurance companies	9,607 (0.186) [0.001]	2,433 (0.047) [0.007]	39,585 (0.767) [0.016]	51,625 (1.000) [0.004]	20,560 (0.171) [0.001]	5,239 (0.044) [0.005]	94,204 (0.785) [0.014]	120,003 (1.000) [0.005]
Life insurance companies	65,912 (0.141) [0.007]		403,043 (0.859) [0.162]	468,955 (1.000) [0.037]	212,897 (0.165) [0.014]	2,169 (0.002) [0.002]	1,076,499 (0.833) [0.164]	1,291,565 (1.000) [0.055]
Central reinsurance company	3,373 (1.000) [0.000]			3,373 (1.000) [0.000]	6,542 (1.000) [0.000]			6,542 (1.000) [0.000]
Property and casualty insurance cooperatives	343 (1.000) [0.000]			343 (1.000) [0.000]	297 (1.000) [0.000]			297 (1.000) [0.000]
Central deposit insurance company	2,343 (1.000) [0.000]			2,343 (1.000) [0.000]	8,009 (1.000) [0.000]			8,009 (1.000) [0.000]
Total	9,738,948 (0.775) [1.000]	343,955 (0.027) [1.000]	2,491,442 (0.198) [1.000]	12,574,345 (1.000) [1.000]	15,753,055 (0.672) [1.000]	1,101,250 (0.047) [1.000]	6,583,740 (0.281) [1.000]	23,438,045 (1.000) [1.000]

Sources: Central Bank of China, *Statistics of Important Business of Financial Institutions* (Taipei, 1990, 1995), Central Bank of China, *Financial Statistics Monthly* (March 1997).

Note: Medium business banks and postal savings systems are included in domestic banks; the other categories are the same as in table 7.2. Numbers in parentheses are horizontal percentages. Numbers in brackets are vertical percentages.

Table 7.4   **Kuomintang-Controlled Financial Businesses, 1997**

Holding Companies	Formal Financial System

Central Investment Holding Co.
  Founded 1971, investing 70 companies
  1995 Assets: NT$40.8 billion; profits $4.4
  billion
Hua Hsia Investment Holding Co.
  Founded 1975 (unofficially, 1991 officially)
  1995 Assets: $7 billion; profits: $680 million
Kuang Hwa Investment Holding Co.
  Founded 1979, investing 51 companies
  1995 Equity: $15.1 billion; profits: $1.7 billion
Asia Pacific Holding Co.
  Founded 1991, overseas investment
Chii Sheng Industrial Co.
  Founded 1988, oversees 17 companies
  1994 Profits: $105 million
Jen Hwa Investment Holding Co.
  Oversees Grand Cathay Securities
King-Dom Investment Holding Co.
  Oversees insurance investments
	Financial institutions
	Commercial banks
	  Sinopad Commercial Bank
	  Chinatrust Commercial Bank
	  United World Chinese Commercial Bank
	Medium business banks
	  Kaohsiung Business Bank
	Investment and trust
	  China Development Corp.
	Life insurance companies
	  Shin Fu Life Insurance Co.
	Property and casualty insurance companies
	  Central Insurance Co.
	Money market
	Chung Hsing Bills Finance Co.
	Capital Market
	Taiwan Stock Exchange Corp.
	Fuh-Hwa Securities Finance
	Securities dealers and traders
	  China Trust Investment Co.
	  Grand Cathay Securities Co.
	  International Investment Trust Co.

	Informal Financial System

	Leasing companies
	  Central Leasing Co.
	Investment companies
	  Central Link Investment Consulting Co.
	  China Investment and Development Co.
	  Global Investment Holding Co.
	  Grand Cathay Venture Capital Co.
	  International Venture Capital Investment
	    Corp.
	  Tai Shin Venture Capital Co.
	  Universal Venture Capital Investment Corp.

Source: Laurie Underwood, "How Big is Big?" *Topics* 27, no. 4 (May 1997): 29–32.

two types, preventive interventions and positive interventions. Preventive interventions are those measures meant to keep the system transparent and to prevent bankruptcy. These measures include reserve requirements, equity ratios, deposit rates, deposit insurance, auditing and disclosure of information, and measures against insider trading. Positive interventions consist of limitations on new financial institutions and products, regulated prices of financial services, and strategic financial policies. In Taiwan, positive measures in the past included strict entry restrictions on private banks, limits on new branches, government ownership of financial institutions, interest rate controls, restrictions on foreign banks, authorization of bank products, and preferential policies for exports, for small and medium-size businesses, and for strategic industries (based on high linkage effects, promising market potential, high tech, high value added, low energy consumption, and low pollution). The strategic financial policies have let the Development Fund of the Executive Yuan create some investment funds and development corporations.

For preventive banking regulation, according to Baltensperger and Dermine (1987), there are three motives: bank safety and overall financial stability, monetary control, and prevention of monopoly activity and concentration. It is widely recognized in Taiwan that the most success has been achieved in terms of monetary control and price stability. There has been total failure in terms of making the system more transparent and preventing monopoly, concentration, and insider manipulation. Results have been somewhat in between in terms of financial safety and stability (see Shea 1994, Yang 1994, 1997; Patrick 1994). The positive interventions have often been criticized as being inefficient and hampering past growth. Specifically, for example, most small and medium-size firms could not obtain funds from the formal financial system or take advantage of the strategic preferential policies, except for export credits. They have had to pursue underground capital bearing a much higher interest rate (see Shea 1994, 233; and fig. 7.2). In general, much of the financial inefficiency and underdevelopment were blamed on the high degree of government intervention in interest rate determination, as well as in financial intermediation, market structure, and banking operations (Shea 1994, 222).

7.3   The Liberalization of Financial Policy

Financial reform in Taiwan is a long and accelerating process. Since the financial system was heavily regulated and broadly criticized as a backward sector damaging the whole economy, the financial deregulation has been under way for a long time. The financial reform embraces liberalization, privatization, and internationalization. Financial liberalization includes interest rate decontrol, market entry deregulation, and so forth. Privatization of government banks has been discussed and the authorities decided to reduce the government's equity in the three biggest commercial banks (First, Hua-Nan, and Chang-Hua) to below 50 percent by offering part of the stock in the market. This policy is controversial because the government will still wholly control the banks by holding some 40 percent of stock. Nevertheless, nothing was done until the end of 1997. While internationalization may not be segregated from liberalization, the government is mainly concerned with policies related to the development of Taiwan into an Asia-Pacific financial center.

The financial liberalization has been going ahead since the mid-1970s and was speeded up in the late 1980s. The major deregulations can be summarized as follows.

1. *Branches:* The regulations governing branching by existing banks were relaxed in 1984, allowing each qualified bank to set up three full-service branches and three limited-service agencies per year, as compared with two of each previously.

2. *Interest rates:* Decontrol has proceeded in several steps since 1975. The fixed and uniform rates (in formal financial markets) were gradually relaxed and were completely floated after 1989 when the new Bank Law was promulgated. However, since most of the major banks are still government controlled, competition is less than complete.

3. *Bank activities:* The 1989 Bank Law granted MOF the power to authorize new financial products. For example, bill transactions formerly conducted only by bill finance companies were opened to some private banks in 1992.

4. *Private banks:* The 1989 Bank Law liberalized regulations concerning the establishment of new private banks. Fifteen new private banks, each with a minimum equity of NT$10 billion required by the law, were granted charters in 1991. By May 1997, nineteen new private banks were established and operating, creating better service attitudes, even in public banks, and more competition in the whole banking industry.

5. *Foreign exchange:* The central bank introduced a floating system in 1978 but still continuously intervened up until the mid-1980s, which resulted in an undervaluation of the NT dollar, huge trade surpluses, short-term speculative capital inflows, and a boosted money supply. In 1987, the authorities phased out most of the controls and liberalized long-term exchange rates, and by 1990 liberalized short-term exchange rates.

6. *Foreign banks:* Before liberalizing private banks owned and operated by Taiwanese, foreign banks were allowed to set up local branches in Taiwan. But only one branch would be approved for each foreign bank before 1986 in Taipei. This was gradually relaxed, and by 1994 there were no more restrictions on the number of branches if the transmitted capital from their head offices is over NT$150 million for the first branch and over NT$1.2 million for each additional branch. Banks were also authorized to open branches in Kaohsiung and Taichung in 1985 and 1990, respectively.

By far the most ambitious reform of Taiwan's financial institutions has been the plan for developing Taiwan into an Asia-Pacific Regional Operations Center (CEPD 1995). The core of the plan is the designation of six specific operation centers—a manufacturing center, sea transportation center, air transportation center, financial center, telecommunications center, and media center. According to CEPD, developing Taiwan as a financial center means "establishing it as a base from which domestic and foreign financial institutions may provide transnational financial services for

the East Asian region" (1995, 22–30). In the short term, the plan emphasizes the development of offshore financial markets, a derivative market,
a gold market, bond and securities markets, the stock market, and the
insurance market. For example, offshore financial markets include the establishment of a regional fund-raising center, foreign exchange market,
offshore banking market, and foreign currency call-loan market.

"Concrete measures," as stated in CEPD, are to relax restrictions on
inward and outward capital transfers, on foreign banks, on the operations
of financing companies, and on "cross-(Taiwan)Strait" regulation, to en-
act reasonable taxation of financial transactions, to speed up the privatization of state-owned banks, which includes enacting the Law Governing
the Administration of State-Owned Financial Institutions and reviewing
the classification and separation of banking activities. Other complementary policies are the training of financial personnel and the establishment
of infrastructure such as building an international financial complex and
improving the quality of telecommunications facilities.

In fact, the idea of a regional financial center began in 1982 when the
Executive Yuan approved the Project of Uplifting Taiwan's Position in
East Asia. In accordance with the project, the Offshore Banking Center
was set up in 1984, but only the International Commercial Bank of China
(Taiwan) established an offshore banking unit. The internationalization
process was very slow before 1987 when exchange controls were relaxed.
The important measures adopted by the end of 1990 consisted of capital
flow deregulation; access to the domestic financial market, for example,
liberalizing branching and activities of foreign banks, creating an offshore
banking center, and setting up financial institutions abroad for which the
restrictions limiting overseas branches by domestic banks were lifted in
1988 by MOF; and establishment of the Taipei Foreign Currency Call
Loan Market. However, if the system of government ownership is not
changed, the prospects for the regional financial center plan can hardly
be optimistic.

7.4 Comparisons of the Financial Development
of Japan, Korea, and Taiwan

One way to understand the Taiwanese financial system, its reform and
problems, is to compare them with those of Japan and Korea. The three
countries share common economic and institutional circumstances and
patterns of development, but they also have certain significant differences.[2]

As for major similarities, commercial banks have been the core of all
three financial systems, and capital markets were developed later and are

2. This section draws heavily from Patrick and Park (1994).

relatively unimportant. The systems have been characterized by separation between the formal and informal sectors and between commercial and investment banking, and within banking by segmentation by borrower and function (e.g., see table 7.1). All three countries pursued export-oriented development strategies while concurrently protecting most of their domestic production from imports to support their preeminent objective of rapid growth. To achieve macroeconomic goals, the financial authorities have used their control of the financial system to channel funds to investment in priority sectors through, for example, central bank rediscount of export trade bills at low interest rates. The three economies all lack reliable accounting and auditing systems and also lack publicly available information on company performance, prospects, and hence creditworthiness. Banks have therefore found it cheaper and safer to require collateral, usually specific real assets, against loans rather than rely on the business performance of borrowers. Accordingly, banks are criticized for "pawnshop" banking. Supervision by the financial authorities has not been transparent. Consequently, these countries have been denounced as "insider societies"—societies taking the existence and utilization of insider information for granted, making few efforts to prevent insider trade, and enforcing few penalties for misuse (Patrick 1994, 338, 353).

Before deregulation began seriously in Japan in the 1970s and in Korea and Taiwan in the 1980s, the financial authorities held interest rates at below-market levels, restricted entry of new financial institutions and creation of new financial instruments, segmented financial markets, and insulated domestic finance from world financial markets. The most important domestic regulations were government-established or sanctioned ceilings for interest rates on deposits, loans, and new bond issues—so-called financial repression. Korea has been the most repressed of the three, Taiwan next, and Japan the least (see table 7.5). Because of the degree and the implementation of the financial repression, the financial system and the indirect intervention by the government have developed differently. Thus the consequences of financial repression were different in the three countries.

In Japan, lending institutions evaded interest rate ceilings by requiring compensating balances or loan-related fee income, so that effective interest rates for the borrower were raised closer to the market level, and the possibilities of inefficient credit allocation and rent-seeking activities by the real sector were reduced accordingly. However, rents accrued to the banks in the form of higher profits, higher wages, less efficient management, and perhaps less risk taking in loan portfolios than would otherwise have been the case (Patrick 1994, 337). In Korea and Taiwan, recipients of rationed credit are major financial supporters of the political apparatus in power. In Korea, with the biggest interest rate gap among the three countries between bank and curb market loans, rationed credit was re-

Table 7.5   Indicators of Relative Financial Liberalization of Japan, Korea, and Taiwan

	Japan		Korea		Taiwan	
Indicator	1965	1990	1965	1990	1965	1990
FIR[a]	3.62	6.62	0.89	4.55	1.61	4.95
Overall level						
Domestic	Low	High	Low	Medium	Low	High
International	Low	High	Low	Low	Low	Medium
Government involvement						
Ownership of banks	Low	Low	High	Low	High	Medium
Credit allocation	Medium	Low	High	High	High	Medium
Interest rate controls	High	Low	High	High	High	Low
Possibility of new bank						
entry	None	None	None	Low	None	High

Source: Patrick (1994, 342).

[a]FIR stands for financial intermediation ratio (ratio of financial assets to GNP).

ceived by big private business groups. The government not only forced the banks to make huge numbers of policy loans to selected firms in designated industries, but foreign funds were also borrowed by the government and relent to those big business groups at interest rates substantially below market rates (Patrick 1994, 330, 335, 349, 351). In Taiwan, state enterprises, which operate in major basic industries as well as public utilities, communications, and transportation, were granted a large share of rationed credit. The rest went to KMT enterprises, for obvious political reasons, well-managed big private enterprises, because of the conservative nature of state-owned commercial banks where severe penalties were readily imposed on bank officials for defaulted loans, and export credits, due to the government's industrial policy.

Korea had a fundamental problem in the real sector because those big private business groups granted substantial profit margins and government subsidies were generally producing "bleeding exports." Japan's financial institutions retained huge profits that inevitably invited all kind of scandals and fraudulent activities contrary to the interest of shareholders. In Taiwan, the profit margins on low-interest loans were partly engulfed by the inefficiency of public enterprises and KMT enterprises and partly embezzled by KMT enterprises and big private enterprises. Obviously the ruling party enjoyed both economic and political gains at the cost of inefficiencies and inequities in the use of financial capital.

Deregulation and liberalization of financial markets and institutions in all three countries has been a conscious, gradual, piecemeal process. Policymakers decided to liberalize financial markets in response to changing circumstances—domestic market forces, changing political constituencies and their concerns, and globalization. Previous forms of repression have become less effective because the economies are now more mature, the curb markets undermined the regulated market, and current account surpluses created domestic liquidity and affected market interest rates. Moreover, foreign pressures have compelled the economies to open their domestic markets to international competition. The authorities have issued timetables to abolish credit and interest rate ceilings, relax entry and financial instrument barriers, and open the economies to international financial flows. These policies have been more or less implemented. Over time, the degree of liberalization has been substantial, at least in Japan and Taiwan, as shown in table 7.5.

Judging from what has happened during the Asian financial crisis of 1997, Patrick (1994) has almost perfectly summarized and distinguished these three countries' financial development. However, two fundamental structural issues in Taiwan have been neglected. One is the spurious nature of privatization and the other is the existence of KMT enterprises. Patrick has made it clear that privatization is not equal to liberalization. He points out that even a decade after the banks were privatized in Korea, the government still appointed new presidents for five of the commercial banks and continued to intrude into banks' lending policies and management (Patrick 1994, 349). However, special problems concerning privatization in Taiwan have been totally neglected in all financial studies (see, e.g., Patrick 1994; Park 1994; Shea 1994; Yang 1994, 1997).

Patrick is very sensitive in the interaction of the financial system and the sociopolitical system. Since finance is a very powerful instrument, when the power to allocate credit lies in the hands of the political and government bureaucratic authorities, the use of finance to support the political apparatus in power, to finance elections, and to reward supporters has been condemned (Patrick 1994, 337, 338, 366). Nevertheless, Patrick does not mention the involvement of the KMT in the financial market, although Yang (1994, 299) briefly describes KMT enterprises in the same volume (Patrick and Park 1994). These and other issues will be addressed in the next section.

7.5 Evaluation of Financial Reform in Taiwan

As mentioned before and as Ito and Krueger (1996, 2) have stated, Taiwan's financial deregulation has been due at least in part to the ineffectiveness of earlier types of regulation that came under stress from worldwide financial integration. In other words, international pressures have played a significant role in the financial liberalization in Taiwan. Hence, before criticizing the financial reform policy, it is worthwhile to point out the importance of internationalization. In fact, the export-oriented strategy itself serves as a built-in ratchet to check all domestic policies that threaten global competitiveness.

It is generally agreed that Taiwan's comparative advantages in setting up a regional financial center include (1) good location; (2) competent marine transportation; (3) massive international trade; (4) huge trade surpluses and cumulative foreign reserves, which are especially beneficial for a regional funding center; and (5) the Hong Kong situation after 1997. Its disadvantages are (1) inefficiency of government administration; (2) poor infrastructure including local communication and transportation; (3) lack of internationally experienced personnel; (4) existing government-owned financial institutions; (5) lack of comparable internationalized financial regulations in such areas as foreign exchange control, international finance, deposits of foreigners and foreign deposits of Taiwanese, and the tax system; and (6) the political difficulty of Taiwan's government joining the international community. Obviously, financial internationalization will solve many of these problems. Moreover, international pressure has always been the best means to liberalize domestic restrictions in Taiwan. A number of historical events support this viewpoint.

U.S. aid to Taiwan after the Korean War had an important influence in creating Taiwan's booming private enterprise system. "Without the intervention of AID (Agency for International Development), private enterprise would not have become, by 1965, the mainspring in Taiwan's economy" (Jacoby 1966, 138). A leading example of AID's promotion of the private sector was the establishment of the China Development Corporation in 1959, which was considered "the most important aid-sponsored industrial finance intermediary . . . with original capital provided by a Development Loan Fund loan" (191).[3]

In the 1980s, due to preferential financial policies toward exports, including an undervaluation of the NT dollar, Taiwan had abundant trade surpluses, which accumulated huge foreign reserves. Although this created substantial inflationary pressure, the belief that "only exports matter" could not be changed. Prolonged criticism by many local economists and some government officials proved of little use. It was in response to pressure from the U.S. government that Taiwan started to liberalize its foreign exchange rate controls (Yang 1997). Also in the 1980s, U.S. pressure played a determinate role in opening markets in banking, insurance, telecommunications, and other service sectors for domestic investors. In fact, in many cases liberalization policies affected foreigners much earlier than they did domestic business. For example, local branches of foreign banks (all privately owned) were welcomed much earlier than private domestic banks, which only became legal in 1989.[4]

Even today, U.S. pressure to open up the telecommunications business

---

3. Interestingly enough, China Development Corporation is now a KMT-controlled venture capital company and serves as the headquarters of the KMT enterprises.

4. The free import of tobacco and wine (made by foreign private firms) coupled with the local Monopoly Bureau of Tobacco and Wine has resulted in the bizarre fact that anyone in the world can produce wine and tobacco to sell in Taiwan except Taiwanese.

in exchange for supporting Taiwan's bid to join the World Trade Organization is playing the primary role in opening the industry to the private sector. Schive and Jan (1997) study the process of financial deregulation in Taiwan during 1990–97 and find this was also true for the financial market. In other words, the shortest way to arrive at the liberalization of domestic markets in Taiwan is follow a path from Taipei via Washington back to Taipei.

A general problem in the Taiwanese financial system is that the informal financial system is still not subject to prudential supervision, while the formal system is subject to insufficient preventive regulations and a lack of strict enforcement of those regulations that do exist. Three more specific structural problems threaten the Taiwanese financial system: first, multiple systems of oversight for the formal financial system; second, KMT-controlled financial institutions; and third, fraudulent privatization. The first two problems have not been dealt with by the financial reform, and the third is expected to be created by the reform.

In the past decade, several ill-functioning financial institutions have suffered runs and even bankruptcy, all of them either credit cooperative associations or credit departments of farmer associations. The problem stems from the multiple systems governing formal financial institutions, one for Postal Remittances and Savings, another for credit co-ops (there is some difference between credit cooperative associations and credit departments of farmer associations), and a third for banks. The multisystem creates an unfair competitive disadvantage for normal banks. As mentioned earlier, credit co-ops were privileged substitutes for commercial banks while private banks were completely prohibited before 1990. The direct authorities over the credit departments of farmer and fishery associations are the Ministry of the Interior and the Council of Agriculture, not the usual financial authorities. The problems are made worse by the fact that farmer and fishery associations have historically been the auxiliary election headquarters of the KMT.[5] The credit departments of farmer associations hold many bad and overdue loans.

The second structural problem, the prominence of KMT-controlled enterprises in the financial system, and the third problem, fraudulent privatization of state enterprises, must be discussed together because they are closely intertwined.

The KMT owns or controls many enterprises in both the formal and informal financial sectors, as shown in table 7.4. In addition, the Central Investment Holding Company used to control two important financial institutions through the KMT's political power without investing any

---

5. The credit departments of the farmer and fishery associations are generally classified as "private" financial institutions (e.g., Shea 1994, 284). However, since the government effectively controls the associations, these credit departments are controlled by the government.

money. The first is the International Commercial Bank of China (ICBC).[6] ICBC was created prior to 1912 in the Ching Dynasty in mainland China as the Bank of the Great Ching. It then became the Bank of China in 1912 after the revolution and was finally "privatized" in 1971 to avoid seizure of its overseas assets by the People's Republic of China when it replaced the Republic of China in the United Nations. From 1971 to 1994, more than 75 percent of ICBC stock shares were owned by the Development Fund of the Executive Yuan. However, the Development Fund entrusted some 30 percent of the ICBC shares to the Central Investment Holding Company (CIHC), registered the shares in its name, and claimed ICBC was a "private" firm (for then the percentage of state-owned shares was below 50 percent). During this period, ICBC was not monitored by the Legislative Yuan and the Control Yuan. ICBC registered its investment in the Chinese American Bank in the United States using the same trick and was found out and fined by the U.S. government in 1997 for false registration. The Development Fund reclaimed the shares held in the CIHC's name in 1994 and sold them. The second case is that of the China Bills Finance Company. The Development Fund held some 35 percent of the shares of China Bills Finance and registered all of them under the CIHC so that China Bills Finance was again claimed to be a private firm. The story is almost the same as that of ICBC. During this period, there were three bill finance companies in Taiwan (the only securities finance company shown in table 7.4 is Fuh-Hwa Securities Finance, which is also owned by the KMT): Chung Hsing Bills Finance, owned by the KMT (see table 7.4); International Bills Finance, owned by ICBC; and China Bills Finance. The KMT thus controlled all of them.

The privatization of the state-owned banks has long been a target. In fact, while ICBC was privatizing in 1971, privatization of the state-owned banks attracted much discussion. Taiwan launched its privatization program in 1989 and started to privatize some state-owned enterprises after 1994. However, these privatizations always ended in one of three results: Type I privatizations are those in which the state maintains control of the "privatized" enterprise (Chang and Olds 1996). Type II privatizations are those in which the "privatized" enterprise becomes a party-controlled enterprise. And Type III privatizations are simply a mix of Types I and II. These privatizations are shown in table 7.6. The privatization of the state-

---

6. In fact, a lot of mistakes are made in distinguishing whether financial institutions in Taiwan are public, private, or KMT enterprises. While ICBC and China Bills Finance are both government owned, they have been controlled by the KMT for a long time. The former was classified as privately owned and the latter as KMT owned (Yang 1994, 298). Farmer and fishery associations are totally controlled by the government, and Fuh-Hwa Securities is KMT controlled; however, all of these were identified as privately owned (e.g., Shea 1994, 284).

Table 7.6   **"Privatized" Public Enterprises**

Enterprise	Date of "Privatization"	Government Shareholding (%)	Party-ization?
Chung Kuo Insurance	March 1994	36.36	
BES Engineering	June 1994	0	Yes
China Petrochemical Development	June 1994	16.20	Partly
China Steel	March 1995	42.10	
Liquidised Petroleum Supply Administration	July 1995	0	Yes
Yang Ming Marine Transportation	February 1996	45.04	

Note: Government shareholding and party-ization are as of 1 May 1997.

owned banks will obviously follow the Type I method of privatization, as stated in Shea (1994, 260). There are other Type I state-controlled enterprises, one of them being ICBC (Yang 1994, 298).

When we say a "publicly" owned and operated firm, the word "publicly" is put in quotation marks by Stiglitz:

In different countries there are different patterns and forms of ownership and control—as we would normally use those terms. While *nominally* all the property may belong to all of the people, the "people" do not directly exercise control, and even in democratic governments, the link between those who actually make decisions and those on whose "behalf" they exercise control may be very weak. In some countries control may be exercised directly from the planning "center" or the relevant industry ministry; in others a plant may be under the control of a large "firm," or the plant may be more directly under the control of its managers. In all of these cases there are myriad influences that affect the decisions, including the interests of the workers at the plant. When plants are establishment controlled, it is more common for the managers to be exercising their control nominally on behalf of the workers, with some limited attention being paid to the remote interest in the state as the provider or "owner" of the capital. (1995, 171)

"Public" companies not working in the public interest is a common theme. In Taiwan, the ruling party (KMT) and the state have been closely intertwined, and the economic system has been designated "KMT-state capitalism" (Chen et al. 1991). The ruling party is particularly powerful because it is a Leninistic party, which means the party overrules government administrators.

As a result of KMT-state capitalism, rumors of rent-seeking activities, insider trading, and, worse, policy insider trading have not ceased. Recently, it was rumored that up to twenty Democratic Progressive Party members of the National Assembly "borrowed" money from the KMT during the 1997 assembly with the understanding that they would collaborate with KMT proposals in place of repayment (*Journalist,* 18 May 1997, 77).

7.6 Concluding Remarks

The business service sector gains importance in a newly industrialized country such as Taiwan. The government seems to be coming to the realization that business service industries are important, because five out of six designated regional operation "centers" in its biggest development plan are in this sector. However, Chinese traditional culture holds this sector in contempt. Typical industrial policy still discriminates against it. To expose the conflicts and structural problems in this sector in Taiwan, I have used the financial system as an example.

The literature devoting itself to Taiwan's financial system typically confronts a paradox because it usually begins from "miracle" economic development experiences (high growth rate, equalized income distribution, low unemployment rate, and stable prices; e.g., Shea 1994, 222–23) and ends up concluding that the financial system is underdeveloped, rigid, and inefficient (e.g., Shea 1994, 266) or that "the maintenance of financial efficiency and financial stability simultaneously becomes a challenge for the government" (Yang 1997). While it may suggest to the third world that an underdeveloped financial system is compatible with an "economic miracle," it is an unsuccessful story from the viewpoint of the Taiwanese because the economic growth of Taiwan is mediocre compared to that of Japan, Hong Kong, and Singapore.

The reform in the financial system reveals that liberalization and internationalization are only half-measures. Privatization is partial and results in "nationalization of private-owned enterprises" and "party-ization." Solutions to the structural problems in the financial system are straightforward. Prospects for such solutions are dim under the current ruling party, however.

References

Baltensperger, Ernst, and Jean Dermine. 1987. Banking deregulation in Europe. *Economic Policy: A European Forum* 4 (April): 63–109.
Baum, Julian. 1994. The money machine. *Far Eastern Economic Review,* 11 August, 62–67.
Bruton, Sandra. 1993. Backlash against money. *Time,* 23 August, 20–22.
CEPD (Council for Economic Planning and Development). 1995. *The plan for developing Taiwan as an Asia-Pacific regional operations center.* Taipei: Executive Yuan, Council for Economic Planning and Development, 5 January.

Chang, Ching-hsi, and Kelly Olds. 1996. The case against partial privatization. In *Proceedings of the National Central University's first international conference on Pacific Basin business and economics,* 385–401. Chungli, Taiwan: National Central University.

Chen, Shih-Meng S., et al. 1991. *Disintegrating KMT-state capitalism: A closer look at privatizing Taiwan's state- and party-owned enterprises* (in Chinese). Taipei: Taipei Society.

Delury, George E., ed. 1987. *World encyclopedia of political systems and parties.* New York: Facts on File.

Hayek, Friedrich August. 1988. *The fatal conceit: The errors of socialism.* Vol. 1 of *The collected works of Friedrich August Hayek,* ed. W. W. Bartley III. New York: Routledge.

Ito, T., and A. O. Krueger, eds. 1996. *Financial deregulation and integration in East Asia.* Chicago: University of Chicago Press.

Jacoby, Neil H. 1966. *U.S. aid to Taiwan: A study of foreign aid, self-help, and development.* New York: Praeger.

Murphy, Kevin M., Andrei Shleifer, and Robert W. Vishny. 1993. Why is rent-seeking so costly to growth? *American Economic Review: Papers and Proceedings* 83, no. 2 (May): 409–14.

Park, Yung Chul. 1994. Concepts and issues. In *The financial development of Japan, Korea, and Taiwan: Growth, repression and liberalization,* ed. H. T. Patrick and Y. C. Park, 3–26. Oxford: Oxford University Press.

Patrick, Hugh T. 1994. Comparisons, contrasts and implications. In *The financial development of Japan, Korea, and Taiwan: Growth, repression and liberalization,* ed. H. T. Patrick and Y. C. Park, 325–71. Oxford: Oxford University Press.

Patrick, Hugh T., and Yung Chul Park, eds. 1994. *The financial development of Japan, Korea, and Taiwan: Growth, repression and liberalization.* Oxford: Oxford University Press.

Schive, Chi, and Fang-Guan Jan. 1997. The relationships of WTO and financial liberalization and internationalization in Taiwan. Paper presented at the Conference on Monetary and Financial Policies, National Taiwan University, Taipei, September.

Shea, Jia-Dong. 1994. Taiwan: Development and structural change of the financial system. In *The financial development of Japan, Korea, and Taiwan: Growth, repression and liberalization,* ed. H. T. Patrick and Y. C. Park, 222–87. Oxford: Oxford University Press.

Shea, Jia-Dong, and Ping-Sing Kuo. 1984. The allocative efficiency of banks' loanable funds in Taiwan (in Chinese). In *Proceedings of the conference on financial development in Taiwan,* 111–51. Taipei: Academia Sinica.

Smith, Adam. (1776) 1976. *An inquiry into the nature and causes of the wealth of nations,* vols. 1 and 2. Edited by Edwin Cannan. Chicago: University of Chicago Press.

Stiglitz, Joseph E. 1995. Privatization. In *Whither socialism?* by Joseph E. Stiglitz, 109–38. Cambridge, Mass.: MIT Press.

Wallis, John Joseph, and Douglass C. North. 1986. Measuring the transaction sector in the American economy, 1879–1970. In *Long-term factors in American economic growth,* ed. S. L. Engerman and R. E. Gallman, 95–161. Chicago: University of Chicago Press.

Yang, Ya-Hwei. 1994. Taiwan: Development and structural change of the banking system. In *The financial development of Japan, Korea, and Taiwan: Growth, repression and liberalization,* ed. H. T. Patrick and Y. C. Park, 288–324. Oxford: Oxford University Press.

———. 1997. An overview of Taiwan's financial system and financial policy. *Revista de Estudios Asiaticos* (Complutense University of Madrid), no. 4 (January–June): 59–73.

Comment   Motoshige Itoh

Ching-hsi Chang offers a good description of the basic characteristics of Taiwan's traditional financial system and the process of its reform under international competition in the financial industry. Like such East Asian countries as Japan and Korea, Taiwan has a financial system that is characterized by various kinds of severe government regulations, such as interest ceilings and entry barriers, and by strong public control of the management of financial institutions. In fact, the paper has a section that compares Taiwan's financial system with those in Japan and Korea.

One of the distinguishing features of Taiwan's financial system is the important portion of financial institutions owned and controlled by a political party. This feature is not found in Japan. It is interesting to know how important this political feature was for the slow pace of financial deregulation in Taiwan. Not only Taiwan but also other countries in Asia have their own reasons for the slow or quick speeds of their deregulation processes. For example, when one discusses the process of deregulation in Japan, one cannot neglect the role of bureaucrats (Ministry of Finance) and their relations with the financial industry. Although Chang does not go into detail about the political elements of the deregulation of Taiwan's financial system, more comment on this issue might make the process of deregulation clearer to readers.

It is interesting to know that the structure of the traditional Taiwanese financial system has many features in common with the systems in Japan and Korea. The three countries also have the common feature that manufacturing industries took off earlier than service sectors. In fact, the three countries achieved strong comparative advantages in their manufacturing sectors in spite of heavily regulated financial sectors. As Chang points out, Asian-style industrial policy, in which financial resources are concentrated in targeted industries and financial support is provided to export-oriented industry, is a vivid feature of Taiwan's financial system; it is very similar to practices in Japan and Korea. There is a vast literature on the effect of industrial policy, especially financial support policy, on the industrialization process; it might be useful to compare the case of Taiwan with other East Asian countries in this context. One might ask the following question: How important is the financial system—in particular, its government-

Motoshige Itoh is professor of economics at the University of Tokyo.

controlled features—to the process of industrialization in Taiwan, and how is the deregulation process related to the stage of economic development in Taiwan? Although the paper emphasizes pressure from the United States as the most important element promoting deregulation, internal factors, especially the stage of economic development, must have an important influence on the structure of the financial system.

After the EASE8 meeting in Taiwan, currency crises hit several Asian countries, and the financial systems in these countries faced serious difficulties. Taiwan was not among this group. It is interesting to see what differences in Taiwan allowed it to stay out of the financial and currency crisis. The paper shows one difference between Taiwan and the other countries. The process of financial system deregulation in Taiwan seems to be slower than in neighboring countries. This slow process of deregulation may have kept Taiwan out of volatile short-term international capital flows.

Comment   Hirotaka Yamauchi

Ching-hsi Chang's paper deals with the regulatory reform of the financial market in Taiwan. The paper is very informative and interesting in that it depicts Taiwan's financial market comprehensively and compares it with those of Japan and Korea. Chang then evaluates Taiwan's financial policy, which raises many obstacles to liberalization, and concludes that the underdeveloped, rigid, and inefficient financial system creates a paradox when taken together with the economic development "miracle" in that country.

According to Chang, financial reform and regulatory policy change is now under way in Taiwan, but the complexity of the financial structure is the main obstacle to promoting real competition in this sector. Taiwan's financial sector consists of a formal system and an informal system. The distinction depends on whether or not a financial institution is subject to regulation by the Ministry of Finance. In the formal system, public ownership plays the main role, and the Kuomintang owns or controls most of the other, nonpublic financial institutions. In this situation, the many differences in competitive position among financial institutions are likely to spur complaints about the straight introduction of competition.

In a sense, it seems quite natural that this sector has a complex industrial configuration. Especially in an industry subject to tight government regulation, vested rights and interests are preserved, and mechanisms that

Hirotaka Yamauchi is professor of transport economics in the Faculty of Commerce, Hitotsubashi University.

curtail malperformance cannot work well. As a result, over time various types of financial institutions have survived, which could make the industry more complex. As Chang indicates, this situation resembles that in Japan—one reason why competition policies in Japan have been very slow in coming.

Recognizing many difficulties, Chang points out that the main forces driving the liberalization of financial markets are "foreign pressures," especially from the United States, and international competition. The "shortest way to arrive at the liberalization of domestic markets in Taiwan is follow a path from Taipei via Washington back to Taipei." And in order to create an international financial center, the government plans to implement a fair and transparent financial policy as well as to prepare the country's infrastructure for international financial trade. This situation is also very similar to that in Japan.

However, it seems to me that Chang's paper overlooks a very important point, which could be one of main sources of change in the industrial configuration. That is the dynamic process of domestic markets. As pointed out in the paper, until now regulatory reform and privatization in Taiwan's financial industry have not been so advanced; but competition, even in its infant stage, is likely to require further liberalization or deregulation, and such momentum has synergic effects on government policy. Individual entities want to act more freely to cope with emerging competitive pressures and therefore demand a more liberal environment. By analyzing explicitly and in detail the emerging competitive process in domestic financial markets, Chang's paper could be a more powerful, more useful study of Taiwan's financial sector.

Interest Rates, Credit Rationing, and Banking Deregulation in Taiwan

Chung-Shu Wu and Sheng-Cheng Hu

8.1 Introduction

Taiwanese financial markets are segmented into an official sector and an unofficial sector. Since the early 1980s, the government has undertaken gradual financial liberalization, leading to an expansion of the official sector. The purpose of this paper is to study the effect of financial liberalization, especially banking deregulation, on the behavior of interest rates.

The official (or formal) financial sector consists of domestic banks and other financial institutions, most of which are either government owned or semigovernment institutions.[1] The official sector also includes local branches of foreign banks (local foreign banks hereafter), whose assets accounted for 7.8 percent of all bank assets in 1987 and 5.5 percent in 1996. Domestic banks and local foreign banks are to some extent segmented. Local foreign banks serve primarily firms engaged in international trade. They rely on the money market rather than on deposits for their supply of funds because they are allowed to have only one branch in addition to their local headquarters.[2] Until the early 1980s, domestic

Chung-Shu Wu is a research fellow of the Institute of Economics, Academia Sinica, Taipei, Taiwan. Sheng-Cheng Hu is a research fellow and director of the Institute of Economics, Academia Sinica, Taipei, Taiwan.

The authors thank Takatoshi Ito, Shinji Takagi, and Moon-Soo Kang for helpful comments and suggestions; Jin-Lung Lin for valuable lessons on the use of the causality test; and Yi-Duang Chen of the Central Bank of China for providing valuable data and information on the market segmentation between domestic and local foreign banks.

1. Examples of financial institutions are credit companies, credit departments of farmers' and fishermen's associations, investment and trust companies, postal remittance and savings banks, insurance companies, and bill and securities finance companies.

2. Foreign banks were allowed to open only a local headquarters but not branches before 1986. They have been allowed to open one branch in addition to their local headquarters since then.

banks benefited from restricted entry, but their operations and their freedom to set interest rates were highly regulated by the government. As a result, they rationed credit by serving primarily large private and government enterprises.

The unofficial (or informal) financial sector takes various forms. "Roscas" (rotating savings and credit associations), *de-shia cheng chuang*s (i.e., underground money shops), postdated checks, unsecured loans from private sources, and individual deposits with firms are but a few examples.[3] According to Shea, Kuo, and Huang (1995), informal financing accounted for 48 percent of total borrowing by private enterprises in 1964. This ratio declined steadily to 27 percent in 1973 and then rose steadily back to 40 percent in 1980. The ratio fluctuated between 35 and 44 percent during the next seven years before it began to fall from 40 percent in 1987 to 25 percent in 1992. Overall, during the period 1964–92, informal financing accounted for slightly more than one-third of total borrowing by all private enterprises (excluding borrowing from money and bond markets). A survey conducted by the Central Bank of China (1996) shows that in 1995, 37 percent of borrowing by small and medium-size firms was from households and other businesses, compared with only 9 percent by large firms.

The informal financial sector also helps consumers overcome credit constraints. This can be illustrated by the fact that despite high housing prices, the home ownership rate in Taiwan has been not only high and rising (around 65 percent in 1980 and nearly 80 percent in 1991) but also quite uniform across the board. Even for the age cohort 30 years or younger, whose members are more likely to be credit constrained, the home ownership rate is nearly 80 percent. Overall, no more than 30 percent of Taiwanese consumers are credit constrained.[4] (See Chan and Hu 1997.)

Since the early 1980s, Taiwan has undertaken gradual liberalization of its financial markets, including banking deregulation, foreign exchange liberalization, establishment of the money market, and development of a financial monitoring system. Banking deregulation measures include abolishment of direct central bank control of bank interest rates, privatization of state banks, liberalization of entry of private banks, and relaxation of regulations with respect to bank business activities and the expansion of branches by existing banks. For example, domestic banks were allowed to open trust divisions and to trade securities beginning in 1987, and both

3. A rosca is essentially a mutual fund. Members of the rosca commit to putting a fixed sum of money into a pot for each period of the life of the rosca. The pot is then allocated to one of the members either randomly or through bidding. The next period, the process repeats itself except that previous winners are excluded from receiving the pot. The process continues until each member of the rosca has received the pot once. At this point, the rosca either is disbanded or begins all over again. See Besley, Coate, and Loury 1993.

4. According to Jappalli and Pagano (1989), the percentage of consumers who are credit constrained is 19 percent for the United States, 35 percent for Japan, and more than 50 percent for Italy, Spain, and Greece.

Table 8.1   **Important Developments in Taiwan's Financial Liberalization since the Early 1980s**

1. *November 1980:* The central bank promulgated and implemented the Guideline on the Adjustment of Bank Interest Rates, which allowed banks to set their own interest rates on negotiable certificates of deposit and debentures as well as on bill discounts. The range between the regulated maximum and minimum lending rates was also expanded.
2. *1984:* Entry regulations governing the branches of existing domestic banks were relaxed by allowing each qualified bank to set up three full-service and three limited-service branches per year, as compared with two each earlier. Effective August 1992, this maximum number of new branches each bank is allowed to set up per year was further increased to five.
3. *March 1985:* The Interest Regulation Act was abolished. Under the new system, the range of lending rates was expanded. In addition, banks were allowed to set their own rates on foreign currencies.
4. *January 1986:* The central bank reduced the categories of deposit rate ceilings from thirteen to four in number, thus allowing banks to set their own rates for various kinds of deposits.
5. *20 July 1989:* The Banking Law was revised effectively. The revised law deleted the remaining regulations controlling maximum deposit rates and maximum and minimum loan rates.
6. *1991 and 1992:* Sixteen new private banks were granted charters and began operation, and Chinatrust was converted from an investment and trust company to a commercial bank.
7. *May 1992:* The Ministry of Finance allowed banks to enter the secondary market to act as dealers and brokers. Before that time, there were only three bill finance companies in the money market.

Note: For more detailed information, see Shea (1992).

domestic and foreign banks were allowed to trade securities and to enter the credit card business beginning in 1988. Foreign banks have also been given more freedom to do business, including setting up a branch in addition to the local headquarters (see n. 2, above). Table 8.1 provides the key dates on which deregulation measures took effect. The government is now embarking on an ambitious plan to turn Taiwan into a regional operation center. The plan calls for the overhaul of the country's financial system and further liberalization and internationalization of its financial markets.

Financial liberalization affects both the quantities of financial transactions (loans and deposits) and prices (interest rates) in each sector by promoting competition, reducing the costs of financial transactions, and influencing the risk-taking behavior of financial institutions. While there have been debates about the welfare effects of Taiwan's financial deregulation (see Shea 1992), the purpose of this paper is to investigate whether financial liberalization has succeeded. We shall focus our attention on banking deregulation. We choose to study the price, rather than the quantity, effect of deregulation because only by studying the behavior of interest rates are we able to determine whether banking deregulation reduces market segmentation. Specifically, we shall study the effect of deregulation on the spreads between bank lending and deposit rates and the differential between official and black market interest rates.

The paper is organized as follows. Section 8.2 briefly describes our analytical framework. Section 8.3 provides the empirical results. Section 8.4 summarizes our main findings.

8.2 Analytical Framework

For analytical purposes, we can think of the banking industry as segmented between an official sector (o) and an unofficial sector (u). The unofficial banking sector is competitive. Entry into the official sector is prohibited; thus existing banks enjoy oligopoly power. In each sector $j = $ o,u, the lending rate is given by

$$(1) \qquad r_\ell^j = r + \rho_\ell^j + \tau_\ell^j,$$

where ρ_ℓ^j is the risk premium to cover the default risk of borrowers and τ_ℓ^j is the transactions cost of handling loans plus the possible oligopoly rents for banks in the official sector that enjoy oligopoly power. The deposit rate r_d^j is given by

$$(2) \qquad r_d^j = r + \rho_d^j - \tau_d^j,$$

where r is the risk-free rate, ρ_d^j is the risk premium (due to the default risk of the depository institutions), and τ_d^j is the transactions cost for handling small deposits plus oligopoly rents for banks if the sector is oligopolistic. In the official sector, since depository institutions are either government owned, or semigovernmental institutions, or local branches of reputable foreign banks, we can take $\rho_d^j = 0$.

From the above two equations, we obtain the spread between the loan and deposit rates:

$$(3) \qquad r_\ell^j - r_d^j = \rho^j + \tau^j,$$

where $\tau^j = \tau_d^j + \tau_\ell^j$, and $\rho^j = \rho_d^j - \rho_\ell^j$ are, respectively, the total transactions cost plus oligopoly rents and the risk premium.

If the official sector were competitive and fully integrated with the unofficial sector and there were no entry barriers, one would expect interest rates for each risk class, and thus average interest rates, to be equalized between the two sectors. The equalization of interest rates across sectors implies that the differential between unofficial (black market) and official interest rates is stationary and therefore that there are no long-term or short-term opportunities for arbitrage. Furthermore, information about interest rates in one market is useful in explaining interest rates in the other market.

In Taiwan, the two sectors are segmented. The official sector is regulated and the government sets an *upper* limit on lending rates; thus official lending institutions ration credit by making mainly low-risk loans (loans to large firms), leaving high-risk loans (loans to small and medium-size firms) to the unofficial sector. As a result, the average (lending) interest rate is higher in the unofficial sector than in the official sector, reflecting the differences in risk premiums as well as transactions costs and oligopoly rents in the two sectors.

The effects of banking deregulation are threefold. First is the (transactions) cost effect: the reduction or even elimination of red tape and restrictions on bank activities leads to a lower transactions cost. Second is the competition effect: the relaxation of barriers to new entry in the official sector reduces the oligopoly rents enjoyed by existing banks. Third is the risk-taking effect: the lifting of the maximum lending rates set by the government encourages risk taking by financial institutions in the official sector.

Equation (3) shows that the first two (cost and competition) effects lead to a lower lending rate and a narrower loan-deposit rate spread in the official sector. Whether the third (risk taking) effect increases the loan-deposit rate spread in the official sector depends on whether banks discriminate among their customers by risk. In the absence of discrimination, interest rate liberalization increases the fraction of riskier loans served by the official sector, leading to a rise in the (average) spread between the lending and deposit rates. If, however, banks do discriminate among their customers by risk, charging small and medium-size firms higher interest rates than they would large firms, the risk premium for each risk class remains unchanged. However, the "average" risk premium will appear to increase as a result of the interest rate liberalization that allows the banks to take riskier loans. Overall, banking deregulation lowers the "average" loan-deposit rate spread in the official sector if the competition and transactions cost effects dominate the risk-taking effect.

The competition and cost effects of banking deregulation cause a narrowing of the differential between unofficial and official interest rates. The risk-taking effect increases the interest rate differential if banks do not discriminate among customers by their risk or if we consider only average interest rates. Thus the overall effect of banking deregulation is to cause the convergence of the (average) interest rates of the two sectors depending on whether the risk-taking effect dominates the cost and competition effects. The official and unofficial rates need not converge. However, if the central bank sets interest rates and thereby causes credit rationing, or if banks have only limited freedom to deviate from the official rates, then interest rate liberalization tends to result in a lower interest rate differential.

Furthermore, if the two sectors are segmented and banks directly set interest rates, the official interest rate is unresponsive, while the unofficial interest rate is responsive, to market conditions. As a result, the interest rate differential fluctuates according to market conditions. Banking deregulation, especially relaxation of interest rate regulation, leads to desegmentation of the two sectors and causes interest rates in the two sectors to respond to the same market conditions in the same manner. As a result, interest rate liberalization increases the variance in interest rates but reduces the variance in the interest rate differential.

The official sector can be further divided into the domestic (d) and foreign (f) segments. Local foreign banks are permitted by the government to engage in only limited banking activities, but they are less regulated in these permitted activities. Whether interest rate spreads are larger for local foreign banks than for domestic banks depends on how risk taking and efficient local foreign banks are. If their risk taking dominates their efficiency, then we expect the interest rate spread to be larger for foreign banks than for domestic banks. Banking deregulation increases the differential between the domestic and local foreign interest-rate spreads if the risk-taking effect dominates the competition and cost effects.

8.3 Empirical Results

As shown in table 8.1, since 1980 a number of important financial liberalization events have taken place, leading to increased competition among domestic banks and between domestic and local foreign banks. The most important event was perhaps the establishment of sixteen new private banks in 1992. As further illustrated in table 8.2, the number of branches of domestic banks increased drastically from 756 in 1991 to 897 in 1992. Since then more than one hundred new branches have been established each year, compared with approximately thirty per year before 1991. Therefore, it is natural to take 1991 as the break point of banking deregulation. Nevertheless, since we do not have monthly data on loan-deposit rate spreads before 1991, we will provide a comparison of the empirical results for the two periods only for the cases where data are available.

That banking deregulation reduces or eliminates the differential between official and unofficial interest rates means that the two interest rates should not drift apart following a shock. And there should be no long-term opportunity for arbitrage. In other words, the two interest rates should be cointegrated and should have a common trend.

In the following subsections, we will first illustrate the pattern of the spreads between loan and deposit rates and the differentials between black market and official interest rates. Next, we will provide unit root tests of whether there exist long-term profit opportunities due to interest rate differentials. Then we will use the causality test to examine the transmission of information across markets. Finally, we will further discuss the market linkage by looking into the impulse response functions among interest rate spreads.

Table 8.2   **Number of Depository Institutions (end of year)**

Year	Domestic Banks H.O.	Domestic Banks Bra.	Medium Business Banks H.O.	Medium Business Banks Bra.	Local Branches of Foreign Banks H.O.	Local Branches of Foreign Banks Bra.	Credit Cooperatives H.O.	Credit Cooperatives Bra.	Credit Departments of Farmers' Associations H.O.	Credit Departments of Farmers' Associations Bra.	Credit Departments of Fishermen's Associations H.O.	Credit Departments of Fishermen's Associations Bra.
1981	15	543	8	171	24	24	74	n.a.	280	n.a.	4	n.a.
1982	16	552	8	171	25	25	75	n.a.	280	n.a.	4	n.a.
1983	16	556	8	189	28	28	75	n.a.	282	n.a.	12	n.a.
1984	16	561	8	197	31	31	75	n.a.	282	n.a.	16	n.a.
1985	16	585	8	203	32	32	75	289	283	565	17	5
1986	16	601	8	212	32	32	75	303	284	593	19	10
1987	16	632	8	236	32	33	74	294	282	603	19	11
1988	16	663	8	240	32	35	74	308	282	614	22	13
1989	16	692	8	261	32	38	74	358	285	665	22	20
1990	16	721	8	275	32	43	74	399	285	713	24	31
1991	17	756	8	290	32	47	74	425	285	754	26	31
1992	32	897	8	315	32	50	74	439	285	770	27	33
1993	33	1,030	8	352	32	55	74	482	285	788	27	34
1994	34	1,174	8	403	32	57	74	530	285	827	27	38
1995	34	1,361	8	446	32	58	74	556	285	886	27	44
1996	34	1,464	8	472	32	65	74	595	285	925	27	47

Source: Central Bank of China, *Financial Statistics Monthly* (various issues).
Note: H.O. = head offices; Bra. = branches.

All the data on interest rates are provided by the Economic Research Department of the Central Bank of China and are available in the *Financial Statistics Monthly,* Taiwan District, Republic of China. The quarterly data are available from 1983:Q1 to 1996:Q4. The monthly data are available only from January 1991 to December 1996. The data on interest rates in unorganized money markets and commercial paper rates are available from August 1987 to December 1996.

The official lending (deposit) rate is taken to be the weighted average of interest rates on loans (deposits) offered by financial institutions, and the unofficial (black market) rate is taken to be the average interest rate on loans against postdated checks in unorganized money markets.[5] Because we wish to show the differences in the behavior patterns of domestic and local foreign banks, we differentiate the interest rates of domestic banks

5. Unofficial or black market interest rates are based on surveys of 213 companies in the three largest cities in Taiwan (Taipei, Kaoshiung, and Taichung) conducted by three commercial banks (First Commercial Bank, Hua-Nan Commercial Bank, and Chang-Hua Commercial Bank) concerning the interest rates the firms paid in unorganized money markets on loans against postdated checks, unsecured loans, and deposits by individuals with the firms. Here we take the black market interest rate as the mean of the interest rates on loans against postdated checks in the three cities.

from those of local foreign banks. Since firms borrow not only from the black market but from the money market as well, when we study the differential between unofficial and official interest rates, we use the thirty-day commercial paper rates in primary markets to represent the official interest rates.

8.3.1   Loan-Deposit Interest Rate Spreads and Black-Market–Money-Market Interest Rate Differentials

As mentioned above, two main factors contribute to the gaps between interest rates. First, increased competition and the decline in the transactions costs cause the spreads between loan and deposit rates to shrink. Second, the risk factor widens the interest rate spreads. Before we analyze the interest rate spreads, we plot in figures 8.1 and 8.2 loan rates, deposit rates, spreads between loan and deposit rates, and differentials between interest rates offered by domestic and by local foreign banks. We also provide the related data in tables 8.3 and 8.4. These graphs and tables show that there does exist a declining trend in the spreads between loan and deposit rates for both domestic and local foreign banks, suggesting that the competition and cost effects due to banking deregulation outweighed the increased risks undertaken by domestic and local foreign banks. Competition and a decline in transactions costs not only cut the spread between loan and deposit rates but also reduced the differential between loan rates and between deposit rates of domestic and local foreign banks.

All test statistics show a significant rejection of the null hypothesis that the mean spreads between interest rates on loans and on deposits and the mean differentials between loan rates and those between deposit rates of domestic and local foreign banks did not change in 1991.[6] Table 8.4 shows interestingly that the differential between black market and money market interest rates has been stable since 1987, though the loan-deposit rate spreads of domestic banks and those of local foreign banks have been declining since the 1980s. The test statistics also show that the means did not change significantly in December 1991. Because the number of new bank branches has increased drastically since the end of 1991, customers have been lured away from unorganized money markets. As a result, funds supplied in the black markets faced higher risks, and the risk premiums had to rise to compensate for the increased risk. This might be the reason why we find such a stable differential between black market and money market interest rates.

Another important fact stands out from the tables. The variances of

---

6. Though the differences in interest rate spreads among domestic banks are relatively small compared to those for local foreign banks, small sample variance causes the test statistic to significantly reject the null hypothesis of equal means between the two periods.

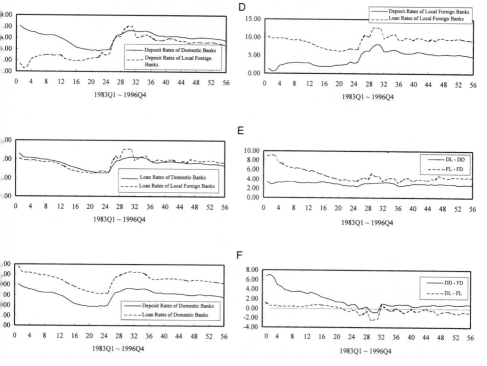

Fig. 8.1   Interest rates of domestic and local foreign banks, quarterly 1983:Q1–96:Q4

Note: *A*, Deposit rates of domestic and local foreign banks. *B*, Loan rates of domestic and local foreign banks. *C*, Deposit and loan rates of domestic banks. *D*, Deposit and loan rates of local foreign banks. *E*, Loan-deposit rate spreads of domestic and local foreign banks. *F*, Differentials between loan rates and between deposit rates of domestic and local foreign banks. See table 8.3 note for abbreviations.

interest rates, the variances of loan-deposit rate spreads, and the variances of interest rate differentials were all significantly larger before than after 1991. This suggests that the competition brought by the increased number of new private banks had a stabilizing effect on not only interest rates themselves but also interest rate spreads and differentials. The decreased volatility of interest rate spreads reduced the uncertainty over interest rates. As a consequence, the spreads between loan and deposit rates declined. On the other hand, although the volatility in the differential between black market and money market interest rates fell from the period July 1987–December 1991 to the period January 1992–December 1996, the increased lending risk surpassed the reduced uncertainty. This is why we find a stable differential between black market and money market interest rates through the period 1983–96.

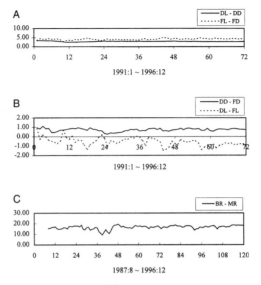

Fig. 8.2   Interest rate spreads and differentials for domestic and local foreign banks and for black markets and money markets, monthly 1987:8–96:12
Note: *A*, Loan-deposit rate spreads of domestic and local foreign banks. *B*, Differentials between loan rates and between deposit rates of domestic and local foreign banks. *C*, Differentials between black market and money market interest rates. BR = black market interest rate; MR = money market interest rate. See table 8.3 note for other abbreviations.

8.3.2   Stationarity of Interest Rate Spreads and Differentials

The preceding subsection showed that the magnitudes of interest rate spreads and differentials before 1991 were significantly different from those after 1991. Test statistics also support the argument that the means of interest rate spreads and differentials did change between the two periods. In this subsection, we will further provide the unit root test to ascertain if these interest rate spreads and differentials are stationary, that is, if we can rule out long-term profit opportunities for arbitrage. If two financial markets are linked, the spreads between loan and deposit rates in each market and the differentials between interest rates in the two markets should not rise persistently over a long period of time. That is, they should have the stationarity property. If interest rate spreads or differentials rise steadily, then they will eventually exceed any finite transactions costs and risk premiums. As a result, arbitrage can take place by lending high and borrowing low. In other words, the stationarity of interest rate spreads or differentials ensures that there is no long-term profit opportunity for arbitrage. (See Lin 1995.)

To check the stationarity of spreads and differentials, we test the hypothesis with three different unit root tests; they are Dickey-Fuller (1979), Phillips and Perron (1988), and Sims (1988). Test results are reported in

Table 8.3   **Deposit Rates, Loan Rates, and Interest Rate Spreads, Quarterly 1983:Q1–96:Q4**

Period	DL-DD	FL-FD	DD-FD	DL-FL	DD	DL	FD	FL
1983:Q1–85:Q4								
Mean	3.258	7.186	4.508	0.574	6.832	10.083	2.323	9.509
Variance	0.029	1.526	2.106	0.053	0.394	0.381	0.768	0.211
1986:Q1–88:Q4								
Mean	2.987	4.526	1.894	0.355	4.234	7.221	2.340	6.866
Variance	0.096	0.546	0.800	0.242	0.408	0.725	0.179	0.311
1989:Q1–91:Q4								
Mean	3.030	4.142	0.260	−0.852	6.639	9.669	6.379	10.521
Variance	0.093	0.294	0.453	1.149	1.006	1.575	1.655	2.930
1992:Q1–94:Q4								
Mean	2.888	4.059	0.668	−0.503	6.249	9.137	5.581	9.640
Variance	0.022	0.122	0.027	0.117	0.037	0.022	0.058	0.097
1995:Q1–96:Q4								
Mean	2.790	4.338	0.765	−0.783	5.924	8.714	5.159	9.496
Variance	0.004	0.010	0.003	0.030	0.034	0.049	0.035	0.044
1983:Q1–91:Q4								
Mean	3.089	5.284	2.221	0.026	5.902	8.991	3.681	8.965
Variance	0.082	2.628	4.204	0.858	2.005	2.483	4.562	3.527
1992:Q1–96:Q4								
Mean	2.849	4.171	0.707	−0.615	6.119	8.968	5.412	9.583
Variance	0.017	0.094	0.019	0.099	0.061	0.076	0.092	0.078
F-test[a]	0.0005	0.0000	0.0000	0.0000	0.0000	0.0000	0.0000	0.0000
T-test[b]	0.0001	0.0003	0.0001	0.0004	0.3753	0.9307	0.0000	0.0606

Note: DD = deposit rates of domestic banks; DL = loan rates of domestic banks; FD = deposit rates of local foreign banks; FL = loan rates of local foreign banks.

[a]F-test for the equality of variance for 1983:Q–91:Q4 and 1992:Q1–96:Q4. Table reports significance levels.

[b]T-test for the difference between two means for 1983:Q1–91:Q4 and 1992:Q1–96:Q4. Table reports significance levels.

table 8.5. As can be seen from the table, all test results show a significant rejection of the existence of unit roots for both periods. The main exceptions occurred in the period 1983–91, in which the Sims (1988) Bayesian test of the differential between domestic and foreign bank interest rates was unable to reject the null unit root hypothesis. In other words, most interest rate spreads and differentials followed a stationary process, and there did not exist a long-term profit opportunity during and after the period of banking deregulation. After banking deregulation, the segmentation between domestic and local foreign banks was not significant.

8.3.3 Cross-Market Causality in Interest Rate Spreads and Differentials

The causality test is often employed to examine the lead and lag relation between asset prices. Such a relation is frequently interpreted as the trans-

Table 8.4   **Black Market and Money Market Interest Rates, Monthly 1987:8–96:12**

Period	BR-CPR	BR	CPR
1987:8–89:7			
Mean	16.2663	21.8733	5.6071
Variance	1.4163	2.4559	3.7412
1989:8–91:7			
Mean	15.0946	24.2183	9.1238
Variance	7.8180	0.2699	8.1797
1991:8–93:7			
Mean	16.9054	24.2417	7.3363
Variance	0.7258	0.0802	1.0347
1993:8–95:7			
Mean	16.9788	23.9350	6.9563
Variance	1.3831	0.1145	1.2569
1995:8–96:12			
Mean	17.4959	23.7765	6.2806
Variance	1.0187	0.0538	1.1697
1987:8–91:12			
Mean	15.8126	23.1336	7.3209
Variance	4.6608	2.5544	7.7941
1992:1–96:12			
Mean	17.0873	24.0093	6.9220
Variance	1.0867	0.1263	1.3096
F-test	0.0000	0.0000	0.0000
T-test	0.0002	0.0003	0.3351

Note: BR = interest rates on loans against postdated checks in unorganized money markets (black market rates); CPR = commercial paper rates in primary market (money market rates).

mission of information across markets. (See, e.g., Engle, Ito, and Lin 1990; Lin, Engle, and Ito 1994.) In this study we will investigate whether interest rate spreads or differentials in one market (domestic banks' loan-deposit market or local foreign banks' loan-deposit market) can provide information useful in explaining spreads or differentials in another market. If two markets are linked, bidirectional, cross-market causality will be displayed.

In order to examine the causality relation between interest rate spreads or differentials, we use the procedure adopted by Caines, Keng, and Sethi (1981) and Liang, Chou, and Lin (1996). First, the order of the bivariate model is chosen to be the one giving minimal final prediction error. Then a stepwise causality test procedure is applied to determine the endogeneity and exogeneity of, or independence between, these two variables. At this stage, the unrestricted bivariate AR model and the restricted model excluding the cross-coefficients are estimated. The likelihood ratio tests are then performed to determine the direction of causality. (For details, see Caines et al. 1981.) Table 8.6 summarizes the empirical results obtained

Table 8.5   **Unit Root Tests**

Test[a]	DDL	DDD	FDL	DLL	DBM
	A. Quarterly 1983Q1–96Q4				
Period 1: 1983:Q1–91:Q4					
ADF(4)	−42.49**	−3.08**	−3.49**	−6.28**	
PP(4)	−9.62**	−0.09**	−2.75*	−9.59**	
SIMS	0.276	0.207	0.353	0.069	
Period 2: 1992:Q1–96:Q4					
ADF(4)	−6.79**	−8.48**	−12.78**	−14.31**	
PP(4)	−9.04**	−8.81**	−14.50**	−15.79**	
SIMS	0.033**	0.060*	0.007**	0.004**	
	B. Monthly 1991:1–96:12				
ADF(4)	−39.42**	−70.14**	−27.87**	−35.99**	−18.18**
PP(4)	−10.76**	−24.89**	−31.36**	−32.99**	−12.99**
SIMS	0.0897*	0.0014**	0.0002**	0.0000**	0.071*

Note: DDL = deposit-loan rate spreads of domestic banks; DDD = deposit rate differentials between domestic banks and local foreign banks; FDL = deposit-loan rate spreads of local foreign banks; DLL = loan rate differentials between domestic banks and local foreign banks; DBM = interest rate differentials between black markets and money markets.

[a]ADF(4) = augmented Dickey-Fuller (1979) unit root test with four lags. Their critical values are obtained from Dickey and Fuller (1979). PP(4) = Phillips-Perron (1988) unit root test with four lags. Their critical values are obtained from Dickey and Fuller (1979). SIMS = Sims (1988) Bayesian unit root test. Numbers in table are significance levels.

*Rejection of unit root null at the 10 percent level.

**Rejection of unit root null at the 5 percent level.

from quarterly data in panel A. As can be seen, during the period 1983:Q1–91:Q4 causality with respect to interest rate spreads ran from local foreign banks to domestic banks, but not the other way around. However, during the period 1992:Q1–96:Q4, there existed no causality relation between the two spreads. This result is also confirmed by the tests using monthly data in panel B. Panels C and D show the causality relations between the loan-deposit rate spreads of domestic and local foreign banks, respectively, and the differentials between black market and money market rates. We see that the causality runs from loan-deposit rate spreads of domestic banks to differentials between black market and money market interest rates, but not the other way around. On the other hand, loan-deposit rate spreads of local foreign banks and differentials between black market and money market interest rates have an interdependent relationship; that is, they cause each other.

Since the early 1970s the authorities in Taiwan have adopted a strategy of "planned gradualism" to liberalize step by step the control of interest rates. The revised Banking Law became effective on 20 July 1989. It practically closed the history of interest rate control in Taiwan. In principle, interest rates on loans, deposits, and other financial instruments are now determined by market forces. However, until 1991, most domestic banks

Table 8.6   **Causality Tests**

Test	χ^2 Test Statistic[a]	Significance Level	Conclusion
**A. Between Domestic Banks' and Local Foreign Banks'**

Test	χ^2 Test Statistic[a]	Significance Level	Conclusion
A. Between Domestic Banks' and Local Foreign Banks' Loan-Deposit Rate Spreads, Quarterly 1983:Q1–96:Q4			
Period 1: 1983:Q1–91:Q4			
T_{10}	(4) 11.058	0.026	$H_0 \geq H_1$
T_{20}	(2) 0.851	0.653	$H_3 \geq H_0$
T_{30}	(2) 10.386	0.006	$H_0 \geq H_2$
T_{12}	(2) 10.207	0.006	$H_3 \geq H_1$
T_{13}	(2) 0.672	0.715	$H_1 \geq H_2$
Period 2: 1992:Q1–96:Q4			
T_{10}	(2) 1.311	0.519	$H_1 \geq H_0$
T_{20}	(1) 0.693	0.405	$H_3 \geq H_0$
T_{30}	(1) 0.463	0.496	$H_2 \geq H_0$
T_{12}	(1) 0.619	0.432	$H_1 \geq H_3$
T_{13}	(1) 0.848	0.357	$H_1 \geq H_2$
B. Between Domestic Banks' and Local Foreign Banks' Loan-Deposit Rate Spreads, Monthly 1991:1–96:12			
T_{10}	(14) 14.399	0.420	$H_1 \geq H_0$
T_{20}	(7) 10.292	0.173	$H_3 \geq H_0$
T_{30}	(7) 4.098	0.768	$H_2 \geq H_0$
T_{12}	(7) 4.106	0.767	$H_1 \geq H_3$
T_{13}	(7) 10.301	0.172	$H_1 \geq H_2$
C. Between Domestic Banks' Loan-Deposit Rate Spread and Black-Market– Commercial-Paper Rate Difference, Monthly 1991:1–96:12			
T_{10}	(4) 10.734	0.0297	$H_0 \geq H_1$
T_{20}	(2) 3.050	0.218	$H_3 \geq H_0$
T_{30}	(2) 7.683	0.021	$H_0 \geq H_2$
T_{12}	(2) 7.685	0.021	$H_3 \geq H_1$
T_{13}	(2) 3.051	0.217	$H_1 \geq H_2$
D. Between Local Foreign Banks' Loan-Deposit Rate Spread and Black-Market– Money-Market Interest Rate Difference, Monthly 1991:1–96:12			
T_{10}	(4) 13.239	0.001	$H_0 \geq H_1$
T_{20}	(2) 3.817	0.011	$H_0 \geq H_3$
T_{30}	(2) 6.363	0.012	$H_0 \geq H_2$
T_{12}	(2) 9.422	0.002	$H_3 \geq H_1$
T_{13}	(2) 6.876	0.009	$H_2 \geq H_1$

Note: An unrestricted model (of order k) is a model of the form

$$
\begin{bmatrix} \psi_{11}(2) & \psi_{12}(2) \\ \psi_{21}(2) & \psi_{22}(2) \end{bmatrix} \begin{bmatrix} x_t \\ y_t \end{bmatrix} = \eta_t,
$$

where the orthogonal process η_t has covariance Σ and the orders of all polynomial entries of $\psi(z)$ not specified to be identically zero are of order k.

Table 8.6   (continued)

Hypotheses are as follows:

$$H_0 : \begin{pmatrix} \psi_{11} & \psi_{12} \\ \psi_{21} & \psi_{22} \end{pmatrix}, \quad H_1 : \begin{pmatrix} \psi_{11} & 0 \\ 0 & \psi_{22} \end{pmatrix}, \quad H_2 : \begin{pmatrix} \psi_{11} & \psi_{12} \\ 0 & \psi_{22} \end{pmatrix}, \quad H_3 : \begin{pmatrix} \psi_{11} & 0 \\ \psi_{21} & \psi_{22} \end{pmatrix}.$$

Tests are as follows:
T_{10}: H_1 is the null hypothesis and H_0 is the alternative hypothesis,
T_{20}: H_3 is the null hypothesis and H_0 is the alternative hypothesis,
T_{30}: H_2 is the null hypothesis and H_0 is the alternative hypothesis,
T_{12}: H_1 is the null hypothesis and H_2 is the alternative hypothesis,
T_{13}: H_1 is the null hypothesis and H_3 is the alternative hypothesis.
[a]Numbers in parentheses are lag orders.

were government owned. Their most important competitors were the more efficient local foreign banks. This might be the reason why we find a causal direction from the spreads of local foreign banks to those of domestic banks. Since 1991, when there was large-scale entry of private banks, government-owned banks have faced competition from all directions. At the same time, local foreign banks, which are under fewer regulations, have greater flexibility, experience, and efficiency. Their customers are mainly export and import firms with good track records. To lower the managing costs, local foreign banks raise funds from the money market rather than from time deposits. In other words, the markets served by domestic and local foreign banks have a certain degree of segmentation. This might explain the empirically weak connection between the two markets in the period 1992–96. Furthermore, by comparing the causal relations among the loan-deposit rate spreads of domestic banks and those of local foreign banks and the differentials between black market and money market interest rates, we find that domestic banks seem isolated from local foreign banks and black markets. This result might reflect the fact that though interest rates have been liberalized, most major domestic banks are still easily influenced by the central bank. Burdened with a long history, the way they run their businesses is still rather inflexible and inefficient compared with local foreign banks and black markets.

8.3.4 Impulse Response Functions

An impulse response function traces the dynamic effects of a shock on an economic or financial variable. Researchers are interested in finding whether there are short-term profit opportunities that investors can exploit by using simple trading strategies based on past information. However, because of the existence of different risk premiums and market friction, unpredictability is too restrictive in most empirical studies. The impulse response function is an alternative way to measure market linkage. Figures 8.3*A* and 8.3*B* plot the impulse response functions of the loan-deposit rate spreads of domestic and local foreign banks with respect

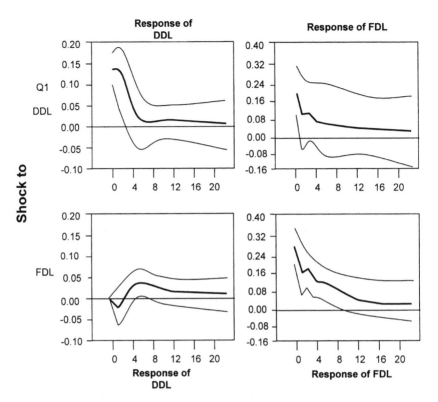

Fig. 8.3A   Impulse response curves for loan-deposit rate spreads of domestic and local foreign banks, quarterly 1983:Q1–91:Q4

Note: See table 8.5 note for abbreviations.

to a one-unit shock to the respective spreads, and their two-standard-error confidence intervals. For comparison, figure 8.3*C* provides impulse response functions for the differentials between loan and deposit rates of domestic and local foreign banks and the differentials between black market and money market interest rates. Figure 8.3*A* shows that before 1991, the interest rate spreads of domestic banks responded significantly only to shocks to the spreads of local foreign banks. After 1991, the responses were insignificantly different from zero (fig. 8.3*B*). The interest rate spreads of local foreign banks also displayed the same pattern; that is, the responses of interest rate spreads of local foreign banks to shocks in the spreads of domestic banks were significant before 1991, but not afterward. These findings are also confirmed by the monthly data in figure 8.3*C*. They suggest that there exists a weak linkage between interest rate spreads of domestic banks and local foreign banks because of the emergence of huge private banks and the customer segmentation between domestic and local foreign banks. The finding of a weak connection between interest rate

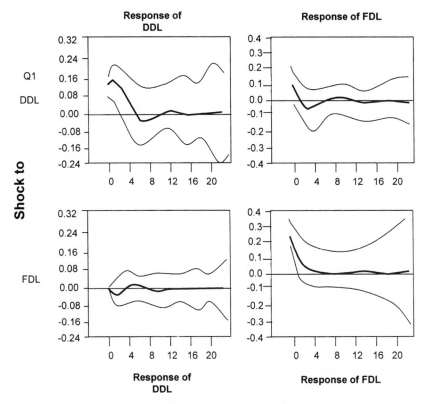

Fig. 8.3B   Impulse response curves for loan-deposit rate spreads of domestic and local foreign banks, quarterly 1991:Q1–96:Q4
Note: See table 8.5 note for abbreviations.

spreads after the banking deregulation is not unique to this study. By comparing Gensaki-Euroyen yield spreads and the difference between Euroyen and Gensaki interest rates, Lin (1995) also found a similar result.

8.4   Concluding Remarks

Our findings can be summarized as follows:

1. Deposit and lending rates of domestic banks and of local foreign banks and black market and money market interest rates experienced greater fluctuations before December 1991 than after.

2. Loan-deposit rate spreads of domestic banks and those of local foreign banks, as well as differentials between lending rates and between deposit rates of domestic banks and local foreign banks all were larger before December 1991 than afterward. Thus banking deregulation and the

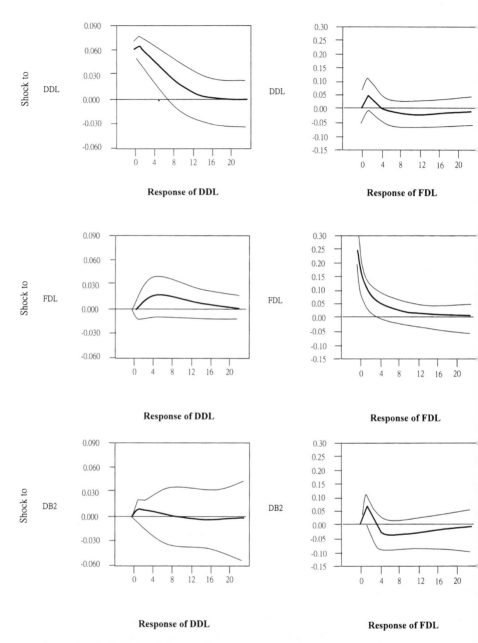

Fig. 8.3C Impulse response curves for loan-deposit rate spreads of domestic and local foreign banks and differentials between black market and money market interest rates, monthly 1991:1–96:12

Note: DB2 = interest rate differentials between black markets and money markets. See table 8.5 note for other abbreviations.

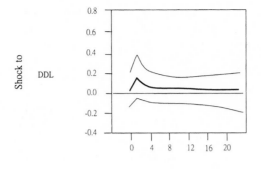

Response of DB2

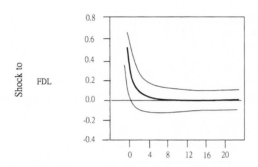

Response of DB2

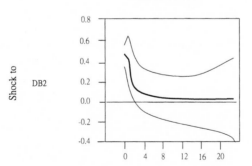

Response of DB2

Fig. 8.3C   (continued)

accompanying sharp increase in the entry of private banks have substantially increased competition among banks, forcing a decline in the loan-deposit rate spread and the differential between interest rates in different sectors.

3. The differential between black market and money market interest rates experienced greater fluctuations before December 1991 than afterward. But the differential did not shrink in the second period despite a decline in its fluctuations. This indicates that the risk-taking effect dominates the competition effect because new banks absorbed funds from the black market and thus face higher risk premiums than government-owned banks do.

4. Most interest rate spreads and differentials followed a stationary process; therefore there did not exist a long-term profit opportunity during and after the period of banking deregulation.

5. During the period 1983:Q1–91:Q4 causality ran from loan-deposit rate spreads of local foreign banks to spreads of domestic banks, but not the other way around. Nevertheless, during the period 1992:Q1–96:Q4, there existed no causal relation between the two spreads. On the other hand, during the second period, loan-deposit rate spreads of local foreign banks and interest rate differentials between black markets and money markets were interdependent.

6. Before 1991, loan-deposit rate spreads of domestic banks responded significantly only to shocks to the spreads of local foreign banks. After 1991, the responses were insignificantly different from zero. Interest rate spreads of local foreign banks also displayed the same behavioral pattern.

In sum, we have found some evidence that banking deregulation may have encouraged competition and reduced costs of financial transactions and may have reduced segmentation of the banking industry. In this sense, banking deregulation in Taiwan is to some extent working.

References

Besley, T., S. Coate, and G. Loury. 1993. The economics of rotating savings and credit associations. *American Economic Review* 83:792–810.
Caines, P. E., C. W. Keng, and S. P. Sethi. 1981. Causality analysis and multivariate autoregressive modeling with an application to supermarket sales analysis. *Journal of Economic Dynamics and Control* 3:267–98.
Central Bank of China. 1996. *Financial survey of public and private enterprises, Taiwan Area, Republic of China, 1995.* Taipei: Central Bank of China.
Chan, V. L., and S. C. Hu. 1997. Financial liberalization and aggregate consumption: The evidence from Taiwan. *Applied Economics* 29:1525–35.
Dickey, D., and W. A. Fuller. 1979. Distribution of the estimators for time series

regressions with a unit root. *Journal of the American Statistical Association* 71:427–31.

Engle, R. F., T. Ito, and W. L. Lin. 1990. Meteor showers or heat waves? Heteroskedasticity intra-daily volatility in the foreign exchange market. *Econometrica* 58:525–42.

Jappelli, T., and M. Pagano. 1989. Consumption function and capital market imperfections: An intertemporal comparison. *American Economic Review* 79: 1088–1105.

Liang, K. Y., W. L. Chou, and J. L. Lin. 1996. Causality between export expansion and manufacturing growth: Further evidence from Taiwan. Taipei: Academia Sinica, Institute of Economics. Memorandum.

Lin, W. L. 1995. Japan's financial deregulation and linkage of the Gensaki and Euroyen deposit markets. *Journal of Applied Econometrics* 10:447–67.

Lin, W. L., F. R. Engle, and T. Ito. 1994. Do bulls and bears move across borders? International transmission of stock returns and volatility. *Review of Financial Studies* 3:507–38.

Phillips, P. C. B., and P. Perron. 1988. Testing for a unit root in time series regressions. *Biometrica* 33:311–40.

Shea, J. D. 1992. The welfare effects of financial liberalization under market segmentation with special reference to Taiwan. *Academia Economic Papers* 20: 697–716.

Shea, J. D., Ping Sing Kuo, and Chi-Tsang Huang. 1995. The share of informal financing of private enterprises. *Academia Economic Papers* 23:265–97.

Sims, C. A. 1988. Bayesian skepticism on unit root econometrics. *Journal of Economic Dynamics and Control* 12:463–74.

Comment   Shinji Takagi

Here Wu and Hu discuss the impact of banking deregulation (i.e., the easing of lending rate ceilings and entry restrictions) on (1) the margin between the deposit rate and the lending rate and (2) the segmentation of the banking sector in Taiwan. The paper should be considered more of an exercise in fact finding than in hypothesis testing because, as it turns out, the quantitative impact of banking deregulation cannot be determined a priori. In this sense, the conclusion that deregulation reduced the interest margin but did not reduce the difference between black market and official market lending rates may not be generalized as a necessary outcome of bank deregulation.

The margin between the deposit rate and the lending rate is influenced by many factors, some of which may well offset each other, including the price of financial intermediation, excess profits, and macroeconomic conditions. The authors recognize that the margin is affected in opposite directions by what they call the risk-taking factor (associated with the incor-

Shinji Takagi is professor of economics at the University of Osaka.

poration of riskier borrowers into the formal sector) and the competition effect (associated with the establishment of new banks and the privatization of existing banks). In finding that the margin did decline during recent years, the authors conclude that the competition effect must have dominated. But the margin is influenced by other factors, notably macroeconomic conditions, so that their conclusion remains only tentative.

The second component of the paper is potentially more interesting because market segmentation is a phenomenon observed in many developing countries. Whether or not bank deregulation helps to integrate the black market into the official market is indeed an interesting topic. Here the authors' assumption is that full liberalization will eliminate market segmentation altogether. On the basis of this assumption they argue that although the participation of riskier borrowers in the official market increases the official market lending rate and the presence of residual high-risk borrowers in the black market also increases the black market lending rate, the increase in the former rate must necessarily be larger than the increase in the latter. Otherwise, the average lending rates in the two markets would never converge.

The problem is that some people in the black market may never be included in the official market. In Japan, there are many legitimate consumer loan companies whose function is to provide unsecured loans to high-risk borrowers who are experiencing a shortage of liquidity. In many countries, including Japan and the United States, interest rates on revolving credit typically are much higher. Thus it seems unrealistic to assume that the official market and what Wu and Hu call the black market will be fully integrated under full liberalization. In fact, the finding that the difference between the two lending rates increased in Taiwan during recent years seems to support the view that, in fact, a complete segmentation of the bank lending market is taking place in Taiwan as a result of (and not in spite of) bank deregulation. In order to clarify this matter, it may be useful to provide evidence on how the relative sizes of the official and black markets changed during the sample period.

Financial Deregulation and Competition in Korea

Moon-Soo Kang

9.1 Introduction

The financial system in Korea has been undergoing structural changes as a result of financial reform and technological innovation. The financial liberalization and internationalization currently in progress may be regarded as deregulation undertaken by the government in response to the needs of financial institutions for financial innovation, and to deal with international pressures and friction resulting from new economic and financial conditions.

Since the early 1980s, the government has gradually changed its policy direction regarding the overall management of the national economy toward a more market-oriented approach. This change regarding the management of the national economy initiated the liberalization of financial policy. Democratization has also accentuated demands for faster financial market deregulation.

Financial deregulation in Korea has been a very cautious and slow process. The authorities have pursued a policy of gradualism in order to give less competitive financial institutions enough time to adjust to a more competitive environment in financial markets. The less competitive institutions include some nationwide commercial banks with a heavy burden of nonperforming assets that had been incurred by bank support for industry rationalization and worsened by the recent economic downturn (see Nam 1994, 184–222). Furthermore, fifteen nationwide commercial banks recorded huge capital losses of 4.5 trillion won in stock investments at the end of 1996 as equity prices declined. Eight investment trust companies

Moon-Soo Kang is senior fellow at the Korea Development Institute.

also suffered from heavy capital losses of 1.8 trillion won in equity investments at the end of March 1997. Given the commercial banks' weakened loan portfolios, it was feared that complete freedom in the determination of bank lending and deposit rates would lead to cutthroat interest rate competition among banks and nonbank financial institutions, with subsequent undue pressures on interest margins, bank profits, and capital adequacy ratios.

Some market observers, disappointed in the slow financial deregulation process, think that "big bang" full liberalization might solve many problems in the financial markets in a single stroke, whereas government authorities have pursued gradual deregulation and have favored restructuring financial institutions in several steps to reduce shocks and uncertainties in the financial markets. At the end of 1995, the government introduced a four-year program, the Revision to the Foreign Exchange Reform Plan, to liberalize capital movements (see OECD 1996, 58–62). The plan includes specific measures and a timetable for implementation. It not only covers long-term capital transactions but also extends the deregulation of short-term capital transactions. In early 1997 the government established the Presidential Commission for Financial Reform, which plans to recommend a big-bang-type full liberalization to the government.

The Hanbo scandal in early 1997 exposed the vulnerability of the Korean financial system by pushing a couple of nationwide commercial banks and dozens of nonbank financial institutions to the wall. The scandal triggered a general public outcry for a comprehensive overhaul of the outdated and inefficient financial system. A sense of urgency has permeated the government's determination to make these changes, with the full-fledged market opening looming large after Korea's accession to the OECD in December 1996 (Kim 1997, 4). Before allowing firms to borrow freely from international capital markets and implementing external liberalization, the government should fully liberalize the national financial market.

The purpose of this paper is to assess the financial deregulation process and its consequences in Korea's financial sector.

9.2 Interest Rate Deregulation

9.2.1 Interest Rate Liberalization

The government implemented the first plan for interest rate deregulation in December 1988, when most bank and nonbank lending rates and some long-term deposit rates, except for those on policy loans, and short-term deposit rates were liberalized. After only about six months, however, the government and the business sector became so concerned about the rise in interest rates that the government again intervened in the financial market, giving tacit consent for financial institutions to collude on interest rates. The interest rate jumps were not directly caused by the deregulation itself but rather by the tight monetary policy being pursued. Thus the first attempt at interest rate deregulation was abandoned and caused some confusion among market participants.

It has become increasingly necessary to liberalize interest rates and reinforce the market mechanism, thereby improving the efficiency of the financial markets as well as the competitiveness of domestic financial institutions. Interest rate deregulation was pursued to handle difficult situations effectively with the global trend of financial liberalization and integration.

The government announced a gradual interest rate deregulation plan in August 1991 (table 9.1). This was the second attempt at deregulating interest rates. The first step of the four-stage interest rate deregulation plan went into effect in November 1991. Interest rates have been gradually liberalized in accordance with developments in the economy as well as in financial markets (fig. 9.1). There has been an attempt to keep a proper balance between the deregulation of deposit and loan rates among different financial products and among different areas of the financial sector in order to minimize any disruption of the financial market's overall stability. In comparison to deposit rates, lending rates have been deregulated relatively faster since they influence fund allocation. Regarding deposit rates, those on large, long-term deposits have been liberalized first to deter an abrupt shift of funds across different financial sectors and to encourage long-term deposits. Under the four-stage approach, demand deposit rates will not be fully deregulated until 1997. The desire of the government and the Bank of Korea to save on borrowing costs as they issue debt instruments is one of the factors that has contributed to the cautious approach toward interest rate deregulation. Monetary authorities do not want to be blamed for instigating a rise in interest rates when they implement the four-phase interest rate deregulation plan.

9.2.2 Behavior of Bank Lending Rates after Deregulation

Just after the deregulation of bank lending rates, lending rates on bank overdrafts and discount rates on commercial bills started to rise between 0.5 and 3.0 percent, reflecting excess demand for bank credit, though these rates then began to drop gradually. Minimum lending rates and maximum rates on general bank loans, however, declined by between 1.5 and 0.5 percent, respectively, just after the deregulation in November 1993. The bank lending rate band between the maximum rate and the minimum rate widened to 6.50 percent at the end of February 1997 from 2.5 percent at the end of 1991 (table 9.2).

Commercial banks' prime lending rates did not move flexibly reflecting market conditions after the deregulation of interest rates. Prime rates of commercial banks are linked to the average funding cost of banks. As of

Table 9.1   **Schedule for Interest Rate Deregulation and Implementation of Selected Measures**

Step	Loans	Deposits	Bonds	Deregulation of Financial Instruments
Step 1: second half of 1991 to first half of 1992	Bank overdraft loan Real commercial bill discounts excluding those rediscounted by Bank of Korea (BOK) Short-term finance companies' commercial paper and trade bill discounts	Negotiable bank certificates of deposit Short-term finance companies' sale of large-size commercial papers and trade bills Banks' sale of large-size real commercial bills Large-size repurchase agreements Some long-term deposits	Corporate bonds with maturities over two years	
Step 2: second half of 1992 to end of 1993	All loans of banks and nonbank financial institutions, excluding loans financed by government and BOK rediscount	Long-term deposits with maturities over two years	Corporate bonds with maturities less than two years Bank debentures with maturities over two years	Auction sales of monetary stabilization bonds and treasury bonds (March 1993) Diversification of short-term instruments (ongoing) Easing of restrictions on short-term financial instruments (maturities and issue limit; ongoing)

Step 3: 1994–96	Loans financed by government and BOK rediscount	Deposits with maturities less than two years (except demand deposits) Further deregulation of short-term market-oriented products Introduction of financial products linked to market rates such as money market certificates	Bank debentures with maturities less than two years Monetary stabilization bonds	Authorization of new short-term products, including money market certificates and money market funds
Step 4: 1997–	1997: Preparation of plan for phased deregulation of remaining regulated interest rates on demand deposits and preferential and company saving deposits with maturities of less than three months		All government and public bonds	1997: Study on abolishing restrictions on short-term instruments

Source: Ministry of Finance and Economy (1991).

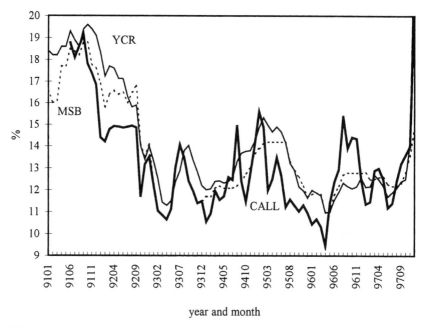

Fig. 9.1   Nominal interest rates
Note: MSB = monetary stabilization bond; YCR = yield on corporate bond.

June 1996, the major commercial banks seem to determine their prime rates based on the following formula (see H. Kim 1996, 22–47)

(1)   Prime rate = Average funding cost + Interest margin

                                – Spread band width/2.

In general, since deregulation, the five major nationwide commercial banks change their prime rates first and then other banks tend to follow them passively (table 9.3). It appears that smaller and regional banks do not have the ability to determine their own rates and do not have a proper risk management system installed. Therefore, they do not want to differentiate themselves much from major leading banks in the financial market. Commercial banks tend to adjust their average lending rates, not by frequently changing prime rates, but by changing interest spreads offered to customers.

9.3   Competition in Banking Markets

9.3.1   Changes in Bank Loan Portfolios

A significant change occurred in bank loan portfolios when phase 2 of the interest rate deregulation plan was implemented. The share of loans to

Table 9.2   Bank Lending Rate Movements after Deregulation (percent per annum)

Deregulation	1990	1991	1992	1993	1994	1995	1996	February 1997
Phase 1: November 1991								
Overdrafts	10.0–13.0	12.0–15.5	10.25–15.0	9.5–13.5	10.0–14.5	11.7–15.5	14.3–16.5	13.4–14.3
Phase 1: November 1991								
Discount on commercial bills	10.0–13.0	12.0–15.5	10.2–15.0	8.5–12.5	8.5–12.5	9.0–12.5	8.5–14.75	8.25–14.75
Phase 2: November 1993								
General loans	10.0–13.0	10.0–13.0	10.0–13.0	8.5–12.5	8.5–12.5	9.0–12.5	8.5–14.75	8.25–14.75
Phase 3: December 1994, July 1995, November 1996								
BOK loans with aggregate credit ceiling	10.0	10.0	10.0	8.5	8.5–9.5	9.0–11.0	8.75–11.0	8.25–14.75

Source: Bank of Korea, *Monthly Bulletin* (various issues).

Table 9.3   Bank Prime Rates and Dates of Change: Leaders and Followers, after April 1996

Prime Rate (%)	23 April 1996	25 April 1996	2 May 1996	7 May 1996	8 May 1996	10 May 1996	23 May 1996
8.75	Top eight banks[a], Donghwa Bank, Boram Bank						
9.0		Koram Bank, Hana Bank	Daegu Bank, Peace Bank	Pusan Bank	Kyongnam Bank		
9.25			Kwangju Bank			Chung-chong Bank	Dongnam Bank

Source: H. Kim (1996).

[a]Includes Chohung Bank, Commercial Bank of Korea, Korea First Bank, Hanil Bank, Seoul Bank, Korea Exchange Bank, Shinhan Bank, and Citizen's National Bank.

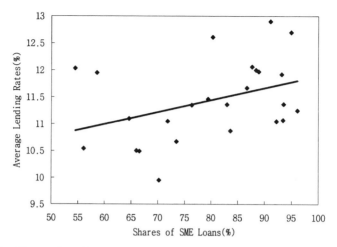

Fig. 9.2   Shares of small and medium-size enterprise (SME) loans and average lending rates of banks

big firms in the loan portfolios of nationwide commercial banks declined considerably, as big firms relied more heavily on funding through securities and the bond market.

On the other hand, the share of loans to small and medium-size firms showed steady growth (fig. 9.2). The share of loans to households rose sharply after interest rate deregulation. Commercial banks have expanded loans to households and small and medium-size firms, to whom relatively high lending rates were applied.

9.3.2   Interest Rate Margins

Next, we investigate the interest rate margin trend in the banking sector. The interest rate margin could be used as an indicator to measure the degree of financial deregulation and competition in the banking market. More competition stemming from a more liberalized financial system will tend to reduce the margin; a bigger margin could be taken as an indicator of a lower degree of financial liberalization.

Interest rate margins of nationwide commercial banks, which measure the difference between the average lending and deposit rates in a given year, came down quite strikingly between 1990 and 1994 (table 9.4). This margin squeeze reflects increased competitive pressures in the bank deposit market that brought about a sharp increase in the average deposit rate after the deregulation of interest rates (fig. 9.3). Interest rate margins of regional banks, however, did not come down as much. This reflects the fact that competitive pressures in the regional banking market are weaker than in the nationwide banking market due to restrictions on the expansion of bank branches. It also reflects the fact that regional banks kept

Table 9.4   **Interest Rate Margins of Banks (percent)**

	Five Major Banks	Nationwide Commercial Banks	Regional Banks	Commercial Banks
1988				
Ave. lending rate	9.14	9.41	11.54	9.79
Ave. deposit rate	5.65	5.74	6.70	5.95
Margin	3.49	3.67	4.84	3.84
1989				
Ave. lending rate	10.28	10.14	12.13	10.48
Ave. deposit rate	5.76	5.80	6.12	5.87
Margin	4.52	4.34	6.01	4.61
1990				
Ave. lending rate	10.37	10.48	11.94	10.74
Ave. deposit rate	6.10	6.23	6.15	6.21
Margin	4.27	4.25	5.79	4.53
1991				
Ave. lending rate	9.83	9.93	11.65	10.28
Ave. deposit rate	7.95	8.15	7.86	8.08
Margin	1.88	1.78	3.79	2.20
1992				
Ave. lending rate	10.28	10.49	12.22	10.82
Ave. deposit rate	8.36	8.70	8.22	8.59
Margin	1.92	1.79	3.99	2.24
1993				
Ave. lending rate	8.73	9.00	10.91	9.36
Ave. deposit rate	7.30	7.58	7.00	7.45
Margin	1.42	1.42	3.90	1.91
1994				
Ave. lending rate	9.39	9.60	11.23	9.91
Ave. deposit rate	7.52	7.77	7.03	7.61
Margin	1.87	1.83	4.20	2.30
1995				
Ave. lending rate	10.41	10.65	11.61	10.82
Ave. deposit rate	7.71	7.88	7.40	7.79
Margin	2.70	2.77	4.21	3.02

Source: Bank of Korea (1995).

extending many more loans to small and medium-size firms than nationwide commercial banks.

9.3.3 Branching

The authorities have maintained controls on the expansion of bank branches in the fear that freedom in bank branching would favor the concentration process. As part of the financial deregulation policies that foster competition through easier market access, the government has gradually deregulated the expansion of branch networks. The Committee for Harmonization of Bank Branching was abolished in 1994, and restrictions

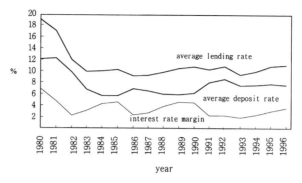

Fig. 9.3   Interest rate margins of commercial banks

Table 9.5   Expansion of Branch Networks of Commercial Banks

Bank Type	1990	1991	1992	1993	1994	1995	1996
Nationwide commercial banks (A)	1,695	1,931	2,149	2,425	2,681	3,476	3,891
		(13.9)	(11.3)	(12.8)	(10.6)	(29.3)	(11.9)
Regional banks (B)	638	746	818	892	1,001	1,081	1,214
		(16.9)	(9.7)	(9.0)	(12.2)	(8.0)	(12.3)
Commercial banks (A + B)	2,333	2,677	2,967	3,317	3,682	4,557	5,105
		(14.7)	(10.8)	(11.8)	(11.0)	(23.8)	(12.0)
Foreign banks[a]	94	94	96	98	95	96	91

Source: Bank of Korea (1996).

Note: Numbers in parentheses are rates of increase (percent) over previous year.

[a]Includes number of branches and representative offices.

on bank branching were lessened. The banks themselves now decide the number of branches that are profitable to operate. In 1995, commercial banks—in particular, nationwide commercial banks—aggressively expanded their branch networks to strengthen their retail operations (table 9.5).

This growth has helped to intensify competition and improve the efficiency of local financial markets that were often characterized by a high degree of concentration. Freedom to open more branches, however, enabled the large nationwide commercial banks to expand their institutional dominance at the expense of smaller local savings institutions and regional banks (table 9.6). These fears prompted regional banks to ask the government to ease territorial restrictions against them. Regional banks are not allowed to open more than ten branches in Seoul and two branches in large cities in provinces other than their home provinces.

Foreign banks, except Citibank, have not expanded their branch networks yet. They do not seem to have strong interest in the retail banking

Table 9.6   Deposits and Assets of Commercial Banks (billion won, period average)

Bank Type	1990	1991	1992	1993	1994	1995	1996
			Deposits[a]				
Nationwide commercial banks (A)	41,585.9	52,152.9	60,122.3	68,593.7	74,518.9	117,097.1	137,715.7
	(82.1)	(81.1)	(81.6)	(80.8)	(79.8)	(83.8)	(84.0)
Regional banks (B)	9,093.2	12,147.1	13,524.9	14,540.7	17,164.9	20,860.8	24,523.3
	(17.9)	(18.9)	(18.4)	(17.1)	(18.4)	(14.9)	(14.9)
Commercial banks (A + B)	50,679.1	64,300.0	73,647.2	83,134.4	91,683.5	137,957.9	162,239.0
	(100.0)	(100.0)	(100.0)	(98.0)	(98.1)	(98.7)	(98.9)
Foreign banks	—	—	—	1,715.1	1,750.9	1,756.0	1,800.7
				(2.0)	(1.9)	(1.3)	(1.1)
Total	50,679.1	64,300.0	73,647.2	84,849.5	93,434.4	139,713.9	164,039.7
	(100.0)	(100.0)	(100.0)	(100.0)	(100.0)	(100.0)	(100.0)
			Assets				
Nationwide commercial banks (A)	96,494.9	119,201.0	144,278.7	172,323.3	217,620.2	299,036.8	363,950.7
	(85.77)	(85.37)	(86.17)	(81.00)	(81.84)	(82.90)	(82.85)
Regional banks (B)	16,007.0	20,421.0	23,147.9	26,164.7	32,651.7	41,506.2	51,487.1
	(14.23)	(14.63)	(13.83)	(12.30)	(12.28)	(11.51)	(11.72)
Commercial banks (A + B)	112,501.9	139,622.0	167,426.6	198,488.0	250,271.9	340,543.0	415,437.8
	(100.0)	(100.0)	(100.0)	(93.30)	(94.12)	(94.41)	(94.57)
Foreign banks	—	—	—	14,246.8	15,630.5	20,161.7	23,861.3
				(6.70)	(5.88)	(5.59)	(5.43)
Total	112,501.9	139,622.0	167,426.6	212,734.8	265,902.4	360,704.7	439,299.1
	(100.0)	(100.0)	(100.0)	(100.0)	(100.0)	(100.0)	(100.0)

Source: Bank of Korea (1997).

Note: Numbers in parentheses are composition ratios.

[a]Includes deposits and certificates of deposit.

business because of the high cost of building a retail network and the regulation of capital movements in Korea.[1] More foreign banks, however, may enter the retail banking business when the Multilateral Agreement on Investment is signed by the OECD member countries.

9.3.4   Market Concentration in the Banking Market

Banking market structure studies apply the structure-performance hypothesis to the banking industry. According to the hypothesis, the degree of competition among banks is influenced by the degree of concentration of output among a few relatively large banks, since a more highly concentrated market structure is assumed to be conducive to more effective collusion. The measures of performance, used as indicators of the degree of competition among banks, include bank profit rates, lending interest rates, and bank deposit rates (see Gilbert 1984, 617–45).

The structure-performance hypothesis implies that there may exist a positive correlation between market concentration and performance. Bank lending rates are influenced by the market structure of the banking industry. According to Jacobs (1971) and Rhoades (1982), bank lending interest rates tend to rise when there is a rise in the market concentration ratio. Thus market concentration seems to have a significant influence on bank lending interest rates.

We apply the structure-performance hypothesis to the banking industry in Korea. We use the Herfindahl-Hirschman index (HHI), better known as the Herfindahl index, to measure the degree of concentration of output in banking markets in Korea. Because of the importance attached to market concentration as an indicator of competition and the relative ease of calculating the Herfindahl index, this index serves as an efficient screening tool for regulators. The guidelines of the U.S. Justice Department, as applied to the banking industry, specify that if a bank merger would result (1) in a postmerger HHI in a market of less than 1,800 or (2) in a change in the HHI of less than 200, it is likely that the market structure would not reach a concentration level high enough or the concentration would not increase enough to give firms in the market the power to maintain prices above the competitive level for a significant period (see Rhoades 1993, 188–89).

After interest rates were deregulated in November 1991, the market concentration ratio in the banking industry, measured by the HHI, steadily declined to 716 at the end of 1996 from 917 at the end of 1990 (table 9.7). The market share of the top five commercial banks also declined steadily to 49.0 percent from 59.7 percent in 1990. These developments seem to reflect the entry of four new banks into the banking market and the homo-

---

1. In general, foreign exchange can only be purchased for approved purposes, primarily current account operations and permitted capital transactions.

Table 9.7   **Market Concentration of Commercial Banks in Korea**

Measure and Bank Type	1990	1991	1992	1993	1994	1995	1996
Herfindahl-Hirschman index							
Nationwide commercial banks	863	803	777	736	684	678	675
Regional banks	55	56	49	52	50	43	41
All banks	917	859	826	788	735	722	716
Top five banks	725	667	629	581	541	511	512
Market share (%)							
Top five banks	59.7	57.3	55.7	53.4	51.7	49.1	49.0

Note: Based on all won-denominated deposits at the end of the period.

geneous competitive market structure. Commercial banks offer similar deposit instruments to firms and households.

Since the deregulation of interest rates, the strong traditional relationship between banks and large firms has weakened. The weight of bank loans in total funding by large firms has shown a substantial decline, as companies increased funding through the corporate bond and commercial paper markets. Bank loans to small and medium-size firms and households have risen sharply to account for a larger share of overall loans. Commercial banks have adopted a new policy in determining lending rates; bank customers who consolidated their financial affairs at one bank started being offered favorable terms for loans and various kinds of free services such as tax consulting. Banks also began to put more emphasis on private banking.

9.4   Financial Deregulation and Monetary Policy

9.4.1   Monetary Policy

The deregulation of financial markets and the modification of regulations governing financial instruments and financial institutions will require changes in the operation of monetary policy, which is based on the monetary targeting of the broadly defined money supply, M2. The complete deregulation of interest rates in financial markets will necessitate a monetary control system based on interest rates. The Bank of Korea (BOK) frequently used repurchase agreements and monetary stabilization bonds (MSBs) for its daily operations. Changes in the operating procedures for monetary policy in the 1990s have led to reliance on the market-based allocation mechanism for open market instruments. The BOK reintroduced a system of auctions for the issuance of MSBs to nonbank financial intermediaries in April 1993 and applied it to banks as well in December 1995. Though very limited in size and frequency, sales of MSBs by auction to the general public, including nonbank financial intermediar-

Table 9.8   Open Market Operations of Monetary Stabilization Bonds (billion won)

Operation	1988	1990	1992	1993	1994	1995	1996
Issuance	16,967	20,262	24,853	29,796	34,879	39,458	30,725
Direct sale	1,575	4,918	10,468	18,917	25,045	27,215	7,019
Auction and acceptance	15,392	15,344	14,385	10,879	9,834	12,243	23,706
Redemption	9,768	22,327	18,085	25,858	33,740	38,974	31,520
Outstanding	15,374	15,241	20,264	24,202	25,340	25,825	25,030
Outstanding/M2 (%)	31.4	22.2	21.1	21.6	17.0	16.8	14.0

Source: Bank of Korea, Annual Report (Seoul, various issues).

ies, were tried by the BOK in 1998 and 1989 (Kang 1993, 201–25). The rate on MSBs issued by competitive bidding applies equally to all successful bidders through the Dutch auction method as with repurchase agreements. The level of discount rates of MSBs is slightly below market interest rates, reflecting the standing of the BOK. The direct sale rate to sixty-four primary dealers is set at a slightly lower rate than the competitive bidding rate (J. Kim 1996, 29–57); see table 9.8. However, mandatory allocations continue to be used to a considerable degree, particularly on special occasions, such as the allocation of MSBs in April 1997 to offset the effects of a cut in the reserve requirement ratio in February 1997. In order to reduce high reserve requirements, bank deposit reserve ratios were lowered in three steps from 11.5 percent in 1990 to 2.0 percent and 5.0 percent for demand deposits and savings deposits, respectively, in 1997 (see IMF 1996, 74). Cuts in deposit reserve ratios also helped to correct the comparative disadvantage of banks relative to nonbank financial intermediaries.

Since 1989, the BOK has made greater use of the sale and purchase of government and public bonds under repurchase agreements in controlling the banks' short-term liquidity. In 1995, about 80 percent of repurchases were implemented using auction-determined rates, the remainder being allocated administratively at slightly lower interest rates. Repurchase operations involve some administrative allocations to banks (see OECD 1996, 70). In order to reduce the banks' access to the BOK's rediscount facility, an overall ceiling on refinancing was introduced in 1994. The outstanding amount of BOK rediscounts was reduced to sterilize the effects of a cut in the deposit reserve ratio in 1997.

In April 1996, the monetary authorities increased the statutory minimum maturity of bank trust accounts. Starting in May 1996, households and firms began to shift out of trust accounts and into bank savings deposits and savings instruments offered by nonbank financial institutions. The portfolio shifts led to a sharp increase in the growth rate of M2. They did not, however, influence MCT and M3.[2] The monetary authorities chose

2. MCT comprises M2 plus certificates of deposit and trust accounts.

to implement a monetary targeting policy based on MCT rather than M2 in 1997.

9.4.2 Interest Rate Deregulation and the Monetary Transmission Mechanism

The income velocity of M2 has fluctuated greatly due to changing regulations and improving transactions technology (fig. 9.4). In contrast, the income velocity of M3 has been more stable, with a standard deviation of 2.15 compared with a standard deviation of 2.64 for M2 during the 1987–96 period.

The money demand equation was specified as

$$(2) \qquad \ln(M/P)_t = a_0 + a_1 \ln r_t + a_2 \ln y_t + a_3 \ln(M/P)_{t-1} + u_t.$$

In the above equation, M/P represents real money stock, r the weighted average of savings and time deposit rates, y the industrial production index, and u the error term. The Kalman filter is applied to update the coefficient a_1. Figure 9.5 delineates movements of the coefficient a_1 for M2 and M3. The interest rate elasticity of demand for M2 seemed to increase remarkably from 1992 due to interest rate deregulation and financial liberalization.

We attempt to estimate the relations, among money supply, output, the inflation rate, and the interest rate to examine whether there has been a significant change in the role of the interest rate in the monetary transmission mechanism in Korea since interest deregulation in the early 1990s. Four variables are included in the vector autoregression (VAR) model:

$$(3) \qquad Y_t = C_0 + \sum_{j=1}^{n} \beta_j Y_{t-j} + U_t,$$

where Y_t is a 4×1 vector of endogenous variables, C_0 is a 4×1 vector of constant terms, the βs are 12×4 matrices of coefficients, and U_t is a

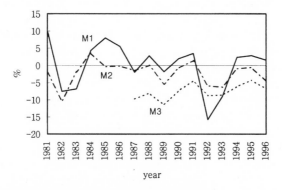

Fig. 9.4   Income velocity of money (percentage change)

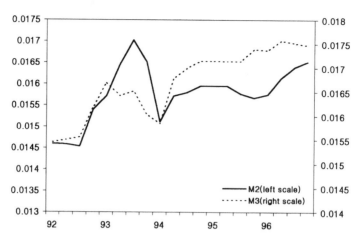

Fig. 9.5   Interest rate elasticity of demand for money

4×1 vector of disturbances. In this VAR model, twelve lags of each variable are included for estimation. Considering the endogeneity of money supply, we chose the following ordering among the four variables: the level of market interest rates, the CPI inflation rate, the industrial output growth rate, and the rate of increase in the money supply (M2; see Hahm and Lee 1997, 51–98).

Based on the estimated coefficients, an impulse response function was used to appraise how the interest rate responds to various kinds of shocks to the economy. In addition, we endeavor to examine whether there is any evidence of change in the monetary transmission mechanism in light of the interest rate deregulation in 1991 and financial liberalization in the 1990s. The sample was split at the end of 1991 (see IMF 1996). The specified VAR model was estimated using monthly, seasonally adjusted time series for two sample periods: 1980:1–96:12 and 1980:1–91:12. The three-year corporate bond yield was used as the market interest rate. The results were similar to those found by IMF studies (see IMF 1996).

Interest rate responses to shocks in the money supply, inflation, and output growth are presented in figure 9.6. The solid lines represent the impulse responses based on the 1980:1–96:12 sample, and the dashed lines represent those based on the 1980:1–91:12 subsample. The results for the two different sample periods are generally similar. The main findings are described below. First, in response to an increase in money supply growth, the nominal interest rate begins to fall steadily in the first three months, with a lag of about two months, and then rises to its original level for the subsample period. The response of the interest rate to an increase in money supply growth is weaker for the whole sample period than for the subsample period. Second, a rise in inflation leads to a significant rise in

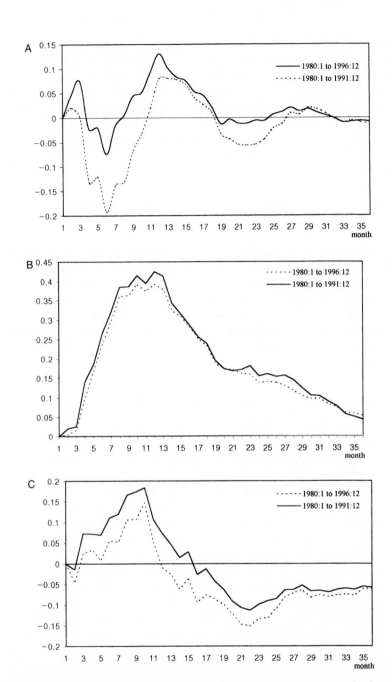

Fig. 9.6   Impulse response of corporate bond rate to contemporaneous shocks in economy

Note: Response to shocks in (*A*) money supply, (*B*) inflation rate, and (*C*) industrial output.

the nominal interest rate. Third, the response of the nominal interest rate to shocks in output growth shows a procyclical pattern.

As an indicator of the stance of monetary policy, the three-year corporate bond rate may not be a good proxy for a short-term interest rate that is directly affected by the BOK through operations in the money market. Therefore, the interbank call rate was used as the market interest rate in the next empirical study. Interbank call rate responses to shocks in money supply, inflation, and output growth are presented in figure 9.7. The sample was split at the end of 1993. The VAR model was estimated using monthly, seasonally adjusted time series for two sample periods: 1988:8–96:12 and 1988:8–93:12. In the second VAR model, six lags of each variable are included for estimation. In response to an increase in money supply growth, the interbank call rate rises in the next month and then declines to its original level for the subsample period. For the whole sample period, the interbank call rate rises steadily in the first four months and then declines to its original level in response to an increase in money supply growth. The puzzling phenomenon that the interbank call rate rises in response to an increase in money supply growth may reflect the expected tightening of liquidity in the money market. The BOK used to tighten monetary policy when M2 growth rates approached or exceeded the annual growth target.

9.5   Financial Deregulation and the Fragility of Banks

The rate of return on total assets of nationwide commercial banks continued to fall from 0.55 percent in 1990 to 0.23 percent in 1996 (table 9.9). The rate of return on total assets of regional banks also declined from 1.11 percent in 1990 to 0.47 percent in 1996. The sharp drop in bank profitability seems to have been due mainly to reduced interest rate margins and significant amounts of nonperforming loans held by commercial banks, some of which stem from recent credit card businesses. Furthermore, commercial banks considerably expanded write-offs of nonperforming loans as the bank supervision authorities suggested they do so.

The share of nonperforming loans of commercial banks steadily declined from 2.1 percent in 1990 to 0.8 percent in 1996 (table 9.10). Nonperforming loans, however, include only loans that are classified as "questionable loans" (Class III) and "estimated loss loans" (Class IV) by commercial banks.[3] The share of "unsound loans," which includes substandard loans (Class II, also commonly known as "fixed loans") and nonperforming loans, amounted to 5.1 percent at the end of 1996.[4] The share

3. Questionable loans are defined as those against which actions of collection or other measures are needed and that are not secured by collateral. Estimated loss loans are defined as bad loans that are judged to be uncollectable.
4. Fixed loans are defined as those against which actions or other measures are needed and that are secured by collateral.

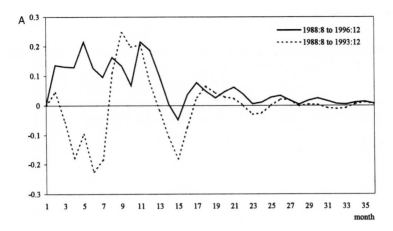

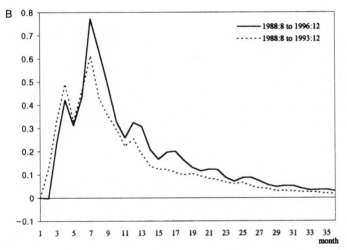

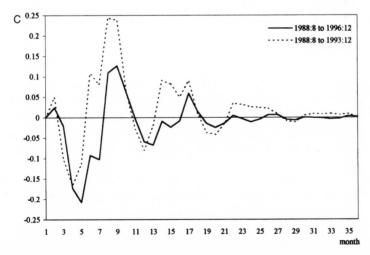

Fig. 9.7 Impulse response of interbank call rate to contemporaneous shocks in economy

Note: Response to shocks in (*A*) money supply, (*B*) inflation rate, and (*C*) industrial output.

Table 9.9   **Rate of Return on Total Assets of Commercial Banks, Trust Accounts Included (percent)**

Bank Type	1990	1991	1992	1993	1994	1995	1996
Top five nationwide commercial banks	0.54	0.49	0.49	0.36	0.38	0.22	0.08
All nationwide commercial banks	0.55	0.54	0.54	0.41	0.40	0.28	0.23
Regional banks	1.11	0.89	0.68	0.67	0.53	0.56	0.47
Commercial banks	0.63	0.59	0.56	0.45	0.42	0.32	0.26

Source: Bank of Korea (1996).

Table 9.10   **Share of Nonperforming Loans (I) of Commercial Banks (percent)**

Bank Type	1990	1991	1992	1993	1994	1995	1996
Nationwide commercial banks	2.2	1.9	1.8	1.9	1.0	0.9	0.8
Regional banks	1.4	1.0	0.9	1.0	0.9	1.0	0.9
Commercial banks	2.1	1.8	1.7	1.8	1.0	0.9	0.8

Source: Bank of Korea (1997).
Note: Nonperforming loans (I) (NPL(I)) = Estimated loss + Questionable.

Table 9.11   **Capital Adequacy Ratios of Banks (percent)**

Bank Type	1990	1991	1992	1993	1994	1995	1996
Five major banks	7.7	7.4	10.24	10.14	10.46	9.21	8.86
Nationwide commercial banks	8.5	8.2	10.40	10.40	10.19	8.97	8.97
Regional banks	13	11.6	16.34	14.86	13.11	11.44	10.15
Commercial banks	9.1	8.7	11.18	11.00	10.62	9.33	9.14

Source: Bank of Korea (various issues).
Note: Capital adequacy ratios are based on Bank for International Settlements criterion from 1992.

of "abnormal loans," which includes "caution-needed loans" (Class I) in addition to "unsound loans," was 14.3 percent at the end of 1996. The current average nonperforming loan ratio of the six major nationwide commercial banks is estimated at around 5 percent by international standards, according to the Presidential Commission for Financial Reform (1997, 2).

The recent economic downturn and the inadequate credit assessment by banks brought about new nonperforming loans and exacerbated the banks' bad-loan problems and pushed down their capital adequacy ratios (table 9.11). There was evidence of deterioration in the balance sheets of commercial banks. In 1997 nonperforming loans of banks increased substantially, as shown in table 9.12.

Table 9.12   **Share of Nonperforming Loans (II) of Commercial Banks (percent)**

	1990	1992	1994	1995	1996	1997	December 1998
NPL (II) ratio	7.5	6.7	5.6	5.2	3.9	5.8	7.4

Source: Financial Supervisory Commission, FSC press release, 3 March 1999.

Note: Nonperforming loans (II) (NPL(II)) = Substandard + Estimated loss + Questionable. Figures from the end of 1996 on include the Housing and Commercial Bank; those from the end of 1997 on include the Long-Term Credit Bank and not the five closed banks.

Rapid increases in nonperforming loans among banks and merchant banking corporations resulting from a series of large corporate bankruptcies have destabilized the financial market and quickly translated into a currency crisis. In order to deal with the increase in nonperforming loans, the government has established a special institution, the Korea Asset Management Corporation, modeled after the Resolution Trust Corporation in the United States, which deals with the resolution of bad loans of commercial banks. The government has also set up a special bad-loan resolution fund of 20 trillion won to finance the operation.

9.6   Concluding Remarks

The strengthening of the international competitiveness of financial markets and institutions has become a major financial policy objective in Korea as in other industrialized as well as in developing countries. The Presidential Commission for Financial Reform was established to accelerate and to broaden the process of financial liberalization and deregulation in early 1997. Priority will be placed on transforming the financial industry into a strategic core industry through competition and structural reorganization (Presidential Commission for Financial Reform 1997, 9).

Financial deregulation has led to an irreversible transformation of the domestic financial environment. Since interest rate deregulation, the difference between market interest rates and bank interest rates has been reduced. Commercial banks began to expand their branch networks in order to strengthen their retail businesses. Five major nationwide commercial banks emerged as market leaders in setting prime lending rates in the banking market. Smaller banks and regional banks have tended to follow the leaders in the banking market in major decisions, which includes setting prime lending rates and fees for services. A significant change occurred in bank loan portfolios. Commercial banks have expanded loans to small and medium-size firms and households since interest rate deregulation. Households are now able to obtain loans from financial institutions more easily than in the past. Interest rate margins of nationwide commercial banks came down strikingly between 1990 and 1994. After the interest rate deregulation in 1991, the market concentration ratio in the banking industry steadily declined in the 1990s. Market concentration through mergers and acquisitions, however, has not occurred yet in the banking market.

Interest rate elasticity of demand for M2 seemed to increase remarkably from 1991 due to interest rate deregulation and financial liberalization. Changes in regulations governing financial instruments recently prompted portfolio shifts between savings instruments of banks and nonbank financial institutions. The portfolio shifts led to unstable demand for M2. Thus the monetary authorities decided to replace M2 with MCT, which comprises M2 plus certificates of deposit and trust accounts, as an intermediate target variable in 1997. Financial liberalization, however, is likely to make the demand for money increasingly unstable. Therefore, there may be advantages to moving the monetary objective away from rigid targeting of M2 or MCT. Deregulation may necessitate the relinquishment of earlier modes of policy implementation that provided some advantages of simplicity and control to the monetary authorities.

The recent economic downturn and the inadequate credit assessment by banks brought about new nonperforming loans and exacerbated the banks' bad-loan problems. Weaknesses in the structure and performance of the corporate governance of commercial banks have surfaced with the Hanbo loan scandal in 1997. The deregulation process may involve transitional risks and costs. Korea's financial system will not become internationally competitive without the presence of some financially and managerially strong banks and other financial institutions.

Restrictions on competition in fees and commissions among members of the stock exchange and insurance companies still limit the scope for price competition in this area of financial services. The government should continue to adopt policies that promote and provide more scope for competition in the financial service market. The government authorities may have to increasingly use the instrument of competition rules in order to dismantle all sorts of cartel agreements in the financial service industry.

The government authorities have pursued gradual deregulation and favor restructuring financial institutions in several steps to reduce the shocks and uncertainties to financial markets. On the other hand, the Presidential Commission for Financial Reform recommended a big-bang-type full liberalization in December 1997. The commission seems to think that such liberalization might solve many problems in Korea's financial markets in a single stroke. It is an open question which approach would offer a better solution in Korea. It remains to be seen whether the commission's recommendation can be implemented in the coming months before the presidential election in late 1997. If not, the recommendations might be handed over to the next government for implementation.

References

Bank of Korea. Office of Bank Supervision. Various issues. *Bank management statistics.* Seoul: Bank of Korea.

Gilbert, R. Alton. 1984. Bank market structure and competition: A survey. *Journal of Money, Credit and Banking* 16 (November): 617–45.

Hahm, Joon-Ho, and Duk-Hoon Lee. 1997. Macroeconomic sources of long-term interest rate differentials. *Journal of Economic Policy* (Korea Development Institute) 19 (1): 51–98.

IMF (International Monetary Fund). 1996. Korea: Selected issues. IMF Staff Country Report no. 96/136. Washington, D.C.: International Monetary Fund.

Jacobs, Donald P. 1971. Business loan costs and bank market structure. NBER Occasional Paper no. 115. Cambridge, Mass.: National Bureau of Economic Research.

Kang, Moon-Soo. 1993. Monetary policy implementation under financial liberalization: The case of Korea. In *Financial opening: Policy issues and experiences in developing countries,* ed. Helmut Reisen and Bernhard Fischer, 201–25. Paris: Organization for Economic Cooperation and Development.

Kim, Hong-Dal. 1996. Interest rate liberalization and determination of lending rates. *Monthly Bulletin* (Bank of Korea), August: 22–47.

Kim, Jae-Chun. 1996. Interest rate deregulation and money market development in Korea. In *Interest rate liberalization and money market development,* ed. Hassanali Mehran, Bernard Laurens, and Marc Quintyn, 29–57. Washington, D.C.: International Monetary Fund.

Kim, Pyung-Joo. 1997. *Financial reform in Korea.* Seoul: Presidential Commission for Financial Reform.

Ministry of Finance and Economy. 1991. *MOF Bulletin,* no. 97 (September).

Nam, Sang-Woo. 1994. Korea's financial reform since the early 1980s. In *Financial reform: Theory and experience,* ed. Gerard Caprio Jr. et al., 184–222. New York: Cambridge University Press.

OECD (Organization for Economic Cooperation and Development). 1996. *OECD economic surveys: Korea, 1995–1996.* Paris: Organization for Economic Cooperation and Development.

Presidential Commission for Financial Reform. 1997. *Financial reform in Korea: The first report.* Seoul: Presidential Commission for Financial Reform, April.

Rhoades, Stephen A. 1982. *Structure-performance studies in banking: An updated summary and evaluation.* Staff Economic Studies no. 19. Washington, D.C.: Board of Governors of the Federal Reserve System.

———. 1993. The Herfindahl-Hirschman index. *Federal Reserve Bulletin* 79 (March): 188–89.

Comment   Shinji Takagi

Moon-Soo Kang discusses the effect of bank deregulation on (1) interest rate margins, (2) market concentration, and (3) the channel of monetary

Shinji Takagi is professor of economics at the University of Osaka.

policy in Korea. The fundamental question here is this: how should we assess the quantitative effect of bank (or banking sector) deregulation? In addition to the three criteria the author examines in the text, one can also suggest, among others, (4) bank profitability, (5) consumer or depositor gains, and (6) arbitrage with market interest rates as additional criteria. I raise these issues because I see no logical necessity that bank deregulation must affect some of these quantitative indicators in a particular way. In fact, many of them are affected not only by deregulation but also by many other factors, including the risk factor, transactions costs, profitability, bank behavior, and general macroeconomic conditions. The findings of the paper, therefore, are probably specific to the macroeconomic, legal, and institutional environment within which Korea's deregulation policy took place.

On a more basic level, one is struck with a parallelism that exists between the experience of Korea and that of Japan. Both Korea and Japan took a slow and gradual approach to financial liberalization. Both are now contemplating a big bang approach to full liberalization. The parallelism, however, ends here. Japan was "forced" to liberalize its financial market because of the need to finance large issues of government bonds resulting from the widening fiscal deficits in the 1970s and because of the liberalization of cross-border capital flows prompted by sustained current account surpluses (and the associated accumulation of foreign assets and foreign pressure to open up the domestic capital markets) in the 1980s. In other words, necessity was the driving force behind Japan's financial liberalization. Likewise for the recently announced big bang (in which the financial system is to be fully deregulated by the year 2001), the government was forced to react to the declining international status of Japanese financial markets and the awareness that Japan's financial industry would be in danger of losing international competitiveness entirely. But what is the driving force for change in Korea?

The Japanese experience has been reasonably explainable in terms of political economy considerations. Government authorities are reluctant to deregulate the financial markets because financial regulation is a significant source of power and authority. Thus deregulation and other institutional change generally occur only as necessity dictates. In the case of Korea, however, there is no such clear picture of forces driving the government authorities to pursue the policy of financial liberalization. Are the Korean authorities driven by their awareness that a deregulated financial system is inherently superior in terms of resource allocation and other efficiency considerations? If so, unlike the Japanese authorities they are driven not by necessity but by reason. Reason *should* be the principle of action in all intelligent beings, but experience tells us that it is often not sufficient to effect a significant institutional change. Was the first attempt at interest rate deregulation abandoned in 1989 precisely because it was conceived by reason and not driven by necessity? If Korea is following the dictates of reason or simply the lead of Japan, one cannot help but be a little skeptical about the future success of the Korean big bang.

Comment   Sang-Woo Nam

Financial deregulation in Korea has indeed been very cautious and slow, as Moon-Soo Kang states in the paper's introduction. Kang assesses that this policy of gradualism has been pursued in order to give less competitive financial institutions enough time to adjust to a more competitive environment in the financial market. The less competitive financial institutions include nationwide commercial banks with a heavy burden of nonperforming loans, which have been the major victims of government industrial policy since the early 1970s. To a large extent, the accumulated nonperforming loans represent a deadweight loss due to broad government intervention in resource allocation. Unlike in the 1970s, most of these nonperforming loans may have resulted from the moral hazard behavior of major *chaebols* and financial institutions rather than direct government intervention. However, if the government's promotion of industry and the way the government has handled corporate financial distress and defaults in the past have induced *chaebols* and financial institutions to believe that they are "too big to die," the government should be held responsible. The neglect of credit evaluation and the moral hazard behavior of banks was also due to the weak governance of the nationwide commercial banks in the midst of continued government intervention in the management of these privatized banks.

The question is how to deal efficiently with this deadweight loss of nonperforming loans. More specifically, we have to ask whether gradualism has been a cost-effective way of dealing with the deterioration of bank loans. Politically, it must have been the most inexpensive way. As the financial sector keeps growing in terms of total credit, the share of nonperforming loans in total credit is supposed to be declining as long as the size of nonperforming loans remains more or less constant. In this way, it was hoped that the problem would ease and, in time, disappear without any attention or criticism from the public. The government would then not need to admit the failure of past policies because the failures would not be exposed explicitly.

This approach, however, seems to have been fairly expensive economically. It has resulted in delays in dealing with insolvent corporations and

Sang-Woo Nam is professor in the School of International Policy and Management of the Korea Development Institute.

in continued resource flows to these firms in distress. The practice of loan repayment guarantees among the subsidiaries of *chaebols* has also contributed to this phenomenon. More important, the delayed and slow process of financial liberalization must have cost the economy a lot. Lack of competition in the financial sector means inefficiencies in the operation of intermediaries and in the allocation of resources among different uses and industries. Stronger governance of commercial banks would have eased the problem of moral hazard on the part of these banks and *chaebols* as well. Cleaning the balance sheet of banks—in other words, separating the nonperforming loans from banks—would have been more cost-effective economically. Freed from the legacies of the past, the banking sector could have been forced to compete rigorously with nonbank financial institutions as well as foreign intermediaries on an equal footing. It is indeed surprising that there has been little serious discussion about how to deal with the deterioration of bank loan portfolios and the potential cost of gradualism in (domestic) financial deregulation. Kang mentions this issue in both the introduction and the conclusion of the paper but leaves out any serious discussion of this important subject.

The paper seems to evaluate the impact of Korea's financial deregulation rather positively in spite of the cautious and slow process of liberalization. The findings include the expansion of commercial bank branch networks, increased loans to small and medium-size firms and consumers, reduced interest margins, and a declining market concentration ratio in the banking industry. Of these, the expansion of commercial bank branch networks may not be desirable if it is simply the result of costly, zero-sum efforts to attract deposits when there is no lack of deposit outlets even in remote areas with agricultural cooperatives, post offices, and other small community-based financial intermediaries.

The evidence of reduced interest margins after interest rate deregulation is not very convincing either. As Kang notes, lending rates have been deregulated faster than deposit rates. This sequence was mainly due to the relatively weak impact of lending rate deregulation on the market, rather than to its expected effect on fund allocation. As is well known, banks generally have ways of circumventing lending rate regulations. For instance, by requiring borrowers to put a portion of what they borrow in deposits (compensating deposit balance), banks can keep their effective lending rates close to market rates. Starting in 1991 there seems to have been a change in the method of calculating the average balance of checking accounts that made the average deposit interest rate much higher. It was only in November 1991 that the first stage of interest rate deregulation went into effect, and only interest rates on time deposits with a maturity of three years and over were deregulated. Thus it is hard to believe that the higher average deposit interest rate in 1991 was due to interest rate deregulation and the consequent increase in competitive pressure for banks. Between 1991 and 1995, the interest margin actually widened from 2.2 to 3.0 percentage points.

Similarly, Kang ascribes the declining rate of return on bank assets to the narrowing of interest margins and the reduced share of nonperforming loans. The real picture seems to be that interest margins widened rather than narrowed, and the reduced share of nonperforming loans might simply reflect increased write-offs of these loans. In the situation where banks were forced to write off large amounts of nonperforming loans and profits were squeezed, they might have no other option than widening interest margins in order to minimize profit deterioration.

Finally, the measured interest rate elasticity of demand for money shows opposite movements for M2 and M3. This may be due to a deficiency in the specification of the money demand equation. As an interest rate variable, the bank deposit interest rate could also be tried in addition to the corporate bond yield for the M2 demand equation. The inflation rate might also be important, as it represents the cost of holding money. Specification of the equation might be improved when the interest rate (and cost) variables are tried in the form $\ln(100 + r)$ (rather than $\ln r$), $\ln[(100 + r)/(100 + r_d)]$, or $\ln(100 + r_p)$, where r_d is the representative bank deposit interest rate and r_p is the inflation rate.

Deregulation, Profit, and Cost in Commercial Banking
The Case of Hong Kong

Yum K. Kwan and Francis T. Lui

10.1 Introduction

Although Hong Kong is often regarded as a classic showcase of the laissez faire economy, the intervening hand of the government is clearly visible in some of its most important sectors. In utilities, public transportation, securities, and housing, the markets are highly regulated. The recent process of democratization has also created significant political pressure to introduce even more regulations in these and other sectors. Nevertheless, between late 1994 and early 1995, a process of deregulating the interest rate cap was imposed by the Hong Kong Association of Banks (HKAB).

The study of deregulation in Hong Kong's banking sector is of interest for several reasons. First, before the deregulation, the HKAB was a powerful cartel, but afterward, its members had to engage in more fierce competition. This shift provides an opportunity for comparing the behaviors of banks operating under different market structures. Second, the transition from monopoly to competition often increases risks and reduces profits. These could cause failures of more vulnerable banks, as happened in the United States after the interest rate deregulation of the early 1980s. On the other hand, Hong Kong's transition has been relatively fast and successful. The banks appear to have absorbed the policy shock smoothly. Analyzing the experience of Hong Kong may shed light on the conditions

Yum K. Kwan is associate professor of economics at the City University of Hong Kong. Francis T. Lui is director of the Center for Economic Development at the Hong Kong University of Science and Technology.

The authors thank Takatoshi Ito, Moon-Soo Kang, and Chung-Shu Wu for useful comments on an earlier draft of this paper. They are also grateful to Jim Wong of the Hong Kong Monetary Authority for help in getting some of the data.

that are needed for a stable transition. Third, having 183 fully licensed banks and with 85 of the world's top 100 banks being represented, Hong Kong is one of the largest international centers of banking. In 1995, its daily foreign exchange trading surpassed that of Switzerland to become the world's fifth most active (Carse 1995a). Events happening in such a major center may have long-lasting effects on the world's financial markets.

The main objectives of this paper are to analyze how Hong Kong banks have optimally responded to the interest rate deregulation and why it has so far not caused any bank failures. To do this, we shall present the arguments in several steps. In section 10.2 we provide the general background of the deregulation of 1994–95. In section 10.3 we present some crude indicators of the banks' new strategies. Section 10.4 discusses the methodology that we use to decompose the changes in the banks' cost and profit functions into (1) the effects of bank-initiated responses to the new regulatory structure and (2) the effects of changes in the external environment. Separating these two effects is important because we can then assess how much of the success is due to luck and how much is due to banks' optimizing behaviors. The empirical results based on this methodology are presented and interpreted in section 10.5. Section 10.6 uses a simple capital asset pricing model (CAPM) to estimate the changes in the risks of banks that are listed on Hong Kong's stock market. This is necessary for completing the argument because risk management is one of the instruments that banks can use to mitigate the impact of deregulation. Finally, concluding remarks are made in section 10.7.

10.2 Institutional Background

The banking cartel in Hong Kong can be traced back a hundred years. In 1897, the Exchange Banks' Association (EBA) was established. It could only be joined by authorized banks, which used it as a forum for fixing banking charges and agreed rates of buying and selling foreign exchange. However, the rules were not mandatory, but similar to a gentlemen's agreement (Ghose 1995).

In the early 1960s there was a cutthroat interest war among the banks in Hong Kong. Some British banks decided to raise the deposit interest rate by 1 percentage point. It was widely interpreted by Chinese banks as an attempt to monopolize the market (*Far Eastern Economic Review,* 22 April 1965). The EBA proposed to form an agreement among all banks, whether they were members of the association or not, for a uniform interest rate structure. After a prolonged process of negotiation and pressure, an agreement materialized in July 1964. There would be no interest paid for demand and seven-day-notice deposits. Interest rates for savings and time deposits of less than one year were to be determined by the EBA.

Loans and advances were not regulated, but it was against the Money Lenders' Ordinance of 1911 to charge an interest rate of more than 60 percent per annum. The agreement was mandatory. Banks contravening it would be denied access to clearinghouse facilities and barred from interbank exchange and fund dealings (Ghose 1995). It is sometimes believed that the agreement at that time probably saved some small banks from collapse (e.g., see Jao 1992, chap. 26).

The EBA was replaced by the Hong Kong Association of Banks in 1980. The Hong Kong Association of Banks Ordinance made this a statutory body, and its rules were legally binding. Bankers were no longer required to observe the rules of the Money Lenders' Ordinance and could lend at any interest rate. A set of rules on maximum interest rates for different types of deposits and minimum bank charges were laid down. Decisions on the maximum base rates were made by the Committee of the HKAB, in consultation with the financial secretary of the Hong Kong government. Banks were free to offer lower rates. Deposits of at least HK$500,000, foreign currency deposits, time deposits of fifteen months and longer, and deposits taken by unincorporated banks were exempted (Ko 1991).

Because the Hong Kong dollar has been pegged to the U.S. dollar at the rate of 7.8 since 1983, interest rates of the former are heavily influenced by the latter. Throughout the 1980s and 1990s, the inflation rate in Hong Kong has been significantly higher than that in the United States. This has created a negative real interest rate situation in Hong Kong for a prolonged period.[1] The public has from time to time pressed for the removal of the "interest rate rules" outlined above. For example, a report issued by the Consumer Council (1994) argued that the spread between the prime rate and the regulated savings (or time deposit) rate was on average about 1.7 percentage points higher than those in other countries. The spread between the prime and the unregulated interbank lending rate was closely in line with international standards. The Hong Kong Monetary Authority (HKMA), the de facto central bank of Hong Kong established in 1993, finally decided to deregulate the interest rate cap in several phases.

On 1 October 1994, the HKMA removed the interest rate cap on all relevant time deposits of maturity more than one month. There was no deregulation of current and savings account deposits. On 3 January 1995, those with a maturity of over seven days were also deregulated (Carse 1995a). The HKMA originally planned to implement the third phase on 1 April 1995. This would have covered Hong Kong dollar time deposits fixed for more than twenty-four hours. However, the short-term volatile environment caused by the Mexican crisis and the Barings collapse

---

1. This is one of the reasons why the proportion of M3 in foreign-currency-denominated assets has been staying at the high level of over 40 percent. Foreign currency deposits are not subject to the interest rate cap (see Jao 1992, chap. 26).

changed the mind of the HKMA. It decided to defer the third phase so that a review of the situation up to the end of June could be done (HKMA 1995). The review led to the conclusion to move one more step. Time deposits of seven days were deregulated. Further deregulation was not entirely off the agenda, but for practical purposes the current program had come to an end. Over 99 percent of time deposits covered by the former interest rate rules had been deregulated.

The HKMA seemed to be cautious in implementing the steps. Fearing that the deregulation could reduce banks' profits by too much, it did not do anything to current and savings deposits. Time deposits of less than seven days' maturity remained regulated so that there would be no destabilizing migration from current and savings deposits to short-term time deposits. The basic problem faced by the HKMA seemed to be how the cap could be removed safely. This concern was based on the belief that the possible erosion of profits could lead banks to take excessive risks that would weaken their positions in times of major external shocks. However, it was judged that the market had absorbed the deregulation well (Carse 1995a). Banks had become more active sellers of their products rather than passive providers of services. More innovations such as electronic and card products were introduced in the competitive and riskier environment (Carse 1995b).

It should also be noted that after the establishment of the HKMA, banks have been required to disclose more of their financial information. This may be important for the public because there is no insurance for bank deposits in Hong Kong. The disclosure requirement has also probably restrained banks from taking positions that are too risky.

10.3   Some Anecdotal Evidence

In this section, we present and discuss some summary statistics that compare banks' situations before and after the deregulation. The purpose is to offer an illustration of the effects of removing the interest rate cap. This also serves to motivate the more rigorous analysis in the later sections of the paper.

Table 10.1 contains appropriate sample means derived from annual data for twenty-four locally incorporated banks before and after the deregulation.[2] Since the deregulation program started in October 1994 and ended a few months later, as an approximation we have taken 1993–94 as the before-deregulation period and 1995–96 as the after-deregulation period. Item 10 of table 10.1 shows that the average real profit rate, which is defined here as the difference between total income (excluding exceptional

2. Data are from annual reports of the banks and from Hong Kong Bank (various issues). Also see the discussion of data in section 10.4.

Table 10.1   **Summary Statistics of Cost, Income, and Rate of Profit (per thousand dollars)**

	Before Deregulation: 1993–94		After Deregulation: 1995–96		Growth Rate (%)	
1. Income from service charges/TA	10.21		10.16		−0.49	
2. Interest income/TA	54.31		68.2		25.6	
Interest income/loans		108.57		126.4		16.4
Loans/TA		522.21		559.12		6.88
3. Exceptional items/TA	2.21		0.8		−63.8	
4. Total income/TA	66.73		79.16		18.6	
5. Operating cost/TA	14.26		12.67		−11.2	
6. Interest cost/TA	30.87		43.98		42.5	
Interest cost/deposits		36.31		51.88		42.9
Deposits/TA		848.38		846.85		−0.18
7. Bad debt provisions/TA	1.42		1.78		25.4	
8. Total cost/TA	46.33		58.42		26.1	
9. Net interest/TA (2 − 6)	23.45		24.22		3.29	
10. Profit rate (1 + 2 − 5 − 6)	19.39		21.71		12	

Note: TA = total assets.

items) and total cost (excluding bad debt provisions), divided by the value of total assets, actually increased by 2.32 percentage points after the interest rate was deregulated. Why did the deregulation, which was meant to take away the monopoly power of the HKAB, fail to lower the profit rate?

Inspection of item 6 readily shows that (real) average interest cost went up from $30.87 per $1,000 of total assets to $43.98. This was an increase of 42.5 percent, confirming the expectation that the more competitive environment forced banks to pay a much higher interest cost. Banks, however, tried to cut operating cost, where there was an 11.2 percent decline.

On the income side, interest income went up from $54.31 to $68.20. The absolute value of this change was almost the same as the corresponding change for interest cost. This implies that the interest rate spread remained relatively stable despite the increase in interest cost. The entries in item 9 support this remark. Closer examination of item 2 suggests that the ratio of interest income to total assets went up for two reasons. One was that banks were able to earn more interest income per unit of loans lent out. The other was that banks tried to lend out more loans.

We should recall that the interest rate rules did not apply to banks' lending interest rate, which was determined in the competitive market even before the removal of the interest rate cap. Why could banks earn more interest after the deregulation? One hypothesis is that banks became more aggressive and less discriminating in offering loans. The result would be an increase in risk. Item 7 shows that bad debt provisions increased by 25.4 percent. This is consistent with the hypothesis that bank risk rose.

Table 10.2	Assets of Banks in Hong Kong (million 1990 HK dollars)		
	Before Deregulation: 1993–94	After Deregulation: 1995–96	Growth Rate (%)
Average	60,952	70,611	15.8
Maximum	870,436	871,246	0.09
Minimum	1,185	1,507	27.2

All the items in table 10.1 are expressed in units per $1,000 of total assets. The table does not tell us whether banks succeeded in attracting more deposits. If this happened, the value of banks' total assets would increase. Table 10.2 shows that the average size of banks went up by 15.8 percent in real terms in the second period. This scale effect, together with the increase in profit rate, would raise total profits by almost 30 percent. The story of Hong Kong's interest rate deregulation cannot be described as one involving erosion of profits.

The above discussion must be regarded as illustrative only. One can always argue that the changes in income, cost, and profit were due to unexplained shocks in the environment rather than to banks' optimal responses to the deregulation. To isolate the effects of the deregulation, we must use better methods. Section 10.4 develops a method to address this problem, and the results are discussed in section 10.5. The method, however, cannot be used to assess the changes in risk. The simple CAPM of section 10.6 can fill the hole in the analysis.

10.4   Profit and Cost Functions

10.4.1   Profit Function

We study the evolution of the industry's operating profits by estimating a translog profit function with three inputs (labor, capital, and deposits) and two outputs (loans and banking services). Variable definitions can be found in table 10.3.

With outputs measured positively and inputs negatively, the profit function is defined as

$$(1) \qquad \pi(p) \ = \ \max\{p'x : x \in T\},$$

where p and x are 5×1 vectors of input-output prices and quantities, respectively, and T is the production possibility set representing the collection of technologically feasible input-output bundles. See Diewert (1982) for theoretical discussions of the profit function. Empirically we adopt a translog specification

Table 10.3   **Variable Definitions**

Variable	Name	Definition
p_1	Price of labor	Salaries and employee benefits divided by number of employees
p_2	Price of capital	Occupancy and fixed asset expenditures divided by net book value of fixed assets
p_3	Price of deposits	Interest expenses plus other operating expenses (unrelated to labor and capital) divided by total deposits including certificates of deposit
p_4	Price of loans	Interest income divided by loans (advances + trade bills − provisions)
p_5	Price of services	Operating income divided by total assets
π	Profits	Interest income + operating income − interest expenses − operating expenses

$$(2) \quad \ln \pi = \beta_0 + \sum_{i=1}^{5} \beta_i \ln p_i + \frac{1}{2}\sum_{i=1}^{5}\sum_{j=1}^{5}\beta_{ij}\ln p_i \ln p_j, \qquad \beta_{ij} = \beta_{ji}.$$

See Lau (1978) and Jorgenson (1986) for surveys of the empirical literature; recent applications to banking can be found in Hancock (1991), Berger, Humphrey, and Pulley (1996), and Humphrey and Pulley (1997),
among many others. From the definition in equation (1) it follows that a
profit function must be linearly homogeneous in prices, a property that
translates into a set of restrictions among the parameters of the translog
profit function:

$$(3) \qquad \sum_{i=1}^{5} \beta_i = 1, \qquad \sum_{j=1}^{5}\beta_{ij} = 0, \qquad i = 1,\ldots,5.$$

Upon differentiating the profit function with respect to prices, Hotelling's
lemma implies a set of input-output share equations

$$(4) \qquad S_i = \beta_i + \sum_{j=1}^{5}\beta_{ij}\ln p_j, \qquad i = 1,\ldots,5,$$

where

$$(5) \qquad S_i \equiv \frac{p_i x_i}{\pi} = \frac{p_i}{\pi}\left(\frac{\partial \pi}{\partial p_i}\right) = \frac{\partial \ln \pi}{\partial \ln p_i}, \qquad i = 1,\ldots,5.$$

The five share equations in (4) are dependent because the shares add to
one by construction; one of them has to be dropped in estimation. Dropping the last share equation, substituting equation (3) into equations
(2) and (4) to eliminate the parameters associated with the last price, and
appending random disturbances to the remaining equations, we obtain a
five-equation system ready for estimation:

(6) $\ln\left(\dfrac{\pi}{p_5}\right) = \beta_0 + \displaystyle\sum_{i=1}^{4} \beta_i \ln\left(\dfrac{p_i}{p_5}\right) + \dfrac{1}{2}\sum_{i=1}^{4}\sum_{j=1}^{4}\beta_{ij}\ln\left(\dfrac{p_i}{p_5}\right)\ln\left(\dfrac{p_j}{p_5}\right) + \varepsilon_0,$

$S_i = \beta_i + \displaystyle\sum_{j=1}^{4}\beta_{ij}\ln\left(\dfrac{p_j}{p_5}\right) + \varepsilon_i, \qquad \beta_{ij} = \beta_{ji}, \qquad i = 1,\dots,4.$

Assuming normally distributed disturbances, a fully efficient maximum likelihood estimate (MLE) can be obtained by Zellner's iterated seemingly unrelated regression (ISUR), with the cross-equation restrictions enforced in computing the residual covariance matrix at each iteration. Moreover, the MLE is invariant with respect to the choice of which share equation to drop. For example, we would obtain the same result if the first share equation, rather than the last one, was dropped.

The underlying technology of production can be inferred from the dual profit function. The Hicks-Allen partial elasticity of transformation can be obtained by differentiating the profit function and applying Hotelling's lemma:

(7) $$\eta_{ij} \equiv \frac{\pi\,\pi_{ij}}{\pi_i\,\pi_j} = \frac{\pi}{x_i x_j}\frac{\partial x_i}{\partial p_j} = \frac{\pi}{x_i x_j}\frac{\partial x_j}{\partial p_i},$$

where π_i and π_{ij} denote, respectively, the first and second partial derivatives with respect to the subscripted prices. The demand (supply) elasticity of input (output) x_i with respect to p_j can be easily calculated, given η_{ij} and share S_j:

(8) $$\varpi_{ij} = S_j\eta_{ij} = \frac{p_j x_j}{\pi}\frac{\pi}{x_i x_j}\frac{\partial x_i}{\partial p_j} = \frac{\partial \ln|x_i|}{\partial \ln p_j}.$$

For the translog function form,

(9) $$\eta_{ij} = 1 + \beta_{ij}/S_i S_j, \qquad i \neq j,$$

$$\eta_{ii} = 1 + \beta_{ii}/S_i^2 - 1/S_i.$$

The translog specification allows a convenient decomposition of profit growth attributed to changes in parameters and prices. Let $\pi(p;\beta)$ and $\pi(p^*;\beta^*)$ be the profit functions for two periods, with price vectors p and p^* and parameter vectors β and β^*, respectively. Consider the identity

(10) $$\frac{\pi(p^*;\beta^*)}{\pi(p;\beta)} = \left[\frac{\pi(p^*;\beta^*)}{\pi(p^*;\beta)}\frac{\pi(p;\beta^*)}{\pi(p;\beta)}\right]^{1/2}\left[\frac{\pi(p^*;\beta^*)}{\pi(p;\beta^*)}\frac{\pi(p^*;\beta)}{\pi(p;\beta)}\right]^{1/2}$$

$$\equiv A \cdot B.$$

The left-hand side (in logarithm) is the growth in profit when (p, β) changes to (p^*, β^*). The right-hand side is a decomposition into marginal effects. The logarithm of A is the average of the two hypothetical cases in which β changes to β^* with prices held constant at p and p^*, respectively. This is the profit growth due to parameter change alone. Similarly, the logarithm of B is the growth in profit due to price change. Using the translog profit function, it is possible to further decompose the four marginal effects. Let $\ln p_k^* = \ln p_k + \Delta \ln p_k$ and $p_j^* = p_j$ for $j \neq k$. It is straightforward to check that

$$(11) \quad E_k(p,\beta) \equiv \frac{\ln \pi(p^*;\beta) - \ln \pi(p;\beta)}{\Delta \ln p_k} = \beta_k + \frac{1}{2}\sum_{j=1}^{5}\beta_{kj}\ln p_j,$$

which is a discrete approximation to the profit elasticity with respect to p_k. Thus

$$(12) \quad \ln \pi(p^*;\beta) - \ln \pi(p;\beta) = \sum_{i=1}^{5}[E_i(p^*,\beta)\ln p_i^* - E_i(p,\beta)\ln p_i],$$

which is a sum of marginal contributions from each of the five prices, with the parameter held constant at β. Similarly,

$$(13) \quad \ln \pi(p;\beta^*) - \ln \pi(p;\beta) = (\beta_0^* - \beta_0)$$

$$+ \sum_{i=1}^{5}[E_i(p,\beta^*) - E_i(p,\beta)]\ln p_i,$$

where $[E_j(p, \beta^*) - E_j(p, \beta)]\ln p_j$ can be interpreted as the jth input-output component of the profit growth due to parameter change, with prices held constant at p.

10.4.2   Cost Function

To study further the impact of deregulation on the cost side, in particular the industry's average cost curve, we estimate a translog cost function with three inputs (labor, capital, and deposits) and one output (loans) of the form

$$(14) \quad \ln c = \beta_0 + \sum_{i=1}^{3}\beta_i \ln p_i + \frac{1}{2}\sum_{i=1}^{3}\sum_{j=1}^{3}\beta_{ij}\ln p_i \ln p_j$$

$$+ \beta_Y \ln Y + \sum_{i=1}^{3}\beta_{Yi}\ln p_i \ln Y + \frac{1}{2}\beta_{YY}\ln^2 Y.$$

Analogous to the profit function case, cost share equations are generated by applying Shephard's lemma and combined with the cost function to form a three-equation system estimated by ISUR, after imposing homogeneity restrictions and dropping the last cost share:

$$(15) \quad \ln\left(\frac{c}{p_3}\right) = \beta_0 + \sum_{i=1}^{2} \beta_i \ln\left(\frac{p_i}{p_3}\right) + \frac{1}{2}\sum_{i=1}^{2}\sum_{j=1}^{2} \beta_{ij} \ln\left(\frac{p_i}{p_3}\right)\ln\left(\frac{p_j}{p_3}\right)$$

$$+ \; \beta_Y \ln\left(\frac{Y}{p_3}\right) + \sum_{i=1}^{2} \beta_{Yi} \ln\left(\frac{p_i}{p_3}\right)\ln\left(\frac{Y}{p_3}\right) + \frac{1}{2}\beta_{YY}\ln^2\left(\frac{Y}{p_3}\right) + \varepsilon_0,$$

$$S_i = \beta_i + \sum_{j=1}^{2} \beta_{ij}\ln\left(\frac{p_j}{p_3}\right) + \beta_{Yi}\ln\left(\frac{Y}{p_3}\right) + \varepsilon_i, \qquad \beta_{ij} = \beta_{ji}, \qquad i = 1,2.$$

The average cost curve (in logarithm) is obtained by simply subtracting $\ln Y$ on both sides of the total cost function (14). Notice that the curvature of the average cost curve is determined by β_{YY}, which is the second derivative of the logarithmic average cost function with respect to $\ln Y$. The cost curve is U-shaped if β_{YY} is positive. Analogous to the profit function case discussed above, the translog specification admits a detailed decomposition of average cost growth attributed to changes in parameter values and input prices. In other words, we decompose the upward or downward shifting of the average cost curve into a number of contributing sources. Since the average cost curve depends on the output level, we choose its minimum as a benchmark by which the shifting of the curve is assessed.

10.5   Discussion of Results

We have estimated the three-input two-output profit function discussed in section 10.4 by using 1993–96 panel data for twenty-four of the thirty-one locally incorporated banks in Hong Kong.[3] New regulations on disclosure have made much more data available for this period. Foreign banks are excluded because they do not have to comply with the same disclosure requirements as local banks. Parameters of the profit function are estimated both for the before- and after-deregulation periods. They are reported in appendix table 10A.1. The demand-supply elasticity matrices for the two periods are presented in tables 10A.2 and 10A.3. We shall refer to the set of parameters for 1993–94 as S1 and that for 1995–96 as S2. The Chow test in table 10A.1 rejects the null hypothesis of no structural shift of the parameters.

The structural shift reveals that the banks' responses go far beyond altering input-output proportions. Humphrey and Pulley (1997) summarize three primary responses from banks that explain the deregulation-induced structural change in banks' production technology. The first response is cost offset and cost reduction. The second response is to transfer some of the higher funding cost and interest rate risk to borrowers (via floating-

---

3. Excluded are mainly investment banks with one or two offices. Their behavior is significantly different from that of the remaining banks, which engage extensively in retail banking.

rate loans) and to purchasers of securities (by securitizing fixed-rate loans). The third response is to expand asset risk in order to reap a higher expected return on loans to a more concentrated, but riskier, set of borrowers. Banks have also become more aggressive in developing and marketing their services (Carse 1995a). The differences between the two sets of parameters therefore reflect the changing strategies of optimizing banks. These banks have to adjust their strategies because the environment is changing.

The profit function formulation assumes perfect competition. Banks are price takers and input-output prices constitute the environment. Deregulation changes the interest rate, which is one of the prices, and therefore affects the environment. We shall refer to the set of prices in the first period as E1 and that in the second as E2.

By having two sets of strategy parameters and two sets of environment variables, we have four different scenarios. We can calculate the profit of an average bank under different scenarios by substituting the four combinations of values into the profit function. We use sample means of the price data for the purpose. Table 10.4 presents the results in a 2 × 2 matrix. It is readily seen that there is substantial growth in profits (6.0903 − 5.8088, the logarithmic difference) by going down the diagonal, or from S1-E1 to S2-E2. This indicates that given the new environment and the new strategies, banks actually made more profits after the deregulation, a phenomenon consistent with what we observed earlier in table 10.1.

The more interesting results are, however, the counterfactual cases of S2-E1 and S1-E2, which isolate the marginal effects of deregulation and banks' responses. Given the new environment E2, if the average bank does not adjust its strategies to S2, then (log) profits will decrease by 5.8088 − 5.5115 = 0.2973. In other words, the marginal impact of deregulation is to reduce an average bank's profits by about 30 percent. Comparing the two strategies S1 and S2 under the new environment E2, we see that the new strategy is able to raise profits by 6.0903 − 5.5115 = 0.5788, which more than offsets the erosion in profits due to deregulation. Similarly, one can obtain a second decomposition of observed profit growth by going through the route from S1-E1 to S2-E1 and then to S2-E2. It should be noted that profits in S2-E1 are larger than in S1-E1. There is the question of why the bank chooses S1 rather than S2 when the environment is E1. Such a seemingly suboptimal choice signals that there must be some hid-

Table 10.4   **Average Bank's Profit in Different Scenarios (logarithmic values)**

	E1	E2
S1	5.8088	5.5115
S2	6.4217	6.0903

den cost to adopting S2. In view of the operating characteristics of financial intermediaries, this is likely to be the cost of risk.

To understand better the relative impact of E2 and S2 on banks' profits, we construct another table. In table 10.5, we decompose the growth in profits of an average firm into its sources. The higher interest cost caused a significant decline in profits due to deposits (-0.3282), but this was completely offset by the banks' new strategies on deposits (1.1963). Much of the growth in profits related to the environment was due to income from providing services (0.1428). It is also readily seen from the table that banks also modified their strategies to take advantage of the services component of profits. The increase in profits due to services in the strategies column was 0.7775. Apparently, banks increased their labor and capital costs and mobilized resources away from loans to expand in the market of providing bank services. These include income from commissions and fees derived from foreign exchange trading, credit cards, trading investments, and other types of services. The new strategy seems to be successful and reasonable. When businesses related to the interest rate are negatively affected, competitive banks look for profit opportunities in other areas. The rapid introduction of new banking services in Hong Kong during the past few years is a testimony to the responsive and flexible nature of local banks.

An implicit assumption in deriving table 10.5 is that all the factors of production are variable. It may be argued that since the duration of the period under study is too short, we should not assume that banks are in their long-run equilibrium. An alternative is to treat capital stock as a fixed input factor of production. We can then estimate a short-run profit function in a similar way. This has been implemented, and we find that the results discussed above are robust. To conserve space, we do not provide the details.

Results from estimating the cost function provide us with additional

Table 10.5   Sources of Profit Growth

Source	Strategies	Environment	Total
Labor	0.0487	−0.0934	−0.0448
Capital	−0.0764	0.0194	−0.0570
Deposits	1.1963	−0.3282	0.8681
Loans	−1.2133	−0.0550	−1.2683
Services	0.7775	0.1428	0.9203
Residual	−0.1369	0.0000	−0.1369
Total	0.5959	−0.3144	0.2815

Note: The values are logarithmic differences of profits. If multiplied by 100, each entry can be approximated as the part of the profit growth rate that is due to changes in the corresponding factors.

Table 10.6   **Sources of Average Cost Growth**

Source	Strategies	Environment	Total
Labor	0.0385	0.0157	0.0542
Capital	0.0559	−0.0063	0.0496
Deposits	−0.1303	0.2474	0.1171
Residual	0.0117	0	0.0117
Total	−0.0242	0.2568	0.2326

Note: The values are logarithmic differences of average costs. If multiplied by 100, each entry can be approximated as the part of the growth rate of average cost that is due to changes in the corresponding factors.

information for understanding how banks responded to interest rate deregulation. The data sources for the estimation are the same as those for the profit function. Again we divide the period in two: 1993–94 and 1995–96. Estimates of the parameters are reported in appendix table 10A.4. The Chow test that we perform also rejects the null hypothesis that there is no structural shift in the parameters.

Table 10.6 shows the decomposition of the sources of growth of the industry's minimum average cost. Changes in the environment caused (minimum) average cost to go up by 23.26 percent. The new strategies only reduced cost by 2.42 percent. It appears the banks did not focus too much on cost reduction. Rather, as discussed above, they became more aggressive in expanding their businesses. The single most important factor that raised cost was the interest cost for bank deposits (24.74 percent). Banks were only able to mitigate part of the increase through their new strategies on deposits (−13.03 percent). It is interesting to note that the prices of labor and capital in the environment remained stable, but banks chose to raise these costs further. This phenomenon is consistent with the picture discussed earlier. Banks strategically expanded into the business of banking services, which is input intensive in both labor and capital. The residual term reported in table 10.6 is 1.17 percent. This means that in addition to the changes in the prices of labor, capital, and deposits, there was an unexplained exogenous increase in cost due to other changes in the environment.

Some interesting results on how banks responded to the deregulation can be seen in figure 10.1, which depicts the industry's average cost curves under the four different scenarios mentioned earlier. The cost function of S1-E1 is above that of S2-E1. The banks could have lowered cost by choosing the new strategies even if the deregulation had not occurred. This result also appears in the profit function discussed earlier. It signals that the new strategies associated with expanding bank services raise the risks of the banks.

Another observation from figure 10.1 is that the new strategies appear

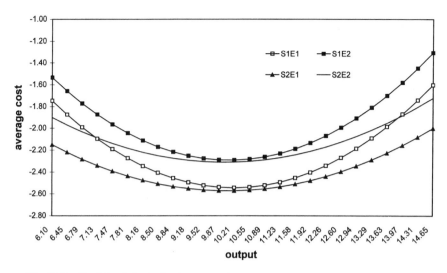

Fig. 10.1   Banking industry's average cost curves

to have flattened the cost curves. This observation is also supported by the statistical test. If the curvature flattens, then the estimate for one of the parameters, β_{YY}, will go down after the deregulation. The result in table 10A.4 supports this hypothesis. The parameter decreases from 0.0949 to 0.0541, and the difference is statistically significant. The flattening of the cost curves can be explained by the fact that competition increased. Banks have recently also engaged in more networking activities among themselves so as to take advantage of any possible economies of scale. The flattening of the cost functions may indicate that banks are moving closer to constant returns to scale.

The main message we get from the empirical results is that banks in Hong Kong seem to be very responsive to changes in the environment and, in this case, the deregulation itself. Their efforts to cut costs did not seem to be successful and they chose the more aggressive strategy of expanding business. We therefore expect their risks to have gone up. To formally test for it, we turn to the next section.

10.6   Changes in Risks

In section 10.5 we only discussed the effects of the deregulation on the costs and profits of the banks. Without knowing what happens to the banks' risks, we cannot conclude that they are better off even when their profits have increased. In what follows, we shall make use of a standard CAPM to find out whether the market believes that the risks of the banks went up after the deregulation (cf. Brooks, Faff, and Ho 1997).

Our estimate of the changes in bank risks is based on the following return-generating process of the CAPM (e.g., see Sharpe and Alexander 1990; Ross 1994):

$$(16) \qquad R_i - R^* = \alpha_i + \beta_i(R_M - R^*) + \varepsilon_i,$$

where R_i is the rate of return of bank i, R^* is the rate of return of a risk-free asset, R_M is the rate of return of a general market portfolio, and ε_i is the random error term associated with bank i. The coefficients α and β can be estimated. If the value of α, also known as Jensen's α, is nonzero, the security of bank i is mispriced. To see whether the market is efficient, we can perform a test for the value of α. The value of β tells us how the market evaluates the risks of the bank. The higher the value of β, the higher the risks associated with the bank.

If a bank chose a riskier position after the deregulation, then its β should have gone up. We collect monthly share price data for all banks listed on the Hong Kong stock market for the period from June 1992 to March 1997.[4] Monthly rates of return for every bank can be derived from these prices. The market portfolio rate of return, R_M, is derived from monthly changes in the Hang Seng Index, which tracks Hong Kong's blue-chip stocks.[5] We use the Fed funds rate to derive the risk-free monthly rate of return, R^*. To implement a test for the change in β, we can add to equation (16) a dummy variable (D) with value equal to one from January 1995 to March 1997 and zero before this period:

$$(17) \qquad R_i - R^* = \alpha_i + (\beta_i + \gamma_i D)(R_M - R^*) + \varepsilon_i,$$

The bigger the increase in risks, the bigger the value of γ.

Table 10.7 summarizes the estimations based on equation (17). There are altogether twelve banks listed on the Hong Kong Stock Exchange. We have eliminated one of these, the Hong Kong Bank, because it has very significant overseas profits that are not affected by the interest rate deregulation. The list in table 10.7 is ranked according to the market shares of the remaining eleven banks. Several results emerge from the table.

First, the t-values of Jensen's α for all eleven banks are insignificant. We cannot reject the hypothesis that they are equal to zero. The securities for all the banks appear to have been efficiently priced both before and after the deregulation. This suggests that the economic profits of the eleven banks are all zero, implying that the increase in bank costs due to the deregulation was offset by the banks' efforts to raise revenue. Second, the t-values of β for all the banks are highly significant, which is a reasonable

---

4. The electronic financial database Extel provides the necessary data (Financial Times 1997).

5. We have properly taken care of dividends and other distributions in computing the rates of return for the banks and the Hang Seng Index.

Table 10.7   **Estimates of Changes in Risks**

Bank	α	β	γ	R^2
Hang Seng	0.4198	0.7592	0.3649	0.634
	0.6	*7.46*	*1.78**$**	
East Asia	0.3427	0.6874	0.4143	0.582
	0.47	*6.46*	*1.93**$**	
Dah Sing	0.997	0.5898	1.077	0.373
	0.75	*3.02*	*2.74***$**	
Dao Heng	0.1801	1.046	0.2263	0.633
	0.18	*4.53*	*0.72*	
HKCB	−0.9063	0.7441	0.1665	0.494
	−0.96	*5.4*	*0.64*	
Wing Lung	0.3344	0.7596	0.2223	0.564
	0.44	*6.78*	*0.98*	
Wing Hang	0.254	0.7184	0.4664	0.452
	0.2	*4.07*	*1.41*$*	
IBA	−0.589	0.8475	0.592	0.52
	−0.43	*3.99*	*1.63*$*	
Union	0.988	0.853	0.8637	0.488
	0.81	*4.76*	*2.39***$**	
First Pacific	0.729	1.0309	0.2022	0.56
	0.56	*5.63*	*0.59*	
Ka Wah	0.076	0.5434	0.7273	0.329
	0.06	*3.12*	*2.07***$**	

Note: Numbers in italics are *t*-values.
*One-tail significance at the 10 percent level.
**One-tail significance at the 5 percent level.
***One-tail significance at the 2.5 percent level.

result. Third, the *t*-values for five of the γs are significant at the 5 percent or 2.5 percent levels, while two of them are significant at the 10 percent level. Although four of the banks do not have a significant γ, it should be noted that the γs for all eleven banks are uniformly positive in sign. These results do suggest that the market believes that the risks of all the banks increased. Risk changes for some of the banks may not be as strong as for others because their strategies may have been different.

The empirical tests from this section support the hypothesis that banks in Hong Kong were more willing to accept risks after the deregulation. Alternatively, at least the market believes that the more competitive environment will create or has created more risks for the banks. This should be regarded as a trade-off for the increase in profits of the banks.

10.7   Concluding Remarks

In this paper, we have examined the changes in profits and costs of Hong Kong's banking industry after the interest rate deregulation from late 1994 to early 1995. It is found that the banks in our sample were all efficiently priced and did not make excess profits before or after the deregulation. Our decomposition analysis shows that banks were responsive to changes in the environment. They made significant adjustments in their business strategies. Within the constraints of the banking production technology, banks were relatively unsuccessful in mitigating the erosion in profits by cost reduction. They instead chose to increase profits by expanding their businesses into relatively interest-independent bank services.

In terms of maintaining growth in profits, the strategy was successful. However, we have also found that the risks associated with most of the banks increased after the interest rate cap was removed. Apparently, changes in interest costs induced them to go deeper into a business that they had been less keen about earlier. Probably because of the general financial health of the economy in the sample period, the increase in risks has not brought about any major crisis yet. The absence of an insurance system for bank deposits and the new regulations on disclosure should also have restrained the banks from taking extremely risky positions.

The process of the deregulation was carried out cautiously in several phases. This gave the banks more time to absorb the shocks and cope with the changes. This could be one of the reasons why the transition was relatively smooth even though the Mexican crisis and the Barings incident occurred in the beginning phases of the deregulation. However, from the analysis in this paper, there seems to have been another reason that was more fundamental. Having operated in a free market environment for a long time, the banks were very nimble in finding new opportunities. This ability has been important in the past and most likely will continue to be important for the banks' survival in the future.

Appendix

Table 10A.1 **Profit Function**

Parameter	Before Deregulation: 1993–94		After Deregulation: 1995–96	
	ML Estimate	Standard Error	ML Estimate	Standard Error
β_0	10.6104	0.2564	10.4735	0.2050
β_1	−0.2199	0.1634	−0.3056	0.0999
β_2	−0.0982	0.0403	−0.0758	0.0252
β_3	−2.1803	0.2412	−2.8537	0.2185
β_4	0.5537	0.1979	1.6257	0.1689
β_{11}	−0.3792	0.0835	−0.2491	0.0584
β_{21}	−0.0378	0.0204	−0.0207	0.0133
β_{22}	−0.0575	0.0087	−0.0183	0.0058
β_{31}	0.0641	0.1141	0.3750	0.0939
β_{32}	−0.0783	0.0335	−0.0108	0.0276
β_{33}	−1.5320	0.2420	−0.6824	0.2913
β_{41}	0.3224	0.0963	0.0018	0.0644
β_{42}	0.1207	0.0286	0.0288	0.0188
β_{43}	1.0633	0.1824	0.3169	0.1900
β_{44}	−0.1739	0.2247	0.3477	0.1999
Log likelihood	332.5182		383.3432	
Sample size	48		46	

Note: Using the pooled sample of all 94 observations gives a log likelihood of 655.1992. The likelihood ratio statistic LR $= -2(655.1992 - 332.5182 - 383.3432) = 121.3244$ rejects the null hypothesis of no structural shift at any reasonable significance level for a χ^2 distribution with 15 degrees of freedom.

Table 10A.2 **Demand-Supply Elasticity Matrix, 1993–94**

−0.7676	−0.0847	−1.9981	2.2811	0.5695
(0.1636)	(0.0400)	(0.2233)	(0.1888)	(0.1215)
−0.2723	−0.7964	−1.3794	2.1528	0.2954
(0.1288)	(0.0551)	(0.2114)	(0.1806)	(0.1095)
−0.5447	−0.1170	−2.0542	2.3449	0.3711
(0.0608)	(0.0179)	(0.1292)	(0.0974)	(0.0665)
−0.3997	−0.1174	−1.5073	1.8531	0.1715
(0.0330)	(0.0098)	(0.0626)	(0.0771)	(0.0335)
−0.4621	−0.0746	−1.1048	0.7944	0.8472
(0.0986)	(0.0276)	(0.1981)	(0.1552)	(0.1537)

Note: Entry $(i, j) = \partial \ln x_i / \partial \ln p_j$, where $x_1 =$ labor, $x_2 =$ capital, $x_3 =$ deposits, $x_4 =$ loans, and $x_5 =$ services. Numbers in parentheses are standard errors.

Table 10A.3   Demand-Supply Elasticity Matrix, 1995–96

−0.7287	−0.0680	−3.2177	3.2092	0.8050
(0.1531)	(0.0350)	(0.2460)	(0.1689)	(0.1192)
−0.2118	−0.9723	−2.1462	2.9789	0.3514
(0.1091)	(0.0475)	(0.2255)	(0.1538)	(0.1113)
−0.5494	−0.1176	−2.9296	3.0722	0.5242
(0.0420)	(0.0123)	(0.1303)	(0.0850)	(0.0630)
−0.3810	−0.1135	−2.1363	2.3222	0.3085
(0.0200)	(0.0058)	(0.0591)	(0.0622)	(0.0251)
−0.5853	−0.0820	−2.2323	1.8895	1.0101
(0.0866)	(0.0259)	(0.2685)	(0.1537)	(0.1565)

Note: Entry $(i, j) = \partial \ln x_i / \partial \ln p_j$, where x_1 = labor, x_2 = capital, x_3 = deposits, x_4 = loans, and x_5 = services. Numbers in parentheses are standard errors.

Table 10A.4   Cost Function

Parameter	Before Deregulation: 1993–94		After Deregulation: 1995–96	
	ML Estimate	Standard Error	ML Estimate	Standard Error
β_0	4.9673	0.7824	3.0198	1.0417
β_1	0.4058	0.0568	0.2258	0.0419
β_2	0.0844	0.0237	0.0174	0.0170
β_Y	0.0761	0.1574	0.4757	0.2029
β_{11}	0.0715	0.0218	0.0689	0.0169
β_{21}	−0.0198	0.0063	−0.0031	0.0046
β_{22}	0.0136	0.0034	0.0055	0.0023
β_{Y1}	−0.0325	0.0055	−0.0169	0.0042
β_{Y2}	−0.0008	0.0024	0.0029	0.0017
β_{YY}	0.0949	0.0160	0.0541	0.0197
Log likelihood	429.1103		456.8197	
Sample size	48		46	

Note: Using the pooled sample of all 94 observations gives a log likelihood of 856.2420. The likelihood ratio statistic LR $= -2(856.2420 - 429.1103 - 456.8197) = 59.3760$ rejects the null hypothesis of no structural shift at any reasonable significance level for a χ^2 distribution with 10 degrees of freedom.

References

Berger, A., D. Humphrey, and L. Pulley. 1996. Do consumers pay for one-stop banking? Evidence from an alternative revenue function. *Journal of Banking and Finance* 20:1601–21.

Brooks, R., R. Faff, and Y. Ho. 1997. A new test of the relationship between regulatory change in financial markets and the stability of beta risk of depository institutions. *Journal of Banking and Finance* 21:197–219.

Carse, David. 1995a. Banking trends in Hong Kong. *Quarterly Bulletin of the Hong Kong Monetary Authority,* November: 38–42.

———. 1995b. Fair trade in financial services: A regulator's perspective. *Quarterly Bulletin of the Hong Kong Monetary Authority,* August: 54–58.

Consumer Council. 1994. *Are Hong Kong depositors fairly treated?* Hong Kong: Consumer Council Steering Group on Financial Services, 28 February.

Diewert, W. 1982. Duality approaches to microeconomic theory. In *Handbook of mathematical economics,* vol. 2, ed. K. Arrow and M. Intriligator. Amsterdam: North-Holland.

Financial Times. 1997. *Extel financial databases.* London: Financial Times, May.

Ghose, T. K. 1995. *The banking system of Hong Kong,* 2d ed. Hong Kong: Buttersworth.

Hancock, D. 1991. *A theory of production for the financial firm.* Boston: Kluwer.

HKMA (Hong Kong Monetary Authority). 1995. Developments in the banking sector. *Quarterly Bulletin of the Hong Kong Monetary Authority,* May: 80–83.

Hong Kong Bank. Various issues. *The banking industry of Hong Kong.* Hong Kong: Hong Kong Bank, Economic Research Department.

Humphrey, David B., and Lawrence B. Pulley. 1997. Banks' responses to deregulation: Profits, technology, and efficiency. *Journal of Money, Credit, and Banking* 29 (1): 73–93.

Jao, Y. C. 1992. *Essays on finance and economics* (in Chinese). Hong Kong: Cosmos.

Jorgenson, D. 1986. Econometric methods for modeling producer behavior. In *Handbook of econometrics,* vol. 3, ed. Z. Griliches and M. Intriligator. Amsterdam: North-Holland.

Ko, S. H. 1991. *Banking regulations of Hong Kong.* Hong Kong: Chartered Institute of Bankers.

Lau, L. 1978. Applications of profit functions. In *Production economics: A dual approach to theory and applications,* ed. M. Fuss and D. McFadden. Amsterdam: North-Holland.

Ross, Steven A. 1994. Finance. In *The new Palgrave dictionary of money and finance,* ed. Peter Newman, Murray Milgate, and John Eatwell. London: Macmillan.

Sharpe, William F., and Gordon J. Alexander. 1990. *Investments,* 4th ed. Englewood Cliffs, NJ: Prentice-Hall.

Comment   Moon-Soo Kang

The Hong Kong Association of Banks cautiously implemented the process of interest rate deregulation in several steps in the 1990s. Kwan and Lui argue that the transition was relatively smooth in Hong Kong. However, their sample period (1995–96) may be too short for them to claim that Hong Kong banks responded optimally to the interest rate deregulation in 1993–94.

Foreign banks are excluded from this study. It would be interesting to investigate how foreign banks responded when local banks raised lending and deposit rates in Hong Kong. The paper does not tell us what happened to local banks' market shares after they raised lending rates.

Moon-Soo Kang is senior fellow at the Korea Development Institute.

The paper argues that local banks expanded into riskier businesses. However, it does not show how much nonperforming loans of local banks increased after local banks adopted new business strategies. When the Hong Kong economy suffers from economic downturns in coming years, local banks may see a considerable increase in nonperforming loans, as Korea has in recent years.

The paper does not tell why local banks in Hong Kong have not been successful in cutting operating costs. Korean commercial banks saw operating profits shrink in recent years when the Korean economy went sour because they could not reduce labor and other operating costs.

11

Telecommunications Liberalization
A Taiwanese Perspective

Shin-Horng Chen

11.1 Introduction

Gone are the days when the telecommunications sectors in most countries were governed as state monopolies. This trend toward telecommunications liberalization has become increasingly apparent since the 1980s and now is taking place in Taiwan. While global deregulation and Taiwan's accession to the World Trade Organization (WTO) carried weight in political minds, there are a few internal self-driving forces at work strengthening the will to liberalize the industry. Critical developmental policies relating to the Asia-Pacific Regional Operations Center and the National Information Infrastructure are characterized by the promotion of institutional reform and soft infrastructure as new competitive parameters. Added to this, changes in industrial parameters, such as scale economies and scope economies, call for the transformation from a state monopoly in a competitive telecommunications market. At the heart of Taiwan's deregulatory process are the organizational separation of the public telecommunications operator from the regulator and the introduction of private competition. Also the reform framework is characterized by a two-tiered regulatory regime for different segments of telecommunications services. Substantial progress has been made, but much remains to be done.

Against this background, this paper examines the policy framework and the implementation of Taiwan's telecommunications liberalization. Its aim is to distill lessons that may add to the current understanding of telecommunications liberalization that has been derived mainly from the developed world, rather than to comprehensively evaluate the whole program.

Shin-Horng Chen is deputy director of the second division of the Chung-Hua Institution for Economic Research, Taiwan.

The remainder of the paper is structured as follows: Section 11.2 reviews the historical background of Taiwan's telecommunications industry prior to liberalization. It is followed in section 11.3 by a discussion of current progress in telecommunications liberalization in Taiwan. In particular, the policy framework is outlined. Section 11.4 puts forward a few criticisms of the liberalization program. Section 11.5 highlights problems arising from market entry. The wrangling over industrial policy versus competition policy in the deregulatory process in Taiwan is taken up in section 11.6. Section 11.7 discusses the emerging issues that warrant the attention of the regulatory authority. Finally, section 11.8 draws conclusions.

11.2 Historical Background

Until recently, virtually all telecommunications services in Taiwan were provided by its public telecommunications operator, the Directorate General of Telecommunications (DGT), under the auspices of the Ministry of Transportation and Communications (MOTC). Based on the Telecommunications Act of 1958, the DGT assumed both regulatory and operational responsibilities. A wide span of business activities, ranging across voice telephonic services, data communications, satellite communications, and training and research, were all operated by the DGT. While the Telecommunications Act of 1977 technically allowed domestic private and public organizations to enter the local telephone service market, this did not really happen, due to the dominance of the DGT. At the same time, a few state enterprises were granted permission by the MOTC to install dedicated telecommunications networks limited strictly to internal communications and monitoring. Also, six international news agencies—Reuters, for example—were allowed to lease direct link circuits from the DGT to communicate with their global news networks. As a result, their subsidiaries in Taiwan acted more or less like value-added network service providers. Nonetheless, these were exceptions. The DGT was mandated to provide comprehensive telecommunications services in Taiwan.

As the administrator and public operator of telecommunications in Taiwan, the DGT was governed as an official body with limited independent authority. Its human resource management and procurement were subject to tight control and scrutiny. Its employees were qualified as civil servants and tended to be vulnerable to the criticism that they demonstrated insufficient customer orientation. Like many public utilities in Taiwan, the DGT was required to meet a return rate of investment, with a profit cap of 11.5 percent. There is a danger that monopolistic utilities such as the DGT, may, under the veil of investment return rates, unduly favor the use of capital relative to other inputs, so that output might be produced at an inefficiently high cost, a scenario known as the Averch-Johnson effect. On top of this, it cannot be taken for granted that the DGT will share its excess profits with customers by reducing tariffs, due to the absence of competition and to delay in the process of changing tariff schemes. Furthermore, like other public telecommunications operators throughout the world, the DGT employed cross-subsidization to provide certain of its telecommunications services at "affordable" prices, as part of its universal service obligations. In this regard, tariffs were priced below cost for local calls but significantly above cost for trunk and international calls and for mobile communications. Though quite common worldwide, there has been concern that this divergence from cost, as a result of cross-subsidization, might distort price signals to the users of telecommunications networks.

Due credit should be given to the DGT for establishing and modernizing the telecommunications infrastructure in Taiwan. Table 11.1 presents a set of performance indicators for the DGT over the period 1991–95. For example, the penetration rate of telephone mainlines in Taiwan was 41.3 per 100 inhabitants in 1995, as against 0.29 in 1950 and 32.1 in 1991, which was close to the OECD average in 1990 (42.58; OECD 1993, 10). Headway has also been made by the DGT in expanding mobile communications services. As a result, 1995 witnessed a penetration rate of 90.8 per 1,000 inhabitants for radio pagers and 27.9 for cellular phones. To date, the completion rates of digitization of local telephone switching, toll trunk exchanges, and toll trunk circuits are all above 90 percent, with toll trunk exchanges having been completely digitized in 1994.

However, it has become increasingly difficult for the DGT to meet mounting demand for communications services. Recently, remarkable growth in mobile communications in Taiwan has resulted in a situation where demand outstrips supply. As a consequence, hundreds of thousands of inhabitants have been on the waiting list to subscribe to cellular phone and radio paging services, due to underestimation of consumer demand on the part of the DGT and to delay in the procurement process. Such a huge unmet demand for cellular phone and radio paging services and hence the long waiting period for connection to the services reflected the deteriorating quality of service provided by the DGT. Ironically, the regulatory authority will not start to monitor and collect data on quality of service until 1998. Having said that, it is estimated that the waiting period for mobile phone and radio paging services is not less than one year, given the long waiting list discussed above. Partly for this reason, mobile communications is the first target for market liberalization, which will be discussed later.

The DGT, though never involved in the manufacturing of telecommunications equipment, had a stake in three local producers of public switching systems (Taiwan Alcatel International Standard Electronics, Siemens Telecommunications System, and AT&T Taiwan Telecommunications). These three firms are international joint ventures led by Alcatel, Siemens, and AT&T, respectively. Of note is the fact that they each enjoyed a de

Table 11.1   Business Performance of Directorate General of Telecommunications, 1991–95

Item	1995	1994	1993	1992	1991
Local telephone exchanges	11,726,572	11,306,386	10,995,646	10,417,616	9,371,406
Local telephone switching digitization (%)	91.5	83.8	70.7	58.7	41.9
Local telephone subscribers	8,773,685	8,209,557	7,662,499	7,137,265	6,583,435
Telephone density (per 100 inhabitants)	41.3	38.9	36.7	34.5	32.1
Resident subscriber density (per 100 households)	110.5	106.3	101.99	97.7	92.8
Public telephones	121,979	119,077	114,151	109,259	106,370
Public telephone density (per 1,000 inhabitants)	5.7	5.6	5.5	5.3	5.2
Radio pager subscribers	1,929,451	1,548,429	1,259,281	1,078,478	885,182
Radio pager density (per 1,000 inhabitants)	90.8	73.5	60.3	52.1	43.2
Cellular phone subscribers	593,869	561,987	472,838	299,690	137,815
Cellular phone density (per 1,000 inhabitants)	27.9	26.7	22.6	14.5	6.7
Toll truck exchanges	833,000	740,000	647,500	563,520	524,380
Toll truck exchange digitization (%)	100	100	99.15	96.8	89.4
Toll truck circuits	668,823	626,303	584,950	480,202	330,006
Toll truck circuit digitization (%)	99.1	98.9	98.8	96.9	94.1
Domestic data communications dedicated line rentals	51,274	44,232	38,401	34,449	27,776
Dial-up data communications subscribers	27,548	21,976	19,698	17,549	15,930
Packet switched data communications subscribers	5,259	4,577	3,935	3,492	2,777
Videotex subscribers	20,122	15,955	13,550	12,334	11,460
Universal database access system	334	360	327	314	252
International telephone direct link circuits	11,173	8,768	6,914	5,684	4,465
International satellite communications circuits	2,241	2,565	2,806	2,257	1,711
International submarine cable communications circuits	16,696	12,951	9,636	7,975	4,953

Source: Directorate General of Telecommunications 1996, http://www.dgt.gov.tw/.

facto spatial monopoly over the provision of public switching systems for the three broad (northern, central, and southern) regions of Taiwan, which is known as the "three systems, three suppliers" policy. This resulted from a government policy introducing digitized switching technology via foreign investment in 1985. It was hoped that the DGT's investment in the three companies might facilitate technology transfer from their overseas parents. However, the extent to which core competencies of digitized switching technology were localized within Taiwan is still open to question. In addition, the three companies were often accused of overcharging for the systems they provided.

11.3   Progress in Telecommunications Liberalization

Since the 1980s, an increasingly significant development on the global telecommunications landscape has been the move from monopolization to liberalization. This trend was pioneered by the United States, the United Kingdom, and Japan in the early 1980s and then followed by many other countries. Taiwan has also followed suit. This move, however, is not just jumping on the bandwagon but reflects a belief that telecommunications liberalization should be an integral part of Taiwan's midterm development policy. In fact, several attempts were made in the late 1970s and early 1980s to provide the statutory basis for the corporatization of the DGT and liberalization of the industry. Relevant draft bills tabled at that time, however, were not enacted, due in part to the resistance of the telecommunications trade union (Cheng et al. 1989, 38–39). These initial efforts did bear fruit, in the liberalization of the customer premises equipment (CPE) market and the regulatory relaxation of access to telecommunications networks that have taken place since 1987. Further momentum was gained as the DGT started to liberalize some segments of value-added network (VAN) services from 1989 onward.

Meanwhile, the issue of the transformation of the industrial structure surfaced when three telecommunications reform bills were drafted. This was due to external pressures and internal self-driving forces. On the one hand, the global trend of deregulation and Taiwan's accession to the WTO carried weight with politicians. On the other hand, critical development policies relating to the Asia-Pacific Regional Operations Center (APROC) and the National Information Infrastructure (NII) were the internal forces at work strengthening resolve. Both programs are at the forefront of public policy in Taiwan's midterm economic development. The APROC plan has two major aspects. First, it aims to promote Taiwan as a center of the Asia-Pacific region by developing regional manufacturing, sea transportation, air transportation, financial, telecommunications, and media centers. Second, it serves to engineer a highly liberalized and internationalized economy. The APROC program proposes to develop Taiwan into a telecommunications center, among others, which will be able to provide reasonably priced, high-quality telecommunications services regionwide. In addition, the NII program aims to construct an information superhighway, preferably led by the private sector through unleashed competition. It embodies the goals of upgrading telecommunications infrastructure, stimulating innovation, introducing novel applications, and setting up an appropriate regulatory framework. To achieve the aims of these two programs, it is necessary for Taiwan to deregulate its telecommunications market. With the passage of the three telecommunications reform bills in January 1996, both the resolve and the means to open up Taiwan's telecommunications sector have emerged. Accordingly, a large-scale telecommunications liberalization program, albeit involving an evolutionary process, is under way in Taiwan.

In addition, evidence on the industrial parameters of the sector, gleaned from other sources, lends support for the introduction of telecommunications liberalization. The concepts of scale economies and scope economies have been used in rationalizing the monopolization of the telecommunications industry. A study supported by the Council for Economic Planning and Development (CEPD 1996) revealed that the cost function of the DGT indeed featured scale economies, but they have been declining over time due to the introduction of new technologies. Moreover, it established no evidence to support the argument that the DGT enjoyed scope economies.

Before 1995, telecommunications liberalization in Taiwan was limited in scale. Over the period 1987–94, the liberalization process focused on deregulating the CPE market, access to telecommunications networks, and VAN services (table 11.2). By the end of 1994, the DGT's monopoly on the supply of numerous items of CPE was rescinded. Subscribers were allowed to obtain their own CPE and in-house lines. As a result, the CPE market was opened to competition. Private competition was also introduced in eight kinds of VAN services. In addition, restrictions on the terms for access and lease of telecommunications networks and circuits were loosened. More recently, CT-2 (second-generation cordless telephone) service was opened to the private sector at the end of 1995. This move went beyond the liberalization of VAN services and served as a prelude to a more radical transformation of Taiwan's telecommunications industry, since, according to the Telecommunications Act of 1996, CT-2 is classified as part of so-called Type I services (common carriers).

Further momentum was gained after the three telecommunications reform acts were promulgated in January 1996 and became law the following month. They are the Telecommunications Act of 1996, the Organizational Statute of the DGT, and the Statute of Chunghwa Telecom Co. Ltd. (table 11.3). The Telecommunications Act of 1996 sets out the framework within which Taiwan's telecommunications industry is to be reformed. The act creates a dichotomy of telecommunications services. Type I services refer

Table 11.2   **Telecommunications Liberalization in Taiwan before 1995**

	Date
Customer premises equipment	
Telephone sets	August 1987
Modems (2,400 bps)	November 1987
Telex terminals	May 1988
Modems (9,600 bps)	June 1988
Modems (9,600 bps)	June 1989
Cellular telephones	July 1989
Radio pagers	February 1990
Access to networks	
Domestic leased circuits shared by value-added network (VAN) service operators and their customers allowed	June 1989
International leased circuits shared allowed	October 1989
In-house lines	July 1990
Connection of domestic leased circuits with local phone systems allowed	March 1994
Restrictions eased on leasing domestic and international leased lines by VAN service providers	December 1994
Telecommunications services	
Domestic VAN services (information storage and retrieval, information processing, remote transaction, word processing, voice mail, e-mail)	June 1989
International VAN services (as indicated above)	October 1989
VAN services (bulletin board system, electronic data interchange)	June 1992
Home/office-based second-generation cordless telephone (CT-2)	August 1994
Public CT-2	November 1994
VAN services (packet switched data services, store and forward facsimile services)	December 1994

Source: Directorate General of Telecommunications, *White paper on telecommunications* (in Chinese; Taipei, 1995), 329–30.

to the installation of telecommunications machinery and line facilities and to services provided through owned circuits and facilities. Those services other than Type I are referred to as Type II. While private firms will be allowed to enter virtually all segments of the telecommunications market, the extent of regulatory control differs between Type I and Type II carriers. Type II carriers need only approval from the DGT to start business, while special approval and a license issued by the MOTC are required for private firms to provide Type I services that are subject to phased liberalization. Under the two-tiered regulatory regime, the planned scenario is that Type II services will be characterized by open competition, but Type I services will involve regulated competition among a limited number of providers. The latter is deemed appropriate on the grounds that the DGT enjoyed scale economies, though they are declining over time (Jang 1993). In addition, this act legalizes the principle of equal access to telecommuni-

Table 11.3   **Outline of Three Telecommunications Reform Acts in Taiwan, 1996**

Telecommunications Act of 1996
1. Delineation of Type I and Type II telecommunications enterprises.
2. Regulations on the extent of liberalization and foreign participation in the two types of telecommunications enterprises.
3. Prohibition on cross-subsidies between the two types of telecommunications enterprises.
4. Establishment and collection of funds for the provision of universal services.
5. Equal access to telecommunications networks.
6. Establishment of a pricing system to allocate radio frequencies.
7. Enhancement of the telecommunications inspection system.

Organizational Statute of the Directorate General of Telecommunications (DGT)
1. Release of the DGT from operational responsibility.
2. Clarification of the roles of the DGT in
    drafting and implementing telecommunications policies,
    approving and reviewing telecommunications tariffs,
    drafting and examining telecommunications technical specifications, and
    inspecting and supervising telecommunications carriers and their activities.
3. Restructuring of the DGT and its subordinate institutions.
4. Establishment of regional telecommunications regulatory stations.
5. Establishment of a telecommunications conciliation committee to settle telecommunications disputes.

Statute of Chunghwa Telecom Co. Ltd. (CHT)
1. Establishment of CHT as a state-owned telecommunications operator.
2. Assignment to CHT of considerable operational discretionary authority, especially concerning organizational structure and regulations, in order to enhance operating efficiency.
3. Application of ex post auditing to CHT's procurements.
4. Preservation of favorable welfare conditions for CHT's employees transferred from the former DGT.

Source: Adapted from Chen (1997).

cations networks and prohibition of cross-subsidies between the two types of services, where applicable. Also provided is a legal basis to develop a pricing system to allocate radio frequencies, given the fact that they have become economic goods (Kelly 1992). On top of these, the act stipulates the extent of foreign participation in Taiwan's telecommunications market. There is no restriction on foreign ownership for Type II carriers, but a 20 percent limit on investment by foreigners is imposed for individual Type I operators (table 11.4). The regulatory framework adopted in Taiwan is similar to that in Japan a decade ago (Sato and Stevenson 1989). While a more liberalized framework has currently been adopted in Japan and such countries as Denmark, Finland, Sweden, and the United States, it is not uncommon in OECD countries for local, national, and international calls and mobile communications, which fall within Type I services in Taiwan, to be handled by firms that have limited competition, and even monopoly status (OECD 1997). Given the proposed liberalization schedule for the

Table 11.4   **Types of Telecommunications Carriers**

Industry Framework	Type I Carriers	Type II Carriers
Business activities	Installation of telecommunications machinery and line facilities and provision of telecommunications services through owned telecommunications circuits and facilities[a]	Telecommunications services apart from Type I
Government regulation		
Start-up of services	Special approval and issue of a license by the MOTC required	Approval by the DGT required
Tariff schedules	Approval of primary tariff schedules by the MOTC required Approval of secondary tariff schedules by the DGT required	Notification to the DGT required
Foreign capital principle	Proportion of total shares held by foreigners limited to 20 percent	Unregulated

Source: Adapted from Chen (1997).

[a]The main items of Type I currently include local calls, toll calls, international calls, mobile communications, satellite communications, broadband switching communications, and high-speed data communications.

next five years, which will be discussed later, it is likely that the two-tiered regulatory framework in Taiwan will remain intact in the near future. Having said that, MOTC, the competent ministry, is inclined to exempt satellite communications from foreign ownership limits.

The other two acts, also outlined in table 11.3, form the statutory basis for restructuring the DGT and establishing a state-owned corporatized telecommunications operator, namely, Chunghwa Telecom (CHT). The Organizational Statute of the DGT demands the DGT be released from its operational responsibility to act merely as a regulatory authority. Among other responsibilities, the DGT is required under this law to establish a telecommunications conciliation committee to settle telecommunications disputes. The Statute of CHT authorizes a spinoff from the DGT to be incorporated as a state-owned telecommunications carrier. It also outlines the corporation's main business activities and basic organizational structure. In particular, the statute gives CHT considerable discretionary authority over its internal management and regulations in order to enhance operational efficiency. It is designed to free CHT from many limitations normally imposed on state enterprises that may not be compatible with commercial best practices.

Following the passage of the three telecommunications reform acts, the restructuring of the DGT took place on 1 July 1996. The business arms of the DGT were spun off to form CHT and incorporated as a state enterprise. The rest of the DGT, staffed by 500 employees or so, has since acted merely as a regulatory authority.

In addition, from 1996 onward, several significant milestones in market liberalization have been planned or realized in the telecommunications sector in Taiwan. First, four mobile communications services, including radio paging, cellular phones, trunked radio, and mobile data communications, have been liberalized. In these segments, a total of fifty-three operating licenses were issued to private operators, in addition to CHT, at the beginning of 1997 (eight licenses each for radio paging and cellular phones, twenty for trunked radio, and seventeen for mobile data communications; Chen 1997). Other segments of Type I services are also scheduled to be liberalized in the next five years (fig. 11.1). The next target for market liberalization is satellite communications, which will take place by the end of 1999. Before July 2001, the rest of Type I services, including local calls, long-distance calls, international calls, broadband switching communications, and high-speed data communications, will be opened to the private sector. More important, CHT will be privatized at that time.

Taiwan is in the middle of liberalizing its telecommunications market. The time is perhaps not ripe for a comprehensive evaluation of the impact of the liberalization program as a whole, but there are signs that market liberalization has started to generate some positive results (Chen 1997). Prominent among them is the reduction of telecommunications tariffs. On the brink of the entry of private mobile communications operators, CHT gained approval from the regulator to rebalance its tariffs (table 11.5). Despite a substantial increase (70 percent) in local call tariffs to eliminate cross-subsidization, tariffs for mobile phones, radio paging, and international calls have fallen. Important reductions of 45 and 25 percent for nationwide and regionwide services, respectively, have occurred. Tariffs for international calls have also decreased, by 3 to 27 percent. However, it is believed that CHT's new tariffs still diverge from costs and hence that room remains for further tariff rebalancing. On top of that, the liberalization is beset by several problems, to which I now turn.

11.4   Criticisms of the Liberalization Program

Criticisms have been leveled against the government's telecommunications liberalization program. First, the breakdown of Type I and Type II services gave rise to controversy. As described above, Type I services refer to the installation of telecommunications machinery and line facilities and

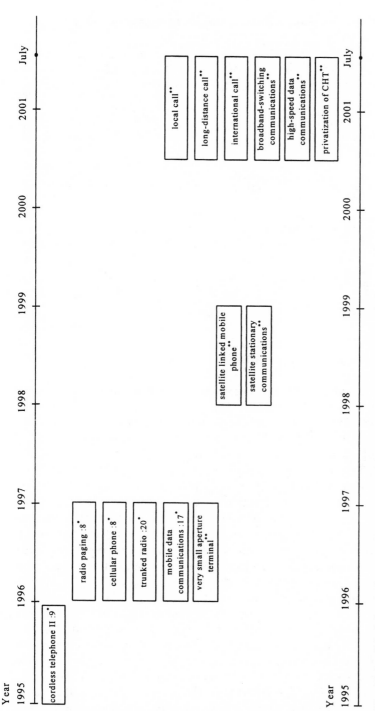

Fig. 11.1 Schedule of telecommunications liberalization in Taiwan, 1995 onward

Source: Adapted from Chen (1997).

*Number of private operators, in addition to Chunghwa Telecom (CHT).

**Scheduled to be liberalized.

Table 11.5   **Changes in Chunghwa Telecom's Tariffs, Effective 1 July 1997**

Category	Old Tariff	New Tariff	Difference (%)
Local calls	NT$1 per 5 minutes	NT$1.7 per 5 minutes (peak time)	+70
		NT$1 per 10 minutes (off-peak time)	−50
Public phone calls	NT$1 per 3 minutes	NT$1 per 2 minutes	+50
Mobile phone calls (nationwide)	NT$6.5 per minute (peak time)	NT$5.6 per minute	−14
	NT$3.3 per minute (off-peak time)	NT$3 per minute	−9
Mobile phone calls (within single region)	NT$5 per minute (peak time)	NT$4.5 per minute	−10
	NT$2.5 per minute (off-peak time)	NT$2 per minute	−20
Radio paging monthly rent (nationwide)	NT$550	NT$300	−45
Radio paging monthly rent (within single region)	NT$200	NT$150	−25
International calls			−3 to −27

Source: Compiled from Chunghwa Telecom press releases.

to services provided through owned circuits and facilities. Services other than Type I are referred to as Type II operations. In other words, the definition of Type II services is characterized by a negative list that allegedly allows for the introduction of new services in line with technological advancement without being unduly hampered by existing regulations. In practice, Type I services—though by law apparently facility based rather than service based—are itemized to include local calls, toll calls, international calls, mobile communications, satellite communications, broadband switching communications, and high-speed data communications. This gives rise to controversy over whether callback and Internet phone services should be legally permissible. Admittedly, these two services have a substantial impact on wireline voice communications, thus public telecommunications operators and even telecommunications authorities throughout the world tend to look on them with hostility. CHT also insists that callback and Internet phone services be banned. However, legally speaking, the prohibition is open to question. While they perform the function of voice communications, callback and Internet phone services by nature appear to be value-added services and hence are, from a legal perspective, closer to Type II than to Type I operations and thus should be opened to private competition. On top of that, CHT's wrangling over the private provision of callback and Internet phone services is at odds with the trend in the telecommunications industry, according to which new technologies often result in productive economic efficiency in the form of lower costs and superior services (Hausman 1996). To capitalize on new technologies available in the marketplace or looming on the horizon, regulations must be continuously upgraded to allow for the reality of complementary and competing services.

Also under attack is the DGT's proposal to regulate Type I carriers with rate-of-return regulation, as opposed to price-cap regulation. Rate-of-return regulation, with a profit cap of 11.5 percent, has been used in Taiwan to regulate public utilities, including telecommunications. By linking allowed revenues to realized or estimated production costs, rate-of-return regulation may weaken incentives on the part of the regulated firm to reduce operating costs and to develop and introduce new and innovative services (Sappington and Weisman 1996, 5). In contrast, in OECD countries rate-of-return regulation is being replaced by price-cap regulation (OECD 1995, 18). At the time of writing, the DGT is indeed in the process of formulating a price-cap regulation. It is generally agreed that price-cap regulation, by controlling the prices charged by regulated firms, provides enhanced incentive for cost reduction relative to rate-of-return regulation. Having said that, the move to price-cap regulation will make the scope of bargaining more explicit (over the productivity offsets, e.g.) between the two sides of the regulatory relationship (Braeutigam and Panzar 1993). Care, therefore, should be taken to enhance the regulatory function and oversight.

More controversial is the 20 percent foreign capital limit imposed on Type I enterprises. Elsewhere I have demonstrated that foreign participation, in terms of business opportunities, in Taiwan's telecommunications market is much wider than implied by the foreign equity cap (Chen 1997), but such tight control on foreign ownership is hard to justify. The main reason for imposing the foreign capital limit appears to rest mainly on the fear that experienced foreign telecommunications carriers may leverage incumbency advantages to dominate the local market; thus economic rents arising from liberalization would be captured mainly by foreign investors at the expense of domestic firms. Such an argument has little merit because economic rents can be preserved for the host economy in a more efficient way by policies other than foreign ownership restrictions (Globerman 1995). Above all, it is preferable to "tax away" economic rents, as far as possible, from private firms, regardless of nationality, by fine-tuning the regulatory regime rather than to take the existence of economic rents for granted. Added to this, the foreign capital limit is at odds with the vision of the APROC plan, which champions the principles of liberalization and internationalization in developing Taiwan into a telecommunications center in the Asia-Pacific region. Since Taiwan is a laggard in global telecommunications, foreign carriers can help Taiwan to fulfill the goals of the APROC plan, particularly the telecommunications center. Tighter control of foreign ownership, however, leaves less room for domestic carriers to forge strategic alliances with foreign firms because such alliances frequently involve equity participation. It is encouraging to learn, at the time of writing, that the authority is reconsidering its position on the foreign investment cap.

11.5   Problems Arising from Market Entry

The initial impact of telecommunications liberalization is open market access, but successful market entry depends on the incumbent's offering interconnection, due to the prevalence of interconnected networks in the industry. In this regard, the literature on telecommunications liberalization is replete with discussions of access pricing regulations (e.g., Doyle 1997). In Taiwan, the issue of interconnection rates has indeed been central to mobile communications liberalization, and opinions are divided between CHT and mobile communications carriers. At the time of writing, CHT and mobile communications operators are still struggling to reach agreement on interconnection rates. While CHT proposes to charge NT$1.86 per minute for interconnection, mobile communications operators are willing to pay only NT$1.01 per minute. This huge gap has something to do with the differences in the two sides' views on which cost items should be included and the accuracy of CHT's cost data.

This is, however, part of the interconnection issue. For mobile communications carriers, interconnection involves a physical link, via E1 leased lines, between their own networks and CHT's public switched telephone network. The demand for installation of the requisite E1 lines, however, outstrips supply due to CHT's poor planning and delay in the procurement process. New entrants in mobile communications may therefore be behind schedule in launching their operations. For this reason, CHT is vulnerable to the criticism that it tactically forecloses entry. Alternatively, mobile communications carriers may opt to bypass to some extent CHT's networks by means of microwave or very small aperture terminal (VSAT) links, which nonetheless remain handicapped by current regulations. The spectrum required for interconnection through microwave has not yet been made available by the DGT and is vulnerable to interference. Neither is the VSAT solution feasible currently because voice communications through VSAT have not yet been liberalized. These interconnection problems raise the fear that mobile communications liberalization may be undermined by incumbent manipulation and out-of-date regulations.

The prospects for new mobile communications carriers are also complicated by other issues such as numbering and portability of numbers. Numbering in the telecommunications industry refers to the arrangement for allocating telephone numbers among carriers to be used by their subscribers. Though seen primarily as a technical issue, it has had economic and regulatory implications (ICCP 1995). Where the incumbent has control over number allocation functions or enjoys proprietary rights over numbers, new entrants may face additional barriers to entry, and thus competition is restrained. The portability of numbers enables consumers to shift completely to other carriers without changing their numbers so that negligible switching costs will be incurred. Lessons distilled from OECD countries show that lack of number portability between carriers has acted as deterrent to competition because it restrains consumers from migrating to a new entrant even if it offers a lower tariff (ICCP 1995). Despite the significant implications for fair competition, these two issues have been low on the DGT's agenda and will not be dealt with technically for two years. New entrants to the mobile communications market will therefore be threatened by a high magnitude of such incumbency advantages at first.

The fortune of some, if not many, of the new mobile communications carriers is also at risk because of "service convergence" among different segments of mobile communications. By service convergence, we refer to the extent to which services provided by different types of communications resemble one another. Thanks to technological progress, cellular phones nowadays can provide short message services that were only available through radio paging before. Two-way communications services developed by CT-2 and radio paging operators duplicate part of cellular phone service. New trunked radios are also able to provide communications services like cellular phones. Looming on the horizon is "personal communications services" (PCS), which is basically a cellular phone including such features as electronic messaging and paging on the same handset. Such examples imply that the functional boundaries between various segments of mobile communications are becoming blurred; thus their markets have overlapped. Two points are particularly noteworthy here. First, to the extent that new services are technologically feasible, their introduction into the marketplace rests on the relaxation of relevant regulations. A manifestation of this point is that the unavailability of spectrum has slowed the introduction of two-way paging in Taiwan. In other words, outworn regulations can be a bottleneck that paralyzes new technologies and services. On the other hand, should those new services become marketable, various kinds of mobile communications would encroach on each other's markets; thus some operators may find their markets being taken away. As a matter of fact, CT-2 operators reportedly have had doubts from the very beginning, due to the functional limitation of CT-2 services and potential market encroachment made by cellular phone and digital enhanced cordless telephone carriers. A few of the nine CT-2 license winners have just started commercial operations but are having difficulty attracting subscribers. A private telecommunications firm, which was the major shareholder in two CT-2 operators, ran into trouble when CT-2 services were available for less than a year. Some may be inclined to position CT-2 services as a "transitional" product. If this is the case, "regulation regimes designed to permit and/or promote entry may well end up achieving little more than a noisy market periphery around a fundamentally uncompetitive core" (Cave 1996, 105). A danger, therefore, is that market entry may fail to deliver economic efficiency in terms of making the best use of resources. Furthermore, Amendola and Ferraiuolo (1995) note that cellular telephony is characterized by technological incrementalism and considerable economies of scope in building and operating different mobile services in the same area. Taking into account these features, they then call for a comprehensive regulatory framework, encompassing the entire field of mobile telephony, rather than regulating each new mobile service as if it were a new separate market. In light of the service convergence discussed above and the fact that the time span of Taiwan's mobile communications licenses is either ten or fifteen years, which is long enough for advanced mobile services, such as PCS, to take root in Taiwan, I echo Amendola and Ferraiuolo's proposal.

11.6   Industrial Policy versus Competition Policy

Telecommunications policy in Taiwan has retained a flavor of industrial policy. A typical case in point is the practice of only procuring systems from local subsidiaries of AT&T, Alcatel, and Siemens in exchange for technology transfer—known as the "three systems, three suppliers" policy. This policy has been criticized for restraining competition in the telecommunications system market without generating much success in technological localization. In addition, most domestic communications firms have been kept from entering the core of the telecommunications equipment industry. Owing partly to this, the lion's share of the business opportunities arising from the liberalization of mobile communications have been out of the reach of local communications firms (Chen 1997).

The implementation of telecommunications liberalization has brought the "three systems, three suppliers" policy under scrutiny. On the one hand, the proliferation of private operators resulting from opening the mobile communications market has made it impossible to sustain the policy. To the extent that private operators are able to compete efficiently in the marketplace, they have to adopt best-practice technology wherever available, rather than merely limit themselves to indigenous supply, if any. On the other hand, binding CHT to the "three systems, three suppliers" policy may sacrifice its competitiveness and the technological performance of the backbone networks in Taiwan. At the time of writing, the "three systems, three suppliers" policy has been exposed to critical review by the Taiwan Fair Trade Commission. The policy might be abandoned. This, however, will not eliminate the possibility that industrial policy considerations will continue to outweigh competition policy in Taiwan's deregulation process. Another case in point is a paging operator's call for government action to fight for medium-speed paging technology, which is currently the dominant standard in Taiwan but is in the process of being replaced by high-speed paging technology. Admittedly, telecommunications liberalization will create enormous business opportunities for service providers and equipment producers. It is difficult to accept the scenario that the lion's share of those business opportunities will be captured by foreign firms. One must bear in mind, however, that service and technological innovations in telecommunications are characterized by continuous flux. Protecting domestic firms by blocking new innovations or technologies runs the risk of decreasing telecommunications competitiveness. Needless to say, the liberalization policy itself could dilute the influence of government mandates because both private and public operators have to fight for their fortunes in a more market-oriented way.

11.7 Emerging Issues

A couple of emerging issues also warrant the attention of the regulatory authority. The first concerns whether or not CHT needs to be divested, by structurally separating the operations of the incumbent. The cost of this separation is to forgo scope economies, but evidence gleaned from a study of the former DGT's cost structure does not support the existence of such economies (CEPD 1996). A more sentimental appeal against the proposed divestiture of CHT seems to rest on the fear that since CHT has just spun off from the former DGT, the more radical reform of separation may cause additional chaos. Therefore, the authority appears to be reluctant to tackle the issue and has decided to leave it to the board of CHT. It should be noted, however, that the structure of the incumbent can have an impact on access pricing and hence on the extent of fair competition between the incumbent and new entrants (Doyle 1997, 86). In Taiwan, competition has not yet encroached on the local and long-distance service markets. The vertical structure of CHT enables it to control the local and long-distance networks while competing with private operators in the mobile communications market, which can lead to foreclosure and predatory action. New entrants in mobile communications are concerned about discrimination in the provision of access to essential facilities and access prices. Indeed, the possibility of predatory action is not remote because information on CHT's operating costs has not been made transparent enough to distinguish its tariff rebalancing policy from a predatory pricing strategy, and regulatory oversight by the DGT remains inadequate (Chou 1996). Of course, this problem may be overcome by other regulatory tools, for example, requiring separate accounting for CHT's operations. Nonetheless, the position taken here is that the issue of decomposing CHT should be addressed by the regulatory authority rather than left in the hands of CHT itself.

The second issue that deserves the attention of the regulatory authority relates to the cross-entry of telecommunications and cable television (CATV). The convergence between telecommunications and broadcasting has been documented, and the two are now segregated mainly by regulation rather than by technology itself (Kelly 1989). A decision to be made by the regulatory authority is whether telecommunications and CATV operators should be allowed to penetrate each other's markets. Likewise in Taiwan, the boundaries between telecommunications and CATV are largely artificial, since these two services are currently governed as separate sectors. Such regulation has little merit in terms of promoting telecommunications competition and developing the NII. CATV provides much wider band transmission services than do traditional telecommunications networks, which presents substantial underexplored potential for providing telecommunications services. To the extent that they are connected by fiberoptic backbones, CATV networks are able to provide broadband services to the home, which is in line with one of the aims of the NII program. In addition, they will form the capacity for promoting network competition in local call services. It is estimated that the penetration rate for CATV in Taiwan is above 60 per 100 households. Removing the artificial boundaries between telecommunications and CATV can facilitate fulfilling the aims of telecommunications liberalization and the NII. It is noted that some may not be so optimistic about the convergence of CATV and telecommunications, but the cross-entry of these two services has been realized in some OECD countries (OECD 1997, 77–79). In Taiwan, a decision has been made to allow CATV operators to explore broadband Internet opportunities over coaxial cable. CATV and telecommunications operators have also developed strong interest in penetrating each other's markets. The possibility of removing market boundaries is therefore not remote. The problem, for one thing, is that CATV operators have a size disadvantage due mainly to a governmental policy to divide the national CATV market into fifty-one sections. This size disparity may shift the balance toward telecommunications operators once cross-entry is permitted.

11.8   Conclusion

The global telecommunications landscape has been shaped by technological, economic, and regulatory forces. Despite having advanced halfway, telecommunications liberalization in Taiwan has already reached the stage where attention should be paid to the essential issue of how to foster fair competition. Above all, market liberalization should go hand in hand with overhauling the regulatory regime. If the regulatory authority in Taiwan is reluctant to adopt the policy of asymmetric regulation in favor of new entrants, it at least has to make sure that they can compete on an equal footing with the incumbent. The opposite, however, appears to be the case. Apart from asymmetric market positions vis-à-vis CHT, the new entrants are beset by problems concerning interconnection, numbering, and so on, due to regulatory slack or ignorance. Such problems have something to do with the dominance of CHT and the extent to which the DGT is willing to break with its past and CHT and reposition itself as a genuine regulator. In essence, central to the telecommunications liberalization policy is the introduction of efficient and effective competition in the market under an appropriate regulatory regime, which is much more than opening the market.

Moreover, the pace of technological and service innovations in the telecommunications industry can quickly outdate policies. This is particularly true for developing countries like Taiwan because they are presented with advanced technologies and services developed elsewhere. This raises the question of what policy changes need to be made to ensure that the benefits of technological change can be fully realized. This question not only is important in its own right but also concerns telecommunications competition. A significant trend in the telecommunications industry is for new technologies to result in lower costs and superior services. The regulatory authority in Taiwan is not unaware of this trend but tends to manage it in a manner that favors CHT, without giving due consideration to its competitive impact and to the needs of the industry and the country. Competition in mobile communications has been restrained because the DGT fails to meet new entrants' needs to bypass CHT's networks via microwave or VSAT links. Service convergence among different segments of mobile communications also challenges the traditional practice of regulating them as separate markets. In addition, the current prohibitions on the provision of callback and Internet phone services and the cross-entry of CATV and telecommunications stifle competition from new complementary and competing networks. The proliferation of new technologies and services will unleash the force of competition in telecommunications but not unless the regulatory regime is continuously upgraded.

References

Amendola, G., and A. Ferraiuolo. 1995. Regulating mobile communications. *Communications Policy* 19 (1): 29–42.

Braeutigam, R. R., and J. C. Panzar. 1993. Effects of the change from rate-of-return to price-cap regulation. *American Economic Review* 83 (2): 191–98.

Cave, M. 1996. Entry, competition, and regulation in U.K. telecommunications. *Oxford Review of Economic Policy* 12 (4): 100–121.

CEPD (Council for Economic Planning and Development). 1996. Report on telecommunications (in Chinese). In *Report on promoting the liberalization of services,* by Council for Economic Planning and Development. Taipei: Council for Economic Planning and Development.

Chen, S. H. 1997. The telecommunications industry. In *The impact of investment rule-making and liberalization,* ed. Chung-Hua Institution for Economic Research. Taipei: Chung-Hua Institution for Economic Research.

Cheng, J., et al. 1989. *A study on the policy and institutional reform for establishing a sound information society* (in Chinese). Taipei: Council for Economic Planning and Development.

Chou, J. 1996. The prospects of Taiwan's telecommunications service industry: Challenges and strategies. In *Proceedings of the Trend and Strategies for Taiwan's Communications Industry Conference,* ed. Industrial Technology Research Institute. Hsinchu: Industrial Technology Research Institute.

Doyle, C. 1997. Promoting efficient competition in telecommunications. *National Institute Economic Review,* no. 159 (January): 82–91.

Globerman, S. 1995. Foreign ownership in telecommunications. *Telecommunications Policy* 19 (1): 21–28.

Hausman, J. A. 1996. Proliferation of networks in telecommunications: Technological and economic considerations. In *Networks, infrastructure, and the new task for regulation,* ed. W. Sichel and D. L. Alexander. Ann Arbor: University of Michigan Press.

ICCP (Information, Computer and Communications Policy Committee). 1995. *The economic and regulatory aspects of telecommunication numbering.* Paris: Organization for Economic Cooperation and Development.

Jang, H. 1993. *Technological change and growth in productivity in Taiwan's electronics industry: Empirical evidence from the telecommunications industry* (in Chinese). Taipei: National Taiwan University, Department of Economics.

Kelly, T. 1989. The marriage of broadcasting and telecommunications. *OECD Observer,* no. 160: 16–18.

———. 1992. What price the airwaves? *OECD Observer,* no. 173: 31–34

OECD (Organization for Economic Cooperation and Development). 1993. *Communications outlook.* Paris: Organization for Economic Cooperation and Development.

———. 1995. *Communications outlook.* Paris: Organization for Economic Cooperation and Development.

———. 1997. *Communications outlook.* Paris: Organization for Economic Cooperation and Development.

Sappington, D. E., and D. L. Weisman. 1996. *Designing incentive regulation for the telecommunications industry.* Cambridge, Mass.: MIT Press; Washington, D.C.: AEI Press.

Sato, H., and R. Stevenson. 1989. Telecommunications in Japan: After privatization and liberalization. *Columbia Journal of World Business* 24 (1): 31–41.

Comment   Ramonette B. Serafica

Shin-Horng Chen provides a good discussion of the reforms undertaken in the telecommunications industry in Taiwan. Figure 11.1, which shows the schedule of telecommunications liberalization in Taiwan from 1995 onward, is particularly interesting because it captures the Taiwanese perspective on telecommunications liberalization. The story behind the sequence and timing of reforms would be a good addition so that readers can gain a deeper sense of the Taiwanese perspective. Another aspect of the paper that I find quite informative is the discussion of the underlying national objectives motivating further liberalization. Indeed, telecommunications is becoming so critical an industry for every nation that it is important for us who are involved in policy research to share the lessons learned and strategies adopted so that our respective economies can be active players in the coming information century.

The objective of the paper is "to distill lessons that may add to the current understanding of telecommunications liberalization outside the developed world." However, given that the reform program in Taiwan is relatively young, I think that what the paper can realistically achieve is to raise the level of awareness of outsiders about the issues confronting Taiwan so that parallelisms can be drawn that will lead to a richer understanding of telecommunications reform worldwide. Since Chen touches on potential problems that may arise from the current policies, he may also want to look at the experiences of other countries that have adopted similar paths and from there distill lessons that may be applicable to Taiwan.

After reading Chen's paper, I realized that despite the differences between Taiwan and the Philippines, particularly in terms of telecommunications network development, we nonetheless share similar concerns with respect to competition in the telecommunications industry. Three issues in particular I think parallel the concerns that have emerged in the Philippines.

Is Divestiture a Prerequisite for Competition?

One of the issues identified in the paper concerns the structure of CHT. Chen notes that CHT's vertical structure allows it to control the local and long-distance markets while competing with private operators in the mobile communications market. Thus he asks whether CHT needs to be divested by structurally separating its operations.

Based on the Philippine experience I can say that the fear of undesirable competitive behavior such as foreclosure and predatory pricing by a vertically integrated incumbent is not entirely unfounded. In 1993, the Philip-

Ramonette B. Serafica is associate professor of economics at De La Salle University, Manila.

pine government decided to open the international long-distance and cellular markets to competition. As a condition for entry in these lucrative lines of business, international gateway facility operators and cellular mobile telecommunications service operators were also required to install fixed lines in both profitable and unprofitable areas, thereby opening the local exchange market to a duopoly. These reforms were introduced to address the huge unmet demand existing at that time. With an asymmetrically competitive industry structure, however, a seamless telecommunications network has so far been unattainable.[1] The Philippine Long Distance Company (PLDT), a private firm that has enjoyed virtual monopoly of long-distance and local exchange service for more that sixty years in the country, has made interconnection difficult for the new local players. Firms have expressed frustration over the delay in getting interconnection lines with PLDT, which owns the most extensive nationwide backbone and network. As the dominant firm, it is able to control the setting of access charges and the pace with which interconnection takes place, to the detriment of competing firms. The regulator generally takes a hands-off stance and lets the individual firms negotiate through bilateral contracts. In a few years, this problem is expected to be less contentious as the networks of the new firms grow. In the meantime, subscriber dissatisfaction brews.

Another topic of hot debate at the moment concerns PLDT's application for rate rebalancing. With the impending reduction of accounting rates from U.S. telecommunications firms, PLDT has petitioned for a restructuring of existing domestic toll service rates (increase in long-haul rates and decrease in short-haul rates) and an increase in existing local exchange service rates. In addition, the company is also planning to adopt metered service rates. Competing firms have argued that the rates proposed by PLDT will allow it to undercut prices in high-revenue and competitive areas, which these firms cannot match because of their government-mandated service obligations in unprofitable areas. With imperfect knowledge of the true cost of service and lack of expertise within the regulatory agency it is difficult to distinguish between tariff rebalancing and predatory pricing.

These two situations illustrate the possibility of exclusionary actions. As Chen has pointed out, divestiture may not be necessary if alternative technologies exist that can bypass bottleneck facilities. It may also be the case that regulatory power is sufficient to discipline the behavior of the dominant firm. In the absence of such conditions, divestiture may be the next best solution. In addition to discussing the cost and benefits of

---

1. According to Sharkey, "Competition is 'asymmetric' if one firm is overwhelmingly larger than each of its potential competitors and if the rules of competitive conduct differ between the large and small firms. . . . The largest firm must also have a dominant market share" (1982, 206).

divestiture in the Taiwanese case, the author may want to consider its implications in light of the final stretch of the reform program scheduled in 2001, which includes the privatization of CHT and the liberalization of the remaining segments of telecommunications. Divestiture may make CHT less attractive to private investors but may draw more players into the liberalization program. The experience of other countries that have successfully introduced reforms in the sector should be examined (see Petrazzini 1995, e.g.).

Regulation of Converging Technologies

The paper cites the convergence of broadcasting and telecommunications. Another convergence would be information technology and telecommunications. And with the creation of the national, regional, and global information infrastructures, all three will converge, at least from the regulatory point of view, because the economics of multimedia will have implications for competition policy. Already the convergence of information technology and telecommunications presents gray areas in terms of ownership and the scope of competition.

To illustrate, value-added services such as the Internet are completely deregulated in the Philippines. Testimony to the fierce competition in the industry is the existence of close to a hundred Internet service providers (ISPs). This situation of unbridled competition is threatened by the potential foreclosure by telecommunications firms who have commercial interests in the Internet business as well. Again, a case in point is PLDT. In 1996, it acquired majority control of INFOCOM Technologies, Inc., the largest ISP in the country. With the impending metering of local telephone rates as spearheaded by PLDT, independent ISPs fear that control of telecommunications facilities by competing ISP firms will unfairly jeopardize their operations. Thus the question arises of whether there is a need to limit ownership and control of complementary goods and services.

Telecommunications Policy in Support of National Goals

Finally, I would like to point out that the Asia-Pacific Regional Operations Center and the NII in Taiwan have equivalent initiatives in the Philippines. The current government would also like to position the Philippines as a center for knowledge-based industries, and the establishment of the NII is likewise part of the national agenda. These two initiatives require advanced telecommunications networks and, therefore, the competition that fosters the innovation needed to deliver the communications requirements of advanced users.

Another national objective in the Philippines, however, merits equal attention. Unlike Taiwan, the telecommunications network in the Philippines is relatively small, as evidenced by the current telephone density rate of about 5 lines per 100 Filipinos. Thus the attainment of universal service is still of paramount concern. Under such conditions, the introduction of competitive forces that tend to concentrate on serving high-revenue customers becomes problematic.

The current strategy by the government is to impose service obligations on new firms in order to increase telephone penetration, particularly in the countryside. By next year, it is hoped that the density rate will double from the current figure as a result of this scheme. As I have argued elsewhere this is not a sustainable solution, and in fact it is contrary to the promotion of competition since, among other things, the dominant firm is not covered by this rule so that new firms operate at a disadvantage vis-à-vis PLDT. The task, therefore, is to think of a better alternative to the current situation. It would be useful for us to learn how universal service can be achieved in the era of competition.

Conclusion

These are just some of the issues that need to be resolved if we are to create a credible competitive environment. I thank the author for providing useful insights from the Taiwanese experience that have enabled me to think of similarities with the Philippine case. Indeed, the technology involved has universal application, so it is easy to understand why similar concerns emerge. The differences lie in the unique social, political, and economic conditions of each country.

References

Petrazzini, Ben A. 1995. *The political economy of telecommunications reform in developing countries.* New York: Praeger.
Sharkey, William W. 1982. *The theory of natural monopoly.* New York: Cambridge University Press.

Competition Policies for the Telecommunications Industry in Korea

Il Chong Nam

12.1 Introduction

In the past fifteen years or so, the world has been witnessing a fundamental change in the way the telecommunications industry operates. For many countries, introducing competition into the telecommunications industry has proved to be much more than allowing additional firms into the industry. It requires the transformation of a monopolistic government business into a competitive industry, which in turn demands the redefinition of the role of the government, creation of a proper regulatory regime, a new set of rules governing who can participate in what parts of the new business opportunity, rules to set rates and access charges, and so on. The process of transformation in Korea has not always been orderly and is still unfolding.

The Korean experience seems to present a unique example of telecommunications deregulation. First, the role of the government has not been clearly redefined. The government opted to allow some private firms into the telecommunications industry while at the same time retaining control of Korea Telecom, which was a monopolistic public enterprise before deregulation.[1] Thus the government put itself in a position to provide ser-

Il Chong Nam is a senior fellow and head of the Law and Economics Department of the Korea Development Institute.

The author thanks Hyun Ok Jung and Jung Hyun Kim for their assistance, as well as those who provided data and other information that made this research possible.

1. A note on public enterprises in Korea is in order. Public enterprises in Korea differ from, say, state-owned enterprises in New Zealand. While state-owned enterprises in New Zealand are commercial companies whose ownership happens to be in the hands of the government, public enterprises in Korea are more like the New Zealand government's business units. They are not allowed to pursue commercial objectives and are required by law to

vices in competition with private entrants. This is in sharp contrast to the comparable cases in the United Kingdom and New Zealand. Second, the regulatory regime has not changed much from the days of government monopoly. Third, omnipresent industrial policies, whose objectives are sometimes ambiguous, have allowed the government to intervene in the industry extensively during the whole process.

The primary purpose of this paper is to evaluate the deregulation of the telecommunications industry in Korea. I also attempt to explain why the deregulation process has produced the outcomes it has. The analysis will also shed some light on how industrial policies affect competition policies in general in Korea. After summarizing major events in the deregulation process, I will analyze the effects of several key policies that have been employed by the Korean government, from the policy toward Korea Telecom, to the policy on entry, rates, access charges, and the regulatory regime. I also discuss the industrial policy of promoting the equipment manufacturing industry.

The paper is organized as follows: In section 12.2 I summarize the history of the industry from government monopoly to its current state. In section 12.3 I evaluate the deregulation process and current policies toward the telecommunications industry in Korea. This section focuses on the effects of past and current policies regarding privatization, entry, rates, access charges, and the regulatory regime. Section 12.4 draws conclusions.

12.2 An Overview of the Deregulation of the Telecommunications Industry in Korea

Telephone services were provided by the Ministry of Communications (MOC) until 1980, when the government created a separate corporation to control telephone services. However, unlike the case of corporatization in New Zealand, this change was made as a restructuring effort within the government and had little to do with market-oriented reform. The resulting public enterprise, Korea Telecom (KT), was viewed as a tool to execute the policies determined by MIC and not as a firm whose objective was to seek profits.[2] MIC's policy at the time was to accomplish universal service as quickly as possible. KT followed the directions given by MIC and achieved universal service in record time. By the end of the 1980s, KT had a monopoly in the international, domestic long-distance, and local exchange markets as well as in the mobile telephone market. However, KT was essentially a government business unit rather than a firm.

---

serve public objectives. In practice, they are close to subsidiaries of the ministries that oversee the industries to which they belong.

2. MOC changed its name to the Ministry of Information and Communication (MIC) in 1996. To avoid confusion, I will henceforth refer to MIC unless there is a need to use the name MOC.

Table 12.1   **International Telephone Traffic and Sales of DACOM**

Measure	1991	1992	1993	1994	1995
Telephone traffic (thousand calls)					
Outbound	754	17,991	26,517	32,253	36,639
Inbound	–	13,165	26,617	34,949	39,540
Sales (hundred million won)					
Outbound	30	714	1,008	1,224	1,422
Inbound	–	415	757	927	964
Total revenue	30	1,129	1,765	2,151	2,386
Market share (%)					
Outbound base	1.0	21.2	26.7	27.2	25.9

Source: Ministry of Information and Communication, *Annual Report of Electro Communication* (Seoul, 1996).

In the early 1990s, MIC announced long-term plans to turn its telephone business into a privatized industry and, as a first step, allowed a private firm, DACOM, to enter the international telephone market. At first, DACOM leased most of the lines and other equipment needed to provide service from KT on favorable terms. Further, MIC set the rate of DACOM's international telephone service substantially below KT's rate. As shown in table 12.1, DACOM quickly penetrated the international market and captured a market share of around 25 percent in a relatively short period of time. DACOM's international telephone traffic on the basis of outbound calls increased by 13.6 percent compared with 1995. Sales also increased, by 10.9 percent. Over the past five years, rates for international calls have been adjusted several times, resulting in a decrease in both the average rate level and the rate differential for the two operators. However, the rates have always been set by MIC.

On the mobile side, KT was forced to divest its mobile phone and paging subsidiary, Korea Mobile Telephone (KMT) in 1994, when a controlling interest was sold to one of the major *chaebols,* the Sunkyung Group.[3] KT has not been allowed to participate in the paging market since then and was barred from reentering the mobile telephone market until it obtained a personal communications services (PCS) license in summer 1996 along with two other *chaebols.* During this period, MIC allowed one more cellular operator, Shinsegi Telecom Inc. (STI), to enter the market. STI was not able to provide service quickly mainly because MIC required as one of the conditions of its license that STI use code division multiple access (CDMA) technology, which was still being developed. This requirement not only delayed the timing of the entry by STI into the mobile market but effectively reduced the size and profitability of entry, while it

3. KMT recently changed its name to SK Telecom (SKT) to make it clear that it belongs to the Sunkyung Group. I will refer to SKT henceforth.

prolonged SKT's monopoly. In late 1996, STI finally began service, but it is still not effective in competing against SKT, which is allowed to use the old analog standard as well as CDMA technology.

In 1996, MOC became the Ministry of Information and Communication (MIC). It issued new licenses for several service areas in what was then viewed by many as the last big business opportunity of the twentieth century. Two licenses for PCS services were granted to two consortia headed by two *chaebols,* Hansol and LG. The third went to a consortium controlled by KT, Freetel. All three new operators were required to use CDMA technology. None of the three has yet begun operations. In addition, MIC allowed Onse, a consortium of many firms without a single controlling firm, to participate in the international market and allowed DACOM to enter the domestic long-distance market. Onse is still preparing for its entry. DACOM started domestic long-distance service in early 1997 but has been able to capture less than 10 percent of the market.

Throughout these years, KT was treated essentially as a business unit of MIC even though MIC periodically announced its willingness to privatize KT and sold some KT shares to private investors in several tranches. Currently, the government owns 71.2 percent of the shares; the rest are owned by a few institutional investors and a large number of small investors. KT is still subject to the Korea Telecom Act, which specifies that KT's objective is to achieve public goals and which gives MIC virtually unlimited power to intervene in the management of KT. This implies that KT does not have a profit incentive, nor does it have any incentive to speak against the decisions made by MIC on issues that could have significant effects on KT, such as rates, access charges, conditions for leasing its facilities to its competitors, and so forth. Thus one cannot view KT as a competitor in any meaningful sense.

Several aspects of the deregulation process attract attention. First, the government did not open major markets fully to anyone who wanted to participate but controlled the number of firms in each market and selected the entrants. In the international telephone market, it allowed only one entrant in 1991, maintained a duopoly until 1996, and then allowed one more entrant in 1996. In the domestic long-distance market, the government maintained the KT monopoly until 1996, when it allowed entry of only one firm, DACOM.[4] The government maintained SKT's monopoly on the mobile side as well, allowing only one more entrant in 1994 and three others in 1995.

Second, in selecting new entrants, the government did not auction off licenses but instead employed complicated scoring systems. For instance,

4. DACOM was seen to be adversely affected by Onse's entry into the international telephone market that it had shared with KT. The decision to allow DACOM to enter the domestic long-distance market appears to have been based partly on MIC's concern about the profitability of DACOM. Onse has not started operation yet.

when MIC was selecting three PCS operators, it evaluated, among other things, the plausibility of business plans as well as the desirability of the applying consortia from a social standpoint. In effect, the government chose the firms that could participate in the market. In addition, the government exercised strong influence on the governance structures of new entrants. Except in selling shares of SKT and in allowing DACOM to enter the international market, the government forced potential entrants to form consortia consisting of many firms.

Third, the government apparently intended to secure a portion of the markets for new entrants and safeguard their financial stability by using its control over KT and its strong rein on the industry, which is guaranteed by law. MIC's rate regulation focused on maintaining rate differentials between the incumbent and new entrants while at the same time preventing overall rate levels from falling to levels that would have been realized under full competition. Its policies toward access charges also appear to have been biased in favor of new entrants. It appears that the government's intention was to create the industry configuration that it wanted rather than let the market decide. Thus the telecommunications industry has multiple firms but is not subject to the forces of competition yet.[5]

Fourth, and most important, MIC has been playing three different and conflicting roles: owner of KT, promoter of industrial policies for the telecommunications industry and the related equipment manufacturing industry, and regulator of the telecommunications industry. As a consequence, KT has been run as an instrument of industrial policy rather than a profit-seeking firm. In addition, an independent regulatory framework has not surfaced yet.

12.3 Evaluation of the Deregulation Process and Current Policies

This section evaluates the effect of the deregulation process and current policies, which have not changed much from the early 1990s. Ever since the entry of DACOM into the international market, which started the deregulation process, rates have gone down and new services have become available. Many investors and firms who were able to participate in the newly created markets made handsome profits. For the business community, opportunities to catch a goose that is supposed to lay golden eggs came every two years. The government heralded the coming of the infor-

---

5. One example that supports this conclusion is the apparent failure of DACOM to achieve superiority in efficiency. Although cost data are not released to the public, leaked pieces of information and the opinions of accountants in this area suggest that DACOM's cost structure is no better than that of KT. Several studies also point out that DACOM managers receive significantly higher salaries than their counterparts at KT. More generally, although not a public enterprise, DACOM is believed by most experts to have serious governance problems, due partly to the protective industrial policies of the government.

mation age. Not surprisingly, there has not been much criticism from the general public of the deregulation process.

However, lower rates and the introduction of new services by themselves are not enough when it comes to a telecommunications industry in which the relevant questions should be: By how much should rates go down? How quickly should new services be introduced? How reliable are the services? Increases in social welfare from telecommunications come from two directions, technological innovation and competition, which are themselves positively correlated. The deregulation of the industry in Korea has not taken full advantage of the merits of competition. In fact, the deregulation process has had problems from the beginning, as I argue below.

12.3.1   Policies toward Korea Telecom

The government did not privatize KT as it introduced competition and has maintained KT as a means to achieve government policies. Since KT has been run as a subsidiary of MIC and has been denied profit incentives, it has had no reason to respond to the new environment. Thus the most important part of the market has been excluded from the forces of competition. With no profit-oriented incentive plans and under a hierarchical structure as rigid and bureaucratic as the government itself, not many KT employees would attempt to improve the efficiency of their organization.

The decision to keep KT as a vehicle of industrial policy when competition was being introduced is in sharp contrast with the cases of the United Kingdom and New Zealand, which privatized British Telecom and Telecom New Zealand, respectively, prior to the introduction of competition. The decision by the Korean government not to privatize KT or to give KT a profit incentive reveals its perception of competition. The decision to keep KT as a vehicle of MIC policy goes directly against the goal of turning the telecommunications market from a government business into a competitive industry. DACOM's entry into the international market in 1991, without a change in KT, signaled the start of an era in which a competitive industry was handmade by the government. After six years of competition, KT is still not allowed to follow commercial objectives.

12.3.2   Regulatory Regime

As the government introduced competition in the telecommunications industry, a need arose for an independent regulatory body. However, no such body has been created. MIC was given the authority to oversee competition policies for the telecommunications industry while continuing all of its original functions. The realm of competition policies in the telecommunications industry has not been clearly defined. This ambiguity has caused tensions between MIC and the Korean Fair Trade Commission. However, MIC was given the authority to draw up and execute the policies concerning entry and exit, operating conditions, rates, and access charges.

It is also widely accepted within the government that MIC, and not the Fair Trade Commission, is primarily responsible for regulating anticompetitive behavior by telecommunications operators. Thus MIC has been playing the three different roles mentioned in section 12.2.

As pointed out in section 12.2, MIC's dual role as the owner of KT and competition authority could lead to conflicts of interests that jeopardize the performance of MIC in both areas. The third function of MIC, to promote industrial policies, further complicates matters. There is no agreement on what the industrial policies are for the telecommunications industry, even among bureaucrats.[6] It appears that the government has chosen the following goals for its industrial policies: (1) making sure that each service is provided by multiple but not too many operators, (2) making sure that each firm has sufficient market share, (3) letting no firm lose money, (4) making Korean operators big enough to be able to compete with foreign operators once the Korean market opens to foreign operators, (5) prohibiting any single party from claiming control of a major operator,[7] and (6) helping related equipment manufacturing firms to become competitive in the world market.

What are the policy variables? The policy variables that the government can employ in pursuing the above objectives include its control over entry, rates, access charges, conditions for operation, and technical standards and its control over the management of KT as the majority shareholder. To promote the equipment manufacturing industry, the government has been using its discretion in the choice of technical standards and R&D subsidies. As one can easily see, some of the objectives of industrial policies overlap with the objectives of competition policies. Further, some industrial policy variables, such as the regulation of rates, access charges, entry, and operating conditions, are the same control variables that an independent competition authority would use to regulate the telecommunications industry.

Consequently, the industrial policies of the government often conflict with its own competition policies. For instance, the government apparently saw that giving DACOM a certain market share within a certain period of time was desirable from the viewpoint of its industrial policy, so

6. This ambiguity surrounding industrial policies is not unique to the telecommunications industry. Generally, industrial policies for an industry are the policies pursued by the ministry in charge of the industry. Often, what a ministry should pursue in an industry is not quite clear. Industry acts that empower the relevant ministries to intervene in an industry state the objectives of policies too generally. Typically, the acts only name "development of the industry" or "preventing disorder in markets" as the objective. As a consequence, the ministries in charge of specified industries enjoy wide discretion and tend to justify their policies or decisions by simply saying that they serve the objectives of industrial policies, which is somewhat tautological.

7. On this point, the government has been inconsistent in the past. While it applied this principle to DACOM and Onse, it permitted *chaebols* to take controlling interests of mobile operators.

it prohibited further entry and set rates in such a way that DACOM would achieve this goal. Another example involves the policies concerning vertical integration between the telecommunications and the equipment manufacturing industries. Up until 1996, when MIC issued PCS licenses to Hansol Telecom and LG Telecom, affiliated with the Hansol Group and the LG Group, respectively, both of which have telecommunications equipment manufacturing subsidiaries, vertical integration in either direction had been prohibited.

The entry of Hansol and LG into the mobile market removed the ban on forward integration as a by-product. However, the ban on backward integration remained. While the policy on vertical integration could have been used as a competition policy, it has been employed as an industrial policy, whose objective was to help some manufacturers. To this day, no explanation has been given for the prohibition on backward integration that selectively applies only to carriers that did not previously have manufacturing subsidiaries. An explanation, if provided, would be based at least partly on assessments of the possibility and the effects of foreclosure.

Industrial policies will work well when the government has all the information about demand and the cost structure of each firm, as well as those of potential entrants, and uses the information to achieve the social optimum. In such an environment, the government will choose the right number of firms and the best firms as participants, choose the optimal size for each firm, and set the most efficient rates and access charges. But this scenario is not about a competitive industry. Rather, it is closer to the old government monopoly. Of course, it was exactly the failure of the government-managed system that led to the transformation of the telecommunications industry into a competitive one worldwide. By not establishing an independent competition authority, the government has failed to create an environment that is consistent with competition in the telecommunications industry.

Another characteristic of industrial policies that deserves attention is that they frequently fail to distinguish between firms and their owners. When large projects are undertaken, they usually involve high sunk costs for which funds must be committed in the early stages of operation, before many uncertainties are realized.[8] However, at the time the uncertainties are realized, the sunk costs are no longer relevant and should not influence the decisions of the firm or the government. For instance, suppose that the government issues a firm a license to operate in the long-distance market, in which there are two incumbents, and that the entrant invests $100 million in facilities that have no opportunity cost, once the investment is

---

8. The telecommunications industry is an example. Building a national network could involve huge costs, and a large part of them may not be of much value for other uses. Many network industries share this property.

made. Suppose also that the marginal cost of each firm is substantially below the range of prices that would prevail as uncertainties about demand and other factors are realized once the entrant starts operation. In such an environment, all three firms will operate and will earn positive economic profits in equilibrium.[9]

However, depending on the realization of the uncertainty, the entrant could find the realized profit significantly smaller than the opportunity cost of $100 million that was available before it committed itself to the facilities. If a large part of $100 million was financed by borrowing, the entrant firm could even go bankrupt though it earns a positive economic profit after entry. In a well-functioning economy, this will not cause any problems.

The firm will continue to operate because it is making a positive economic profit. Only the firm's shareholders will take a loss on the unfortunate investment if the firm can still pay the interest on borrowed capital. If the operating profit, before deducting interest payments, is smaller than the interest payments, banks too will have to take a loss. However, all these losses have nothing to do with economic efficiency and involve only the financial well-being of the shareholders and creditors. There is no reason for the firm to deviate from the level of operation in equilibrium. There is no need for the government to intervene either.[10]

However, industrial policies in Korea frequently call for government intervention when realized profits are smaller than the levels expected at the time of entry.[11] A popular method used by the government is to limit competition and secure financial stability for the entrant.[12] The government claims that such interventions are necessary to ensure a strong domestic industry and sometimes goes as far as to say that they are necessary to induce competition in the industry in the long run, although such intervention only affects investors' financial well-being and has no impact on efficiency in the post entry game, as shown above. Limiting post entry competition may have an effect on the efficiency of investment prior to the entry decision. As potential entrants see that the government will help their profitability in the post entry game if the realization of uncertainties is unfavorable, they have incentives to overinvest.

Such industrial policies have a long history in Korea. While interventionist industrial policies generally are fading in Korea, they started only

---

9. This can be shown in a noncooperative game model in which firms first commit to investment under uncertainty and play a Cournot-type game with capacity constraints after the uncertainties are realized.

10. Except possibly to reduce transactions costs involved in reorganization once insolvency occurs.

11. I.e., before the realization of uncertainties.

12. Another widely used method is to force banks to ease the conditions on lending. This policy has been used extensively since the modernization drive started in the early 1960s and has resulted in huge problems for the financial sector.

a few years ago in the telecommunications industry and are showing no signs of diminishing in either scope or strength. The remainder of this section will investigate in more detail the effects of the government's policies on the efficiency of the telecommunications industry in the areas of entry, rates, access charges, and vertical integration.

12.3.3 Entry, Rates, and Access Charges

The government's policy on entry can generally be characterized as "one entrant each time, guaranteed market shares and profitability." Such a policy is bound to affect not only entry itself but rates, access charges, and other relevant variables. Tables 12.2 and 12.3 below provide information about the rate regulation that has been applied to the international market since the entry by the second carrier, DACOM. As shown in table 12.3, MIC initially set DACOM's rates 5 percent lower on average than KT rates, reduced the differential to 3 percent as DACOM's market share came close to 30 percent, and reduced it again to 1 percent.

In addition, MIC maintained rates for international call services at levels far higher than the standalone costs of providing them. This, combined with the asymmetric rate regulation explained above, enabled DACOM to secure the market share needed for profitable operation.

Table 12.2   **Sales Revenue and Market Share Trends (billion won)**

Company and Measure	1992	1993	1994	1995
Korea Telecom				
Total sales revenue	4,487.6	4,907.6	5,389	6,361.5
International services revenue	444.8	420.5	505	580.5
International services market share (%)	86	70.4	70	70.8
DACOM				
Total sales revenue	227.5	325	345	369.8
International services revenue	71.6	176.5	215	238.7
International services market share (%)	14	29.6	30	29.2

Source: Korea Information Society Development Institute.

Table 12.3   **Effect of Competition on International Service Price Index of Korea Telecom**

Measure	1988	1989	1990	1991	1992	1993	1994	1995
International service price index	190.32	140.05	129.02	129.02	129.02	104.32	104.32	100
Price differential between Korea Telecom and DACOM (%)	–	–	–	–	5	3	3	1

Sources: Ministry of Information and Communication and Korea Telecom.

Table 12.4   **Comparison of Long-Distance Call Rates** (won per three minutes)

Measure	Within 30 km		Within 100 km		Over 101 km	
	DACOM	KT	DACOM	KT	DACOM	KT
Basic rate	41.6	41.6	164	182.6	250	277.3
Difference between rates (%)	–		11.3		10.8	

Source: DACOM.

Table 12.4 shows the differences in call rates based on distance in the long-distance call service market. While the government has claimed that rate reductions became possible as a result of introducing competition, rate reductions were actually caused by its decisions about rates.[13] There was no price competition since the rates for each firm were set by the government. It is also worth noting that the government forced KT to lease the facilities needed for DACOM's rapid expansion on favorable terms. Consumers also contributed to DACOM's growth by paying higher rates.

Rates of essentially all the major telecommunications services are set by MIC.[14] Traditionally, rates for international and domestic long-distance calls have been set at levels higher than the standalone costs of providing those services, and rates for local calls have been set lower than their accounting costs.[15] Although no reliable figures are available, it is generally believed that the rate for local exchange service in Korea is substantially below those in the other OECD countries while the rates for international and domestic long-distance calls are significantly higher. As one can see from table 12.5, the ratio of the rate for a long-distance call to the rate for a local call in Korea is much higher than the ratios in other countries.[16] This suggests that the size of the subsidy from the long-distance market to the local exchange market is much larger in Korea than in the other countries.

Considering that the rates for international and domestic long-distance calls are set by the government and that the government has maintained a rate differential between KT and DACOM, past and current rate policies

13. The government could have made the rate reduction much bigger by simply ordering KT to reduce rates without introducing DACOM into the market.

14. MIC officially regulates only rates for services of dominant carriers. These consist of KT's local exchange, domestic long-distance, and international calls and SKT's cellular calls.

15. There is a subtle point in discussing costs of local calls. Accountants claim that they can separate the costs of local calls by allocating joint costs to different services. However, their claim has little truth. If a cost is separable, it would not be a joint cost. However, one may say that KT's local exchange operations are not profitable in the sense that if its international and long-distance divisions had no profits, KT would face a big loss from its local exchange operations at current prices.

16. Here the rate for a long-distance call made to destinations within 30 km is used as a proxy for the rate for a local call.

Table 12.5   **Differences in Telephone Rates Due to Distance**

	Korea	United Kingdom	United States	Japan	Germany	Australia
Ratio[a]	7.8	1.4	1.4	4.5	3.0	3.0

Source: Korea Information Society Development Institute.
[a]Ratio of long-distance call rates (over 101 km / within 30 km) in each country.

must have created ample room for DACOM's profit. Since DACOM took away a sizable portion of the lucrative market that used to subsidize the local exchange operation and other money-losing businesses required by the government, KT's profit levels have been decreasing.

On the mobile side, SKT has been enjoying a monopoly position aided by the policy on technical standards that requires newcomers to use the CDMA system.[17] The rate regulation on SKT appears to have been more generous than the rate regulation on KT.[18] Although SKT is much smaller than KT in size and in the amount of capital initially invested, it earned greater profits than KT did last year. Since the second mobile carrier started operation this year and three more PCS operators are still in the preparatory stage, it is hard to discuss policies on mobile service rates.

The final topic of our discussion of rate regulation is predatory pricing. The rationale behind the rate regulation described above, according to MIC, is the possibility of predatory pricing. In other words, MIC argues that if it does not set rates, the incumbent will set rates below costs and drive the new entrant out of the market. Predatory pricing is illegal according to Korean antitrust laws. Predatory pricing, if found to have occurred, would be punished by the Korean Fair Trade Commission. Thus MIC's rate policies, designed to prevent predatory pricing in advance, are somewhat ad hoc. In other oligopolistic industries, one would normally be more concerned about the possibility of collusion than that of predatory pricing. In our view, MIC's rate regulation has more to do with its industrial policy goals than with the competition policy goal of preventing predatory pricing.

17. SKT would have preferred the group special mobile standard, which is far better than CDMA in terms of the cost of investment and quality, had there been no competitor in sight. But STI had obtained a license and was preparing to enter the mobile market. The government's decision to allow only CDMA technology as the digital standard for mobile services would both delay STI's entry and reduce the magnitude of its entry, in addition to increasing its costs. SKT recognized that the benefits from the adoption by the government of CDMA technology would far outweigh the costs it would entail. Consequently, SKT actively advertised the need for the country to adopt the CDMA standard even though it would increase its own costs substantially.

18. It is believed that regulation of SKT has been generous because it is providing a new service that many view as a luxury good and also because there had been excess demand for quite a while. On the other hand, KT's rates for local calls were much harder to raise due to political constraints.

Let us now turn to the policy on access charges, probably the single most important factor in regulating the telecommunications industry. The nature of the access charge problem depends on the relationship between KT and the firm that wants to access KT's local network. DACOM's services are substitutes for the services provided by KT, while SKT's services are by and large complementary. By providing access to DACOM, KT loses revenue from its long-distance and international businesses. On the other hand, the mobile market is a market that neither SKT nor KT can profit from alone. Consequently, KT and SKT are in a joint-venture bilateral monopoly situation in which each needs the other to take advantage of a new opportunity.

MIC's approach to access charges between DACOM and KT was initially based on the retail tariff rate but changed to a fully distributed cost approach in 1994. On the other hand, MIC's handling of access charges between KT and SKT has proved more difficult. Access charge settlement between KT and SKT was "bill and keep" initially. In 1993, however, MIC changed the rule and required that access charges be determined based on historical fully allocated cost, as between KT and DACOM since 1994, through its decree on interconnection. As the problem with this new rule became evident, MIC gave up this approach and has been trying to come up with yet another method.[19] As a consequence, KT and SKT have been giving access to each other in the land-to-mobile and mobile-to-land markets without any agreement on how they settle on access charges. Table 12.6 shows the trends of access charge rates between KT and SKT, STI, and DACOM.

The problems with accounting-cost-based access charges are well known. They do not reflect true costs or demand conditions. Further, they leave too much to the arbitrariness of bureaucrats and accountants. In addition to these general problems, MIC's access charge policies may have been affected by its industrial policies favoring new entrants. Although much of the cost data are confidential, and the process of determining access charges is not open to the public, experts generally believe that charges have tended to favor firms other than KT. It is worth mentioning that no economic approach, such as an efficient component pricing rule (ECPR) or a global price cap, has been considered by the government thus far.[20]

Access charges between KT and SKT should be interpreted as a profit-sharing rule in a joint venture. However, MIC refused to accept this interpretation and chose to set access charges based on the accounting costs of providing access services. In the early stage, when accounting-cost-based

---

19. The problem is explained below. The explanation will provide a good example of how wrong accounting-cost-based access charges can be.

20. ECPR and its properties are well summarized in Baumol and Sidak (1995), Economides and White (1995), and Laffont and Tirole (1996). Laffont and Tirole (1996) also suggest an approach that can be viewed as a generalization of Ramsey-Boiteux pricing.

Table 12.6   Access Charge Rate Trends (won/minute)

Year	Type[a]	SKT		STI	DACOM	
		Land to Mobile	Mobile to Land	Land to Mobile	Type	Interconnection
1992					Per call	25
1993					Per call	30
1994	Local	13.33	45.03		Per call	40
	Long distance	49.42				
1995	Type A	Undecided	32.04		Local	26.34
	Type B	Undecided	46.83		Long distance	45.03
	Type C		3			
1996	Type A	22.52	22.52	13.27	Long distance	25.02
(expected)	Type B	35.06	35.06	23.67	International	25.08
	Type C		3			

Source: Marketing Division of Korea Telecom.
[a]Translation type.

Table 12.7   **Estimates of Korea Telecom's Access Charge Revenue, 1996**

	Access Charge (hundred million won)				
Company	Charge for Local Call	Charge for Long-Distance Call	NTS Share of Expenses Compensating Deficits[a]	Total	Ratio of Share of Expenses to Sales (%)
KT					
Long distance	4,116	0	4,970	9,086	58.75
International	87	116	107	310	4.33
DACOM					
Long distance	525	490	Exemption	1,015	41.08
International	25	33	30	88	3.34
SKT	453	497	556	1,506	5.96
STI	24	38	Exemption	62	4.65
Total	5,230	1,174	5,663	12,067	22.20

Source: Marketing Division of Korea Telecom.

[a]Non-traffic-sensitive (NTS) expense can roughly be understood as the cost of providing universal service.

access charges were being studied, KT and SKT did not pay access charges and simply used the bill-and-keep method, as directed by MIC. This way of settlement was biased in favor of SKT because most calls were made from mobile to land. The new way of settlement based on the accounting cost of providing access, introduced in 1993, defined both KT and SKT as providers of access services and dictated that each firm receive from the other an access charge equal to the average accounting cost of providing access.

However, SKT's average accounting cost of providing the access to KT needed to complete a land-to-mobile call turned out to be higher than the rate for a call. Thus KT, as a seller of land-to-mobile call services, was to pay more in access charges than it receives as the price for its service.[21] SKT and KT are currently negotiating yet another way of settling access charges.

Table 12.7 summarizes estimated access charges for KT, DACOM, SKT, and STI for 1996. The low ratios of access charges paid to revenue for DACOM and SKT seem to confirm our claim about access charges.[22]

21. This may be interpreted as an example of how arbitrary an accounting approach can be. SKT's cost of providing access services can vary widely depending on the way it allocates costs of capital investment, etc. It also seems that accountants have considerable discretion in qualifying acceptable costs.

22. The ratio of the access charges paid by DACOM to its revenues from the international market is extremely low, compared to those of long-distance carriers in the United States, which range from 40 to 50 percent. The ratio for SKT is also significantly lower than ratios in the OECD countries, which range between 30 and 50 percent.

12.3.4   Vertical Integration

The current policy on vertical integration, allowing forward integration by equipment manufacturers while prohibiting backward integration by carriers, seems to have no economic basis. There is little possibility that KT, DACOM, or SKT could become a dominant firm in manufacturing even if backward integration were allowed. Thus the expected loss of efficiency from vertical foreclosure effects that may arise when these carriers are allowed to integrate backward appears insignificant.

On the other hand, from the past behavior patterns of *chaebols,* it is highly probable that LG Telecom and Hansol Telecom will purchase most of their equipment from the telecommunications equipment manufacturing subsidiaries of LG Group and Hansol Group, respectively, thus foreclosing a substantial portion of the markets both upstream and downstream. Thus the current policy on vertical integration regulates the backward integration whose expected harm to the economy is smaller than the expected harm of the forward integration by nonregulated manufacturers.

Another industrial policy pursued by MIC deserves attention when discussing the vertical relationship between the telecommunications industry and the equipment manufacturing industry. MIC has been playing a key role in subsidizing the equipment manufacturing industry through the R&D programs of service providers downstream. The policy, supported by law, requires telecommunications operators to spend a certain percentage of their revenues on R&D, a large part of which has supported R&D in telecommunications equipment, but does not allow them to commercialize the results. This policy has the effect of taxing services and giving the tax revenue to the R&D part of the equipment manufacturing industry.

Before, when vertical integration in both directions was prohibited, the only issue surrounding the policy was the effect on consumers in the telecommunications market and the effectiveness of the subsidy in helping equipment manufacturers to gain competitiveness in the world market for telecommunications equipment. However, the entry by LG and Hansol led to the possibility that the carriers that are not vertically integrated would subsidize their competitors that are vertically integrated. Such a subsidy will undoubtedly distort competition in the telecommunications industry.

12.4   Basis for Reform

As the above discussions demonstrate, deregulation of the telecommunications industry in Korea has been severely constrained by the industrial policies of the government. As a result, effective competition among carriers seeking profits in a noncooperative way has yet to occur. As long as the present regulatory framework prevails, loss of allocative efficiency as well as internal efficiency of the carriers will continue.

If a more efficient, low-cost telecommunications sector is to be achieved, changes in the structure of incentives facing the management of KT are necessary. Privatizing KT would be the best way to achieve this goal. However, privatization could prove to be a long process, as the history of privatization efforts in Korea shows. Thus, before full privatization takes place, it is important that KT be run as a profit-seeking entity even while the government remains a large shareholder.

One way of giving proper profit incentives to KT would be to separate the ownership role of the government from the regulatory role and establish an independent authority for the telecommunications industry, similar to the Office of Telecommunications in the United Kingdom or the Federal Communications Commission in the United States. The regulatory body would then be charged with regulation of entry, rates, and access charges and other related issues such as universal service.

For mobile telecommunications, an alternative to the present policy would be to sell the spectrum, letting an auction determine who could most profitably and efficiently enter the market. For the wired markets, further relaxation of entry regulation may lead to improvement in allocative efficiency, at least in the long-distance markets.

Reform of regulation on rates and access charges is a complex issue. Factors to be considered include the restructuring of rates to minimize cross-subsidies and, at the same time, the provision of a rate structure that would yield an adequate return when firms are efficient. There also are issues with regard to the allocation of access charges to be divided among KT and mobile operators.

References

Baumol, W. J., and J. G. Sidak. 1995. *Toward competition in local telephony.* Cambridge, Mass.: MIT Press.

Economides, N., and L. White. 1995. How efficient is the "efficient component pricing rule"? *Antitrust Bulletin,* no. 3.

Laffont, J. J., and J. Tirole. 1996. Creating competition through interconnection: Theory and practice. *Journal of Regulatory Economics* 10 (3): 227–56.

Comment   Ramonette B. Serafica

The basic argument of the paper is that telecommunications policies in Korea have not created a competitive industry. Il Chong Nam supports this contention by discussing various forms of government intervention. In particular, several instances of how the Ministry of Information and Communications (MIC) has stepped in to influence market outcomes directly are described. Such an open and honest account of the extent of government intervention is not found in most papers, so the author deserves credit for sharing this information.

To create a more complete and balanced view of the Korean reform program, however, Nam could give some background on the government's motivation for opening up the market. It would be useful to know, for example, what the impetus was for the reform of the sector. Was it due to the immense dissatisfaction of consumers with the old system, or a change in some national or industrial policy goal, or is it simply a response to the changing technologies? What is the rationale for deregulation? Based on the author's discussion, one is inclined to believe that regulation is driven by industrial policies. It would therefore help to know what the actual policy pronouncements of the government are with respect to telecommunications. Thus a discussion of (1) what triggered telecommunications deregulation and (2) what is driving it forward should help the reader gain a view of the forest that is the Korean telecommunications reform program.

After reading through the paper one is convinced that there is indeed a lot of room for the introduction of competitive forces in the industry. Acting as regulator, promoter of industrial policies, and owner of the dominant firm, MIC has been able to use its powers to carve out an environment that guarantees *results* rather than the mere *opportunity* to participate in such a dynamic industry. If this is true, then there is certainly the danger that such a low-powered incentive structure will not encourage optimal behavior from the privileged few.

A case in point is the policy on market entry, which Nam describes as "one entrant each time, guaranteed market shares and profitability." I agree with the author that it is only with perfect information on cost and demand conditions that a central planner has any chance of accurately determining the best candidate. However, as we all know, such a situation does not exist. In fact, as economists have always maintained, it is the process of competition that is the most efficient "discovery procedure" for eventually separating the winners from the losers.[1]

Of course, there is some merit in ensuring the economic viability of new

---

Ramonette B. Serafica is associate professor of economics at De La Salle University, Manila.

1. Snow (1997) provides a good discussion of the debate regarding natural monopoly vs. competition in telecommunications networks.

entrants. It reduces their risks and encourages investment in the sector. But even as a select few are chosen, competitive forces can be introduced into the selection process by adopting competition *for* the market instead of competition *in* the market. Through a bidding process, the candidate that offers the best combination of price, quality, and product variety is chosen to enter the market first. Phasing of licenses can then be used as a stick to discipline an erring operator and as a carrot to entice prospective entrants to offer better, more innovative packages of services as a condition for entry.[2] This option may be explored as an alternative to the current system.

It must be noted that the case for asymmetric regulation in favor of entrants has been stressed in other countries. The British and U.S. experiences show that initial support for entrants was necessary in order to create a credible competitive environment. Based on the actions of MIC perhaps the interventions are aimed at creating a competitive industry, and thus it may be premature for Nam to declare "that telecommunications policies in Korea have not created a competitive industry." The fact that rates have gone down and that new services have become available in international long distance reveals that slowly competition is taking root. As I have said, the author has done a good job of convincing me of the enormous potential for the introduction of competitive forces in Korean telecommunications. As a next step, the author may want to look at how other countries have managed to help new firms in the name of creating a level playing field and still been able to promote efficiency in the process.

The contribution of government or government-run operators in the development of telecommunications networks should also not be totally disregarded. I think that government-run post, telegraph, and telephones (PTTs) were successful in achieving universal service in some countries (and thus government was able to correct a potential market failure under a private monopoly situation). Even Nam acknowledges that this is true for Korea, and chapter 11 on Taiwan can attest to this fact as well. In addition, it is incorrect to claim that "it was exactly the failure of the government-managed system that led to the transformation of the telecommunications industry into a competitive one worldwide." In fact, the single most important impetus for the transformation of the telecommunications industry into a competitive one is the change in the cost structure of providing telecommunications services attributable to technological innovation. Thus "failure of the government-managed system" can perhaps explain the return of PTTs to the private sector, but it is technology that makes competition possible.

Finally, in the last section of the paper, Nam makes several recommendations for restructuring the regulatory framework for the industry. Given

2. See Glynn's (1994) proposal.

the complexity of telecommunications, it would be impossible to provide an adequate treatment of the subject matter in one paper (much less one section of a paper). As a guide, the International Telecommunication Union lists the following as important elements of telecommunications policy, regulation, and legislation:

1. *Market structure:* What are the monopoly services and which ones can be provided under competition?

2. *Ownership of operating entities:* What is the extent of private sector participation and of foreign participation?

3. *Conditions and rules of market entry and exit:* What are the obligations of operating entities, technical standards, rules for interconnection, mechanisms for entry, and so forth?

4. *Pricing principles and cost recovery guidelines:* What are guidelines for monopoly and competitive services, allowable rates of return and so forth?

5. *Institutional roles:* What are the location of authority, the process to establish policy, and the process to monitor and enforce compliance with policy?

Each of these elements needs to be thoroughly studied, individually and in conjunction with the other aspects, in order to come up with a complete and coherent reform program for telecommunications.

References

Glynn, Simon. 1994. How many cellular licenses should there be? The economic feasibility. *Telecommunications Policy* 18 (2): 91–96.
Snow, Marcellus. 1997. Testing for natural monopoly in telecommunications systems and networks. In *International communication: A trade and development perspective—Essays in honor of Meheroo Jussawalla,* ed. Donald Lamberton. New York: Hampton.

13

China's Telecommunications Infrastructure Buildup
On Its Own Way

Ding Lu

In many aspects of its market-oriented reform, China has been moving forward on its own way. The regime's gradualist, trial-and-error reform defies the big bang approach recommended by some Western gurus for transitional economies. Nevertheless, the Chinese economy has proudly displayed spectacular growth and rising living standards, in sharp contrast to the painful transition in the Eastern European and the former Soviet states. Between 1978 and 1995, China's economy chalked up an average annual real growth rate of 9.7 percent. The economy grew at double-digit rates for four consecutive years from 1992 to 1995.

The uniqueness of the Chinese experience is equally, if not more, impressive in the country's telecommunications industry. Opening of telecommunications markets and privatization of telecommunications services have become worldwide trends as technological progress redefines the nature of the industry. China's telecommunications sector, however, remains centrally planned, state-owned, and monopolistic in major service areas. Unlike most other Chinese sectors, the telecommunications sector still shuts its door to direct foreign equity investment and foreign operation of businesses. The hierarchical business empire under the Ministry of Posts and Telecommunications (MPT) still maintains an old-style tariff structure based on redistribution and cross-subsidization. The emergence of non-MPT domestic (also state-owned) carriers, although challenging, has not posed a serious threat to the MPT's monopolistic hold on the industry.

Despite all these apparent shortcomings, China's telecommunications

Ding Lu is senior lecturer in the Department of Economics, National University of Singapore.

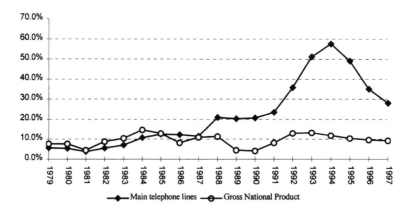

Fig. 13.1   Growth rates of GDP and main telephone lines
Sources: China Statistical Yearbook (various years) and *Yearbook* (various years).

infrastructure has been growing at an astonishing rate. Figure 13.1 shows
that there has been a sudden speed-up in telecommunications infrastructure development since the late 1980s. From 1991 to 1995, China installed
more than 73 million phone lines, more than all the rest of the developing
world combined. This has made China one of the largest telecommunications networks in the world. In the past decade, the growth of the telecommunications business has dwarfed the nation's already spectacular GDP
growth by a four-to-one margin. The telephone penetration rate (measured by number of telephone terminals per 100 persons) rose sharply
from 0.6 to 4.66 in a decade (fig. 13.2). In urban areas, the rate reached 17
percent by 1995. Many coastal cities, in particular, raised their telephone
penetration level from 2 to 3 percent to above 30 percent by 1995, in less
than a decade's time.[1]

Compared to other developing countries, to what extent has China been
an overachiever in building up its telecommunications infrastructure?
How did China manage to develop its telecommunications infrastructure
in leaps and hops while maintaining a centrally planned and monopolistic
regime? Has China achieved this in an efficient way? This paper tackles
these questions. Section 13.1 contrasts China's telecommunications statistics with those of other developing countries. Section 13.2 discusses the
incentive structure facing Chinese telecommunications enterprises. Section 13.3 examines government policies to mobilize capital and encourage
telecommunications investment. In section 13.4 I comment on the efficiency of China's investment in telecommunications and try to identify

1. The statistics in this paper, if not otherwise noted, are from *Yearbook of China Transportation and Communications,* hereafter *Yearbook* (various years).

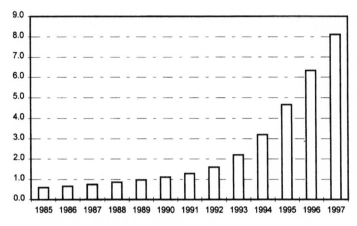

Fig. 13.2   Telephone terminals per 100 residents
Source: Yearbook (various years).

the factors at work. In the concluding section I speculate about the impact of the development experience on Beijing's future industrial and trade policy toward domestic and foreign competition, in particular, its stance on issues related to China's World Trade Organization membership.

13.1   A Leap Forward in Infrastructure Buildup

The current phase of hyper economic growth in China started around the end of the 1970s when the country embarked on market-oriented reform. In 1982, Beijing announced an ambitious plan to modernize the economy and quadruple the nation's annual gross output within two decades, by the year 2000. Concerned about the economy's weakness in infrastructure and technology, this plan highlighted three "strategic foci" for development. One was energy and transportation, the second was agriculture, and the third was education and science. Economic reform was instrumental in raising efficiency and restructuring the economy for further growth (*Documents* 1982).

Like other infrastructure services, telecommunications was one of the worst bottlenecks in the economy when the aforementioned plan was launched. The Centre for Economic and Technological Development of the MPT did research based on econometric modeling showing that the marginal contribution to the national economy brought by adding one dollar of investment in information resources was 15.8 times that brought by investment in physical resources (Yang 1991). The center used data from twenty-nine countries to regress telephone line density on factors such as per capita GNP, average educational level, and relative size of

Table 13.1   **Telecommunications Infrastructure: Targets Hit**

Sixth Five-Year Plan: 1981–85	Planned for 1985	Achieved by 1985
Urban switchboard capacity (lines)	2.7 million	3.37 million
Long-distance phone lines	28,011	37,551
Telephone terminals per 100 residents (up from 0.43 in 1980)	n.a.	0.6
Average annual growth rate of postal and telecommunications turnover (%)	5.0	9.8

Seventh Five-Year Plan: 1986–90	Planned for 1990	Achieved by 1990
Urban switchboard capacity (lines)	6.35 million	8.26 million
Long-distance phone lines	109,615	112,437
Telephone terminals per 100 residents	n.a.	1.11
Average annual growth rate of postal and telecommunications turnover (%)	11.05	22.5

Eighth Five-Year Plan: 1991–95	Planned for 1995	Achieved by 1995
Urban switchboard capacity (lines)	18 million	54.56 million
Long-distance phone lines	350,000	735,545
Telephone terminals per 100 residents	Above 2.0	4.66
Average annual growth rate of postal and telecommunications turnover (%)	20	35.1

Sources: China Statistical Yearbook (various years), *Yearbook* (various years), MPT Planning Department (1987, 1993, 1996), and Liu S. (1992).

service industries. The regression result was compared with China's relevant data, and it was concluded that only half of the social demand for telecommunications was met in the 1980s.

To safeguard the national economic plan, the MPT in 1983 proposed to increase the number of telephone terminals tenfold by the year 2000. Meanwhile the telephone penetration rate was to reach 2.8 percent by the turn of the century (*Almanac of China's tertiary industry* 1993, 543).

With comfortable margins, the MPT successfully reached the targets set in the Sixth Five-Year Plan, for 1981–85 (see table 13.1). Compared to earlier decades, the growth of telecommunications infrastructure in this period was unprecedented. Increased fixed capital in these five years amounted to Rmb 4.2 billion, equivalent to two-thirds of the total increased fixed capital in the three decades from 1949 to 1980.[2] The investment generated 1.37 million lines of urban switchboard capacity, compared to a total increase of 1.69 million lines from the 1950s to the 1970s.

---

2. The official exchange rate in 1990 was US$1.00 = Rmb 4.78. After the Chinese currency (yuan or renminbi) was made partially convertible in 1994, the exchange rate was about US$1.00 = Rmb 8.6. Since then the Chinese currency has gradually appreciated against the U.S. dollar. As of 30 April 1997, the exchange rate was about US$1.00 = Rmb 8.29.

Notwithstanding that, growth of the telecommunications sector failed to beat overall economic growth during the first half of the 1980s (fig. 13.1).

Telecommunications infrastructure development sped up in the mid-1980s after the government introduced stimuli into the industry (see section 13.2 for details). The growth rate of main telephone lines was twice the rate of GDP growth from 1988 to 1991 and rose to above 30 percent after 1992.

Table 13.1 shows that the telecommunications sector has developed much faster than was planned by China's central planners. Again and again the explosive growth of the industry has turned government blueprints into poor forecasts. Take switchboard capacity, for example. For the Sixth Five-Year Plan, capacity built was 25 percent higher than what was planned. During the Seventh Plan period, the target was overshot by 30 percent. In 1995 capacity reached a level 200 percent higher than specified in the Eighth Plan!

With such astonishing growth, China has effectively caught up with the rest of the world in telecommunications infrastructure buildup. To evaluate this effect, we statistically estimated the correspondence between teledensity (defined as main telephone lines per 100 residents) and GNP per capita (see appendix B for details of the modeling) for low-income and middle-income countries. We then used the estimated models to forecast China's teledensity levels corresponding to the country's per capita GNP for the years 1987 and 1994. In 1987, China had a per capita GNP of US$290 and a teledensity figure of 0.3741, which was about 17 percent higher than its forecast level (0.3202). By 1994, however, with a per capita GNP of $530, China had reached a teledensity level of 2.2865, about 53 percent higher than the forecast level (table 13.2). The implication is that in 1987 China had a telecommunications infrastructure compatible with its income level. By 1994 the country had become more developed in telecommunications than in income level.

The figures in table 13.3 also show that China has become an overachiever among low-income countries in developing telecommunications infrastructure. The gap between China and the middle-income countries in teledensity is quickly being closed. Between 1984 and 1994, the quantity of China's main telephone lines grew at a compound annual rate of 25.7

Table 13.2   **China's Forecast Teledensity Compared with Actual Teledensity**

	1987	1994
Per capita GNP (US$)	290	530
Forecast teledensity	0.3202	1.4974
Actual teledensity	0.3741	2.2865
Gap (forecast compared to actual)	16.83% higher	52.70% higher

Source: Appendix B.

Table 13.3   Catching Up in Teledensity

Country	Teledensity	Compared to China's Teledensity
1987		
China	0.3741	
Low-income country average	0.2911	22.2% lower
Middle-income country average	5.2724	13.3 times higher
1994		
China	2.2865	
Low-income country average	1.6040	29.8% lower
Middle-income country average	13.4885	4.9 times higher

Sources: Yearbook (1991, 1996) and ITU (1995a).

Note: According to the World Bank classification, countries with per capita GNP below US$500 in 1987 or with per capita GNP below US$750 in 1994 are low-income countries. The per capita GNP range for middle-income countries is US$500–$6,000 for the year 1987, while the range is US$750–$8,500 for the year 1994.

percent, the highest in the world (ITU 1995b). In comparison, the average growth rate for low-income countries was 17.4 percent, and the world average was 5.2 percent. In 1995, China's main telephone lines increased by another 49 percent. While China's population increased almost 13 million in that year, the country's teledensity rose from 2.2865 to 3.3607 lines per 100 residents.

13.2   Incentives Inside the State Monopoly

China's telecommunications sector took off with a series of fundamental institutional changes and strong centrally planned initiatives during the 1980s and early 1990s. These developments fundamentally changed the incentive structure of telecommunications enterprises and their business environment.

In the Mao era (the 1950s to the 1970s), the telecommunications infrastructure received low priority in the heavy-industry-oriented development plans. The telecommunications sector was seen purely as a tool to serve administrative needs. Its "nonprofit feature" was reflected in the fact that the state-owned monopoly was in the red eight out of ten years in the 1970s (fig. 13.3). Telecommunications expenses were classified as "nonproductive" and often subject to cuts during hard times. Subscribing to a residential telephone line used to be an exclusive political privilege reserved for high-ranking officials. The state-owned telecommunications system was semimilitary and had a rigid administrative structure (Yang 1991; Gao 1991).

When China started its economic modernization program in the late 1970s, the telecommunications sector was a visible bottleneck in the econ-

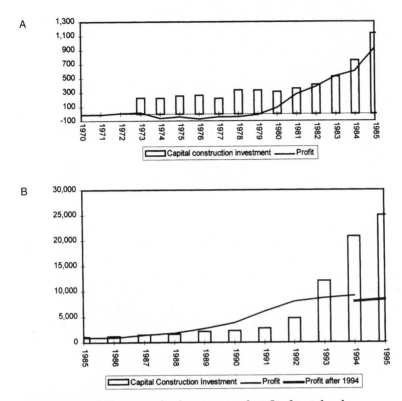

Fig. 13.3   Capital construction investment and profit of postal and telecommunications enterprises, 1970–85 (A) and 1985–95 (B)
Sources: China Statistical Yearbook (various years) and *Yearbook* (1996).
Note: "Profit" refers to pretax profit. The 1994 tax reform changed sales-related taxes.

omy. This caused serious concern to policymakers. In an instruction issued in 1984, the State Council acknowledged that the sector was "seriously backward" and there existed a "remarkable gap between supply and demand" (*Yearbook* 1986, 243). The government introduced a series of reforms to rectify the problem starting in the late 1970s.

13.2.1   Organizational Revamp

The first step was to restructure the formerly semimilitary administration in the MPT system. The Ministry of Posts and Telecommunications is the functional organ of the State Council responsible for nationwide postal and telecommunications services. The prereform system was highly centralized with little autonomy and financial accountability at the local enterprise level. All enterprise revenues were handed over to the authorities along the administrative hierarchy. Expenses were claimed from higher authorities in the hierarchy. The MPT centrally allocated nationwide investment. During the chaotic Cultural Revolution (1966–76), the MPT was dissolved in 1969 and the telecommunications sector was put under the regional military administrations. When the MPT was restored in 1973, it was not able to immediately regain centralized control of the national postal and telecommunications network. From 1973 to 1979, the governments at the levels of province, municipality, and prefecture had actual control over the planning for the postal and telecommunications business in their domains. This fragmented administrative structure caused many coordination problems in the industry (MPT 1986, 342).

In 1979, the State Council issued a directive to make the MPT the dominant central planner of nationwide postal and telecommunications development. Local postal and telecommunications enterprises (PTEs) were put under the "dual leadership" of provincial governments and the MPT, with the latter the main decision maker. Meanwhile, administration of daily business operations was to be decentralized with the introduction of primary financial accountability at the local level. As stipulated by the directive, in this sector government administration and business management should be separated. The postal business and the telecommunications business should also be separately administered. Enterprises should have their own accounts and should be made financially independent.[3]

In line with the above principles, local postal and telecommunications administrations (PTAs) were set up at the provincial level under the dual leadership of the MPT and the provincial governments. From 1983 to 1985, the MPT introduced a new accounting system, known as "enterprise own revenue," to define an elaborate methodology for calculating the income of an individual PTE (Guo and Xu 1992; Xu 1996). By the mid-1980s, all the PTEs had built their independent accounts and started to operate on a system of contractual responsibility in which their earnings were linked to their business performance.[4]

Since then, the administrative structure of China's telecommunications sector has been basically a vertically organized hierarchy. The national ministry at the top is responsible for overall planning and management of the industry. It controls international and interprovincial communications. It also sets and enforces technical standards and formulates key policies and plans. At the provincial level, the PTAs perform a similar role within the province. Below them are hundreds of municipal and prefecture postal and telecommunications bureaus (PTBs). Next, more than 2,000 county-

---

3. In Chinese: "Zheng qi fen kai, you dian fen ying, qiye hesuan, zi ji ying kui" (Gao 1991).
4. The accounting system for long-distance service commenced in 1985 with a simple record of the firm's long-distance revenue and operation costs. Since telecommunications service is a two-way exchange, the increase of real business revenue at one location may not necessarily reflect the growth of service quantity provided by the firm at that location. Therefore, the system was adjusted and improved in 1988 on a concept of network revenue (Lu 1994).

level PTEs operate local service networks in the county capitals and extend lines into the surrounding rural areas. Below them are tens of thousands of branch offices operating exchanges at the village level. There are also many private branch exchanges (PBXs) owned and operated by work units and rural villages (Mueller and Tan 1997).

The MPT system underwent a deeper revamp in 1988 amid a major state enterprise reform initiative taking place nationwide (Mueller and Tan 1997). Beijing announced the "sixteen-character policy" for telecommunications infrastructure development. The policy was summarized by sixteen Chinese characters,[5] which outline four principles:

Overall planning of industrial development should be unified under the MPT.

Ministerial administration should be coordinated with regional authorities.

Responsibilities should be defined and shared among different administrative levels.

Construction of infrastructure should mobilize resources from all concerned.

Following these principles, the MPT granted its national manufacturing, construction, and purchasing departments the status of separate legal entities or greater independence in financial accounting and human resource management. Meanwhile the MPT set up the Directorate General of Telecommunications (DGT) and the Directorate General of Posts (DGP) to incorporate business enterprise functions. The DGT is now known as China Telecom, which comprises twenty-nine provincial PTAs, all of which offer local and long-distance services. The PTAs in Beijing, Shanghai, and Guangdong also offer international services. The MPT itself handles regulatory matters through its Department of Policy and Regulation. Its other governmental functions were distributed among its Telecommunications Administration Department, the Department of Science and Technology, and the Department of Finance.

This was an important step toward complete separation between government administration and business management in the industry. In most areas, however, the local PTB is a combined government branch and business company. Until recent years, at the city and county level the local PTBs in some provinces did not even have business licenses, not to mention the status of legal persons. The definition of "enterprise" used to be very blurred in the postal and telecommunications industries (Xiao 1992). In 1995, the MPT's China Telecom formally registered with the government for the first time as an enterprise legal person (*Yearbook* 1996, 234).

---

5. In Chinese: "Tong chou guihua, tiao kuai jiehe, fen ceng fu ze, lianhe jianshe."

Nowadays most PTEs are still in the process of "corporatization" to restructure themselves into independent accounting entities that conform with China's Corporation Law (Li 1996).

13.2.2   Financial Stimuli

In parallel with organizational reforms, various financial stimuli came to promote infrastructure development and industrial performance. Traditionally, the MPT centrally controlled the pricing of most services, which included monthly rent and communications charges. The tariff policy before the 1980s was to underprice telephone services. Upward adjustment of rates was rare. Due to the underpriced rates, before 1980 the postal and telecommunications sector was in the red for more than ten years.

In October 1984, the State Council stipulated a "six-point instruction" to give priority to postal and telecommunications development. In this document, the government gave the green light to the MPT to adjust its service rates (State Council 1986, 243). During the period 1986–90, the MPT made adjustments to a wide range of telecommunications service rates. Consequently, the rate of capital return in the industry increased from 9 percent in 1986 to 17 percent in 1990, somewhat higher than the average rate of capital return for all industries. According to the World Bank, the rate of return of China's telecommunications industry in 1989, adjusted for accounting differentials, was equivalent to 12 percent by Western business standards (Ma 1992). Under the existing price structure, the rate of return is lower for local (intracity) services and higher for long-distance and international services.[6] At the end of 1990, intracity telephone rates were widely adjusted. The ministry set a price cap according to local telephone companies' average costs with a markup for profit. Local telecommunications companies were authorized to set their own intracity rates not exceeding the cap, subject to the approval of the local government's price control authorities (Sun 1992).

A pivotal stimulus for building up telecommunications infrastructure at the local level was the authorization of local telephone companies to determine and charge cost-based line installation fees. In 1980, the central government authorized PTAs to collect installation fees within ranges set by the MPT. For commercial phone lines, the installation fee ranged between Rmb 1,000 and Rmb 2,000 per terminal. For residential users, the charge was between Rmb 300 and Rmb 500 (Ministry of Finance 1986, 344–45). In 1990, the MPT adjusted its guidelines for telephone installation fees. The installation fee charges have since then been based on line

6. An MPT source disclosed that in 1993 the profit margin on local service was only 2 to 3 percent, while the margin on long-distance calls was 25 percent and on international calls 75 percent (Mueller and Tan 1997, 41).

connection costs. The decision making regarding installation charges has been decentralized to the local level. In the early 1990s, the installation charges varied from around Rmb 2,000 to more than Rmb 5,000 per line (Wu 1992). In comparison, the average annual wage in China was only Rmb 2,140 in 1990.

Along with the above fee adjustments, the management of moneys collected was organized in a system of "special funding accounts." The source (credit) side of these accounts consists of "earmarked grants" from the government and "specialized funds," which are collected by the enterprises themselves. The proportion of government grants in postal and telecommunications investment declined sharply from 59 percent in 1980 to 29 percent in 1981. It continued to drop, reaching 10 percent in 1989. The use (liability) side of these accounts divides funds into specialized purposes such as line maintenance and upgrading, new technology development, and local telephone line construction and connection. The system ensured that the funds collected (such as installation fees) were used solely for their earmarked purposes (such as line construction; *Yearbook* 1990, 270–71).

As for service operation, the accounting reform in the mid-1980s provided the basis to contract performance responsibilities to enterprise managers and employees. A PTE's own revenue is accounted as

$$EOR = \sum P_i Q_i \cdot \beta + \Delta R \cdot \gamma + LR,$$

where *EOR* is enterprise own revenue, Q_i is the firm's *i*th (interregional) service output, P_i is the unified national accounting rate, β is the regional cost coefficient, and *LR* refers to local (intracity) telephone revenue and other miscellaneous income. The item ΔR is the increased operating revenue over the previous year's basis. The item γ is a uniform "retaining ratio," which was set at 20 percent in 1989 (MPT 1989a, 617). The retaining ratio acts as an extra factor to encourage the enterprise to increase revenues.

In the early 1990s, the accounting rate was calculated according to 1987's average cost and profit tax rate in the industry. A catalog issued by the MPT lists the accounting rates of more than 140 service products. The regional cost coefficient β was estimated by regressing thirty-two provincial telecommunications companies' real costs against seven factors such as per capita income, weather conditions, telecommunications infrastructure investment, and the like (Zhang 1991). Net contributing PTEs have a coefficient $\beta < 1$ while the net receiving PTBs have a $\beta > 1$.

Based on the above formula, the ministry contracted performance responsibilities to the local PTEs. By 1995, most PTEs had completed three contracting periods, namely, 1985–88, 1989–91, and 1992–95. The more recent contracts included supplementary evaluative criteria such as communications quality and capital investment. Beginning in 1991, some contracts have included terms of "asset responsibility," which define managers' responsibility for maintaining and improving the state assets in their charge (Liu Z. 1992).

An important incentive incorporated in these contracts was to link PTBs wage fund increases to their service output increases. Starting in 1988, PTBs' wage fund increases were calculated as

$$\Delta W = s(0.5 \cdot G + 0.5 \cdot g) \cdot W,$$

where g is the PTB service quantity growth rate, G is the MPT service quantity growth rate, W is the previous year's total wage, and s is a "floating ratio coefficient," which is 0.7 for each PTB and 0.8 for all PTBs (MPT 1989b, 614–15). The weight of PTB service quantity growth increased to 60 percent in 1993 and further increased to 70 percent in 1994. The rationale for this arrangement is that the local company's service not only contributes to its own revenue but also to the revenue of the entire network. In 1994, all quantity growth rates in the formula were replaced by revenue growth rates (*Yearbook* 1995, 247).

How much employees and managers can actually get paid from the wage fund depends on evaluation of four aspects of performance with different weights of marking: communications quality (40 marks), communications quantity (20 marks), profit level (20 marks), and labor productivity (20 marks). If, for instance, the total evaluation is below 85 marks, 1 percent will be deducted from the wage fund increase. If communications quantity increases 5 to 10 percent over the previous year, the wage fund will get an additional percentage point of increase. In 1994, some other factors, including asset value and wage-profit ratio, were added to the marking in order to encourage greater efficiency.

13.2.3   Privileged Status

To facilitate telecommunications development, a policy of "three 90 percent" was developed upon the State Council's "six-point instruction" of 1984 (Gao 1991; Wu and Zhang 1992). According to this policy:

Ninety percent of profit was to be retained by the MPT (in other words, the tax rate is 10 percent, well below the 55 percent tax rate for other industries).
Ninety percent of foreign exchange (hard currency) earnings were to be retained by the MPT.
Ninety percent of central government investment was not considered as repayable loans.

In addition, PTEs and PTBs might also enjoy favorable interest rates when they got loans from state banks (Luo 1992).

In 1994, China introduced a major tax reform aiming to unify corporate tax rates into an across-the-board 33 percent rate for all enterprises and to simplify the tax levy structure. Meanwhile, after a reform to unify foreign exchange rates and make Chinese currency convertible for current account transactions, enterprises benefit little from retaining their foreign exchange earnings. The preferential "three 90 percent" policy has since no longer been relevant (Luo 1996).

In summary, after delegation of greater management autonomy, the PTEs face an incentive structure that strongly encourages business expansion. All revenues from local (intracity) telephone services are kept by the PTEs. Their revenues from (interregional) services are determined by unified national accounting rates and a regional cost coefficient. On top of that, the PTB retains 20 percent of the increased operating revenue over the previous year's basis. For PTB employees and managers, the effective way to increase their wage fund is to increase the output or revenue of the enterprise and of the MPT's national network by generating more telecommunications traffic. Until some changes in 1995, the other factors of performance evaluation played only a secondary role in wage determination. Therefore, there have been strong incentives for output and revenue maximization.

When service prices and tariffs for long-distance telecommunications are set by the MPT and local rates and installation charges are capped, revenue maximization is equivalent to output maximization. Therefore, the PTEs must increase revenue by expanding quantity of sales. Given the low teledensity, strong and growing demand, and infrastructure bottleneck, China's telecommunications market has been a supply-constrained one until recently. The PTEs have no alternative but to make all-out efforts to increase their supply capacity by improving the local telecommunications infrastructure.

Meanwhile the system of special funding accounts (before 1993) separated the PTEs' capital expenses and operating expenses. Under the rigid specification of fund uses according to fund sources, once capital was raised, the marginal investment cost appeared to be zero or external to the PTEs. As long as the PTEs and PTBs could raise capital from the state, banks, or users, investment in telecommunications network capacity would be risk free. This made it rational for the PTEs and PTBs to raise as much capital as possible to invest in infrastructure buildup. Beginning in 1993, the capital account system replaced the special funding accounts to allow PTEs more freedom to manage infrastructure development funds.

The shortcomings of the incentive structure are obvious. It provided very little incentive for PTEs to economize on operating expenses and investment expenses. Nor did it give enough stimuli for firms to improve service quality and to introduce new service products. However, the structure did give a big push to the expansion of the telecommunications sector through infrastructure investment, which has also been supported by a series of external incentives.

13.3   External Incentives to Infrastructure Investment

According to the "sixteen-character policy," telecommunications development should "mobilize resources of all concerned in telecommunications infrastructure development." One important policy is called "mobilizing four resources together ("sige yiqi shang," in Chinese), namely, the resources of government fiscal expenditure, user contributions, enterprise finance, and domestic and foreign loans (Wu and Zhang 1992).

13.3.1   High Fees, Strong Demands

In 1980 the State Council adopted a policy of developing intracity telephone service with intracity telephone revenue. Since then, intracity telephone service revenue has been fully retained by the local company. On top of that, local telephone companies were authorized to charge installation fees. In 1990, they were allowed to determine the installation charge according to the full installation cost. Installation fee revenue became a major financial source of intracity telephone development (Gao 1991). Wu Jichuan, the minister of the MPT, estimated that in 1995 the revenue from installation fees collected from installing 15 million telephone terminals amounted to Rmb 45 billion. This revenue accounted for about half of the annual investment capital in 1995.[7] By this estimation, the average installation fee per telephone terminal was Rmb 3,000 in 1995. Relative to the country's per capita income, China's installation charge is the highest in the world. Some experts worried that the extraordinarily high installation fee could become an impediment to residential telephone development (Wu and Zhang 1992). When infrastructure is built, a slow increase in subscribers may lead to underutilization of network capacities and thus undermine network externalities (Hu 1996). Notwithstanding that, the high installation fee policy has successfully financed infrastructure investment for intracity telephone services.

A footnote to this success is the equally impressive privatization of residential phone service subscription. Telephone service is no longer only an administrative tool of the state, but rather has become a private good for business operation and household consumption. In 1991, of all residential phone subscribers, private ones accounted for 75 percent. In more than ten provinces and municipalities, residential phones accounted for more than one-third of all phones (Hong and Qian 1992). In 1995, more than 80 percent of the increase in telephone exchange capacity was for residential uses.[8]

7. Wu Jichuan, interview, *Yazhou Zhoukan* (International Chinese News Weekly), 19 May 1996, 58.
8. Wu Jichuan, interview, *Yazhou Zhoukan* (International Chinese News Weekly), 19 May 1996, 57–58.

13.3.2   Attracting Non-MPT Investors

According to the "sixteen-character policy," the State Council has clearly defined the division of responsibilities between the MPT and local government. The MPT should invest in equipment and machinery while local government should invest in cable and line construction (Gao 1991). Telecommunications infrastructure development was incorporated into provincial development plans. Most provincial legislative bodies have passed laws and regulations to define the division of responsibilities between the MPT and local governments (*Yearbook* 1992, 181).

Financing postal and telecommunications investment was largely decentralized in the late 1980s. The Seventh Five-Year Plan (1986–90) stipulated that intraprovince telecommunications projects should mainly rely on local financing. Institutions or individuals should be encouraged to contribute to infrastructure investment. Those who invested in telecommunications projects could benefit by receiving priority in being connected to the network and lower charges for telecommunications services. In rural areas, whoever invested in infrastructure facilities could manage and operate the local exchange (You 1987).

The multi-investor feature of joint venture projects called for well-defined property rights. In July 1993, all PTEs established the capital account system to replace the earlier system of special funding accounts. The new system ensures that a PTE can raise capital in various ways and behaves as a legal person who manages the invested capital (*Yearbook* 1994, 235). In 1994, the MPT specified two measures to reward non-MPT investors in trial joint ventures. One is fixed-rate remuneration, and the other is dividend distribution (MPT 1995b, 513).

13.3.3   State Support

One state policy to facilitate telecommunications investment is to allow the postal and telecommunications sector a faster pace of capital depreciation. The State Council's six-point instruction of 1984 promised to gradually raise the accounting capital depreciation of the postal and telecommunications sector to 7 percent (State Council 1986, 243). From 1980 to 1990, the government adjusted the capital depreciation rate upward three times (*Yearbook* 1990, 271). A new reform of the PTE accounting system in July 1993 again raised the capital depreciation rate.[9] In 1995, the gross fixed capital depreciation rate was as high as 16 percent. The capital depreciation amounted to Rmb 40 billion, accounting for more than 40 per-

---

9. The detailed deprecation scale is five to seven years for telecommunications equipment, six to eight years for power equipment, ten to fifteen years for communications cables, and thirty to forty years for buildings (*Yearbook* 1994, 235).

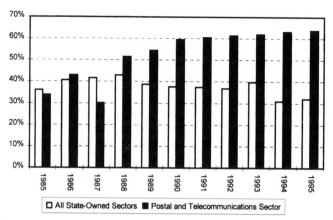

Fig. 13.4   Weight of technical upgrading and transformation: total fixed capital investment
Sources: China Statistical Yearbook (various years) and *Yearbook* (1991, 1996).

cent of total fixed capital investment.[10] Capital depreciation is the main source of technical upgrading and transformation (TUT) investment. The higher depreciation rate in the postal and telecommunications sector led to a higher than average weight of TUT investment in total fixed capital investment. Thanks to the policy, the weight of TUT investment has increased over the years in postal and telecommunications fixed capital investment (fig. 13.4).

To encourage telecommunications investment, imports of telecommunications equipment have received preferential tariff treatment. In 1985, for instance, the import tariff rate on automatic exchanges and telefax equipment was cut from 12.5 to 9 percent (*Almanac* 1986, 129). For projects involving foreign investment, import tariffs are usually exempted. In comparison, China's arithmetical average tariff rate was 39.9 percent before 1994. By 1996, the average tariff rate went down to 23 percent. Domestic producers of telecommunications equipment also enjoy better sales-related tax treatment, as shown in table 13.4.

In 1991 China introduced the "coordinating tax for directions of fixed capital investment," which is levied on indigenous enterprises. A zero tax rate applies to projects "urgently needed by the state." These projects include fixed capital investment in agriculture and water conservancy, the energy industry, transportation, postal and telecommunications, some important raw material industries, geological prospecting, certain medical projects, certain electronic and machinery projects, pollution control, urban public utilities, and some storage facilities. For those projects encour-

10. Wu Jichuan, interview, *Yazhou Zhoukan* (International Chinese News Weekly), 19 May 1996, 58.

Table 13.4   **Burden of Sales-Related Taxes of Industrial Enterprises by Sector (billion renminbi)**

Sector	Pretax Profit	Posttax Profit	Sales-Related Tax	Effective Rate (%)
	1990			
Heavy industry	102.891	34.684	68.207	7.59
Manufacturing	38.247	17.517	20.73	5.13
Special purpose equipment	3.195	1.557	1.638	5.44
Electronic and telecommunications	4.255	2.294	1.961	3.77
Instruments, meters, cultural and official machinery	1.166	0.592	0.574	5.69
National total	194.588	55.981	138.607	8.25
	1995			
Heavy industry	313.26	112.98	200.285	6.48
Manufacturing	110.94	42.60	68.34	4.79
Special purpose equipment	10.16	2.69	7.471	4.55
Electronic and telecommunications	18.50	11.68	6.819	2.81
Instruments, meters, cultural and official machinery	2.62	0.69	1.927	4.62
National total	505.03	163.49	341.54	6.45

Source: Lu (1997, 73–74).

aged by the state but constrained by energy supply and transportation facilities, the low 5 percent tax rate applies. For those projects inefficient in scale, using outmoded technologies, or making products already in excess supply, the state policy is to strictly control their development, and therefore the highest rate of 30 percent is applied.[11] All the other projects should be taxed at a rate of 15 percent (State Council 1992).

13.3.4   Foreign Investment but No Foreign Involvement

China's policy toward foreign investment in the telecommunications sector is twofold. On one hand, the government is keen to use foreign capital to develop the country's telecommunications industry. On the other hand, it bans foreign equity investment or direct operational control over ventures in China's telecommunications sector (MPT 1993, 455). Most foreign capital comes from government loans and loans by such international organizations as the World Bank, the Asian Development Bank (ADB), and the International Monetary Fund. There are also cases of borrowing of foreign businesses' export credit. Meanwhile, the manufacturing of telecommunications equipment has been open to foreign direct investment. In this field, Bell Shanghai and Shenda Telecom (in Shen-

11. Based on the same principle, the state has also promulgated a list of forbidden projects.

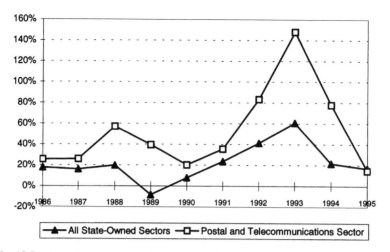

Fig. 13.5   Annual growth rate of fixed capital investment
Sources: China Statistical Yearbook (various years) and *Yearbook* (1991, 1996).

zhen) are the two earliest manufacturing joint ventures in China (Zhou 1991). The 1994 reform in foreign exchange management made Chinese currency virtually convertible for current account transactions and greatly reduced the exchange risk in using foreign capital.

Policies to mobilize capital for telecommunications infrastructure development have been very successful. Figure 13.5 shows that investment in the postal and telecommunications sector increased by leaps and bounds in the decade after 1984.[12] The growth was spectacular in the first half of the 1990s. Fixed capital investment in the sector during the Eighth Five-Year Plan period was twelve times that invested during the Seventh Five-Year Plan period (Wu 1996). According to the MPT, during the first half of the 1990s, investment in telecommunications infrastructure was mainly financed through three sources. One was installation fees collected from users, which accounted for 40 percent of the capital. The second was domestic and foreign government loans, accounting for about 30 percent of total capital. The remaining 30 percent came from PTEs' profits and capital depreciation (*Lianhe Zaobao* [United Mornings, Singapore], 8 April 1994, 23).

13.4   Efficiency of Infrastructure Buildup

An interesting issue is whether China's mammoth investment in the postal and telecommunications sector has increased supply capacity cost-

---

12. Investment in telecommunications accounts for about 80 percent of total fixed capital investment in the postal and telecommunications sector.

effectively. To examine this issue, we estimate a regression model to evaluate the cost-effectiveness of telecommunications investment to increase telephone lines in the Asia-Pacific region during the period 1988–94 (see appendix C for technical details). The model is used to forecast China's main telephone line increase during the same period based on official statistics of investment in the postal and telecommunications sector. The forecast figures are compared with real figures of main telephone line increase to evaluate investment efficiency.

The forecast figures in the upper panel of table 13.5 are based on U.S.-dollar-denominated (deflated) investment figures published by the International Telecommunication Union (see appendixes A and C for a definition). The results show that China's telecommunications investment has been surprisingly cost-effective. It has increased telephone lines three times more than the forecast figures. Because of the drastic devaluation in the official exchange rate of the Chinese currency from U.S.$1.00 = Rmb 3.72 in 1987 to Rmb 8.62 in 1994, we reestimated the figures using Rmb-denominated figures published by the Chinese authorities. After being deflated by China's retail price inflation rates, these figures were converted into U.S. dollars using the exchange rate of 1987. The resulting figures in the lower panel of table 13.5 still show that China's investment has been on average two times more effective in increasing telephone lines than forecast.

For comparison, table 13.6 lists the average percentage differences between the forecast line increase and the actual line increase for other countries and regions. China's extraordinary performance in telecommunications investment is more evident by this comparison. Of the seventeen countries and regions, the actual figures of five are within about ±30 percent of the forecast values. Three see their actual figures about 55 to 75 percent below forecast values. Five managed to achieve line increases more than 50 percent higher than forecast levels. The highest is Iran, whose line increase was 1.1 times higher than the forecast level. This achievement, however, still appears to have been far below the Chinese performance.

The impact of statistical discrepancy on the reliability of these results is uncertain. All investment figures (including China's) used in this model include investment in land and buildings. On one hand, Chinese statistics may undervalue land cost since the accounting procedure only records the official compensation price if the land is acquired from the original users. Since the property market was underdeveloped until the early 1990s, the official valuation of the land compensation rate might be far from realistic.[13] It is noteworthy that Chinese telecommunications investment has been intense in coastal cities, where actual land costs are no longer cheap

---

13. Since July 1993, China's PTEs have adopted international standards in accounting assets and liabilities (*Yearbook* 1993, 234–35). How effective the change has been in improving asset accounting remains an unresolved issue.

Table 13.5   China's Forecast Main Telephone Line Increases Compared with Actual Line Increases (thousand)

	1988	1989	1990	1991	1992	1993	1994	1995	Average
	Based on Fixed U.S. Dollar Values and Nominal Exchange Rate								
Lines	4,727.00	5,680.40	6,850.30	8,450.60	11,469.1	14,074.0	27,230.00	40,706.00	
Forecast line increase	318.45	399.96	525.40	471.31	631.49	1,171.25	2,882.98	3,689.11	
Actual line increase	730.00	953.40	1,169.90	1,600.30	3,018.50	2,604.90	13,156.00	13,476.00	
Percentage difference	129	138	123	240	378	122	356	265	219
	Based on Renminbi Values Deflated by China's Price Index and Fixed Exchange Rates								
Forecast line increase	318.64	339.51	405.44	481.54	715.90	1,321.01	3,027.32	4,846.88	
Actual line increase	730.00	953.40	1,169.90	1,600.30	3,018.50	2,604.90	13,156.00	13,476.00	
Percentage difference	129	181	189	232	322	97	335	178	208

Note: The forecast in the upper panel is made on the investment figures published by the International Telecommunication Union, deflated by the U.S. producer price index. The forecast in the lower panel is made on the investment figures published in the *Yearbook of China Transportation and Communications*. The investment figures are first deflated by China's price index and then converted to U.S. dollars based on the 1987 exchange rate (US$1.00 = Rmb 3.72).

Table 13.6   Average Percentage Difference between Forecast Main Telephone Line Increases and Actual Line Increases, 1987–94

Country	Average Percentage Difference	Teledensity 1987	Teledensity 1994	Digitization 1987	Digitization 1994
Australia	−74.20	43	50	26[a]	51
New Caledonia	−59.43	16	23	80[a]	100
New Zealand	−58.21	41	47	37	98
Bahrain	−50.68	18	25	49	100
Taiwan, China	−44.59	31	40	31[a]	84
Singapore	−36.62	33	47	24	100
Israel	−34.16	32	39	22	81
Macau	−28.63	18	36	80	100
Hong Kong	−12.50	35	54	61[b]	100
Oman	10.94	4	8	44[a]	100
Korea (Rep.)	23.51	20	40	14	59
Indonesia	39.30	0.4	1.3	36[a]	92
United Arab Emirates	54.78	18	33	100[a]	100
Malaysia	64.84	7	15	78[a]	93
India	72.16	0.4	1.1	30[a]	70
Sri Lanka	104.38	0.6	1.0	67[a]	96
Iran	110.77	3	7	13[a]	49

Source: Appendix C.

[a] 1990 or 1991 data.

[b] 1989 data.

by international standards. On the other hand, however, China's statistics for investment costs could be biased upward because they refer to total investment in both the postal sector and the telecommunications sector. Meanwhile, we have used the official exchange rate in 1987 to convert the renminbi into U.S. dollars to get the results in the lower panel of table 13.5. This exchange rate (US$1.00 = Rmb 3.72) largely overvalued the renminbi and hence might again have inflated capital costs.

A plausible factor behind the apparently higher investment effectiveness in China might be low labor cost. Both low land cost and low labor cost in many Chinese regions may have saved the Chinese PTEs some capital costs. However, since the late 1980s labor costs in the coastal areas have been escalating rapidly with the standard of living. On top of that, our model includes teledensity as an independent variable, which is highly correlated with per capita GNP (see appendix B). This feature of the modeling has already largely controlled for the impact of low labor cost and land cost due to underdevelopment.

Another possible factor may be that China's population density data are averaged over the entire nation while most new telephone lines were laid in coastal urban areas, where the population density is much higher. Given the relatively small estimated value of the population density vari-

Table 13.7   Percentage of Telephone Lines Connected to Digital Exchanges, 1994

Country/Region	Percentage
United States	69.00
Europe	52.86
Africa	67.75
Latin America	81.09
Asia-Pacific region	72.43
Japan	75.00
Taiwan	83.79
China	97.2
Singapore and Hong Kong	100

Source: ITU (1995a).

able's coefficient, however, this factor may only play a secondary role if China's investment effectiveness has been overestimated.

Being a "late starter" in telecommunications infrastructure development may have been a favorable factor. The inclusion of teledensity in the model has only partly taken care of this factor. In table 13.6, we note that all eight overachievers had low teledensities (≤ 20) in 1987 and either raised their digitization rate considerably during the period or kept a high digitization rate all through.

As described in section 13.3, Beijing has followed a policy of giving the green light to telecommunications equipment imports and lightening the tax burden on domestic equipment manufacturers. Thanks to this state policy, China's telecommunications sector has faced low barriers to equipment trade and competitive domestic equipment supply. Between 1988 and 1993, while China's main telephone lines grew at a compound annual rate of 19.9 percent, its telecommunications equipment imports grew at a compound rate of 26.6 percent.[14] Telecommunications investors, therefore, enjoyed the advantages of being able to employ state-of-the-art technologies at good prices.

In the earlier analysis of the PTE incentive structure, we noted that the PTEs behaved like output or revenue maximizers who did all they could to expand supply capacity. Investment costs and risks involving the purchase of new and expensive equipment were minimal or external to them. All this might have encouraged them to employ and import whatever technology would be most effective and efficient in increasing supply capacity (number of main lines). Table 13.7 shows that China's telecommunications network is already at the forefront compared to other countries.

The last but not the least factor in cost-effectiveness could be the MPT's ability to enforce unified planning in China's telecommunications develop-

14. Calculated according to ITU (1995a, 1995b).

ment. Despite some reports of connection problems between the MPT's public network and private networks developed by non-MPT departments, China's public network has been built on the unified MPT standard. This may have helped China avoid costs arising from incompatibility of different network standards.

13.5   Concluding Remarks

From the above discussion, we can conclude that the speedy buildup of China's telecommunications infrastructure has been a market-oriented development with strong state initiatives. China's central planners played a pivotal role in introducing a variety of innovative measures to push the industry onto the takeoff track. Meanwhile, local driving forces riding on soaring market demand have repeatedly overshot centrally planned targets. Financial accountability of enterprises, prices and fees reflecting costs and scarcity, and government support with local initiatives, all have contributed to the spectacular growth of the telecommunications business. On top of these factors, the unique incentive structure for PTEs and PTBs has provided great stimuli to supply capacity expansion.

Looking into the future, we are interested in whether and how long China will keep this momentum in telecommunications infrastructure buildup. On the demand side, according to a study by an MPT research institute, in the late 1980s every dollar of investment in telephony service could increase national output by $6.78. The 6.78 output-input ratio is much higher than Japan's 2.5 ratio and India's 4.0 ratio (You 1987). China's policymakers and central planners are well aware of the importance of telecommunications to modern economic development. China's Ninth Five-Year Plan (1996–2000) aims to triple telecommunications infrastructure capacity in five years (table 13.8). The MPT plans to keep the telecommunications sector growing twice as fast as the national economy until the year 2010.

Table 13.8   **Main Telecommunications Targets of China's Ninth Five-Year Plan: 1996–2000**

Ninth Five-Year Plan: 1996–2000	Planned for 2000	Achieved in 1995
Urban switchboard capacity (lines)	150 million	54.56 million
Long-distance phone lines	2,800,000	735,545
Main telephone lines	123 million	44 million
Mobile phone lines	18 million	3.6 million
Telephone terminals per 100 residents	National: 10	4.66
	Urban: 30–40	
Average annual growth rate of postal and		
telecommunications turnover (%)	20	35.1 in 1991–95

Source: Zhang (1996).

Uncertainty may arise in capital financing. The Economist Intelligence Unit in Hong Kong has estimated that the telecommunications targets set in the Ninth Five-Year Plan would require U.S.$60 to $80 billion to fulfill. In comparison, a total of $29 billion was invested in telecommunications infrastructure between 1991 and 1995 (EIU 1997). During the period 1991–95, foreign capital accounted for about 20 percent of the MPT's total telecommunications investment. The main sources were supplier credits, commercial investment, government soft loans, and international loans from the World Bank and the ADB. The OECD countries reached an agreement in 1993 to cut government soft loans to telecommunications projects in China. The World Bank and the ADB, too, will gradually eliminate loans to telecommunications projects in China (Mueller and Tan 1997, 108). If China continues to ban foreign equity investment and forbid direct foreign operational control, it must find innovative ways to raise capital. One such way is to raise capital in overseas stock markets. For instance, in October 1997, China Telecom (Hong Kong) launched the biggest initial public offering in Hong Kong Stock Market history to raise HK$540 to $718 billion (*Business Times* [Singapore], 14 October 1997, 1).

On the supply side, the ongoing corporatization of PTEs and the development of plural ownership of asset investment reinforce the momentum of infrastructure development. As discussed earlier, the incentive structure for PTEs strongly encourages revenue maximization and business expansion. In view of the shortcomings of this incentive structure, the MPT reformed the wage fund formula in 1995. The new formula links 30 percent of wage increases to national network revenue, 50 percent to the enterprise's per employee operating revenue, and 20 percent to national network profit and the enterprise's cost-revenue ratio. The new formula is intended to restrain enterprises from hiring new staff and to encourage cost savings (*Yearbook* 1996, 235). Since revenue increase is still the dominant factor in wage determination, the incentive structure will continue to be proexpansion.

When infrastructure development goes into less densely populated areas, the cost per line must go up. In this regard, competition may play a crucial role in containing the cost rise by bringing in new technologies.

In recent years, China has tasted the benefits of competition, albeit limited, in the telecommunications market. Starting around 1988–89, the government deregulated some parts of the telecommunications industry. The reform in 1988 shifted more decision-making authority regarding procurement, operations, network development, and financing from MPT headquarters to municipal and county PTEs. In 1989, the MPT instructed all province-level PTAs to set up telecommunications regulatory bodies. Meanwhile, the introduction of terminal equipment licensing under the MPT largely deregulated the terminal equipment used by customers of the network (*Yearbook* 1996, 232). As a result, the PTEs could choose among

Table 13.9   **Main Telephone Lines, Mobile Phones, and Pager Subscribers (thousand)**

Year	Main Line	Mobile Phone	Pager
1990	6,850	18	437
1991	8,451	48	874
1992	11,469	117	2,220
1993	17,332	638	5,614
1994	27,295	1,568	10,330
1995	40,706	3,629	17,392
1996	54,950	6,850	25,360
1997	70,310	13,240	29,690

Source: Yearbook (various years).

competing domestic and even foreign equipment suppliers. The purchasing and production of network equipment became highly competitive. This will continue to work together with low trade barriers to equipment imports to constrain investment cost increases.

Non-MPT suppliers of value-added services, mobile telephone services, and satellite communications services emerged and prevailed in many regions during the early 1990s. In 1993 the State Council formally deregulated the mobile telephone service market and very small aperture terminal communications by authorizing the MPT to license these service suppliers (State Council 1994, 468–69). By the end of 1995, the MPT had licensed 2,136 mobile telephone service suppliers and 68 interprovince telecommunications service providers (*Yearbook* 1996, 231–32). Thanks to competition in this market section, China has made great progress in developing its mobile telephone business (table 13.9).

In 1993, the State Council made a landmark decision to award a basic telecommunications license to China United Telecom (or Unicom, Beijing; MPT 1995a, 512). It was set up by the Ministry of Electronic Industries, the Ministry of Railways, the Ministry of Electric Power, and thirteen major companies. The carrier intends to compete with the MPT in the long-distance and international services market. Another player is Ji Tong Communications Co. Ltd. (Beijing), a value-added network (VAN) operator set up by the State Economic and Trade Commission. Its charter is to build a nationwide backbone linking the networks belonging to government ministries, universities, and research and state-owned organizations. It also is supposed to offer VAN services to government departments and the private sector. Both new players are shareholder based but largely state owned and controlled.

In 1994, Beijing announced the "eight policies of telecommunications development" (*Yearbook* 1995, 225), which outlined China's strategies of developing the sector:

1. Giving priority and policy support to the telecommunications sector
2. Planning network and service development centrally
3. Focusing on the construction of a unified nationwide public network
4. Licensing value-added and mobile telecommunications services; deregulating equipment manufacturing market; open tender for network projects
5. Requiring independent accounting and hierarchical administration for PTEs; linking employee rewards to enterprise performance
6. Supporting PTEs to raise capital from various ways and collect installation fees
7. Promoting network modernization and human resource development
8. Importing foreign equipment and technology and utilizing foreign fund sources

In these policies, one can observe a gradual approach toward a less regulated and less monopolized market. The future of China's telecommunications business lies in a new telecommunications law, which is being drafted by the MPT. As pointed out by Liu Cai, director general of policy and regulation of the MPT, Chinese telecommunications development is hampered by outmoded legal and regulatory constraints (China's MPT director general 1996). According to him, the legislation will address the following objectives:

Maintaining the current pace of business expansion, focusing on telecommunications' role as a multiplier of economic growth
Decentralizing the present structure of telecommunications enterprises
Assuring availability of advanced technology, both from foreign sources and expanded domestic R&D facilities
Strengthening competition among foreign and domestic suppliers of network equipment, including the possible introduction of open bidding
Encouraging improvements in financing telecommunications expansion, including changes in user-pricing patterns

Regulatory reform at the central government level will endorse the reform process initiated in the 1980s by legally defining what Liu called "the three separations." They are (1) separating the MPT's postal and telecommunications units, (2) separating the MPT's regulatory and operational functions, and (3) separating telecommunications manufacturing functions from service obligations. Therefore, the MPT will be set up as solely a regulatory body and China Telecom as an operational body. The two organizations will be completely separate. Compatible with the new law, the Ministry of Electronic Industries is likely to be transformed into a trade association. More network development decisions will be devolved to provincial and municipal administrations. The legislation is expected to be submitted to China's State Council for approval in 1997. These coming changes will surely be a boost to domestic competition in the telecommunications sector.

As for letting foreign companies get involved in China's telecommunications sector, the MPT still believes conditions are not yet ripe. It has set the year 2010 as the earliest date for a possible change in the policy banning foreign involvement and direct investment stakes. A major argument for maintaining the policy is that "the development of the telecommunications sector is still dictated largely by government policy rather than market economics, and therefore unsuitable for foreign involvement."[15] The past success of rapid development has obviously become a subtle excuse for not opening the door sooner.

The existing policy toward foreign equity investors conflicts with China's bid to join the World Trade Organization (WTO). The WTO's acceptance of China will hinge on whether China agrees on terms that mandate opening up its service sectors, including the telecommunications market. If China intends to commit itself to meeting the standards set in the WTO's hard-won Global Telecommunications Pact, the new telecommunications legislation must allow more room for reform than that suggested by "the three separations."

It remains a question whether China is ready to play by the WTO rules by opening the telecommunications sector to foreign competitors. China's remarkable success in telecommunications development so far contributes to policymakers' reluctance to allow foreign equity investment in this lucrative industry. Given its successful experience in the past decade, China may well keep going on its own way to building a world-class telecommunications infrastructure.

---

15. Wu Jichuan, statement reported by AFP, *Straits Times* (Singapore), 27 August 1997, 45.

Appendix A

Table 13A.1   **Basic Statistics of China's Telecommunications Industry, 1994**

Statistic	China	Asia	World
Financial data, 1992 (U.S.$)			
Income[a] per main telephone line	228.83	889.97	1,253.52
Expense[b] per main telephone line	205.07	787.82	834.69
Investment[c] per main telephone line	246.32	284.00	225.10
Tariff structure for residential users, 1994 (U.S.$)			
Installation charges	540.00	108.40	132.36
Monthly subscription	4.00	5.67	6.30
Local call rate (three minutes)	0.03	0.08	0.09
Residential subscription tariff as percentage of			
per capita GNP	0.8	1.4–162.8	0.2–162.8
Basic quantity data, 1994			
Main lines per 100 residents	2.29 (3.36)[d]	4.79	11.57
Long-distance calls per main line[e]	249.0[d]	35.45 (India)	330.41 (Brazil)
Outgoing international traffic (minutes			
per subscriber)	43.0	56.8	85.0
Waiting time for subscription[f] (years)	0.3	1.1	1.4
Satisfied demand[g]	94.4	91.6	93.4
Completion rate (long distance; %)	45		
Completion rate (local; %)	58		

Sources: ITU (1995a, 1995b) and *Yearbook* (various years).

Note: U.S. dollar figures are reached by applying the average annual exchange rate to the figure reported in national currency.

[a]Income consists of all telecommunications revenue earned during the financial year under review, including income from subscribers and other national and foreign telecommunications administrations after deduction of payment to other administrations or organizations for outgoing telecommunications traffic. It does not include moneys received by way of loans or moneys received from refundable subscribers' contributions or deposits.

[b]Expense refers to expenditure other than investments. It includes operational expenditure, depreciation, interest, taxes, etc.

[c]Investment means expenditure associated with acquiring ownership of property and plant. Due to difficulties of interpreting the concepts of depreciation among different countries, only gross investment figures are available. The "investment per main telephone line" figure for the world may be a slight underestimate since a few small countries' investment figures are not available.

[d]1995 data.

[e]"Long-distance calls per main line" is obtained by dividing trunk (toll) traffic by the number of main lines. Since Asia average and world average figures are not available, figures for India and Brazil are used.

[f]Waiting time is approximate number of years applicants must wait for a telephone line to be connected.

[g]Satisfied demand is obtained by dividing the number of main lines by the total demand for main telephone lines.

Table 13A.2	Main Events in China's Telecommunications Industry since 1979
Date	Event
June 1979	State council approved the Ministry of Posts and Telecommunications' (MPT's) proposal of administrative reform to set up a system of "dual leadership" of the MPT and provincial governments over telecommunications sector. MPT became the dominant central planner of nationwide postal and telecommunications development. A vertically organized hierarchy of MPT, postal and telecommunications administrations (PTAs), and postal and telecommunications bureaus (PTBs) emerged.
January 1980	MPT and State Urban Development Bureau decided to incorporate telecommunications infrastructure development into urban planning and construction code.
June 1980	MPT and Ministry of Finance authorized local PTAs to charge telephone installation fees amounting to Rmb 300–2,000 for each residential line. "Special funding accounts" system was introduced to manage telecommunications infrastructure maintenance and development.
March 1982	State Council approved MPT's proposal to • Allow urban telephone enterprises to retain all profits • Reduce other PTEs' profit submission rate from 20% to 10% • Adjust postal and telecommunications service rates and decentralize the setting of nonbasic local service rates • Raise fixed capital depreciation rate to 7%
October 1984	State Council stipulated a "six-point instruction" to give priority to postal and telecommunications development, which endorsed a policy of "three 90 percent" (see section 13.3 for more details).
1984–86	With accounting reform, the MPT contracted performance responsibilities to local PTAs and PTBs.
1985	The Seventh Five-Year Plan (1986–90) stipulated that intraprovince telecommunications projects should mainly rely on local financing.
1986–1990	MPT made adjustments to a wide range of telecommunications service rates and raised capital depreciation rate.
August 1988	MPT linked PTBs' wage fund increases to their revenue increases.
October 1988	MPT adopted a new formula to calculate "enterprise own revenue."
1988	Beijing announced the "sixteen-character policy" for telecommunications infrastructure development (see section 13.3). MPT granted its national manufacturing, construction, and purchasing departments the status of separate legal entities or greater financial and managerial independence. MPT set up the Directorate General of Telecommunications (DGT) and the Directorate General of Posts (DGP).
1989	MPT instructed all province-level PTAs to set up telecommunications regulatory bodies. MPT introduced terminal equipment licensing scheme, which deregulated the use of terminal equipment.
December 1990	Intracity telephone rates were widely adjusted. Local telecommunications companies were authorized to • Set their own intracity rates not exceeding the cap set by the MPT • Charge cost-based installation fees

(continued)

Table 13A.2	(continued)
Date	Event
1990–93	Non-MPT suppliers of value-added services, mobile telephone services, and satellite communications services emerged and prevailed in some regions.
June 1992	MPT stipulated the Re-statement on Forbidding Joint Operation of Postal and Telecommunications Business with Foreign Companies.
July 1993	All postal and telecommunications enterprises (PTEs) established the capital account system to manage infrastructure development funds.
	(Accounting) depreciation of telecommunications capital accelerated (equipment, 5–7 years; network, 10–15 years).
September 1993	State Council formally deregulated the mobile telephone service market and very small aperture terminal communications by authorizing MPT to license these service suppliers.
April 1994	MPT awarded a basic telecommunications license to China United Telecom and a value-added network operating license to Ji Tong Communications Co. Ltd. (Beijing).
	Nationwide tax reform unified corporate tax rates into an across-the-board 33% rate for all enterprises. Renminbi became convertible for current account transactions
1994	MPT froze all subsidiaries' employment and revised PTEs' wage-fund–revenue linkage formula to give larger weight to local revenue.
	The government announced the "eight policies of telecommunications development" (see section 13.6 for details).
September 1994	MPT specified two measures to reward non-MPT investors in trial joint ventures: fixed-rate remuneration and dividend distribution.
1995	MPT's China Telecom (DGT) formally registered with the government for the first time as an enterprise legal person.
	Local PTEs started the process of "corporatization" under China's Corporation Law.
	MPT revised PTEs' wage-fund–performance linkage formula to restrain employing new staff and encourage cost control.
October 1997	China Telecom launched 144 million initial public offer shares on Hong Kong Stock Market.

Source: Yearbook (various years).

Appendix B

Correspondence between Teledensity and Per Capita GNP

Objective

The objective is to test the correspondence between teledensity and GNP per capita for low-income and middle-income countries. See the note to table 13.3 for the World Bank definition of low- and middle-income countries.

Data

Teledensity statistics (defined as main telephone lines per 100 residents) are from ITU (1995a). Per capita GNP data are from the World Bank

(1989, 1996). There are 81 observations for the year 1987 and 93 observations for the year 1994.

Estimated Regressions for 1987 and 1994

The following equation is estimated by regressing the logarithmic values of teledensity data (TELDEN) on the logarithmic values of per capita GNP data (LNPCGNP):

$$\text{LNTELDEN}_{it} = \alpha + \beta \cdot \text{LNPCGNP}_{it} + \varepsilon_{it}.$$

Table 13B.1   **Regression Results for 1987**

	Statistic	Value
	Multiple R	.9026
	R^2	.8147
	Adjusted R^2	.8124
	Standard error	.6769
	Observations	81

ANOVA	df	SS	MS	F	Significance F
Regression	1	159.2067	159.2067	347.4170	1.18E-30
Residual	79	36.2024	0.4583		
Total	80	195.4091			

	Coefficient	Standard Error	t-Statistic	P-Value	Lower 99%	Upper 99%
Intercept	−9.2258	0.5064	−18.2170	5.16E-30	−10.5625	−7.8890
LNPCGNP	1.4263	0.0765	18.6391	1.18E-30	1.2243	1.6283

Table 13B.2   **Regression Results for 1994**

	Statistic	Value
	Multiple R	.8401
	R^2	.7057
	Adjusted R^2	.7025
	Standard error	.9096
	Observations	93

ANOVA	df	SS	MS	F	Significance F
Regression	1	180.5663	180.5663	218.2365	6.6548E-26
Residual	91	75.2923	0.8274		
Total	92	255.8587			

	Coefficient	Standard Error	t-Statistic	P-Value	Lower 99%	Upper 99%
Intercept	−7.1391	0.5642	−12.6544	9.06E-22	−8.6234	−5.6548
LNPCGNP	1.2025	0.0814	14.7728	6.65E-26	0.9883	1.4166

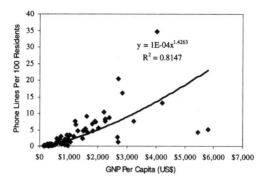

Fig. 13B.1   Teledensity vs. per capita GNP, 1987

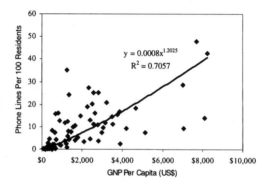

Fig. 13B.2   Teledensity vs. per capita GNP, 1994

Appendix C

Telecommunications Investment and Increase of Main Telephone Lines

Objective

The objective is to find the effectiveness of telecommunications investment in increasing main telephone lines in the Asia-Pacific region during 1987–94.

Data

Main telephone line statistics and telecommunications investment statistics for seventeen Asia-Pacific countries (China not included) during 1987–94 are from ITU (1995a). According to the ITU definition, investment means expenditure associated with acquiring ownership of property and plant. This includes expenditure on initial installations and on additions to existing installations where the usage is expected to be over an extended period of time. Data are gross investment figures, which include cost of land and buildings. Investment figures are deflated by the U.S. producer price index. There are 114 observations. Population density (number of persons per square kilometer) and teledensity (main telephone lines per 1,000 persons) statistics are from World Bank (1995) and ITU (1995a).

Regression Model

The logarithmic value of annual line increase (unit: thousand lines), LOGLINC, is regressed on three variables:

1. Previous year's logarithmic value of telecommunications investment (unit: million U.S. dollars), LOGINV
2. Relative teledensity in sample countries, RTELDEN (individual country's teledensity divided by average teledensity)
3. Relative population density, RPOPDEN (individual country's population density divided by average density)

$$LOGLINC_{it} = \alpha + \beta_1 LOGINV_{it-1} + \beta_2 RTELDEN_{it}$$
$$+ \beta_3 RPOPDEN_i + \varepsilon_{it}.$$

RTELDEN is included in the model on the assumption that countries with low teledensity can save capital cost of infrastructure as "late starters." They tend to be more efficient in increasing telephone lines than the earlier starters. This is partially because earlier starters also have to incur

Table 13C.1   Regression Results

	Statistic	Value
	Multiple R	.8962
	R^2	.8032
	Adjusted R^2	.7978
	Standard error	.8258
	Observations	114

ANOVA	df	SS	MS	F	Significance F
Regression	3	306.1180	102.0393	149.6116	1.13E-38
Residual	110	75.0231	0.6820		
Total	113	381.1411			

	Coefficients	Standard Error	t-Statistic	P-Value	Lower 95%	Upper 95%
Intercept	−1.1882	0.2929	−4.0569	9.33E-05	−1.7686	−0.6078
LNINV	1.0544	0.0525	20.1019	1.26E-38	0.9505	1.1584
RPOPDEN	0.0992	0.0341	2.9072	0.0044	0.0316	0.1669
RTELEDEN	−0.2527	0.1172	−2.1562	0.0332	−0.4850	−0.0204

higher replacement cost in investment to upgrade their existing networks. Late starters do not have the earlier starters' burdens of replacing out-of-date facilities, and they can use the latest technologies to build their telecommunications networks. Low teledensity is also associated with low per capita income levels, which in turn may imply lower land cost and labor cost in infrastructure construction. For these reasons, we expect the coefficient of RTELDEN to be negative.

High population density should have a positive impact on the cost-effectiveness of telecommunications investment. With fixed-line telephony, the connection cost per telephone line in a densely populated area is usually cheaper than in a sparsely populated region. Therefore, we expect the coefficient of RPOPDEN to be positive. With development of wireless telephony, however, the significance of this impact is likely to be weaker.

References

Almanac of China's foreign economic relations. 1986. Beijing: Foreign Trade and Economic Cooperation Press.

Almanac of China's tertiary industry. 1993. Beijing: China Statistics Press.

China's MPT director general outlines issues for new telecom law. 1996. International Communications Studies Program web page. 11 December. Available at http://www.csis.org/ics/.

China statistical yearbook. Various years. State Statistics Bureau. Beijing: China Statistics Press.

Documents of the twelfth national congress of the Communist Party of China. 1982. Beijing: People's Press.

EIU (Economist Intelligence Unit). 1997. Telecommunications: Easier access. In *Business Report: China,* 15–18. Hong Kong: Economist Intelligence Unit.

Gao Yangzhi. 1991. Shanghai's telephone network: Status quo and development strategy. *P & T Economy* 16:22–28.

Guo, R. C., and Y. Xu. 1992. *Business accounting system for postal and telecommunications enterprises* (in Chinese). Beijing: Beijing University of Posts and Telecommunications Press.

Hong Xiuyi and Qian Yongwei. 1992. The trend of residential telephone development in China (in Chinese). *P & T Economy* 21 (4): 19–23.

Hu Shiliang. 1996. Some thoughts on the reform of telecommunications fees in China (in Chinese). *P & T Economy* 34 (1): 19–21.

ITU (International Telecommunication Union). 1995a. *ITU statistical yearbook, 1987–94.* Geneva: International Telecommunication Union.

———. 1995b. *World telecommunication development report.* Geneva: International Telecommunication Union.

Li Guohua. 1996. Post and telecommunications business in new transition (in Chinese). *P & T Economy* 37 (4): 10–15.

Liu Shuping. 1992. Introduction to the Eighth Five-Year Plan of postal and telecommunications sector (in Chinese). In *Yearbook of China transportation and communications,* 168. Beijing: China Transportation and Communications Society.

Liu Zhaoquan. 1992. The development of P & T and reform of asset management (in Chinese). *P & T Economy* 18 (1): 2–4.

Lu, Ding. 1994. The management of China's telecommunications industry: Some institutional facts. *Telecommunications Policy* 18 (3): 195–205.

————. 1997. *State intervention and business in China: The role of preferential policies.* London: Elgar.

Luo Guilin. 1996. Correctly deal with several issues in the transformation of telecommunications growth mode (in Chinese). *P & T Economy* 37 (4): 5–7.

Luo Yunchao. 1992. The monopoly nature of P & T industry and its effects on operation. *P & T Economy* 21 (4): 15–17.

Ma Qiang. 1992. Ways to estimate telecommunications rates and an international comparison of rates (in Chinese). *P & T Economy* 18 (1): 27–30.

Ministry of Finance, Ministry of Posts and Telecommunications, and State Bureau of Price. 1986. Directive on urban telephone installation fees (June 1980). In *Yearbook of China transportation and communications.* Beijing: China Transportation and Communications Society.

MPT (Ministry of Posts and Telecommunications). 1986. Proposal to reform postal and telecommunications administration system (April 1979). In *Yearbook of China transportation and communications.* Beijing: China Transportation and Communications Society.

————. 1989a. Instruction on improved accounting system for PTEs (October 1988). In *Yearbook of China transportation and communications.* Beijing: China Transportation and Communications Society.

————. 1989b. Measures to link PTA wage funds to revenues (August 1988). In *Yearbook of China transportation and communications.* Beijing: China Transportation and Communications Society.

————. 1993. Re-statement on forbidding joint operation of postal and telecommunications business with foreign companies (20 June 1992). In *Yearbook of China transportation and communications.* Beijing: China Transportation and Communications Society.

————. 1995a. Approval of China United Telecom's scope of business (14 April 1994). In *Yearbook of China transportation and communications.* Beijing: China Transportation and Communications Society.

————. 1995b. Instruction on trial joint venture projects to speed up telecommunications development (September 1994). In *Yearbook of China transportation and communications.* Beijing: China Transportation and Communications Society.

MPT Planning Department. 1987. Main goals of China's postal and telecommunications development in the Seventh Five-Year Plan period (in Chinese). In *Yearbook of China transportation and communications,* 8–9. Beijing: China Transportation and Communications Society.

————. 1993. Postal and telecommunications sector (in Chinese). In *Yearbook of China's tertiary industry.* Beijing: China Statistics Press.

————. 1996. Goals of China's postal and telecommunications development in the Ninth Five-Year Plan period (in Chinese). In *Yearbook of China transportation and communications,* 542–43. Beijing: China Transportation and Communications Society.

Mueller, M., and Z. Tan. 1997. *China in the information age: Telecommunications and the dilemmas of reform.* Westport, Conn.: Praeger.

State Council. 1986. Instruction to the postal and telecommunications management (12 October 1984). In *Yearbook of China transportation and communications.* Beijing: China Transportation and Communications Society.

————. 1992. The provisional regulation on the PRC's direction-adjustment tax on fixed capital investment (16 April 1991). In *Almanac of China's economy*, 693–700. Beijing: Economic Management Press.

———. 1994. Approval of the MPT's proposal to enforce regulation of telecommunications service markets (3 August 1993). In *Yearbook of China transportation and communications*. Beijing: China Transportation and Communications Society.

Sun Yaming. 1992. Issues related to pricing policies regarding P & T new services (in Chinese). *P & T Economy* 18 (1): 36–37.

World Bank. 1989. *World development report*. New York: Oxford University Press.

———. 1995. *World development report*. New York: Oxford University Press.

———. 1996. *World development report*. New York: Oxford University Press.

Wu Changgeng and Zhang Xuan. 1992. An analysis of the seemingly high profit in the industry (in Chinese). *P & T Economy* 18 (1): 6–9.

Wu Houzeng. 1992. Discussion of the installation fee for private residential telephones (in Chinese). *P & T Economy* 20 (3): 44–46.

Wu Jichuan. 1996. Carefully study the experience of fulfilling the Eighth Five-Year Plan, work hard to fulfill the Ninth Five-Year Plan, and strive for making China a country with the most advanced postal and telecommunications sector by the year 2010 (in Chinese). In *Yearbook of China transportation and communications*, 16–17. Beijing: China Transportation and Communications Society.

Xiao, Jinxue. 1992. Views on the transition of operational mechanism of posts and telecommunications enterprises (in Chinese). *P & T Economy* 21 (4): 17–19.

Xu Yan. 1996. Competition without privatization: The Chinese path (in Chinese). Paper presented at the eleventh biennial conference of the International Telecommunications Society, Seville, Spain, 19 June.

Yang Peifang. 1991. On the goals and ways of a harmonic development of telecommunication (in Chinese). *P & T Economy* 16 (3): 2–4.

Yearbook of China transportation and communications. Various years. Beijing: Yearbook House of China Transportation and Communications.

You Zhengyan. 1987. Status of postal and telecommunications sector and industrial policies (in Chinese). In *Yearbook of China transportation and communications*, 766–68. Beijing: China Transportation and Communications Society.

Zhang Chenshuang. 1996. Strategic choice towards the 21st century for postal and telecommunications sector (in Chinese). In *Yearbook of China transportation and communications*, 543–44. Beijing: China Transportation and Communications Society.

Zhang Xuan. 1991. A discussion of perfecting the economic mechanism of telecommunications enterprises (in Chinese). *P & T Economy* 16 (3): 5–7.

Zhou Zhiqun. 1991. The usage of foreign investment in P & T business (in Chinese). *P & T Economy* 16 (3): 36–37.

Comment   Shang-Jin Wei

Ding Lu's trademark is lucidity. In this well-written paper, Lu provides a very informative account of how China's telecommunications industry has developed during the past two decades.

Shang-Jin Wei is associate professor of public policy at Harvard University and a faculty research fellow of the National Bureau of Economic Research.

According to Lu, the Chinese reform has several important features. First, the old central planning system was partially dismantled in the early 1980s. The single Ministry of Posts and Telecommunications has been broken down into several *state-owned* corporations competing with each other. Second, there is virtually no foreign direct investment in the sector.

Lu concludes that the result of the reform is a spectacular improvement in China's telecommunications infrastructure. In fact, China has overachieved its targets set in its five-year plans for every such plan in the past two decades. Using a regression analysis, Lu infers that China's teledensity has evolved from substantially below the world norm relative to its per capita GNP in the mid-1980s to 93 percent above the world norm in 1994.

I have two comments or questions about the paper. First, what is the lesson of the telecommunications sector in China? Second, is China truly an overachiever in teledensity?

Let me start with the first question. It is interesting to compare the telecommunications reform with energy sector reform. The reform measures are apparently similar in the two sectors. Both had what Lu calls "limited deregulation and controlled competition": the production and sale functions of the ministries were converted into a few state-owned corporations; no foreign direct investment was visible. Yet the results in the two sectors are very different: the reform in the telecommunications sector appears successful, while the energy sector is subject to severe shortages, bottlenecking the rest of the economy. Why?

My guess is that the degree of competition makes a big difference. In the energy sector, price remains controlled and the distribution channel remains monopolized. The incentive for private entry into production is not too great. In contrast, in the telecommunications sector, the government has wisely allowed local companies to charge market prices for installation fees, which helps to increase the supply and to equilibrate supply and demand. Maybe partly out of luck, the emerging and quickly booming cellular phone business does not depend on the existing state-owned telecommunications network, so the nature of the technology makes the state monopoly relatively easy to break. The lesson is that deregulating the price system and allowing free entry and more competition should also help the energy and other currently state-monopolized sectors (such as banking).

Let me turn to my second comment on China's teledensity. To see how China's actual teledensity compares to the world norm, Lu uses a two-step strategy. In step one, he runs a regression of teledensity on the level of GNP per capita and uses the fitted value to establish a benchmark. In step two, he compares China's actual teledensity with the prediction of the regression. Using this procedure, Lu infers that China's teledensity has become higher than the international norm.

This inference could be wrong if the benchmark is misspecified. A potential source of misspecification exists: the regression has no intercept. If the true relationship has a positive intercept, then the true slope would be smaller than what Lu estimated. Since China's per capita GDP is likely below the average in the sample, China's teledensity could be below the world norm in truth while it appears above Lu's estimated line. Therefore, it may make sense for Lu also to report a benchmark regression with an intercept.

Another point: Lu may want to transform per capita GDP into logarithmic form before putting it in the regression. It is my hunch that this would improve the fit of the regression by making the error closer to homoskedasticity. But it can be easily checked.

Comment   Tsuruhiko Nambu

The objective of this paper is to inquire into China's secrets or sources of success in building up its telecommunications network so rapidly in the 1980s and early 1990s. Ding Lu gives an excellent description of governmental policies toward the telecommunications industry. The main points are as follows:

Incentive induced investment: This includes the "three 90 percent" rule, the accelerated depreciation rule, and the freedom to set installation fees.

Hierarchical structure of regulatory system: The relationship between the MPT and local governments is structured so that PTAs govern PTEs and PTBs govern local telephone companies.

MPT's strong guidance on unified network construction

The success of the MPT is not surprising to the Japanese because Nippon Telephone and Telegraph, Inc. (NTT) achieved the same thing in the twenty years from 1952 to 1977. During this period, the backlog of telephone installation demand disappeared and direct dialing throughout the country was realized.

But the situation China faces is totally different. In the case of Japan, network construction was done in the 1960s and 1970s when the basic technology was simple: it was wireline technology and few alternatives were in sight. From now on, technology will be diverse and the future is full of uncertainties. The competition between wireline and wireless makes it difficult to guess the future.

The MPT itself faces risks in investing in wireline. Clearly, mobile telephone is emerging as a threat to wireline telephone. Wireline may be efficient as a backbone network, but in local telephony, wireless technology might well be more efficient, especially in the huge country of China.

The future of the telecommunications industry will be dominated by the

Tsuruhiko Nambu is professor of economics at Gakushuin University.

demand side. The essence of telecommunications service lies in interconnection between users. Unlike electricity, users generate their own demand and telecommunications circuits serve only as intermediary equipment. This is becoming more obvious with the recent development of Internet communication.

Although the Chinese government has built its network its own way, Chinese telephone users may also build their own communications network. What is most needed is to restructure and build in mechanisms that are fully adjustable to the shifting demand structure. On the other hand, installation fees are so high that they constitute an important part of the investment fund. What kind of policy measures can be applied to let this fee be reduced to a level affordable to the average customer?

Internet expansion is based on easy access to the network, and future development depends especially on accessibility to the local network. At this moment the nature of competition is changing dramatically from the long-distance market to the local telephone market. It is most important to understand the process by which of local competition emerges and to evaluate the role of government in letting competition loose or forestalling the dynamic competitive process. I will give a brief outline of local loop competition in Japan since the privatization of NTT in 1985.

Competition in the Local Loop

In the early 1980s everyone believed that competition in telecommunications would be limited to the long-distance market and that local telephony would remain monopolistic. This prediction has become groundless since technological innovations have been realized to the extent that the incumbent monopolist has been challenged by newcomers like CATV operators and wireless businesses.

In Japan the Telecommunications Business Law, enacted in 1985, gave the regulatory framework within which competition would be introduced into the telecommunications industry. It is notable that entry into the local market was not restricted by the law, unlike the Modified Final Judgment (MFJ) dichotomy ruling in the United States. The law could be interpreted as saying that any firm could enter the local loop if it could meet the conditions imposed on Type I carriers by Japan's Ministry of Posts and Telecommunications (MPT). Type I carriers are defined as those who own telecommunications facilities for their own use. Because entry into the long-distance market was encouraged by MPT, one could reasonably expect that some firms may have entered providing both local and long-distance services. In reality, it did not happen.

Subsidiaries of electricity companies entered the local markets in their own regulated business areas. Japan has nine electricity companies, which are given the status of local monopolies. They had the capability to challenge NTT, but they encountered two difficulties.

First, MPT did not allow rate rebalancing as was done in the United

Kingdom, and accordingly the local rate was kept intact: NTT could not raise its local rate. This allowed little room for profitable entry into the local market.

Second, the nine electricity companies were already interconnected for the purpose of wheeling their electricity services and well prepared to provide telecommunications services jointly in a technological sense. But they found, or believed they had found, that interconnecting telecommunications services across the country was prohibited by MPT. Not until 1995 did an MPT officer declare from the seat of the Regulatory Reform Committee that MPT had never banned interconnection of telecommunications services among subsidiaries of electricity companies. Indeed, the Telecommunications Business Law contains no formal restrictions on such interconnection.

There then emerged several regulatory disasters that prevented entry or the potential threat of entry into the Japanese local telephone market. First, rate rebalancing was flatly put aside by MPT. The ministry argued that NTT was a fat company and could cope with the problem of cross-subsidy from long distance to local service even when facing competition in the long-distance market. Along with the Telecommunications Business Law, the NTT Corporation Law was enacted, and NTT was made responsible for continuing universal service as it had in the days of public monopoly. The focus was always on whether NTT could be profitable enough to provide universal service. It was the judgment of MPT that NTT could continue to provide universal service by cutting its organizational redundancy, and rate rebalancing was out of the question until MPT found adequate evidence of efficiency enhancement in the NTT corporate structure.

From the social point of view it is difficult to say whether the Japanese approach or the British approach—where British Telecom was given an opportunity for rate rebalancing under a price-cap regime (retail price index minus 3 percent)—was better. But from the viewpoint of an economist, it was necessary to introduce rate rebalancing in order to realize competition and reshape the telecommunications industry as a whole. The problem of an inefficient incumbent monopolist is another issue to be tackled separately. The confusion at MPT between squeezing NTT from a regulatory standpoint and restructuring service prices was a source of delay in attempts to invite local competition.

The second regulatory problem was the Japanese nontransparent, implicit guideline procedure—often called *gyoseishido.* This term was associated with the industrial policy of the Ministry of International Trade and Industry (MITI). No one knows whether this procedure was successful, but MPT seems to have adopted this custom when it began regulating the telecommunications industry. A careful reading of the Telecommunications Business Law was not sufficient to honor the intent of MPT bureaucrats. Other detailed documents were published, and business firms had to consult with bureaucrats in each section of the ministry when they made business decisions. It is not surprising that electricity companies took for granted that they could not enter local telephony.

Because the local rate was kept unchanged (10 yen per three minutes) the entry of electricity companies was unprofitable, and those companies naturally wanted to enter the long-distance business. They argued for deregulating the telecommunications industry, and the Regulatory Reform Committee gave a formal opportunity for discussing this problem. It was a kind of accident that the MPT top official confessed that MPT did not intend to regulate entry into long distance by electricity companies and that they could be interconnected nationwide.

This episode gives insight into the uncertainties created by the discretion of bureaucrats. If there had existed a transparent guideline, electricity companies and others might have begun to supply full line service or at least might have brought different strategies to the telecommunications business. MPT's implicit policymaking, and its policy agenda subject to no time constraints, constituted another source of delay in bringing about local telephone competition.

Competition among Technologies

Wireline technology used to be regarded, whether coaxial or fiberoptic, as a dominant technology with no close substitute. Quite recently, however, wireless technology has become a challenger to wireline. It was developed mainly in the Scandinavian countries but now has no particular location. The inertia of older telephone subscribers may be the highest barrier to its development, but this resistance will be easily broken in the coming years. Cable television (CATV) providers have become wireline competitors to incumbent telephone monopolists. They can exploit economies of scope in providing broadcasting and telephone services. At the same time computer technology development has made it possible for a small exchange to compete with the local exchange of the incumbent. Satellite is another source of potential competition to the old telephone network. Many problems must be solved for it to become a stable competitor, but its competitive threat is so great as to enhance local as well as long-distance competition.

In the face of these new technical opportunities, institutional architecture plays a decisive role in encouraging competition. The Nordic countries placed no regulation on technology choice, and the evolutional development of the wireless business has been witnessed in the past fifteen years. After the duopoly review in 1991, the British CATV industry experienced rapid growth, and it has become a real threat to the British Telecom telephone network. In the United States, the 1984 act of deregulating CATV relieved CATV operators of providing public broadcasting services and it paved the road to extend its business from broadcasting to telephony.

In Japan MPT was an efficient brakeman to this kind of development. The CATV industry was strictly regulated in several ways:

1. CATV tariffs had to be based on accounting cost and could not be lowered in order to attract new customers. As a result, CATV service was expensive enough to restrict the number of subscribers.

2. CATV used to be defined as a rescue service for broadcasting in a limited area. As public broadcasting it had to observe rules that prohibited entertainment services. Also there existed unprofitable "local content" regulation. The CATV industry was not given business opportunities in general.

3. CATV operators did not have the right of way to access subscribers. This was the greatest obstacle to expanding their businesses.

In 1994 MPT deregulated the CATV industry to some extent. The narrowly defined business areas were relaxed to enable multifranchise operators in certain regions. Foreign capital restraints were lifted to the extent that foreign companies could contribute up to one-third of total capital. But everything came too late. CATV operators are now going to start telephone service under a new regime of interconnection with NTT. It is quite probable that they will become competitors to NTT, but Japanese customers must wait and continue to lose much until local competition emerges.

The experience of the wireless industry gives a clear and simple example how regulation can be a deterrent to the healthy development of telephone business. Until recently there existed price regulation on wireless services: cellular telephone and personal communications services. Their prices used to be too high to attract subscribers. Then a few years ago, MPT lifted these regulations and the wireless markets exploded. This should have been easily anticipated simply because of the examples of many other countries. The Japanese people wasted much time and many resources through untimely regulation.

Uncertainty Created by a Divestiture Argument

In this year the argument over NTT divestiture was settled: NTT should be reorganized as a holding company to which two regional companies (NTT East and NTT West) and one long-distance company belong as subsidiaries.

It was in 1985 that the decision whether to break up NTT was postponed. In 1990 again no conclusion was reached, and the discussion was postponed until 1996. During that period the environment surrounding the telecommunications industry changed completely. The dichotomy between local and long distance has proved meaningless; technology is constantly changing, and no one can foresee the future; bundling or full line service might be necessary for large operators to survive; entry from other fields like electricity and gas has become a real threat; and so forth.

It appears that MPT paid little attention to these changes and continued to insist upon the necessity of divestiture. Wrong or right, it created great uncertainty about the telecommunications infrastructure. Because holding companies were prohibited by the Antimonopoly Law, it was impossible to imagine NTT as an integrated organization in the name of a holding company. MPT took a political risk by proposing the idea of restructuring NTT as a holding company, along with reforming the Antimonopoly Law.

It may take a few years to reshape NTT, while such countries as the United Kingdom, United States, and Singapore will not miss the opportunity to develop at higher speeds. Japan does not have time to lose. How to deregulate or break up regulations is an urgent issue for the Japanese.

Last, I will touch on the harmonization problem with regard to interconnection and accounting rules. By nature the telecommunications business is global. There is no obstacle to international communications but institutional restraint. Needless to say, interconnection is the key to realizing full competition. In every country now, interconnection rules are being discussed, and in the United Kingdom and United States there have emerged certain proposals to deal with this problem. In Japan the report of MPT on interconnection was recently published.

Each country has its historical background to account for differences in its price structure that cannot be harmonized in the short run. As a starting point, we must have common accounting rules to allow us to understand correctly the financial situation of each country. And based on transparent accounting rules, we can calculate interconnection charges that can be shared among countries.

14

Telecommunications Liberalization
The U.S. Model

Robert W. Crandall

The United States has been in the process of liberalizing telecommunications for at least thirty years and perhaps more. Private microwave licenses were first considered in 1956 and granted in 1959. Competitive entry into certain long-distance communications common carriage was first sought by Microwave Communications Incorporated (now MCI) in 1963; the Federal Communications Commission (FCC) approved its entry in 1969. Terminal equipment ("customer premises equipment") was finally liberalized in 1977. Entry into ordinary, switched long-distance first occurred without FCC authorization in 1974, but it was another four years before this entry (by MCI) was upheld by the courts despite the FCC's vehement protests.[1]

Finally, in 1996, the U.S. Congress passed and the president signed the 1996 Telecommunications Act, which included, among other provisions, a requirement that *state* regulators permit entry into the delivery of local telecommunications services and—eventually—intrastate long-distance calls. This act also frees the Bell operating companies to enter long-distance markets under prescribed conditions, allows all local exchange companies to enter the video distribution business, and eliminates much of the formal rate regulation of cable television. Most of current U.S. telecommunications policy attention is quite understandably focused on implementing this 1996 act, but a thorough understanding of the American "model" of liberalization requires an examination and understanding of thirty years of trying to open telecommunications markets to competition.

Robert W. Crandall is senior fellow in economic studies at the Brookings Institution.

1. *MCI Telecommunications Corp. v. FCC*, 561 F.2d 365 (D.C. Cir. 1977), *cert. denied*, 434 U.S. 1040 (1978); *MCI Telecommunications Corp. v. FCC*, 580 F.2d 590 (D.C. Cir. 1978), *cert. denied*, 439 U.S. (1978).

Liberalization and deregulation of trucking and airlines occurred much more swiftly in the United States. Why should telecommunications take so long?

14.1 Monopoly, Regulation, and the Distortion of the Rate Structure

Until recently, telecommunications has generally been thought to be a network industry characterized by economies of scale and density that make it a natural monopoly, but this view has rarely been afforded a market test because most nations have provided legal protection of a single, national (and typically government-owned) carrier.[2] The United States was an exception because it never had a government-owned telephone system, and it even permitted open entry into telephony in the early part of this century.

Competition soon fell victim to a series of mergers and acquisitions and a government regulatory policy that was erected in lieu of antitrust enforcement.[3] By the 1930s, the industry was essentially a set of regulated private monopolies comprising the American Telephone and Telegraph Company (AT&T) and a few smaller, independent operating companies. State regulatory commissions had the authority to control intrastate rates (local service and intrastate long-distance calls) of the local operating companies while the FCC exercised loose authority over interstate long distance provided solely by AT&T. The implicit premise of this regulation was one of franchised monopoly, natural or not, protected from entry as long as it served the "public interest."

In practice, U.S. regulators—like those in most countries—protected the franchised monopolies from entry while requiring that they price their services in response to political forces.[4] Over time, this meant that long-distance rates would be set at levels substantially above cost while local connections, particularly for residences, were priced below their long-run incremental cost. Equally important, most states required that rates be *lower* in rural and exurban areas than in urban areas despite the obvious fact that incremental costs of these connections were higher in less densely populated areas.[5] Finally, residential connection rates were generally far

2. There are numerous studies of the economies of scale and scope in telecommunications. For a useful summary, see Waverman (1989, table 8).

3. For a review of this history, see Brock (1981). An alternative view may be found in Temin (1987).

4. In most countries, the telephone company has been a public enterprise, often part of the postal, telegraph, and telephone authority. These enterprises have generally pursued the same practice of keeping local access charges low and long-distance rates artificially high. Most developed countries and even many developing countries are now in the process of privatizing their telephone companies and establishing independent regulatory authorities like those found in the United States.

5. Most developed countries have local monthly rates that do not vary by geographic area. However, Canada had rates that were more distorted than those in the United States prior to recent regulatory actions. See Crandall and Waverman (1996).

lower than monthly charges to businesses for the same service in the same area.

These regulatory distortions in the rate structure were not widely understood in an era in which no one tried to compete with the established telephone monopolists. However, once the FCC began to admit entry into interstate services in the 1970s, these distortions became visible and even controversial, creating artificial incentives for entrants to attack the overpriced interstate service markets. The implicit subsidy from these interstate services to local residential service that was once accomplished largely through internal transfers within AT&T was made explicit in the form of "access charges" paid by long-distance carriers to local companies for originating and terminating their calls. When AT&T was broken up in 1984 to settle an antitrust suit brought by the federal government, the FCC began a protracted policy of reducing the subsidies flowing through these access charges. However, the states moved far less aggressively and were generally hostile to allowing entry into intrastate markets. As a result, even today—nearly thirty years after telecommunications liberalization began with MCI's entry into long-distance services—U.S. telephone rates do not even approximate the long-run incremental cost of services.

14.2   The Requisites of Successful Liberalization

The United States essentially stumbled into the liberalization of telecommunications in the 1960s and 1970s. There was no carefully drawn plan to introduce competition into any market, nor was there legislation requiring such liberalization. Rather, the FCC responded to a variety of political pressures and direct petitions from those desiring to offer long-distance service or competitive terminal equipment.[6] As the distinctions between telecommunications and computer services began to blur, the commission was forced to draw the line between regulated "telecommunications" services and unregulated computer-like terminal equipment.

Competition developed in the long-distance market by a combination of FCC rules and a series of accidents.[7] The FCC decided in 1969 and again in 1971 to allow "specialized" carriers to offer dedicated interstate service—private lines—to business customers. It did not, however, grant MCI or subsequent entrants the right to offer ordinary, switched long-distance services to any subscriber, business or residential. Nevertheless, MCI began to offer switched services in 1974 by terminating its calls over Bell company connections designed for other purposes. When the FCC

6. See Crandall (1981). "Terminal equipment" or "customer premises equipment" is that equipment used by the telephone subscriber to connect to the network. It includes telephone handsets, private branch exchanges (PBXs), modems, fax machines, and answering machines.
7. This history is reviewed in Brock (1981) and, more recently, in Crandall and Waverman (1996).

attempted to block MCI from offering these services, the federal appellate court refused to enforce its order, citing the absence of a procedural record that showed that MCI's service was not in the public interest. When AT&T attempted to deny MCI and other entrants use of its local circuits to originate and terminate such calls, a variety of antitrust suits were filed, including the 1974 Sherman Act suit that would eventually culminate in the breakup of AT&T.

Obviously, the U.S. government did not have a clear plan to introduce competition into telecommunications. Rather, liberalization lurched forward through a series of uncoordinated regulatory and legal actions. Had a liberalization plan been devised, once the government decided that competition was feasible in a network industry such as telecommunications, it should have contained at least the following:

1. An early end to rate distortions created by decades of government regulation
2. Assurances that incumbent carriers cannot utilize their control of "bottleneck" facilities to disadvantage entrants
3. Market incentives, but no direct or indirect subsidies, for entrants to build new facilities
4. A commitment to phase out regulation very soon after entry occurs

In the United States, trucking, airline, and—on a more limited basis—railroad liberalization satisfied these four conditions. As we shall see, U.S. telecommunications liberalization has not and is now proceeding in a direction that violates at least three of them.

14.3 Telephone Rate Distortions

All government regulation is a political process. As a result, political considerations generally lead regulators to craft a variety of cross-subsidies in the regulated rate structure to benefit various favored constituent groups. Obviously, such cross-subsidies cannot withstand liberalization because competition drives the above-cost rates toward cost, thereby depriving regulators of the sources of funds for such subsidies. The U.S. airline regulator, the Civil Aeronautics Board, began to purge the regulated rate structure of these cross-subsidies almost a decade before deregulation. In telecommunications, a large share of these cross-subsidies remain, serving as impediments to full liberalization. Despite a substantial body of research that demonstrates such cross-subsidies are an inefficient and largely ineffective mechanism for inducing subscribers to remain on the network, these subsidies are still defended as necessary to achieve "universal service."

The magnitude of cross-subsidy in U.S. telecommunications can be shown quite succinctly with two charts. Local service is generally priced

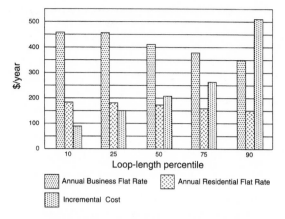

Fig. 14.1   Average U.S. business and residential local rates, 1994

on a flat-rate basis—allowing callers to make unlimited calls within a local area—that declines with the increase in incremental cost of providing it.[8] Figure 14.1 shows the average residential and business charges arrayed by "loop length," the distance of the subscriber from the local switch.[9] Subscribers in less densely populated areas require more copper wire (or copper plus fiber) to serve them, yet in the United States rates for both businesses and residences decline with the increase in the incremental cost of service that is driven by declining population density. In addition, as figure 14.1 shows, businesses typically pay twice as much for the same service in any given geographic area despite the fact that the incremental cost of business lines is generally somewhat lower than the incremental cost of residential lines in the same geographic area.[10]

The historical (book) cost of providing local connections is less relevant to pricing decisions in an industry with some long-lived assets and rapid technical change than for others, but these historical accounting costs provide at least an indication of the *average* level of costs that must be recovered in a regulated industry. In 1995, the local exchange companies that submitted their financial results to the FCC reported a total of $51.2 billion in noncapital costs for 148.4 million switched lines, or about $345 per line. Not all of these costs were dedicated to providing subscriber access,

8. Flat rates are slowly giving way to measured rates as carriers begin to petition their state regulators for a more rational rate structure in the face of prospective entry.

9. These data are drawn from NARUC (1994a) and a "benchmark cost" study of local network costs funded by several local and long-distance carriers.

10. These are obvious generalizations about *average* rates across the lower forty-eight states. Businesses are generally closer to the central office, but they generally account for more busy-hour minutes of use than do residential subscribers. On balance, before the Internet complicated life for all telecommunications providers, business and residential rates should have been about the same in any given geographic location.

Table 14.1   Average Local Telephone Rates in the United States, 1995

Service	Rate ($)
Installation charge	38.10
Monthly residential rate (unlimited calling)	19.54
Monthly single-line business rate (unlimited calling)[a]	41.77
Local call rate[a]	0

Source: FCC (1997, tables 8.4 and 8.5).

[a]A few states do not permit flat-rate unlimited calling for businesses; the average business rate shown here is either the flat rate or the rate that includes 200 five-minute business-day calls per month. The zero local call rate is therefore the modal rate, but not the average rate.

but a large share undoubtedly were. In addition, these companies had about $150 billion in net undepreciated plant in service, or slightly more than $1,000 per line. Assuming a 25 percent capital charge for the before-tax cost of capital plus depreciation, this suggests an annual capital cost of about $250 per year. Thus total accounting costs for the U.S. local companies are nearly $600 per year, most of which is required to build and maintain local access facilities. By comparison, the average U.S. residential rate was $19.54 and the average single-line business rate for flat-rate service was $41.77 in 1995 (see table 14.1).[11]

The second chart (fig. 14.2) shows the enormous gap between the charges paid by long-distance carriers to the local telephone companies for connecting their calls and the local companies' incremental cost of originating and terminating these calls.[12] Because of this wide gap, both for interstate and intrastate calls,[13] long-distance rates are artificially high and most local residential rates are artificially low. Average long-distance rates in the United States remain far above the long-run incremental cost of the service, which is likely between 5¢ and 7¢ per minute.[14] To some extent, the disparity between interstate rates and costs reflects the failure to account for competitive discount plans. Even with these discounts, however, table 14.2 shows that average *transactions* prices for all custom-

11. Several states no longer offer flat-rate service for business customers. Therefore, the data in table 14.1 reflect either the flat rate or the rate for a single line generating 200 five-minute business-day calls per month.

12. These data are taken from the FCC's periodic *Telephone Trends* reports produced by the Industry Analysis Division of the Common Carrier Bureau.

13. Interstate rates are regulated by the FCC; intrastate rates are regulated by the state commissions. The FCC recently acted to reduce interstate (per minute) access charges, but this action may well be appealed to the courts, thereby delaying its implementation.

14. This estimate is the subject of considerable dispute. Robert Crandall and Leonard Waverman in an affidavit prepared for Ameritech's application for entry into in-region long-distance services in Michigan contend that the long-run incremental cost of long-distance service, excluding marketing and administrative costs, is between 1.5¢ and 2.5¢ per minute, including the cost of originating and terminating calls on local company networks. Even if marketing and overhead costs are 5¢ per minute, long-run incremental costs plus average marketing and overhead costs should be no more than 7.5¢ per minute.

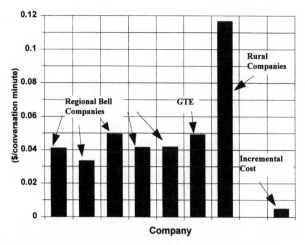

Fig. 14.2   Interstate access charges versus incremental cost, 1998

Table 14.2   Average Discounted Rates for Interstate Long-Distance Service, 1985–95

Year	Average Rate ($/minute)
1985	0.37
1986	0.30
1987	0.25
1988	0.24
1989	0.22
1990	0.19
1991	0.18
1992	0.17
1993	0.17
1994	0.16
1995	0.15

Source: Hall (1997).

ers, business and residential, are still above long-run incremental costs. Approximately 5¢ of this difference is due to the regulatory overpricing of local company access charges; the remaining 3¢ to 5¢ appears to be rents retained by the long-distance carriers or dissipated in nonprice rivalry reflected in marketing expenses.

There is considerable disagreement over the degree to which long-distance rates have fallen in the United States because of the growth in discount pricing plans and the absence of accurate data on minutes of calling. Nevertheless, most data sources provide substantial evidence of real rate declines since 1984, driven in large part by the FCC's reduction of access charges from more than 17¢ per conversation minute in 1984 to

6¢ per minute in 1995 (see table 14.3). The most important issue is whether rates continued to decline in the 1990s after the FCC initiated price caps and the growth of MCI and Sprint (the third largest carrier) slowed. The real list prices for the major carriers have actually risen since 1990 while Hall's MCI data on average revenue per minute show a continuing decline.

The reduction in long-distance access rates has been effected through the phasing-in of a "subscriber line charge" that is now $3.50 per month for residences and as much as $6 per month for businesses. Despite this new charge, however, real local rates—including the subscriber line charge—have not risen in the past decade (figure 14.3).

There are other sources of cross-subsidies for local telephone rates in

Table 14.3   Average Long-Distance Rates in the United States (dollars per minute)

Distance	AT&T Undiscounted Interstate Rate, 1997	AT&T Undiscounted Interstate Rate, January 1984	Bell Company IntraLATA Rate, December 1994[a]	Bell Company Intrastate Rate, December 1983[b]
25 km	0.28	0.26	0.15	0.15
100 km	0.28	0.32	0.25	0.34
200 km	0.29	0.41	0.29	0.38
1,000 km	0.30	0.47	n.a.	n.a.

Sources: FCC (1997) and NARUC (1996b).
Note: Table reports rates for five-minute daytime call. n.a. = not applicable.
[a]See n. 19.
[b]Predivestiture.

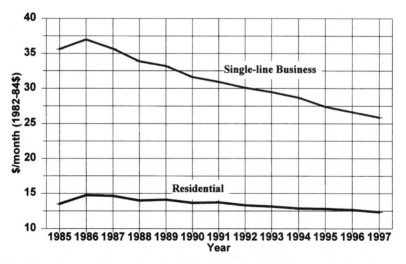

Fig. 14.3   Average U.S. real local residential rates, 1985–97

the United States: vertical services, high-bandwidth services, and even advertising in the Yellow Pages. However, figures 14.1 and 14.2 capture the essence of the cross-subsidies in the period before and immediately after the passage of the Telecommunications Act of 1996.

If liberalization is to proceed, it is obvious that these cross-subsidies cannot remain. While regulators cannot know carriers' costs with any precision, they should be making their best efforts to unwind these subsidies before unleashing the forces of competition. However, these U.S. regulators had little formal idea of the structure of carriers' costs until the 1996 act required that local carriers lease their facilities to new entrants *at cost*. Now, every state commission is involved in lengthy regulatory proceedings to determine its local carriers' costs for setting *wholesale* rates while failing to move *retail* rates toward these costs. Indeed, the FCC's first set of rules under the 1996 act established guidelines for these cost determinations that were extremely controversial and immediately subjected to court appeal.[15] I turn to some of the issues raised in this appeal in the next section, but before doing so it is necessary to stress that many U.S. regulators continue to try to enforce a politically motivated set of subsidies to rural subscribers in general, and residential subscribers in particular, from a distorted *retail* rate structure while promoting competition.

14.4   Telephone Penetration and Usage

Telephone pricing policies in the United States and most other countries have been devised with the purported goal of encouraging "universal service." Nevertheless, telephone subscriber penetration (per 100 persons) is only marginally greater in the United States than in most other high-income OECD countries (table 14.4). Of all countries, Sweden has the highest number of main telephone lines per 100 population, but the United States and Canada are somewhat above the European average in this regard. Canada's local line rental rates are somewhat below those in the United States and its free-calling areas are generally larger, but its average per capita income is somewhat below the U.S. equivalent. However, a larger percentage of Canadian households have at least one telephone line than do U.S. households (Crandall and Waverman 1996, table 1-8).

Because the United States has generally used flat-rate charges for monthly line rentals and local calling, particularly for residences, U.S. residences and most business establishments face a zero marginal cost for local calls. These artificially low local call charges obviously stimulate very intensive use of the local network by U.S. telephone subscribers. In table

15. The U.S. Court of Appeals for the Eighth Circuit ruled on this appeal in July 1997, deciding against the FCC on virtually every important issue, but the Supreme Court reversed the court of appeals in *AT&T v. Iowa Utilities Board* in January 1999.

Table 14.4   **Telephone Lines per 100 Population, 1994**

Country	Lines per 100 Population
Belgium	44.9
Canada	59.2
Denmark	60.4
France	54.7
Germany	48.3
Italy	42.9
Japan	48.0
Netherlands	51.1
Norway	55.4
Sweden	68.3
United Kingdom	48.8
United States	60.2

Source: International Telecommunication Union (1996).

Table 14.5   **Telephone Calls per Line in the United States and Other OECD Countries, 1994**

Country	Local Calls per Line	National Long-Distance Calls per Line
Germany	787	559
Japan	1,165	273
Netherlands	528	639
United States	3,250	583

Sources: Non-U.S. data, International Telecommunication Union (1996); U.S. data, FCC (1997).

14.5 I show average calls per line for the United States and for a few other OECD countries for which data are available. Clearly, U.S. telephone subscribers make far more local calls than do German, Japanese, or Dutch subscribers. Moreover, given extended-area local service in many U.S. states, many of these calls would be considered long-distance calls in many countries. Thus the total number of national long-distance calls in the United States is somewhat understated in table 14.5 relative to the numbers in other countries.[16]

Modern telephone technology provides extremely reliable service as long as the telephone plant is maintained and sufficient switching and transmission capacity is provided. In the 1990s, the Bell operating companies have averaged less than 1 second of service disruption per access line per quarter, or about 3 seconds per line per year (Kraushaar 1996). Al-

16. These data are at best illustrative given the problems in the data and the differences in approaches to collecting them across countries.

most all service quality complaints today are related to delays in scheduling installation or maintenance calls.

14.5 The Bottleneck

In any network industry, there may be "essential bottleneck" facilities that incumbents control to the temporary or permanent disadvantage of new entrants. Transportation carriers may control sections of track, bridges, or terminal facilities that they refuse to make available to competitors. In the United States, such actions may violate the antitrust laws, but relying on antitrust enforcement may substantially slow liberalization of heretofore regulated monopoly industries. As a result, regulators must address the problems raised by such bottlenecks.

In telecommunications, bottlenecks allegedly arise for two reasons.[17] First, a subscriber may be connected to the network through a single line or interface that is controlled by the incumbent carrier. Even if a new carrier replaces the incumbent, this new carrier may now control an essential bottleneck with the same effect on competition in various markets. Second, new entrants may require substantial capital and time to duplicate certain facilities that incumbents already possess. To provide true network service, the entrant has to be able to interconnect its new subscribers with all other subscribers. The entrant may be forced to build the facilities required to accomplish this interconnection. As a result, the entrant may claim that many of these facilities should be offered him by the incumbents on reasonable terms—at least until the entrant can replicate them. The crucial policy issues involve defining the scope of these essential facilities and the period of time for which they should be available from the incumbent.

14.5.1 Long-Distance Services

In the United States, AT&T used its control of local bottleneck facilities to deny to subscribers connections of quality equivalent to those provided to its own (Long Lines) long-distance operations. In part, this occurred because AT&T's local switching capacity—like that of most monopolists of the time—was built in the 1960s and 1970s under the assumption that there would be no long-distance competition. Without modifying these switches, AT&T could not offer equal, trunk-side connections to its new rival(s).

After AT&T was divested of its operating companies as the result of an antitrust suit brought in 1974 and settled in 1982, the divested "regional Bell operating companies" were required to modify their switches to pro-

---

17. For an exhaustive analysis of the potential for bottleneck abuse, see Bernheim and Willig (1996).

Table 14.6   **Market Shares in the U.S. Long-Distance Market, 1984–95 (percentage of revenues)**

Year	AT&T	MCI	Sprint	All Others
1984	90.1	4.5	2.7	2.6
1985	88.3	5.5	2.6	5.6
1986	81.9	7.6	4.3	6.3
1987	78.6	8.8	5.8	6.8
1988	74.6	10.3	7.2	8.0
1989	67.5	12.1	8.4	12.0
1990	65.0	14.2	9.7	11.1
1991	63.2	15.2	9.9	11.8
1992	60.8	16.7	9.7	12.9
1993	58.1	17.8	10.0	14.2
1994	55.2	17.4	10.1	17.3
1995	53.0	17.8	10.0	19.2

Source: FCC (1997).

vide equal access to all long-distance competitors. The other local companies were required to follow shortly thereafter. This conversion to equal access took place in the 1984–87 period, and the resulting effect on competition was dramatic, as table 14.6 shows. AT&T began to lose market share much more rapidly after 1984 than in the previous decade when MCI was laboring against an integrated AT&T that did not provide equivalent access.

Many observers use the results in table 14.6 to argue that integration between the provision of local access and other telecommunications services is necessarily adverse to the development of competition in the latter sectors. However, AT&T could have been required to provide equal access by the FCC even without the antitrust divestiture. Indeed, the Canadian telephone companies continue to be integrated but are now required to offer equal access to long-distance competitors. As a result, competition has developed extremely rapidly in Canada without vertical divestiture— indeed even more rapidly than was the experience in the United States.

The United States went too far in mandating "equal" access, requiring local companies to offer connection services to AT&T and its rivals at the same rates despite the fact that the local companies' costs of connecting AT&T calls were lower than the costs of connecting the new competitors' calls because AT&T delivered its calls in quantities and at locations that were less expensive to connect. This implicit subsidy was deemed to be desirable in order to give new entrants a competitive advantage. Similarly, in earlier years, when new carriers could not obtain equal-quality connections, they were provided enormous discounts that apparently overcompensated for this disadvantage.

14.5.2   Local Exchange Access Services

Until the 1996 Telecommunications Act, most states did not allow competition for local services except in the form of new "competitive access providers" who built fiberoptic rings to serve business customers in large cities. Indeed, there were few requests for entry into suburban or rural areas, probably because of the distorted retail rate structure.

The 1996 act now requires that all local companies "unbundle" their networks and offer the various components or "network elements"—switching, transport, signaling, the local loop, and so forth—to any and all entrants at rates that reflect some measure of cost. Thus local incumbents must lease *any* facility, whether a bottleneck or not, to new entrants. In addition, incumbents must interconnect at any technically feasible point with new entrants.

These requirements for unbundling and leasing all network elements to entrants create enormous controversy over the number of such elements into which the network must be divided and the rates to be charged for each. Surely, the only true bottleneck in the local network is the final subscriber line (local loop) or the interface between the subscriber's line and the rest of the network. To encumber the process of liberalization with the requirement of complex new regulations concerning the piecemeal division of incumbent networks preserves regulation more than it fosters liberalization.

The appropriate policy for interconnecting local networks is less obvious. It is possible that incumbents could design an interconnection system that makes interconnection with entrants difficult because the latter have more modern technology and therefore different interconnection requirements. Reciprocal interconnection agreements have worked successfully for decades for adjacent networks, but few countries have imposed them on *competing* networks in the same geographic area. Some regulation may be necessary to assure that incumbents do not frustrate competition, but the U.S. 1996 act's requirement for interconnection at all "feasible" points may be excessive.

On the other hand, any interconnection requirement is likely to be controversial. If a carrier changes its technology, as it must periodically in the face of such rapid technical progress, any rival carrier may complain that the changes have the effect of and were even designed to frustrate competition if the changes alter interconnection conditions. Given the absence of full competition in local telephone services anywhere in the world, we simply have too little experience to be sure that we know how to navigate through these choppy seas.

14.6 Encouraging Facilities-Based Entry

Network industries are often very difficult to enter because of the enormous scale of investment required. It might be argued that some subsidy is required to encourage entrants or to overcome first-mover advantages in the provision of terrestrial network or even satellite services. Yet, in the United States, four new entrants have built competing national fiberoptic networks, and at least one other company is preparing to build another one despite the apparent existence of excess transmission capacity. Similarly, there are several direct broadcast satellite systems in operation in the United States and more to come. More to the point, there are at least four proposed low- or medium-orbiting satellite systems being designed or built to offer global wireless communications. Thus there would appear to be little grounds for providing subsidies to encourage entry into such services where the markets are very large and the technology is constantly improving, thereby reducing the incumbent's first-mover advantages.

In smaller countries, competition among terrestrial networks may not develop without some direct or indirect subsidies, but even in these countries such subsidies are surely questionable. If scale economies are great and the markets are small, subsidies may only encourage inefficient entry that requires permanent subsidy for survival. While there could be welfare gains from such a perpetual subsidy system, the political economy of maintaining it surely argues for caution.

The most contentious single issue in implementing the 1996 Telecommunications Act in the United States is the measure of cost to be used in setting rates for wholesale unbundled elements. In August 1996, the FCC ruled that states should base such rates on "forward-looking" estimates of long-run incremental costs, where the basis for such costs is the most modern technology found anywhere in an incumbent's network. This requirement to price at TELRIC—"total-element long-run incremental cost"—means that incumbents must offer their networks for lease at rates below their own embedded costs because of the rapid technological change in telecommunications.[18] Unless the incumbent has been depreciating its plant rapidly to reflect the rate of obsolescence and charging accordingly for its services, it will be unable to recover its costs from the new forward-looking wholesale rates. The FCC's ruling was initially overturned by the U.S. court of appeals on jurisdictional grounds, but many state regulators nevertheless used some form of forward-looking wholesale pricing in their implementation of the 1996 act.

The U.S. policy of requiring the unbundling of all local network elements and pricing them at forward-looking costs rather than historical

---

18. This requirement has been dubbed TELRIC-BS (total-element long-run incremental cost—blank slate) by Alfred Kahn (1998).

embedded costs has exceedingly unfortunate effects on entry incentives. Why should entrants assume the costs and risks of building their own network facilities when they can lease any combination of incumbents' facilities at prices that reflect engineers' assessments of the lowest costs currently available through new construction? The FCC's ruling may have this effect at first—inhibiting entry through the construction of new facilities. One and a half years after the passage of the 1996 act, there were few major new entrants into local services, but more recently entry has accelerated.

14.7 Deregulation

In many countries mere privatization is a step forward in telecommunications policy. In others, some liberalization—such as allowing competition in "value-added" services—is a major advance. Ultimately, however, liberalization must be accompanied by forbearance or deregulation if the benefits of competition are to be realized.

Perhaps the most important mistake made by the United States in liberalizing its telecommunications sector has been the perpetuation of a burdensome regulatory regime while extolling the virtues of market competition. Unlike most other countries, the United States has a divided system of regulation that derives from its federalist origins. Intrastate communications is regulated by the states; interstate communications is regulated by the FCC. The Congress could easily alter this regime by eliminating state regulation, federal regulation, or both. Unfortunately, the recent Telecommunications Act extended this complex regulatory system and even made it worse by mandating new FCC rules to guide the states, rules that have become the centerpiece of lengthy court appeals.

Both the states and the FCC are responsible for the unfortunate rate distortions described above. Both have continued to regulate competitive portions of the telecommunications sector far too long. After many years of contentious proceedings, the FCC was able to prevail in requiring the states to deregulate the sale or lease of terminal equipment—the handsets, PBXs, answering machines, modems, and other equipment with which we communicate over the network. Subsequently, the FCC waited eleven years after the AT&T divestiture to deregulate AT&T fully. Between 1989 and 1995, AT&T was regulated by a price-cap regime whose principal objective was to prevent AT&T from abusing its market power by *reducing* rates to the disadvantage of rivals. Such regulation is more likely to cartelize an industry characterized by open entry than to prevent the reappearance of monopoly.

Many states still regulate long-distance communications within their borders even though the longer calls have been opened to competition for more than a decade. The 1996 act requires the states to liberalize entry into providing the shorter calls, but only after the regional Bell companies are permitted to enter the longer-call market.[19]

Indeed, most of the arguments for continuing regulation after liberalization come from new entrants who see the regulatory process as a mechanism for constraining the incumbent and reducing the probability of price competition. In the United States, the new long-distance carriers have long opposed the decision by the FCC to discontinue formal tariff filings that announce price changes in advance. They were successful in court as long as AT&T was under rate regulation, but having deregulated AT&T, the FCC is now apparently able to deny all carriers the right to file tariffs in advance of rate changes.

The 1996 act should have provided for immediate deregulation of retail telephone rates once entry was opened and a set of wholesale prices were established for unbundled elements and interconnection. Dozens of studies of the effects of regulation in rivalrous industries demonstrate that regulation generally prevents prices from adjusting to costs and protects certain seller or buyer groups, often through deliberate cross-subsidies. Even though the 1996 act mandates the introduction of competition into most telecommunications markets that are not now competitive, it also continues and even extends the regime of cross-subsidies, instructing the FCC to assure that they be explicit and competitively neutral. This mandate plus the extensive new requirements for regulating wholesale rates and interconnection provide far too many opportunities for participants in the regulatory process to engage in rent seeking. It also provides for adverse incentives.

For example, the new 1996 act requires that states and the FCC certify that local exchange and access markets are reasonably open to competition before allowing the regional Bell companies to enter the long-distance market. As a result, three of the most likely entrants into local services—the largest long-distance companies—have a perverse incentive to refrain from investing in local facilities or from aggressively pursuing local customers so that they can claim that the local Bell companies have failed to open their networks sufficiently to allow them to enter. Similarly, the Bell companies may be persuaded to delay local competition in their territories because the states are not required to open intraLATA (intrastate) long-distance services to competition until the Bell companies are granted entry

---

19. The details of these market divisions are perhaps too complicated to describe fully in this paper, but they derive from the 1984 AT&T divestiture. After divestiture, the regional Bell companies were allowed to provide only local access and exchange services and long-distance services within their "local access and transport areas" (LATAs). Larger, more populous states have two or more such LATAs; hence, the Bell companies cannot provide *intrastate* long-distance services between these areas. The 1996 act allows the Bell companies into the *interLATA* market after they have complied with a "competitive checklist" for facilitating entry into their local markets.

into in-region interLATA services, which, in turn, is likely to be delayed by the FCC for several years.[20] Equally important, the continuing regulation of incumbent local carriers makes it difficult for them to respond to market conditions by changing their rates or service options. These carriers are still subject to lengthy state regulatory processes to adjust these rates or service conditions. As a result, low residential rates are likely to remain for some time, particularly in suburban and rural areas, reducing the incentive for new carriers to enter these markets except on a selective basis to attract heavy users of long-distance, vertical, or Internet services.

14.8   Conclusion

To some observers, the fact that the United States has had the longest experience with telecommunications liberalization suggests that it might be a model for other countries to follow, particularly in the growth-oriented Pacific basin. However, observers should ask why liberalization is still not complete in the United States thirty years after it began. The answer is quite clearly that U.S. politicians have been reluctant to shed the notion that telecommunications regulation should be retained in order to move rents among political constituent groups—most notably between urban and rural subscribers. The committees of Congress that control telecommunications policy are dominated by representatives from rural areas, and even conservative Republicans from these areas are willing to combine with liberal Democrats to use telecommunications policy to redistribute income. This redistributionist goal, achieved largely through internal cross-subsidies, will be difficult to achieve if full liberalization occurs. As a result, regulation remains an important and counterproductive force.

Other countries may learn several lessons from the U.S. experience in attempting to liberalize telecommunications:

1. Reduce rate distortions as much as possible *before* attempting to introduce competition.

2. Require only limited unbundling of "essential" facilities for a limited time. Otherwise, encourage entrants to build their own facilities.

3. Establish a certain date for deregulating rates after entry barriers are lowered and entrants begin to offer services.

20. In the nineteen months since the act was passed, only two Bell companies were able to persuade their state commissions that they have met the competitive checklist required for entry into in-region interLATA long-distance services, and both have been denied entry by the FCC. It may be several years before any Bell company is able successfully to run the gauntlet of state, Department of Justice, and FCC clearances for in-region long-distance entry. In the interim, many may simply decide that the prize is not worth the cost of ceding market share in their own local markets.

4. Limit regulation to the requirement of reciprocal interconnection after retail rate and service deregulation occurs.

The United States has been trying to liberalize telecommunications for thirty years. This fact, by itself, provides ample testimony against the U.S. "model." Indeed, in countries where national telecommunications carriers are notoriously inefficient, the U.S. model of a long adjustment period and continued regulation can be justified as providing the "safeguards" against the rapid loss of jobs that is required for carriers to become efficient. The United States never had a government-owned telecommunications monopoly; therefore, it has fewer excuses for continuing telecommunications regulation this long. Estimates of the static economic losses from regulatory rate distortions in the U.S. industry range from about $10 billion to $30 billion per year. With wireless costs falling so rapidly, it seems unlikely that any temporary or even permanent exertion of monopoly power that might be unleashed by total deregulation could reduce economic welfare by as much.

References

Bernheim, B. Douglas, and Robert D. Willing. 1996. *The scope of competition in telecommunications.* Washington, D.C.: American Enterprise Institute, October.

Brock, Gerald W. 1981. *The telecommunications industry.* Cambridge, Mass.: Harvard University Press.

Crandall, Robert W. 1981. *After the breakup: U.S. telecommunications in a more competitive era.* Washington, D.C.: Brookings Institution.

Crandall, Robert W., and Kenneth Flamm, eds. 1989. *Changing the rules: Technological change, international competition, and regulation in communications.* Washington, D.C.: Brookings Institution.

Crandall, Robert W., and Leonard Waverman. 1996. *Talk is cheap: The promise of regulatory reform in North American telecommunications.* Washington, D.C.: Brookings Institution.

FCC (Federal Communications Commission). 1997. *Statistics of communications common carriers, 1995/96.* Washington, D.C.: Federal Communications Commission.

Hall, Robert E. 1997. Affidavit submitted on behalf of MCI in the Federal Communications Commission's Docket no. cc 97–121, April.

International Telecommunication Union. 1996. *World telecommunications indicators.* Geneva: International Telecommunication Union.

Kahn, Alfred E. 1998. *Letting go: Deregulating the process of deregulation.* Lansing: Michigan State University, Institute of Public Utilities.

Kraushaar, Jonathan. 1996. *Update on quality of service for the local operating companies aggregated to the holding company level.* Washington, D.C.: Federal Communications Commission, Common Carrier Bureau, Industry Analysis Division, March.

NARUC (National Association of Regulatory Utility Commissioners). Annual-a.

Bell operating companies exchange service telephone rates. Washington, D.C.: National Association of Regulatory Utility Commissioners.
————. Annual-b. *Bell operating companies long distance message telephone rates.* Washington, D.C.: National Association of Regulatory Utility Commissioners.
Temin, Peter, with Louis Galambos. 1987. *The fall of the Bell system.* Cambridge: Cambridge University Press.
Waverman, Leonard. 1989. U.S. interexchange competition. In *Changing the rules: Technological change, international competition, and regulation in communications,* ed. Robert W. Crandall and Kenneth Flamm. Washington, D.C.: Brookings Institution.

Comment   Shin-Horng Chen

When talking about liberalization, one may expect free competition with few regulations. This is not the case in telecommunications. Market opening in telecommunications around the world is often followed by regulation or, to be more precise, re-regulation. In his paper, Robert Crandall tries to show us that according to the U.S. experience, regulations can undermine market opening. He begins by listing four requisites of successful liberalization, namely, no rate distortion, elimination of facility bottlenecks, market incentives only for promoting entry, and a commitment to phase out regulation very soon after entry occurs. For the benefit of readers, Crandall may need to elaborate on those requisites.

However, in the United States and many other countries, rate distortion does occur because of cross-subsidies and, more important, because of universal service requirements. Like it or not, universal service has been considered essential to telecommunications. Thus arises the question of how regulators should deal with the universal service requirement if they are to eliminate rate distortion.

Crandall also suggests regulators get rid of facility bottlenecks mainly in terms of interconnection. In this regard, equal access may be required. However, he has observed that the FCC went too far in mandating "equal access," requiring local carriers to offer connection services to AT&T and its long-distance call rivals at the "same" rate. This gave AT&T's rivals an advantage because local carriers' costs of connection to AT&T were generally cheaper than those to AT&T's rivals. On the surface, setting interconnection fees at the same rate for AT&T and its rivals may be fair, but it ignores the marginal cost pricing principle. Having said that, the above observation may also mean that AT&T has enjoyed advantages over its rivals in terms of getting access to interconnection, which seems to be the legacy of AT&T as the incumbent in the United States. How long

Shin-Horng Chen is deputy director of the second division of the Chung-Hua Institution for Economic Research, Taiwan.

should the regulator and new entrants live with such an incumbency advantage without taking any action?

Crandall also suggests that apart from the interconnection requirement, regulators can encourage facility-based entry to promote network competition. This may be desirable and feasible for a large country such as the United States, but for a small country such as Taiwan, facility-based entry and network competition may be limited to some extent by its territory and market size. As a matter of fact, we have seen operators around the world forge strategic alliances and mergers to provide interconnected services. This may mean that network competition need not take the form of facility integration.

The 1996 U.S. Telecommunications Act requires regulators to regulate the rates for wholesale services provided by local call carriers on the basis of forward-looking estimates of long-term incremental costs. This rule together with the policy requiring the unbundling of all local network elements, according to Crandall, has prohibited entry into local call services through the construction of new facilities. However, if historical embedded costs are used to determine the rates for wholesale services, different problems may arise. For example, we in Taiwan asked Chunghwa Telecom (CHT), the incumbent, to rebalance its tariffs. CHT has done so by basing its new tariffs on historical costs. However, one may argue that CHT's historical costs probably include the costs of X-inefficiency, which are the legacy of CHT as the state monopoly. As a result, CHT's new tariff structure may not reflect productive efficiency. Therefore, using the historical cost approach to determine tariff rates may not be appropriate.

In principle, we all agree that liberalization means allowing market forces to prevail, but I am not entirely convinced by Crandall's call for a governmental commitment to phase out regulation very soon after entry occurs—while how soon is open to interpretation. It is feasible and desirable to introduce competition into the telecommunications industry. Having said that, the industry has retained the features of scale and scope economies in certain segments of the market. Also, there are incumbency advantages against new entrants. Certain regulations or regulatory oversight may therefore be needed for some time to foster an environment of fair competition.

Comment   Tsuruhiko Nambu

In 1996, the U.S. Telecommunications Law was revised from its 1934 form. What was most impressive to me at that time was the spirit of the newly

Tsuruhiko Nambu is professor of economics at Gakushuin University.

revised law, captured in the following: "The objective of this law is not to protect competitors but to protect or enhance competition." Last summer, however, we got the orders of the FCC, and I was totally surprised to see that the spirit of the law had more or less faded. Robert Crandall's paper is an excellent exposition of the basic problems of the U.S. situation. I will summarize the relevant issues.

1. FCC regulation may have the effect of inhibiting facility-based entry into the local market.

2. This follows from the orders of the FCC saying that interconnection should be done at the forward-looking cost. Forward-looking cost means the best technology available in the foreseeable future.

3. If regional Bell operating companies (RBOCs) always interconnect newcomers on the basis of forward-looking cost, newcomers will lose the incentive to invest in the local loop simply because investment is meaningless when they are guaranteed the best technology at the cheapest cost by the incumbents.

It is my understanding that the present situation was brought about by the deep-rooted conflict between RBOCs and long-distance carriers, which is traceable to the accidental decision of the AT&T breakup. The difficulties now stem from confused decisions at that time. The LATA concept is an example. Artificial lines were drawn between local areas partly based on the advice of AT&T. It became a big burden on telecommunications players. But the situation is more or less the same in Japan, where the dispute over the desirability of breaking up Nippon Telephone and Telegraph (NTT) continued until 1997.

Summing up, the U.S. model has traits that are highly colored by the historical accidents of the AT&T antitrust case. My feeling is that the U.S. experience cannot be a useful model for developing countries because in such countries government or public monopoly is a major player and antitrust forces are not at work.

The Japanese model might be more applicable to these countries because, in Japan, a public monopoly (NTT) was privatized and competition was introduced. But I must also stress that government is a dangerous thing. Yesterday, government was like a chicken, but in my view, government is now like a cat in telecommunications regulation.

Finally, I will touch on the divestiture problem. The main points are stated in Nambu (1997). In my view, the divestiture plan was doubtful in that it may help create more competitive structure in the future. On top of that, the AT&T breakup teaches us a lesson. After divestiture the RBOCs and AT&T became true opponents and mutual mistrust developed. Now the RBOCs and long-distance carriers are discussing interconnection rules.

Huge documents exist on the study of different engineering models:

Hatfield I, II, III; the benchmark cost model I, II, III; the Strategic Planning Policy Alliance model; and so forth. Some of them are sponsored by the RBOCs, others by long-distance carriers. The results of calculations of reasonable charges are totally diverse. Of course, there cannot be an absolutely accurate figure for interconnection charges. The fatal problem is the insurmountable mistrust between the RBOCs and long-distance carriers. Divestiture may well create this kind of difficulty as a by-product.

I stress the peculiarity of telecommunications networks, where the platform of interconnection plays a decisive role for developing the industry. If people put too much weight on competition policy where divestiture is the choice for promoting competition, they may lose sight of the economic losses caused by the selfish and myopic behavior of telecommunications carriers.

Reference

Nambu Tsuruhiko. 1997. Is "bottleneck" a viable concept for the breakup of NTT? *Telecommunications Policy* 21 (2): 113–26.

Contributors

Ching-hsi Chang
National Taiwan University
Department of Economics
21 Hsuchow Road
Taipei, Taiwan

Shin-Horng Chen
Chung-Hua Institution for Economic
    Research
No. 75 Chang-Hsing Street
Taipei 106, Taiwan

Leonard K. Cheng
Hong Kong University of Science
    and Technology
Department of Economics
Clear Water Bay
Kowloon, Hong Kong

Robert W. Crandall
Brookings Institution
1775 Massachusetts Avenue NW
Washington, DC 20036

Sheng-Cheng Hu
Institute of Economics
Academia Sinica
Nankang, Taipei 11529, Taiwan

Takatoshi Ito
Institute of Economic Research
Hitotsubashi University
Naka 2-1, Kunitachi 186-8603
Tokyo, Japan

Motoshige Itoh
Faculty of Economics
University of Tokyo Bunkyo-ku,
    7-3-1 Hongo
Tokyo 113, Japan

Moon-Soo Kang
Korea Development Institute
POB 113
Chong Nyang
Seoul, Korea

Anne O. Krueger
Department of Economics
Stanford University
579 Serra Mall
Landau Economics Bldg., Room 153
Stanford, CA 94305

Yum K. Kwan
Department of Economics and
    Finance
City University of Hong Kong
Tat Chee Avenue
Kowloon, Hong Kong

Ding Lu
National University of Singapore
Department of Economics
10 Kent Ridge Crescent
Singapore 119260

Francis T. Lui
Hong Kong University of Science
  and Technology
Department of Economics
Clear Water Bay
Kowloon, Hong Kong

Thomas Gale Moore
Hoover Institution
Stanford University
Stanford, CA 94305

Sadao Nagaoka
Institute of Innovation Research
Hitotsubashi University
2-1 Naka, Kunitachi
Tokyo 186-8603, Japan

Chong-Hyun Nam
Department of Economics
Korea University
5-1 Anam-dong, Sungbuk-ku
Seoul 136-701, Korea

Il Chong Nam
Korea Development Institute
POB 113
Chongnyang
Seoul, Korea

Sang-Woo Nam
KDI School of International Policy
  and Management
PO Box 184
Chungyang
Seoul, Korea

Tsuruhiko Nambu
Faculty of Economics
1-5-1, Mejiro, Toshima-ku
Tokyo 171, Japan

Roger G. Noll
Department of Economics
Stanford University
Stanford, CA 94305

Ramonette B. Serafica
Economics Department, LS 207
Dela Salle University
2401 Taft Avenue
Manila 1004, Philippines

Shinji Takagi
Faculty of Economics
Osaka University
1-7 Machikaneyama Toyonaka
Osaka 560-0043, Japan

Shang-Jin Wei
JFK School of Government
Harvard University
79 JFK Street
Cambridge, MA 02138

Frank A. Wolak
Department of Economics
Stanford University
Stanford, CA 94305

Changqi Wu
Department of Economics
Hong Kong University of Science
  and Technology
Clear Water Bay
Kowloon, Hong Kong

Chung-Shu Wu
Institute of Economics
Academia Sinica
Nankang, Taipei, Taiwan

Hirotaka Yamauchi
Faculty of Commerce
Hitotsubashi University
2-1 Naka, Kunitachi City
Tokyo 186-8601, Japan

Author Index

Subject Index